Lecture Notes of the Institute for Computer Sciences, Social Informatics and Telecommunications Engineering 646

Editorial Board Members

Ozgur Akan, *Middle East Technical University, Ankara, Türkiye*
Paolo Bellavista, *University of Bologna, Bologna, Italy*
Jiannong Cao, *Hong Kong Polytechnic University, Hong Kong, China*
Geoffrey Coulson, *Lancaster University, Lancaster, UK*
Falko Dressler, *University of Erlangen, Erlangen, Germany*
Domenico Ferrari, *Università Cattolica Piacenza, Piacenza, Italy*
Mario Gerla, *UCLA, Los Angeles, USA*
Hisashi Kobayashi, *Princeton University, Princeton, USA*
Sergio Palazzo, *University of Catania, Catania, Italy*
Sartaj Sahni, *University of Florida, Gainesville, USA*
Xuemin Shen ⓘ, *University of Waterloo, Waterloo, Canada*
Mircea Stan, *University of Virginia, Charlottesville, USA*
Xiaohua Jia, *City University of Hong Kong, Kowloon, Hong Kong*
Albert Y. Zomaya, *University of Sydney, Sydney, Australia*

The LNICST series publishes ICST's conferences, symposia and workshops.
LNICST reports state-of-the-art results in areas related to the scope of the Institute.
The type of material published includes

- Proceedings (published in time for the respective event)
- Other edited monographs (such as project reports or invited volumes)

LNICST topics span the following areas:

- General Computer Science
- E-Economy
- E-Medicine
- Knowledge Management
- Multimedia
- Operations, Management and Policy
- Social Informatics
- Systems

Zhaolong Ning · Song Guo · Xiaojie Wang
Editors

Communications and Networking

19th International Conference, ChinaCom 2024
Chongqing, China, November 2–3, 2024
Proceedings, Part II

Editors
Zhaolong Ning
Chongqing University of Posts
and Telecommunications
Chongqing, China

Song Guo
The Hong Kong University of Science
and Technology
Hong Kong, China

Xiaojie Wang
Chongqing University of Posts
and Telecommunications
Chongqing, China

ISSN 1867-8211   ISSN 1867-822X (electronic)
Lecture Notes of the Institute for Computer Sciences, Social Informatics
and Telecommunications Engineering
ISBN 978-3-032-03214-0   ISBN 978-3-032-03215-7 (eBook)
https://doi.org/10.1007/978-3-032-03215-7

© ICST Institute for Computer Sciences, Social Informatics and Telecommunications Engineering 2026

This work is subject to copyright. All rights are solely and exclusively licensed by the Publisher, whether the whole or part of the material is concerned, specifically the rights of translation, reprinting, reuse of illustrations, recitation, broadcasting, reproduction on microfilms or in any other physical way, and transmission or information storage and retrieval, electronic adaptation, computer software, or by similar or dissimilar methodology now known or hereafter developed.
The use of general descriptive names, registered names, trademarks, service marks, etc. in this publication does not imply, even in the absence of a specific statement, that such names are exempt from the relevant protective laws and regulations and therefore free for general use.
The publisher, the authors and the editors are safe to assume that the advice and information in this book are believed to be true and accurate at the date of publication. Neither the publisher nor the authors or the editors give a warranty, expressed or implied, with respect to the material contained herein or for any errors or omissions that may have been made. The publisher remains neutral with regard to jurisdictional claims in published maps and institutional affiliations.

This Springer imprint is published by the registered company Springer Nature Switzerland AG
The registered company address is: Gewerbestrasse 11, 6330 Cham, Switzerland

If disposing of this product, please recycle the paper.

Preface

We are delighted to introduce the proceedings of the 19th European Alliance for Innovation (EAI) International Conference on Communications and Networking in China (ChinaCom 2024). Hosted by Chongqing University of Posts and Telecommunications, China, the conference was held from November 2–3, 2024. The conference aimed to bring together researchers and practitioners from China and worldwide and promote extensive discussion about the progress of applications and theories in communications, networking, signal processing, and related areas.

The technical program of ChinaCom 2024 consisted of 37 full and 5 short papers in oral presentation sessions at the main conference tracks. These papers were selected from 98 submissions. Each submission was reviewed following a double-blind process with a minimum of 3 reviews per paper. The conference tracks were: Track 1 - Wireless Communications and MIMO Systems; Track 2 (A) - Unmanned Aerial Vehicles and Augmented Reality; Track 2 (B) - Edge Computing and the Internet of Things; Track 3 (A): Signal Processing and Optimization Algorithms; and Track 3 (B): Task Scheduling and Blockchain. Aside from the high-quality technical paper presentations, the technical program also featured three keynote speeches, and three invited talks. The three keynote speakers were Bo Ai from Beijing Jiaotong University, China, Mingchun Tang from Chongqing University, China, and Feifei Gao from Tsinghua University, China. The invited talks were presented by Li Zhou from the National University of Defense Technology, China, Liangtian Wan from Dalian University of Technology, China, and Lu Sun from Dalian Maritime University, China.

Coordination with the steering chairs, Changjun Jiang, Qianbin Chen, and Honghao Gao, was essential for the success of the conference. We sincerely appreciate their constant support and guidance. It was also a great pleasure to work with such an excellent organizing committee team for their hard work in organizing and supporting the conference. In particular, the Technical Program Committee, led by our TPC Co-Chairs, Yan Zhang and Xiaojie Wang, completed the peer-review process of technical papers and made a high-quality technical program. We are also grateful to Conference Manager Timea Madarova for her support and to all the authors who submitted their papers to the ChinaCom 2024 conference.

We strongly believe that the ChinaCom conference provides a good forum for all researchers, developers, and practitioners to discuss all science and technology aspects that are relevant to communication networks. We also expect that future ChinaCom conferences will be as successful and stimulating as indicated by the contributions presented in this volume.

Zhaolong Ning
Song Guo

Organization

Steering Committee

Qianbin Chen — Chongqing University of Posts and Telecommunications, China
Honghao Gao — Shanghai University, China
Changjun Jiang — Tongji University, China

Organizing Committee

General Chair

Song Guo — Hong Kong University of Science and Technology, China

General Co-chair

Zhaolong Ning — Chongqing University of Posts and Telecommunications, China

TPC Chairs and Co-chairs

Xiaojie Wang — Chongqing University of Posts and Telecommunications, China
Yan Zhang — University of Oslo, Norway

Sponsorship and Exhibit Chair

Behrouz Jedari — Nokia, Finland

Local Chair

Yunjian Jia — Chongqing University, China

Workshops Chair

Amr Tolba   King Saud University, Saudi Arabia

Publicity and Social Media Chair

Qingqing Wu   Shanghai Jiao Tong University, China

Publications Chair

Miaowen Wen   South China University of Technology, China

Web Chair

Ling Yi   Chongqing University of Posts and Telecommunications, China

Posters and PhD Track Chair

Yuxuan Yang   University of Sydney, Australia

Panels Chair

Limei Peng   Kyungpook National University, South Korea

Demos Chairs

Xingguo Zhang   Tokyo University of Agriculture and Technology, Japan
Chengchao Liang   Carleton University, Canada

Technical Program Committee

Yueyue Dai   Nanyang Technological University, Singapore
Yishuo Chen   Chongqing University of Posts and Telecommunications, China
Peiran Dong   Hong Kong Polytechnic University, China
Cheng Guo   Dalian University of Technology, China
Xiangjie Kong   Zhejiang University of Technology, China

Chengming Li	Advanced Institute of Chinese Academy of Sciences, China
Qianwen Liu	Chongqing University of Posts and Telecommunications, China
Laisen Nie	Macau University of Science and Technology, China
Weijing Qi	Chongqing University of Posts and Telecommunications, China
Azizur Rahim	National University of Sciences and Technology, Pakistan
Jiaxin Ren	Chongqing University of Posts and Telecommunications, China
Lu Sun	Dalian Maritime University, China
Amr Tolba	King Saud University, Saudi Arabia
Wei Wang	Sun Yat-sen University, China
Guangjun Wu	Institute of Information Engineering, CAS, China
Minqiang Yang	Lanzhou University, China
Yao Yu	Northeastern University, China
Ke Zhang	University of Electronic Science and Technology of China, China
Yuzhen Zhang	Chongqing University of Posts and Telecommunications, China

Contents – Part II

Edge Computing and the Internet of Things

Communication Efficient Reinforcement Learning-Based Federated Pruning 3
   Weishan Zhang, Jiakai Wang, Yuming Nie, Hongwei Zhao, Yuru Liu, Haoyun Sun, Tao Chen, and Baoyu Zhang

Semi-asynchronous Federated Dynamic Mutual Distillation in Vehicular Networks 18
   Xiaoge Huang, Yali Xiao, Wenjing Li, Chengchao Liang, and Bin Shen

Computation Offloading and Resource Allocation in Multi-constraint Edge Environments Using DRL 33
   Junjie Zhang, Bing Xiong, Zhiqin Huang, Zhengxin Yu, Wang Miao, and Zheyi Chen

Anomaly Traffic Detection in Edge with Multi-scale Aggregated Transformer 47
   Longxiang Xue, Junjie Zhang, Xiaowei Shi, Hongju Chen, and Zheyi Chen

Communication Efficient Fuzzy Clustered Graph Federated Learning 62
   Weishan Zhang, Ziyu Wang, Hongwei Zhao, Zhicheng Bao, Yuru Liu, Haoyun Sun, Tao Chen, and Baoyu Zhang

A Distributed Container-Based Internet of Things (IoT)-Enabled Autonomous E-Healthcare System for Development and Operations (DevOps) 78
   Qinglong Dai, Guangjun Qin, and Ran Li

Signal Processing and Optimization Algorithms

Weakly Supervised Multimodal Video Anomaly Detection Based on Knowledge Distillation 93
   Lulu Yang, Xiaoyu Wu, and Simin Li

A Combined Phase Optimisation and Clipping Reduction PAPR Technique for LCSS System 110
   LuShuang Liao, Lin Zheng, and Chao Yang

A Structure of MWC Based on Overlapping Window Method for Wideband
LFM 120
    Juejia Liang, Chao Yang, and Lin Zheng

STFT Spectrograms and Statistical Features Fusion for Emitter
Identification Based on Deep Learning 136
    Qi Cheng, Hongyujie Xiao, Julei Ye, Heng Liu, and Liu Yang

A Fast Rivet Detection Algorithm Based on VanillaNet Network
and Computer Vision 148
    Juntian Zheng and Peiyan Yuan

A Cepstral Domain Radio Frequency Fingerprint Extraction Method
for LTE-V2X 163
    Ying Chen, Aiqun Hu, and Yang Yang

SEQ-Track: Detecting Web Tracking with Sequences of Packet Lengths
and Time Intervals 177
    Yong Yuan, Ziling Wei, Lin Liu, Shuhui Chen, and Jinshu Su

Enhanced Feature-Based Approach to Identify and Classify Android
Encrypted Malware Traffic 190
    Jiaqi Gao, Yaru He, Mingrui Fan, Yueming Lu, and Yaojun Qiao

An Energy Efficient and High Accuracy Detection Scheme for Dual
Function Radar and Communication Systems 206
    Pengzun Gao, Long Zhao, and Kan Zheng

Task Scheduling and Blockchain

A Network Intrusion Detection Method Based on Multi-scale
Spatiotemporal Feature Extraction 223
    Yushu Zhang, Xuanrui Xiong, Yuan Zhang, Tianyu Li, Canpu Liu,
    and Xiaolin Fan

Investigating the Correlation Between Choice of Spreading Factor
and Duty Cycle Calculations on Energy Consumption Profiles for LoRa:
Insights from Optimized Image and Audio Data Transmission in Beehive
Monitoring 241
    Ephrance Eunice Namugenyi, Julianne Sansa Otim, Marco Zennaro,
    Stephen Wolthusen, Mary Nsabagwa, and David Tugume

GPT Promotes Intelligent Autonomy in Communication Networks 262
    Yifan Yang, Zheng Yang, Jie Zeng, Yuran Dan, Zhenming Bai,
    and Chen Xu

Multipath Transaction Scheduling for Payment Channel Networks 276
  *Xiaojie Wang, Zhonghui Zhao, Yu Wu, Hailin Zhu, Ling Yi, Li Zhou,
  and Zhaolong Ning*

An Energy Payment Transaction Scheduling Solution for Electric Vehicles
Based on Off-Chain Computing 291
  *Ziyi Liu, Yu Wu, Qi Guo, Qianwen Liu, Yuzhen Zhang, Xinfeng Deng,
  Qiuping Li, and Xuanrui Xiong*

Local Descriptors Aided Few-Shot Learning for Wireless Spectrum Status
Recognition 306
  Zixin Wang, Bianzheng Wang, Xin Wang, Yue Li, and Bin Shen

A Variational Bayesian Based Adaptive Kalman Filter Time-Scale
Algorithm for Atomic Clock Ensemble 318
  *Buyun Ma, Zhengkang Wang, Yiyi Yao, Jiahui Cheng, Xinyu Miao,
  and Yaojun Qiao*

Cost-Optimized Dynamic Offloading and Resource Scheduling Algorithm
for Low Earth Orbit Satellite Networks 327
  Jinhong Li, Kangan Gui, Chengchao Liang, and Rong Chai

Author Index 341

Contents – Part I

Wireless Communications and MIMO Systems

Near-Field Non-stationary Channel Estimation for Wideband Extremely
Large-Scale MIMO 3
   Xingkuan Li

Pilot Optimization for mURLLC in CF mMIMO Systems Under $\kappa - \mu$
Shadowed Fading 16
   Shiyu Zhang, Jie Zeng, Tiejun Lv, Yuting Zhang, Zhipeng Lin, and Xin Su

Study on Frequency Compatibility Analysis Methods Between NGSO
Constellations and GSO Systems 29
   Xiang Gao, Ying Li, Xiujuan Yao, Xue Li, Yiwei Qi, Yuanhao Ma, and Zhen Li

Joint Resource Optimization for a Dual System Assisted by UAVs and RIS 46
   Xuehao Feng, Xin Liu, and Jihan Feng

A Method of Inter-Base Station Synchronization for Cooperative
Integrated Sensing and Communications in Indoor 2.2 GHz Scenarios 56
   Xiaoqian Wang, Shuang Jin, Tao Jiang, Rongyan Xi, Hongjun He, Liang Xia, and Guangyi Liu

Gibbs Sampling Based Channel Estimation Under Magnitude
Measurements 68
   Zhaorui Jiang and Shengchu Wang

Frame Synchronization Algorithm Based on Cyclic Prefix and Signal
Sparsity in Delay-Doppler Domain for OTFS System 82
   Haiyan Yang, Junsheng Zhuo, Mingjun Zhang, Jianfei Tong, Heng Liu, and Zheng Ma

An Effective Signal Processing Method for OFDM-Based ISAC System 93
   Qihui Tao, Bei Liu, Xin Su, and Xibin Xu

Active RIS-Enhanced Wireless Powered Communication Network
in Hybrid Near- and Far-Field 108
   Zhengyu Zhu, Jiaxue Li, Zheng Chu, and Chongwen Huang

Deep Reinforcement Learning-Based Secure Transmission
for UAV-Mounted RIS Aided ISAC Systems 120
  Gangcan Sun, Kaihao Wang, Zhengyu Zhu, Zheng Chu, and Zheng Li

Energy Efficiency Optimization Based on DRL for RIS-Assisted
Heterogeneous Networks with Human-Machine-Object Hybrid Access 134
  Sai Huang, Ke Lv, Ruixin Fan, Yuanyuan Yao, Liyan Li, and Zhiyong Feng

Temporal Beam Prediction for MmWave MIMO Systems Based on Deep
Learning 152
  Yan Zhao, Long Zhao, Jiayi Xu, and Hongrui Shen

Unmanned Aerial Vehicles and Augmented Reality

Enhancing UAV Relay System Security: A Joint Optimization Algorithm
for Power Allocation and Trajectory Planning 169
  Xiaoge Huang, Hongshidi Liu, Yuyang Luo, Chengchao Liang,
  and Qianbin Chen

A Bibliometric Analysis of Cloud-Based Augmented Reality 184
  Joseph U. Oju, Olufunke R. Vincent, Gregory O. Onwodi,
  John N. Inekwe, and Grace E. Jokthan

A Joint Optimization Method for Urban Edge User Task Offloading
and UAV Energy Consumption in the Space-Air-Ground Integrated
Network 203
  Xiaolin Fan, Xuanrui Xiong, Tianyu Li, Haihong Huang, Yushu Zhang,
  Canpu Liu, and Dan Hu

A Path Recommendation System Based on UAV Swarm Missions 218
  Shouze Tang, Yu Wu, Yishuo Chen, Kai Shao, Yuzhen Zhang, Jiaxin Ren,
  and Li Zhou

An Advanced UAV Perspective Object Detection Algorithm Based
on Multi Scale Feature Reconstruction 233
  Tianyu Li, Xuanrui Xiong, Xiaolin Fan, Haihong Huang, Dan Hu,
  and Yushu Zhang

Simultaneously Tracking Skeleton Points of Body and Hands in Virtual
Reality 248
  Boxian Li, Xin Su, Bei Liu, and Xibin Xu

HyMSCA: A Hybrid Multi-Scale Convolutional Attention Model
for Hyperspectral Image Classification 259
　　*Dan Hu, Xuanrui Xiong, Weiqin Lin, Tianyu Li, Xinfeng Deng,
　　Xiaolin Fan, and Mengting He*

Author Index 275

Edge Computing and the Internet of Things

Communication Efficient Reinforcement Learning-Based Federated Pruning

Weishan Zhang(✉)❶, Jiakai Wang❶, Yuming Nie❶, Hongwei Zhao❶, Yuru Liu❶, Haoyun Sun❶, Tao Chen❶, and Baoyu Zhang❶

Qingdao Institute of Software, College of Computer Science and Technology, China University of Petroleum (East China), Qingdao, China
zhangws@upc.edu.cn, zhw@s.upc.edu.cn

Abstract. By enabling decentralized model training, federated learning allows sensitive data to remain on local devices, significantly reducing privacy and security risks. In real-world applications, federated learning faces key challenges, such as high communication costs, device heterogeneity, and the varying computational capacities of devices, all of which negatively impact training efficiency and limit the generalization capabilities of the global model. In this paper, we propose a novel framework called Reinforcement Learning-Based Federated Pruning (RLBFP), including a Reinforcement-Based Generalization Pruning (RBGP) process and a Federated Sparse Aggregation (FedSA) process, which can dynamically adjust pruning rates and apply efficient sparse aggregation strategies. RLBFP can not only reduces communication costs but also improves model sparsity and performance. Comprehensive experiments conducted on benchmark datasets such as CIFAR-10, MNIST, and Fashion-MNIST demonstrate that RLBFP surpasses existing federated learning approaches in terms of sparsity, accuracy, and convergence speed. FedSA further enhances model sparsity by up to 18.9% without compromising performance.

Keywords: Federated Learning · Reinforcement Learning · Model Pruning · Communication efficiency

1 Introduction

The proliferation of the Internet of Things (IoT) and the increasing ubiquity of smart devices have resulted in the generation of vast amounts of data, necessitating advances in distributed machine learning techniques. Federated Learning (FL) has emerged as a promising paradigm to address privacy concerns by enabling decentralised model training directly on edge devices, eliminating the need for centralised data collection and storage. However, while FL offers privacy benefits, it also poses significant challenges in terms of communication efficiency,

---

This work was supported in part by the National Natural Science Foundation of China (62072469).

especially when applied to large-scale IoT networks. The frequent transmission of model updates between edge devices and a central server during FL training can consume significant network bandwidth, resulting in increased communication overhead. This in turn leads to increased network latency and affects the overall efficiency of the learning process.

Communication costs are a critical bottleneck in FL because the constant exchange of large model parameters puts a strain on the network infrastructure, especially when dealing with resource-constrained edge devices. These devices often have limited bandwidth, storage and processing power, making it difficult to maintain timely and efficient communication during the model training process. As deep learning models typically have a large number of parameters and complex structures, making training and inference on resource-constrained edge devices extremely difficult [1].

The heterogeneity of edge devices in an FL system, combined with the variability of local data distributions, introduces additional communication challenges. Devices can have widely varying network conditions, processing capabilities and data quality, making it difficult to synchronise and aggregate model updates. These factors lead to asynchronous communication patterns and can slow down model convergence, limiting both scalability and overall performance of the global model. Addressing these communication-related challenges is crucial for improving the practicality and scalability of FL, especially in resource-constrained environments.

This paper proposes a novel Reinforcement Learning-Based Federated Pruning (RLBFP) framework to optimise communication efficiency in federated learning (FL) systems. RLBFP integrates reinforcement learning and model pruning techniques to minimise communication overhead during FL training. Its key components, Reinforcement-Based Generalisation Pruning (RBGP) and Federated Sparse Aggregation (FedSA), work together to improve efficiency. RBGP uses reinforcement learning to dynamically adapt pruning to the communication constraints of heterogeneous edge devices, reducing the number of model parameters exchanged. FedSA further improves sparsity by aggregating only non-zero weights, minimising redundant communication between devices and the server. Together, these methods reduce communication overhead while preserving model performance, enabling more scalable and efficient FL systems. The main contributions of this paper are as follows:

1) A reinforcement learning-based pruning mechanism is proposed that dynamically adapts to the data distribution on different devices, ensuring the generalization capabilities of the pruned model while significantly reducing the communication resources required for model transmission.
2) A federated sparse aggregation method is proposed to minimize redundant communication during federated training, improving model sparsity, thereby further reducing communication costs and enhancing the efficiency and accuracy of the global model.

3) Evaluation of the proposed method using three datasets and two pruning models in image classification tasks, assessing its accuracy, sparsity, and trade-offs in performance loss.

The rest of the paper is organized as follows. Section 2 will present the related work on model pruning and federated pruning Sect. 3 will present the details of the overall architecture and methodology of RLBFP. Section 4 will present the experiments and results of RLBFP, RBGP and FedSA. Section 5 will present the conclusion and future work.

2 Related Work

2.1 Model Pruning

As the size and complexity of deep learning models continue to grow, the demand for computational and storage resources has surged, posing significant challenges to their deployment on resource-constrained devices. While deep models such as AlexNet and VGG have demonstrated outstanding performance across various tasks, their large number of parameters and high computational complexity create considerable obstacles for devices with limited computational power, such as smartphones and tablets, especially in terms of power consumption and latency.

To address this challenge, researchers have explored solutions from both hardware and algorithmic perspectives. On the hardware side, specialized neural network processing units [2] have been designed to enhance computational efficiency. On the algorithmic side, model compression techniques, particularly pruning methods, have emerged as an effective approach. Pruning reduces the size of models, accelerates inference, and decreases power consumption by removing insignificant weights and connections in neural networks. This concept mirrors the sparse connectivity observed in the human brain. Although early pruning methods like Optimal Brain Damage (OBD) [11] and Optimal Brain Surgeon (OBS) [5] occused primarily on shallow neural networks, the rapid growth of deep learning has reignited interest in pruning techniques.

Current research on pruning primarily focuses on three key areas: pruning granularity (such as weight, channel, or convolution kernel pruning), pruning methods (e.g., neuron importance assessment and layer-wise pruning ratio determination [14]), and the timing of pruning (e.g., integrating pruning with the training process). For instance, NISP [20] achieves fine-grained pruning by calculating neuron importance scores, while CPrune [10], proposed by Kim et al., supports target-aware efficient execution of deep neural networks, SimGNN [15] reduces redundant information in both GNN models and input graphs, Liu et al. proposed DCP [13] method to efficiently compress deep networks by selecting the most discriminative channels and kernels, Guo et al. proposed PCP [3] framework to accelerate convolutional neural networks by iteratively selecting and pruning a small number of channels, and Li et al. proposed EagleEye [12] method for efficiently evaluating pruning based on adaptive batch normalisation, which can quickly find the best pruning candidates without fine-tuning. Existing pruning techniques typically rely on global data distribution, leading to prolonged training times and high computational costs, making them unsuitable for federated learning systems with decentralized data. These methods struggle to operate effectively on resource-constrained mobile and IoT devices. Maintaining model performance during pruning, automatically determining pruning sparsity, and extending these techniques to broader tasks remain unresolved challenges.

2.2 Federated Pruning

The advent of Federated Learning (FL) [15] has provided a solution to the vexing issues of data privacy concerns and the problem of data silos. This machine learning framework facilitates the collaborative training of models across disparate clients, orchestrated by a central server, with the objective of developing a superior quality shared global model while assiduously safeguarding data privacy.

In the context of integrating federated learning with model pruning techniques, the research area of federated pruning has seen a significant increase in activity. This approach combines the strengths of both FL and pruning, enabling model compression and simplification, which significantly reduces communication and computational costs. Current research on federated pruning explores several avenues, including improving pruning algorithms [4] and integrating them with quantization techniques [16] to enhance accuracy and efficiency.

To illustrate, Prakash et al. [16] put forth GWEP, which markedly enhances communication efficiency by concurrently applying quantization and pruning. Nevertheless, the delegation of the pruning task to clients may result in an increase in the computational burden. In contrast, Yao et al. [19] introduced FedHM, which distributes heterogeneous low-rank models to clients and aggregates them into a full-rank global model, thereby reducing communication and computational overhead. Similarly, Jiang et al. [8] proposed CS pruning mechanism, which performs complementary pruning between the server and clients, aiming to achieve a balance between low overhead and high accuracy. Zhu et al. proposed FedLP [22] framework to optimise computation and communication in federated learning through hierarchical pruning. These methods often rely on fixed pruning ratios, which may lack adaptability to varying environments and could potentially fail to meet the demands of different scenarios.

To address these issues, FedDUAP [21] [19] employs server-contributed data for dynamic updates and performs adaptive pruning based on dimension and importance. Jiang et al. proposed FedMP [9] framework to improve the efficiency and performance of federated learning on heterogeneous edge devices through adaptive model pruning and residual recovery in synchronous parallel, and Wen et al. proposed FedDrop [18] to reduce the communication overhead and computational load of federated learning through a stochastic model pruning scheme. These methods risk under- or over-pruning, potentially degrading model performance. Developing more flexible and adaptive federated pruning techniques remains a challenge in current research.

3 Methodology

3.1 Overall Architecture

In the RLBFP architectural framework, model generalization capabilities are initially employed to direct the reinforcement learning pruning process, thereby enhancing model generalisation. Subsequently, the pruning process is abstracted to form a generic reinforcement learning pruning method, which is capable of adapting to different pruning environments and avoiding the necessity for retraining when changing datasets and models. RBGP is capable of incremental optimisation and enhanced effectiveness through a process of iterative pruning and updating. FedSA serves to enhance the sparsity of the model by fusing solely the non-zero weights and reducing the impact of the 0 weights on the global model. The overarching architecture of RLBFP is illustrated in Fig. 1.

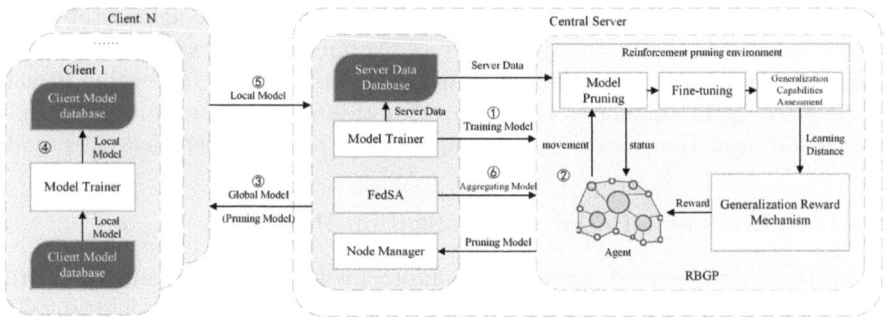

Fig. 1. The overall architecture of RLBFP.

For the purposes of this discussion, it is assumed that the RLBFP framework proposed in this paper is being deployed in a federated learning system comprising a single server and N clients. Similarly, the server is equipped with training data, which is used to facilitate reinforcement learning. Let D_n represent the local dataset of client $n \in \{1, 2, ..., N\}$. The objective of federated learning is to identify the model weights w that minimise the global empirical loss $F(w)$. The relevant formulas are provided in Eqs. (1) and (2).

$$\min_w F(w) := \sum_{n=1}^{N} p_n F_n(w) \qquad (1)$$

$$F_n(w) := \frac{1}{|D_n|} \sum_{i \in D_n} f_i(w) \qquad (2)$$

where p_n is the weight of the client n and $\sum_{n=1}^{N} p_n = 1$, $f_i(w)$ are the loss functions of the client n for the samples i of its dataset.

The reinforcement-based generalization pruning method RBGP and the federated sparse aggregation method FedSA are integrated into the original federated learning training process to form RLBFP. As shown in Fig. 1, the training process of RLBFP consists of multiple rounds, and each round consists of six steps, and the training steps of the t-th round are described as follows: if $t = 0$, step ① is executed, and server S initialises the model parameters and uses the server data to train the initial dense model $M_G^t(M_G^0)$.

S In step ④, the client n receives the global model D_n and performs local fine-tuning using the local data D_n to generate M_n^t. Subsequently, the local model M_n^t is transmitted to the server via step ⑤ and model aggregation is performed using FedSA to obtain a new global model M_G^{t+1} to complete step ⑥. In Reinforcement Generalised Pruning RBGP, the agent selects an action to perform each time based on the current state, which is represented as performing a pruning operation with a pruning rate of p on the global model M_G^t. Subsequently, the reinforcement pruning environment performs unstructured pruning on M_G^t based on the action selected by the agent, obtains the agent state transfer, and calculates the learning distance of the model using the server data for model fine-tuning and generalization capabilities assessment. The generalization reward mechanism calculates the reward for this action based on the learning distance and uses the reward value to update the reinforcement learning model.

3.2 Reinforcement-Based Generalization Pruning

This section introduces the proposed Reinforcement-Based Generalization Pruning (RBGP) method, which formulates pruning as a reinforcement learning (RL) problem, using model generalizability to guide pruning decisions. By generalizing the RL model, RBGP can be applied to various pruning tasks, avoiding the computational costs of retraining and enhancing pruning efficiency and scalability. While magnitude-based pruning (MBP) is a simple yet effective technique, it serves as the foundation for the pruning module in RBGP due to its demonstrated success in modern neural network architectures. Building on the findings of He et al. [7], which identified the sparse double-drop phenomenon and the link between learning distance and model performance, this work prioritizes model generalizability as a key metric for pruning. The goal is to achieve a more accurate pruning strategy that reduces model complexity while preserving or enhancing performance on unseen data.

In this paper, the learning distance D is defined as the distance between the model and its initialisation. The smaller the learning distance, the higher the model generalisation. Defining $W_{init} \in R^d$ as the initialised weights of the dense model and $W_{finetune} \in R^d$ as the fine-tuned model weights after pruning, the formula for the learning distance D is given in Eq. (3).

$$D(W_{finetune}) = ||W_{init} - W_{finetune}||_2 \tag{3}$$

In reinforcement learning, it is crucial to increase the training speed and avoid excessive pruning. For this purpose, the range of single pruning and the sparse upper limit of the model need to be set to control parameter tuning. Directly searching for the optimal pruning rate within the set range faces the problems of large search space, long time and difficulty. In addition, the RL model needs to be re-trained when changing the pruning object or dataset, which consumes a huge amount of resources, and the pruning rate may be close to 0, which makes it difficult to reflect the effect.

To solve these problems, this system abstracts the pruning problem into a one-dimensional scene exploration problem. In this scene, the agent moves from point A to point B, and receives rewards associated with the current position at each step. The agent needs to try different sequences of actions to explore the optimal path and collect environmental information to maximise the reward.

RBGP first samples at a set range and takes the point with the highest generalization capabilities as the RL initial state point. Let the pruning rate of the initial state point be p_0, at which time the pruned and fine-tuned model is W_{p_0}. At the moment t, let the model pruning rate be p_t. Determine the end point of the agent by Eq. (4).

$$\left| \frac{D(W_{p_t})}{D(W_{p_0})} - y \right| < \varepsilon \qquad (4)$$

where parameters y and ε are hyperparameters, which in this paper are set to 1.05 and 0.015, respectively. The implication of this formula is to maintain the generalization capabilities of the model after pruning in a certain interval, with the aim of increasing the pruning rate while minimising the amount of variation in generalization capabilities.

The neural network pruning task is modelled as Markov Decision Process (MDP). In this paper, we formulate and construct each element of MDP tuple such as state, action, strategy and reward as detailed below:

(1) State is the position of the agent in the environment and reflects the situation of the agent. In this paper, we use an integer to denote the state of the agent, whose specific meaning is the distance of state s from the initialisation s_0. $s = s + 1$ when the pruning rate increases by one step long, otherwise, $s = s - 1$.
(2) The action space in this environment is discrete, allowing the agent to either increase or decrease the pruning rate. The action step size is set to 0.05% to allow precise pruning adjustments and optimise overall performance.
(3) The reward function provides feedback on the agent's actions. In a one-dimensional setting, rewards are based on the agent's proximity to the target: positive rewards for moving closer, small negative rewards for moving away, and a large positive reward for reaching the target. In the context of problem abstraction, the reward function is no longer directly related to generalization capabilities, and the reward function is calculated using Eq. (5):

$$R(a) = \begin{cases} r - 1 & s \notin [0, uplimit] \\ r + 1 & s = end \\ r + a * 0.5 & else \end{cases} \qquad (5)$$

where *uplimit* is the set upper limit of pruning and *end* denotes the end point of pruning determined by Eq. (5). Using this reward function encourages the agent to keep moving to the right to increase the pruning rate until it reaches the set endpoint.

To implement the proposed Markov Decision Process (MDP), this paper adopts the Deep Q Network (DQN) algorithm as the core solution. The operation mechanism of DQN consists of randomly selecting an action and performing a pruning operation, evaluating the rewards and the new states, and then depositing the transfer tuples into the experience pool. The agent is trained by randomly selecting samples from the experience pool and gradually updating the network parameters by narrowing the deviation between the predicted and actual Q values until convergence. This process ensures the efficiency and accuracy of the algorithm in dealing with complex problems.

Algorithm 1: RBGP algorithm based on DQN

---
1 Initialise the experience pool D with the capacity N;
2 Initialise the action-value function Q and the objective function Q using random weights θ and θ^-, respectively;
3 **for** *episode*=1 *to* M **do**
4   Initialise the exploration strategy to obtain the initial state s_0;
5   **for** t=1 *to* T **do**
6   Execute action a_t to prune and fine-tune the target network and determine whether to terminate based on the learning distance;
7   Compute reward r_t and new state s_{t+1} Store the transfer tuple (s_t, a_t, r_t, s_{t+1}) to D;
8   Make $s_t = s_{t+1}$;
9   Randomly draw *minibatch* of transfer tuples from D;
10   **for** j=1 *to minibatch* **do**
11

$$y_j = \begin{cases} r_j & s_{j+1} is terminal \\ r_j + \gamma max Q(s_{j+1}, a', \theta^-) & others \end{cases}$$

            Perform gradient update $(y_j - Q(s_j, a_j, \theta))^2$ on network parameters θ
12   **end**
13   Every C steps let $\theta^- = \theta$
14   **end**
15 **end**

3.3 Federated Sparse Aggregation

The main goal of model aggregation is to combine model updates from different clients to produce an updated global model. In FedAvg, this aggregation is usually achieved by a simple weighted average. The server receives the model parameters from each participating training client and subsequently computes the average of these parameters. FedAvg uses Eq. (6) to aggregate the local model parameters into global model parameters.

$$w_{t+1} = \sum_{k=1}^{M} \frac{m_k}{m} w_{t+1}^k \qquad (6)$$

where w_{t+1} is the global model parameters obtained from the $t+1$ round of aggregation, M represents the number of clients participating in the aggregation, m_k is the number of samples from client k in the $t+1$ round of aggregation, m represents the total number of samples from the M clients participating in the training, and w_{t+1}^k is the local model parameters of client k in the $t+1$ round of aggregation.

Once the weighted average is computed, the server updates the global model with this new global model parameters and distributes it back to the individual clients for the next round of training. In federated learning environments, especially when model pruning is involved, the sparsity of the model is usually different across clients. Traditional FedAvg algorithm uses an undifferentiated parameter averaging strategy when dealing with these models with different sparsities, which may ignore model sparsity and thus affect performance and efficiency.

To overcome this limitation, this paper proposes the Federated Sparse Aggregation (FedSA). FedSA performs weighted averaging of only the non-zero parameters during model aggregation, which avoids ineffective computation of the zero weights and more accurately reflects the features and structure of the global model, thus improving the overall performance. When implementing FedSA, each client model is first analysed for sparsity to accurately identify its sparse structure. Subsequently, the algorithm focuses on non-zero parameters for weighted averaging to ensure that the aggregated model focuses on important weights and exhibits better performance. The formulation is shown in Eq. (7).

$$w_{t+1} = \sum_{k=1}^{M} \frac{\frac{m_k}{m}}{\sum_{k}^{M} \frac{m_k}{m}} w_{t+1}^k \quad \left(w_{t+1}^k \neq 0\right) \qquad (7)$$

4 Experiment

To fully validate RLBFP, this paper uses diverse datasets and methods for testing. Since most of the existing federated pruning studies focus on the image domain, the use of image datasets helps to conduct comparative experiments with the existing baselines, clearly demonstrating the advantages of RLBFP in terms of performance, and further confirming its generality and effectiveness. The experiments are conducted in a FL system consisting of 100 clients and a central server, with 10 devices randomly selected for training in each round.

4.1 Datasets and Metrics

Datasets. In this paper, RLBFP is evaluated using CIFAR-10, MNIST and Fashion-MNIST datasets. CIFAR-10 contains 60,000 32×32 colour images divided into 10 categories (e.g., aeroplanes, automobiles, etc.), and the dataset is divided into 50,000 training images and 10,000 test images. The MNIST dataset contains 60,000 handwritten digital images of 28×28 (training samples) and 10,000 test samples. Fashion-MNIST contains 60,000 clothing images of 28×28 (training samples) and 10,000 test samples. These datasets provide the basis for evaluating the performance of the models in different image classification tasks.

Metrics. The evaluation metrics used in this section are model generalization capabilities, sparsity and loss. Generalization capabilities refer to the capability of the model to perform on unseen data, measured by accuracy - the ratio of correctly predicted samples to total test samples. Higher accuracy indicates better generalisation. The formula for accuracy is given in Eq. (8).

$$Accuracy = \frac{\sum_{i=1}^{N} TP_i}{Total} \tag{8}$$

where N denotes the number of classes of samples in the dataset, TP_i denotes the number of data in class i that were correctly classified, and $Total$ denotes the total number of samples.

Sparsity is the percentage of zero weights of the model, and higher sparsity reduces the storage space of the model as well as improves the computational efficiency. The formula for model sparsity is shown in Eq. (9).

$$Sparsity = \sum_{i=1}^{m} \frac{\tau_i}{M_i N_i} \tag{9}$$

where m denotes the number of model layers, τ_i denotes the number of zero weights in the model parameters of layer i, and M_i, N_i denote the number of rows and columns, respectively, in the model parameter matrix of layer i.

Finally, the loss is calculated using the cross-entropy loss function, the formula for which is given in Eq. (10).

$$Loss = -\frac{1}{N} \sum_{i=1}^{N} y_i \log(p_i) \tag{10}$$

where N is the number of sample categories, p_i denotes the probability that the sample belongs to the i-th category, and y_i denotes the probability distribution of true labels, which is a one-hot coding vector. When the sample belongs to the i-th category, $y_i=1$, otherwise $y_i=0$.

4.2 Pruning Models and Baselines

Pruning Models. In this paper, we use VGG-19 [17] and ResNet-18 [6] as pruning models. VGG-19 consists of 16 convolutional layers, 5 pooling layers, and 3 fully-connected layers, and uses a small convolutional kernel to reduce the number of parameters. ResNet-18 solves the gradient vanishing problem through residual blocks and short-circuit connections, which improves training efficiency.

Baselines. Baseline methods include PruneFL, a technique that combines federated learning with model pruning, PQSU, which integrates structured pruning, weight quantisation and selective updating, and FedAvg, a widely used federated learning algorithm.

4.3 Evaluation of FedSA

To evaluate the performance of FedSA in the federated pruning task, this section compares FedSA with the widely used FedAvg method. In the experiments, the other components of RLBFP are kept unchanged and only the central aggregation method is replaced to verify the advantages of FedSA.

The experimental results are summarised in Table 1, demonstrating the best accuracy and sparsity of the global model for both aggregation methods with different models and datasets. The goal of model pruning is to improve the sparsity of the model while maintaining the accuracy. The results show that the accuracy of FedSA is 0.57% lower than FedAvg, but FedSA achieves an average sparsity of up to 18.9% while maintaining accuracy. This shows that FedSA is more effective in dealing with model aggregation with different sparsities in federated learning, overcoming the shortcomings of traditional aggregation methods when facing model sparsity and achieving more accurate model aggregation.

Table 1. FedSA Evaluation Results Table

Dataset	Maximum accuracy/sparsity			
	ResNet-18		VGG-19	
	FedAvg	FedSA	FedAvg	FedSA
Cifar10	88.92/0.435482	83.64/0.722253	77.45/0.470041	79.08/0.750887
MNIST	99.54/0.21574	99.51/0.311692	99.57/0.304456	99.55/0.387588
Fashion-MNIST	92.6/0.245904	92.68/0.26976	92.44/0.324078	92.60/0.693178

4.4 Model Generalization Capabilities Assessment

In order to fully assess the generalisation capabilities of the model, this study uses multiple datasets to compare the performance of RLBFP with the baseline approach in terms of global model accuracy. PQSU baseline reference RLBFP sets the same pruning rate to ensure a fair comparison. Figure 2 demonstrates the comparison of global model accuracy between RLBFP and the baseline method on different datasets. When the pruning model is VGG19, RLBFP significantly outperforms the other federated pruning baselines, with an accuracy close to that of FedAvg trained dense model, proving that RLBFP is effective in maintaining model performance during the pruning process.

When the pruning model is ResNet18, PQSU pruning operation leads to a severe performance loss of the model, which fails to converge efficiently, and the accuracy drops significantly. This highlights the advantage of RLBFP in pruning, which is able to better preserve the key information of the model and avoid the performance loss caused by excessive pruning. On MNIST and FMNIST datasets, the accuracy gap between PruneFL and RLBFP decreases due to the excellent performance of ResNet18 itself. Despite the fact that the curves of the two almost overlap in Fig. 2(e), the accuracy of RLBFP is still slightly higher than that of PruneFL, with an average difference of 0.43%.

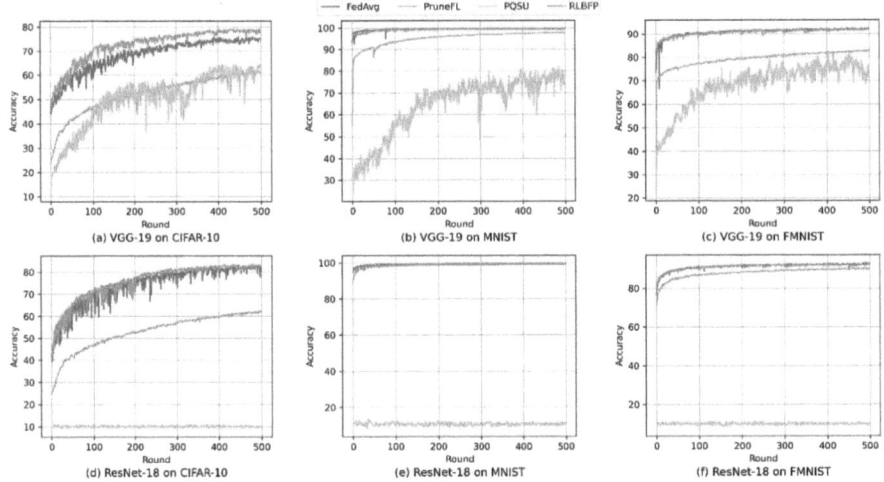

Fig. 2. Accuracy Test Result Graph of RLBFP.

4.5 Convergence Analysis

After rigorous experimental validation, this study compares the performance of RLBFP with multiple federated pruning baseline methods on different datasets. The experimental results are shown in Fig. 3 and Tables 2, 3, both of which demonstrate the significant advantages of RLBFP in federated pruning.

As shown in Fig. 3, the loss profile of RLBFP is consistently lower than that of other federated pruning baseline methods during model training. Although in some cases other methods such as PQSU achieved lower losses, RLBFP maintained a steady advantage and significantly outperformed other methods on other datasets. In addition, RLBFP has comparable loss levels to the unpruned federated learning process, further demonstrating its success in achieving pruning while maintaining model performance.

The Ra columns in Tables 2 and 3 then demonstrate the minimum number of rounds required for each method to achieve the specified accuracy. From the experimental results, RLBFP requires significantly fewer training rounds than

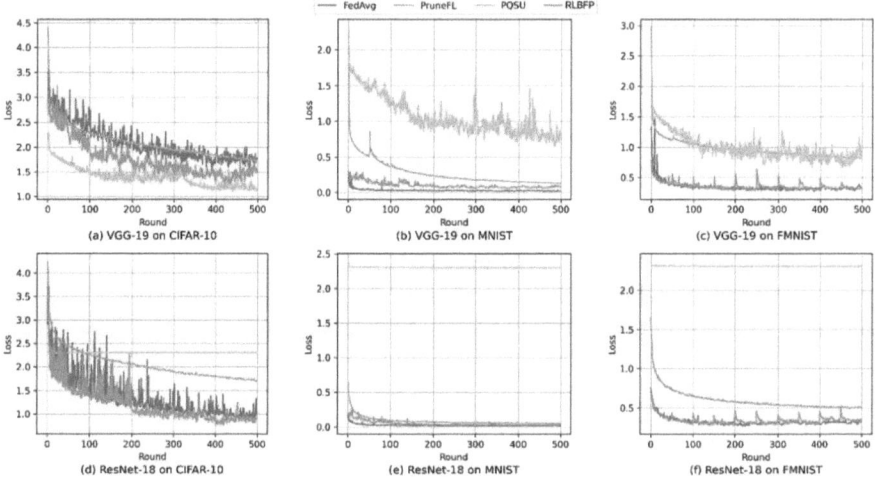

Fig. 3. Loss Comparison Chart of RLBFP and Baselines.

Table 2. Comparison Results Table of RLBFP and Baselines under VGG19 Model

Method	Cifar10(vgg19)			MNIST(VGG19)			FMNIST(VGG19)		
	R0.5	R0.6	R0.7	R0.95	R0.98	R0.99	R0.75	R0.8	R0.9
FedAvg	6	54	177	4	5	61	2	3	57
PruneFL	156	433	-	153	-	-	37	222	-
PQSU	112	-	-	-	-	-	157	446	-
RLBFP	5	36	102	2	36	91	1	1	83

the other methods to achieve the same accuracy rate and achieves to reach a higher accuracy rate.

In summary, based on the analysis of the experimental results, it can be concluded that RLBFP can not only effectively improve the accuracy and training efficiency of the model, but also achieve fast convergence while maintaining low loss.

Table 3. Comparison Results Table of RLBFP and Baselines under ResNet18 Model

Method	Cifar10 (ResNet18)			MNIST (ResNet18)			FMNIST (ResNet18)		
	R0.6	R0.7	R0.8	R0.95	R0.98	R0.99	R0.75	R0.8	R0.9
FedAvg	27	97	313	2	13	47	1	2	68
PruneFL	402	-	-	10	52	340	4	13	431
PQSU	-	-	-	-	-	-	-	-	-
RLBFP	26	81	257	3	38	108	1	2	60

5 Conclusion

In this paper, RLBFP, a federated reinforcement learning-based model pruning method, is proposed to address the high communication overhead and model generalization capabilities in federated learning systems, including a reinforcement-based generalization pruning method, RBGP, and a federated sparse aggregation method, FedSA, and reduces the model size while maintaining high performance through intelligent pruning and sparse aggregation strategies. Experimental results show that RLBFP outperforms existing federated pruning baseline methods by performing well on multiple datasets and models, significantly improving model sparsity and maintaining good accuracy and generalisation. This provides a new solution for federated learning system deployment on resource-constrained edge devices.

Our future research will focus on optimizing the reinforcement learning model within RBGP to improve its intelligence and automation capabilities, investigating more efficient federated sparse aggregation algorithms for large-scale federated learning systems, and extending the application of the RLBFP framework to a broader range of real-world scenarios to further evaluate its effectiveness and robustness.

References

1. Chen, J., Ran, X.: Deep learning with edge computing: a review. Proc. IEEE **107**(8), 1655–1674 (2019)
2. Esmaeilzadeh, H., Sampson, A., Ceze, L., Burger, D.: Neural acceleration for general-purpose approximate programs. In: 2012 45th Annual IEEE/ACM International Symposium on Microarchitecture, pp. 449–460. IEEE (2012)
3. Guo, J., Zhang, W., Ouyang, W., Xu, D.: Model compression using progressive channel pruning. IEEE Trans. Circuits Syst. Video Technol. **31**(3), 1114–1124 (2020)
4. Han, S., Pool, J., Tran, J., Dally, W.: Learning both weights and connections for efficient neural network. In: Advances in Neural Information Processing Systems, vol. 28 (2015)
5. Hassibi, B., Stork, D.: Second order derivatives for network pruning: optimal brain surgeon. In: Advances in Neural Information Processing Systems, vol. 5 (1992)
6. He, K., Zhang, X., Ren, S., Sun, J.: Deep residual learning for image recognition. In: Proceedings of the IEEE Conference on Computer Vision and Pattern Recognition, pp. 770–778 (2016)
7. He, Z., Xie, Z., Zhu, Q., Qin, Z.: Sparse double descent: where network pruning aggravates overfitting. In: International Conference on Machine Learning, pp. 8635–8659. PMLR (2022)
8. Jiang, X., Borcea, C.: Complement sparsification: low-overhead model pruning for federated learning. In: Proceedings of the AAAI Conference on Artificial Intelligence, vol. 37, pp. 8087–8095 (2023)
9. Jiang, Z., Xu, Y., Xu, H., Wang, Z., Qiao, C., Zhao, Y.: Fedmp: federated learning through adaptive model pruning in heterogeneous edge computing. In: 2022 IEEE 38th International Conference on Data Engineering (ICDE), pp. 767–779. IEEE (2022)

10. Kim, T., Kwon, Y., Lee, J., Kim, T., Ha, S.: CPrune: compiler-informed model pruning for efficient target-aware DNN execution. In: Avidan, S., Brostow, G., Cissé, M., Farinella, G.M., Hassner, T. (eds.) ECCV 2022. LNCS, vol. 13680, pp. 651–667. Springer, Cham (2022). https://doi.org/10.1007/978-3-031-20044-1_37
11. LeCun, Y., Denker, J., Solla, S.: Optimal brain damage. In: Advances in Neural Information Processing Systems, vol. 2 (1989)
12. Li, B., Wu, B., Su, J., Wang, G.: EagleEye: fast sub-net evaluation for efficient neural network pruning. In: Vedaldi, A., Bischof, H., Brox, T., Frahm, J.-M. (eds.) ECCV 2020, Part II. LNCS, vol. 12347, pp. 639–654. Springer, Cham (2020). https://doi.org/10.1007/978-3-030-58536-5_38
13. Liu, J., et al.: Discrimination-aware network pruning for deep model compression. IEEE Trans. Pattern Anal. Mach. Intell. **44**(8), 4035–4051 (2021)
14. Liu, Z., Sun, M., Zhou, T., Huang, G., Darrell, T.: Rethinking the value of network pruning. arXiv preprint arXiv:1810.05270 (2018)
15. McMahan, B., Moore, E., Ramage, D., Hampson, S., Arcas, B.A.: Communication-efficient learning of deep networks from decentralized data. In: Artificial Intelligence and Statistics, pp. 1273–1282. PMLR (2017)
16. Prakash, P., et al.: IoT device friendly and communication-efficient federated learning via joint model pruning and quantization. IEEE Internet Things J. **9**(15), 13638–13650 (2022)
17. Simonyan, K., Zisserman, A.: Very deep convolutional networks for large-scale image recognition. arXiv preprint arXiv:1409.1556 (2014)
18. Wen, D., Jeon, K.-J., Huang, K.: Federated dropout–a simple approach for enabling federated learning on resource constrained devices. IEEE Wirel. Commun. Lett. **11**(5), 923–927 (2022)
19. Yao, D., et al.: Fedhm: efficient federated learning for heterogeneous models via low-rank factorization. arXiv preprint arXiv:2111.14655 (2021)
20. Yu, R., et al.: NISP: pruning networks using neuron importance score propagation. In: Proceedings of the IEEE Conference on Computer Vision and Pattern Recognition, pp. 9194–9203 (2018)
21. Zhang, H., Liu, J., Jia, J., Zhou, Y., Dai, H., Dou, D.: Fedduap: federated learning with dynamic update and adaptive pruning using shared data on the server. arXiv preprint arXiv:2204.11536 (2022)
22. Zhu, Z., et al.: Fedlp: layer-wise pruning mechanism for communication-computation efficient federated learning. In: ICC 2023-IEEE International Conference on Communications, pp. 1250–1255. IEEE (2023)

Semi-asynchronous Federated Dynamic Mutual Distillation in Vehicular Networks

Xiaoge Huang[✉], Yali Xiao, Wenjing Li, Chengchao Liang, and Bin Shen

School of Communications and Information Engineering, Chongqing University of Posts and Telecommunications, Chongqing 400065, China
huangxg@cqupt.edu.cn

Abstract. Federated Learning (FL) is a distributed machine learning method with great potential for the Vehicular Networks. However, traditional FL involves frequent exchanges between RSUs and vehicles, causing high communication overhead. Additionally, the Non-IID nature of vehicle data, due to varying driving habits and environments, reduces model accuracy. To address these issues, this paper proposes a Semi-Asynchronous Federated Dynamic Mutual Distillation (SFMD) method. It first selects the top N vehicles for model updates based on processing time and forces inactive vehicles to join training. Secondly, teacher and student models perform mutual knowledge distillation with dynamic intensity to improve generalization and training. Finally, a data sharing mechanism based on differential privacy reduces model bias from Non-IID data. Simulations show SFMD improves model accuracy and reduces communication overhead.

Keywords: Semi-Asynchronous federated learning · Dynamic knowledge mutual distillation · Non-IID · Data sharing

1 Introduction

According to authoritative statistics, the global penetration of Connected and Automated Vehicles (CAVs) has surpassed 400 million, leading to a significant demand for data processing. Machine Learning (ML) is essential for CAV tasks like perception, planning, and control, as it extracts "complex patterns and insights" from data [1]. However, ML training requires access to CAV data, raising concerns about privacy and the communication overhead from large datasets [2].

Federated Learning (FL) is a decentralized ML approach that allows multiple CAVs to train a global model without sharing private data, protecting privacy and security. McMahan et al. introduced the FedAvg algorithm [3], where all nodes send their model updates after each training round, causing heavy communication loads. Xie et al. proposed FedAsync [4], where the global model updates immediately after receiving a local model. However, frequent updates lead to high communication costs, and inconsistent update speeds cause outdated local models, reducing accuracy. Zhang et al. [5]

This work is supported by the National Natural Science Foundation of China (62371082), Guangxi Science and Technology Project (AB24010317), Natural Science Foundation of Chongqing (CSTB2023NSCQ-MSX0726, cstc2020jcyj-msxmX0878).

and Wu et al. [6] proposed methods like CSAFL and SAFA, which set specific time windows or thresholds for updates, allowing some nodes to synchronize updates while others update asynchronously. To reduce communication overhead, Jeong et al. [7] proposed Federated Distillation, which shares only the model output logits. Li et al. [8] further enhanced this with the FFSD algorithm, using feature fusion and self-distillation to improve model training.

Although FL has advantages in communication between CAVs, it lacks the ability to handle Non-Independent and Identically Distributed (Non-IID) data. The differences in driving environments and operating conditions of CAVs lead to data that exhibit Non-IID characteristics, causing model bias and reducing model accuracy [10,11].

To address these challenges, this paper introduces Semi-Asynchronous Federated Dynamic Mutual Distillation (SFMD), which integrates Semi-Asynchronous FL, knowledge distillation, and data sharing to lower communication costs and enhance model accuracy. The key contributions are:

- To improve training efficiency, a Semi-Asynchronous FL method is proposed. The RSU selects the top N CAVs for model updates based on their processing time. Model updates include training and aggregation, and CAVs that skip multiple rounds are forced to participate.
- A dynamic mutual knowledge distillation method is proposed, where teacher and student models are trained simultaneously on the CAV using training data and exchanged soft labels. Dynamic distillation intensity enhances model generalization and training effectiveness.
- Data sharing mechanism based on differential privacy boosts low-quality CAV training data, protects privacy, and reduces model bias from Non-IID data.
- The data sharing mechanism based on differential privacy aims to increase low-quality training data for CAV models, protecting data privacy while mitigating model bias caused by Non-IID data.

The paper is organized as follows: Sect. 2 describes the system model. Section 3 presents the SFMD algorithm, covering Semi-Asynchronous FL, dynamic mutual distillation, and data sharing. Section 4 shows the simulation results, followed by conclusions in Sect. 5.

2 System Model

In this section, we discuss the network model and working process of SFMD.

2.1 Network Model

The SFMD double-layer vehicular network architecture consists of a CAV layer and an edge layer, as shown in Fig. 1

CAV Layer: The CAV layer comprises the CAVs participating in FL, which have limited computing and storage resources. The set of CAVs can be represented as $\mathcal{V} = \{V_1, V_2, \cdots, V_i, \cdots, V_I\}$. During driving, CAVs collect data through onboard sensors to support the training of local student and teacher models.

Edge Layer: The edge layer consists of RSUs deployed alongside roads, which have higher computing and storage capabilities and are used to process models uploaded by CAVs, facilitating data sharing among CAVs.

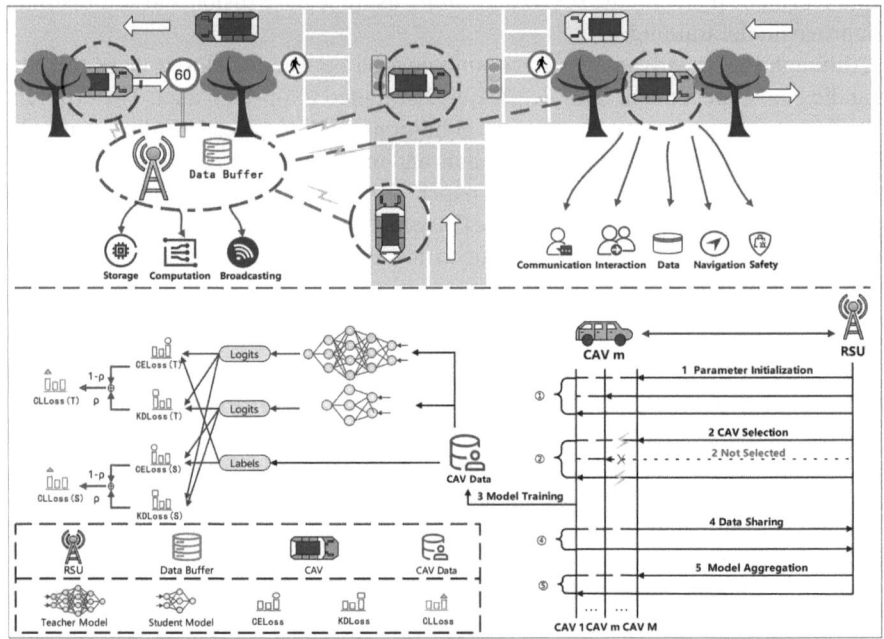

Fig. 1. Semi-Asynchronous Federated Dynamic Mutual Distillation in Vehicular Networks.

2.2 Working Process of SFMD

SFMD algorithm consists of the following five steps:

Parameter Initialization. The RSU sets the number of CAVs participating in model updates to N based on model quality requirements and resource constraints, and broadcasts this information to all CAVs. Subsequently, each CAV randomly initializes its teacher model and student model.

CAV Selection. The model processing time of the CAV is calculated, which consists of model training time and transmission time. The RSU selects the top N CAVs based on model processing time and adds them to the CAV candidate set V_{agg}, which will participate in this round of model updates. If a CAV is not selected in the current round, its laziness increases by one. The laziness of all CAVs are checked, and any CAV that exceeds the laziness threshold is forced to participate in the current round of model update.

Model Training The CAVs in the set V_{agg} train their student model and teacher model. The teacher model will only be trained locally, while the student model will be uploaded to the RSU for global model update. During this process, the CAVs calculate task loss $L^{CE}(w)$ based on real labels and model soft labels, and distillation loss $L^{KD}(w)$ based on student and teacher model soft labels. Distillation intensity is defined as the contribution of task loss and distillation loss to the combined loss $L^{CL}(w)$, and it is dynamically adjusted based on the training rounds using an exponential decay function.

Data Sharing. When the accuracy difference between the student models of the CAVs in two consecutive training rounds exceeds the set threshold, the data sharing mechanism based on differential privacy is triggered. At this time, all CAVs randomly select part of their local data, add Laplace noise, and upload it to the data buffer of RSU to protect data privacy. The data buffer is then forwarded to the corresponding CAVs for local training to improve the accuracy of their student models. The new task losses for the student and teacher models are then uploaded to the RSU.

Model Aggregation. The RSU adjusts the weights of the student models based on the task losses of the teacher models, aggregates the global model, and sends the updated global model to the CAVs. The RSU and CAVs then proceed to the next iteration of training, continuing until the number of training rounds reaches the termination condition.

3 Semi-asynchronous FL

Unlike synchronous FL, Semi-Asynchronous FL does not need to wait for all CAVs to complete local training to perform model aggregation. In this scenario, the CAV candidate set is generated based on the CAV model processing time to determine which CAVs are involved in each round of training.

Model processing time includes: model training time, model uploading time, model aggregation time and model distribution time. Model aggregation and model distribution time are relatively short and negligible, model training and model uploading time primarily depend on CAV computing capabilities and communication resources, which can be calculated by the following equations, respectively:

$$t_i^{comp} = \theta log_2(\frac{1}{\varepsilon})\frac{C_i|D_i|}{f_i} \quad (1)$$

$$t_i^{upload} = \frac{s}{r_i} = \frac{s}{Blog_2(1+\frac{P_ig_i}{N_0})} \quad (2)$$

where θ is a constant determining the upper bound of local iterations, ε represents the expected accuracy, $\theta log_2(\frac{1}{\varepsilon})$ is the number of iterations required to achieve the desired model accuracy, C_i is the number of CPU cycles required for local training of one sample, D_i is the number of training data samples for V_i, f_i is the CPU frequency used for training V_i's model, B is the transmission bandwidth allocated to V_i, P_i is the transmission power of V_i, g_i is the channel gain from V_i to RSU, N_0 is the noise power. The model processing time for V_i is:

$$t_i = t_i^{comp} + t_i^{upload} \tag{3}$$

Due to the differences in network transmission quality, CAV computing power, and other factors, some CAVs take a longer time to complete the local model training and uploading, which will lead to an increase in model processing delay. Therefore, only the first N CAVs with shorter model processing time are selected for this round of training in this scenario. However, some CAVs may not be selected for multiple rounds, resulting in their model versions lagging behind the latest global model, reducing the model performance of CAVs. The laziness is defined as the number of consecutive times the CAV does not participate in training, and the laziness is added 1 when the CAV is unselected. When V_{agg} is generated, the RSU will check the laziness of all current CAVs, and if the laziness of the CAV exceeds the threshold value, the RSU will send the current global model to the CAV and notify it to perform the model update.

3.1 Dynamic Mutual Knowledge Distillation

In the dynamic knowledge mutual distillation approach both teacher and student models are trained locally, and the models are helped to learn by local data and soft labels that are transferred to each other.

Mutual Knowledge Distillation. Specifically, at the kth round, for category c, the output soft labels of the student model and the teacher model obtained from V_i training are denoted as $y_{s,i}^k(c)$ and $y_{t,i}^k(c)$, and the true label vector is $y_i^k(c)$. $L_{s,i}^{k,CE}(y_i^k(c), y_{s,i}^k(c))$ and $L_{t,i}^{k,CE}(y_i^k(c), y_{t,i}^k(c))$ denote the task loss of the student model and teacher model, calculated by the following equation:

$$L_{s,i}^{k,CE}(y_i^k(c), y_{s,i}^k(c)) = -\sum_c y_i^k(c) \log(y_{s,i}^k(c)) \tag{4}$$

$$L_{t,i}^{k,CE}(y_i^k(c), y_{t,i}^k(c)) = -\sum_c y_i^k(c) \log(y_{t,i}^k(c)) \tag{5}$$

The output soft labels of the student model and the teacher model are the corresponding normalized model output vectors, which are expressed as:

$$p_{s,i}^k(c) = \frac{\exp(y_{s,i}^k(c))}{\sum_z \exp(y_{s,i}^k(z))} \tag{6}$$

$$p_{t,i}^k(c) = \frac{\exp(y_{t,i}^k(c))}{\sum_z \exp(y_{t,i}^k(z))} \tag{7}$$

where z represents the category index and is used to iterate through all possible categories. The distillation loss formula for the kth round is as follows:

$$L_{s,i}^{k,KD}(p_{t,i}^k(c)\|p_{s,i}^k(c)) = \sum_c p_{t,i}^k(c) \log\left(\frac{p_{t,i}^k(c)}{p_{s,i}^k(c)}\right) \tag{8}$$

$$L_{t,i}^{k,KD}(p_{s,i}^k(c)\|p_{t,i}^k(c)) = \sum_c p_{s,i}^k(c) \log\left(\frac{p_{s,i}^k(c)}{p_{t,i}^k(c)}\right) \tag{9}$$

The weight of task loss and distillation loss are adjusted by dynamic distillation intensity, the formula for which is described in the following section. The combined loss of the student model and teacher model are defined as follows:

$$L_{s,i}^{k,CL}(w_{s,i}^k, w_{t,i}^k) = (1-\rho^k)L_{s,i}^{k,CE}(y_i^k(c), y_{s,i}^k(c)) + \rho^k L_{s,i}^{k,WL}(p_{t,i}^k(c)\|p_{s,i}^k(c)) \tag{10}$$

$$L_{t,i}^{k,CL}(w_{t,i}^k, w_{s,i}^k) = (1-\rho^k)L_{t,i}^{k,CE}(y_i^k(c), y_{t,i}^k(c)) + \rho^k L_{t,i}^{k,WL}(p_{s,i}^k(c)\|p_{t,i}^k(c)) \tag{11}$$

The student model and teacher model are updated according to the stochastic gradient descent method:

$$w_{s,i}^k = w_{s,i}^{k-1} - \eta \nabla L_{s,i}^{k,CL}(w_{s,i}^k, w_{t,i}^k) \tag{12}$$

$$w_{t,i}^k = w_{t,i}^{k-1} - \eta \nabla L_{t,i}^{k,CL}(w_{t,i}^k, w_{s,i}^k) \tag{13}$$

where η is the learning rate, which determines the step size of the parameter update.

Dynamic Distillation. The knowledge mutual distillation process involves local data training and inter-transferred soft label-assisted training, with a combined loss function of task loss and distillation loss. The distillation intensity regulates knowledge transfer from the teacher to the student model. The teacher model, having more parameters and a deeper structure, learns finer features and improves accuracy. To enhance the student model's learning, it should focus on insights from the teacher model. However, as training progresses and the student model matures, the impact of mutual knowledge distillation decreases. Since the teacher model's knowledge is derived from local CAV data and student model feedback, it is fully utilized during early training. Therefore, the distillation intensity must be dynamically adjusted to optimize the student model's knowledge absorption, using an exponential decay function based on the number of training rounds:

$$\rho^k = \rho_0 e^{-\lambda k} \tag{14}$$

where ρ_0 is the initial distillation weight and λ is the decay rate.

3.2 Data-Sharing

The use of Non-IID data collected by CAVs for training will result in significant discrepancies among the local models. In order to improve the model performance under Non-IID data, a data sharing mechanism based on differential privacy is proposed, which will be activated when the accuracy difference between the CAV student models in two consecutive rounds exceeds a set threshold. All CAVs need to add Laplace noise to part of the raw data and upload them to the RSU data buffer to construct the shared data set. With more data in the data buffer, CAVs will select the most suitable data from these data for model correction. Therefore, the importance of each round of shared data in model correction needs to be calculated, and based on this, the proportion of shared data in each round is decided.

When V_i triggers data sharing mechanism, the global model parameters are all stored in the RSU, denoting the number of rounds of data sharing as $\mathcal{H} = \{1, 2, \cdots, h, \cdots, H\}$, and the global model at the hth round of data sharing is w^h. w^* is the global model with the lowest loss. The model bias is quantified by calculating the difference between w^* and the jth parameter of the hth round global model, which can be denoted as:

$$d^{h,j} = ||w^*(j) - w^h(j)|| \tag{15}$$

A smaller $d^{h,j}$ indicates that the global model update in that round is close to the optimal training direction and its training data is more globally characterized, so the corresponding shared data uploaded in round h is assigned a higher training ratio. In addition, the importance of the jth parameter to the model performance is calculated by Fisher's information matrix $F^{h,j}$. The jth parameter is used to calculate the importance of model performance:

$$F^{h,j} = -E[\frac{\partial^2 L_{s,i}^{h,CE}}{\partial w(j)^2}] \tag{16}$$

A larger $F^{h,j}$ means that the parameter has a greater impact on the model output and the parameter has a higher importance in the model, and vice versa for a lower importance. Based on $d^{h,j}$ and $F^{h,j}$, the proportion of shared data in the model correction is adjusted. To optimize the shared data ratio, the optimization problem can be modeled as:

$$\begin{aligned}\min_{x^h}(&\sum_{h=1}^{H} g(x^h) \sum_{j}^{J} F^{h,j}(d^{h,j})^2) \\ \text{s.t.: } &\sum_{h=1}^{H} g(x^h) = 1 \\ &g(x^h) > 0\end{aligned} \tag{17}$$

where $g(x)$ is the Sigmoid function, defined as:

$$g(x) = \frac{1}{1+e^{-x}} \tag{18}$$

By optimizing the proportional adjustment parameter x^h, making $f^h = g(x^h)$, the optimal shared data ratio f^h for the hth round can be obtained. To sum up, Algorithm 1 summarizes the SFMD algorithm.

Algorithm 1 Semi-Asynchronous Federated Dynamic Mutual Distillation

---

1: **Input:** Training rounds K; Initial student model w_s^0; Learning rate η; Initial distillation weight ρ^0; Decay rate λ; Laziness threshold LA_0, number of candidate CAVs N;
2: **Output:** Optimal student model w_s^*;
3: **Initialization:** Initialize aggregating CAVs N;
4: **for** $k = 1$ to K **do**
5:    **for** CAV $i \in M$ **do**
6:       Calculate model training time t_i^{comp} and model upload time t_i^{upload}, and calculate model processing time t_i
7:    **end for**
8:    Select the top N CAVs based on t_i to add them to the CAV candidate set V_{agg}
9:    Record the CAV laziness LA_i and add the CAVs exceeding the laziness threshold to the candidate V_{agg}
10:   **for** CAV $i \in V_{agg}$ **do**
11:      Calculate task losses for the student model and teacher model $L_{s,i}^{k,CE}(w)$ and $L_{t,i}^{k,CE}(w)$
12:      Calculate distillation losses for the student model and teacher model $L_{s,i}^{k,KD}(w)$ and $L_{t,i}^{k,KD}(w)$
13:      Calculate the ratio of task loss and distillation loss ρ^k
14:      Calculate weighted losses for the student model and teacher model $L_{s,i}^{k,CL}(w)$ and $L_{t,i}^{k,CL}(w)$
15:      Update student model $w_{s,i}^{k+1}$ and teacher model $w_{t,i}^{k+1}$
16:   **end for**
17:   **if** CAV i triggers the data sharing mechanism **then**
18:      CAV $i \in V_{agg}$ uploads α portion of original data to the data buffer, adds Laplace noise
19:      Calculate model bias and Fisher information matrix
20:      Calculate the proportion of data shared in each round
21:   **end if**
22:   Calculate the proportion of data shared in each round
23: **end for**

---

4 Simulation Performances

In this section, the performance of the proposed SFMD algorithm is evaluated in various aspects by comparing other algorithms. Three typical FL algorithms are used as comparison algorithms: FedAvg [3] and FedAsync [4] are described in Sect. 1. FedProx [12]introduces a regularization term based on FedAvg to reduce the performance degradation caused by Non-IID data.

4.1 Simulation Setting

To validate the SFMD algorithm's performance in training Convolutional Network (CNN) models on the MNIST and Traffic Signs Preprocessed (TSP) datasets, the MNIST training set has 60,000 handwritten digit images (0 to 9) and a test set of 10,000 images. The TSP training set consists of 86,989 images of 43 traffic sign classes, with 12,630 test images. Both teacher and student models use CNN: 1) Teacher model: three convolutional layers with max pooling and two fully connected layers; 2) Student model: two convolutional layers with max pooling and one fully connected layer. The meta-learning rates are 0.005 for meta-training and 0.001 for meta-updating, with a batch size of 64, 200 training epochs, and an initial distillation intensity ρ_0 of 1.

4.2 Performance Evaluation

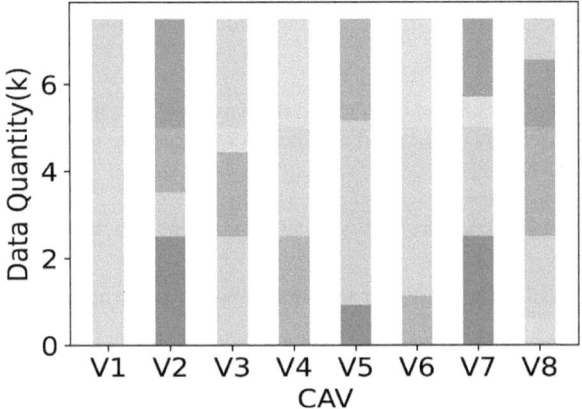

Fig. 2. Data distribution of CAVs on Mnist dataset

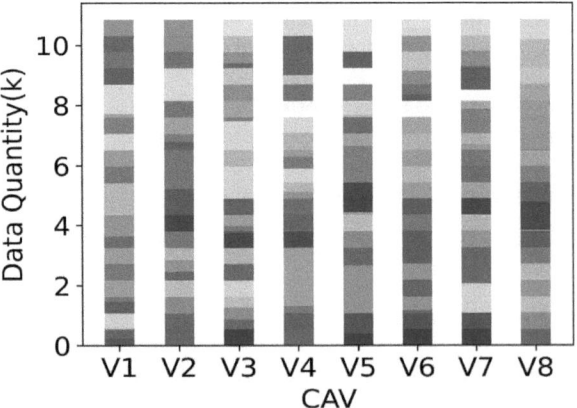

Fig. 3. Data distribution of CAVs on Tsp dataset

The data distribution of CAV on different datasets is shown in Fig. 2 and Fig. 3. The MNIST and TSP datasets are used to demonstrate the Non-IID characteristics of the data collected by CAV, respectively. Different colors in the figure represent different types of data, and it can be seen that the composition of each of the data types collected by the CAV is different, and this difference stems from the fact that the CAVs are in different road environments, the CAV status, and other factors.

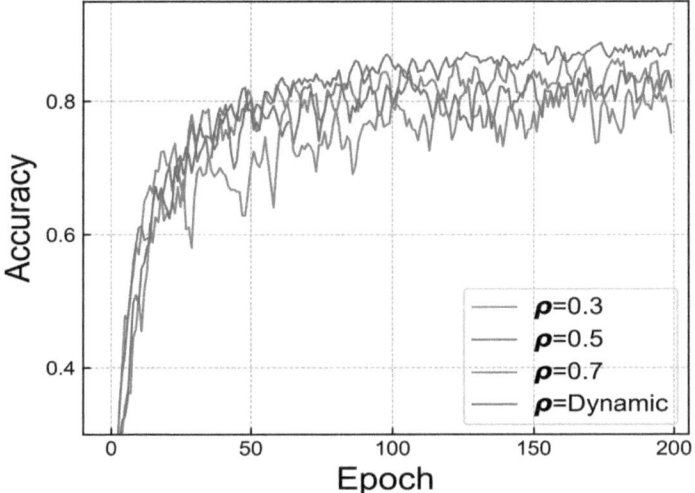

Fig. 4. Acc on Different Distillation Intensities

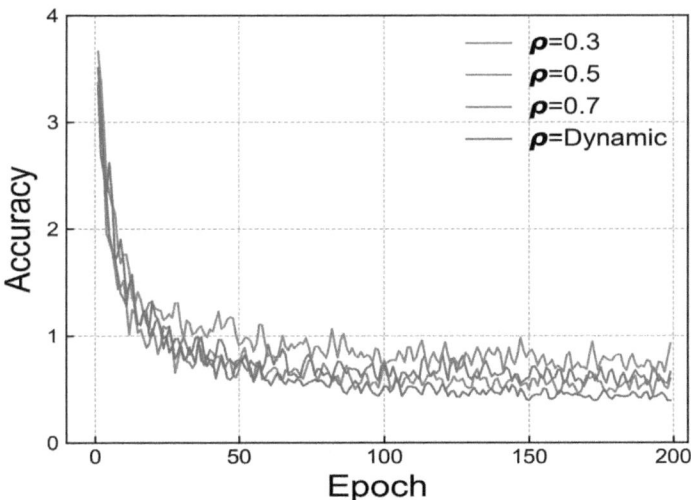

Fig. 5. Loss on Different Distillation Intensities

Figure 4 and Fig. 5 demonstrate the effect of different distillation intensities on the model performance. As shown in the figure, the dynamic distillation intensity based on knowledge mutual distillation approach performs more superior in both model accuracy and stability. The teacher model shows higher performance due to its ability to learn more detailed features, but its knowledge is mainly based on local data and feedback from the student model, and this knowledge will be gradually fully explored in the training process. Therefore, in the late stage of knowledge mutual distillation, the distillation intensity can be dynamically adjusted to enable the student model to transition from relying on the guidance of the teacher model to strengthening its own learning ability. Therefore, the performance of the knowledge mutual distillation method based on dynamic distillation intensity tends to stabilize with deeper training, while the model accuracy using fixed distillation intensity still has significant fluctuations.

Figure 6 and Fig. 7 compare the accuracy and loss with the number of iterations for different algorithms on the TSP dataset. From the figure, it can be found that the proposed algorithm achieves higher model accuracy and lower loss compared to the other three compared algorithms. FedAsync consistently fails to converge in a limited number of rounds, while both FedAvg and FedProx model accuracies are below 90%. After 200 rounds of model training, the accuracies of FedAsync, FedAvg, FedProx, and the SFMD method with different N values (N is 3, 5, and 7) are 74.6%, 84.8%, 86.2%, 88.5%, 89.6%, and 91.4%, respectively. Meanwhile, the volatility of the model accuracy curve decreases as the number of CAVs involved in training increases. This is due to the fact that more CAVs are involved in the training, resulting in richer data for

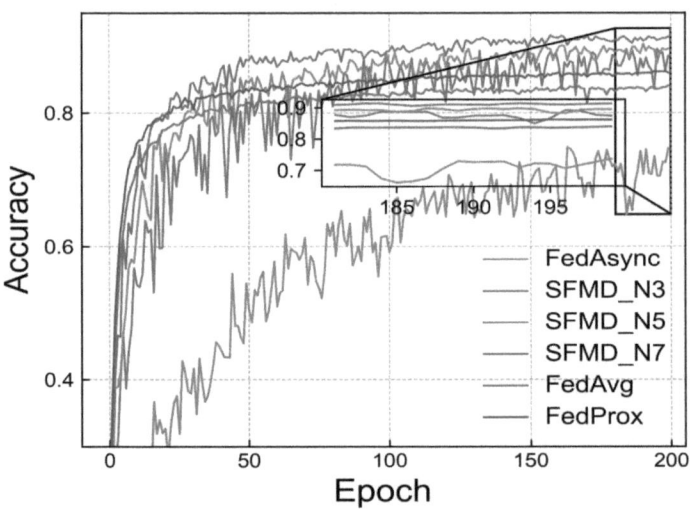

Fig. 6. Acc of Different Algorithms in Non-IID

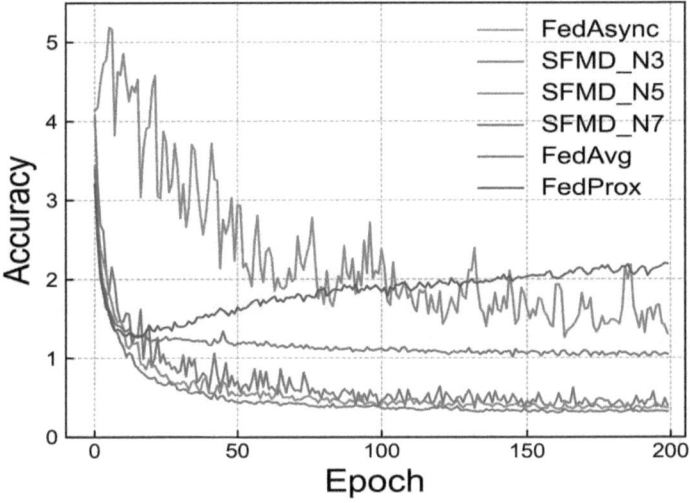

Fig. 7. Loss of Different Algorithms in Non-IID

the model training process, which provides more diverse and comprehensive features and improves the generalisation ability of the model.

Table 1. Communication Overhead in Non-IID (MB)

Data	Acc	FedAsync	SFMD	FedAvg	FedProx
Tsp	70%	139	18	51	41
	80%	491	45	180	113
	85%	-	80	-	503
	88%	-	144	-	-
	90%	-	251	-	-
Mnist	75%	87	11	64	50
	85%	239	25	193	143
	92%	676	78	507	336
	95%	-	128	1050	700
	97%	-	301	-	-

Table 1 shows the communication overhead of different algorithms on different datasets in MB. For example, the target accuracy is set to 70%, 80%, 85%, 88%, and 90% for the TSP dataset. The proposed SFMD algorithm incurs additional communication overhead due to data sharing, but it remains lower than the three previously mentioned algorithms, mainly due to optimizations in communication frequency and data volume. On the one hand, Semi-Asynchronous FL reduces the number of uploaded models by selecting only N CAVs to participate in global aggregation; on the other hand, knowledge mutual distillation greatly reduces the number of parametric quantities for model transmission. Notably, when the number of participating training CAVs is small, more training rounds are required to achieve the target model accuracy due to the lack of data diversity, which increases the communication overhead. However, as the number of participating training CAVs increases, the communication overhead per round of aggregation will also increase, but the number of training rounds will decrease. Therefore, the optimal balance between communication overhead and model accuracy can be found by optimizing the number of participating training CAVs.

Figure 8 and Fig. 9 illustrate the impact of data sharing strategies on model accuracy and loss. It can be seen that compared to models without data sharing, models with data sharing perform better in terms of accuracy. For example, when the sharing ratio is 0.15, the model achieves the accuracy of 91.4% after 200 training epochs, while without data sharing, the accuracy is only 89.5%. When the data sharing ratio is increased to 0.25, there is an initial improvement in accuracy compared to 0.15, but the final convergence accuracy does not significantly increase. This is because although increasing the data sharing ratio can accelerate the model's learning progress in the early stages, in the later stages of training, the model may have already acquired sufficient information. Therefore, further increasing the data sharing ratio has limited effect on further improving the model performance.

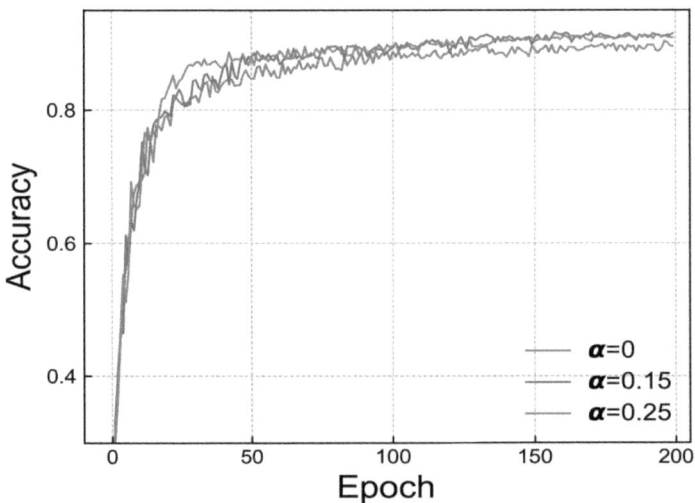

Fig. 8. Acc Under Different Data Sharing Ratio

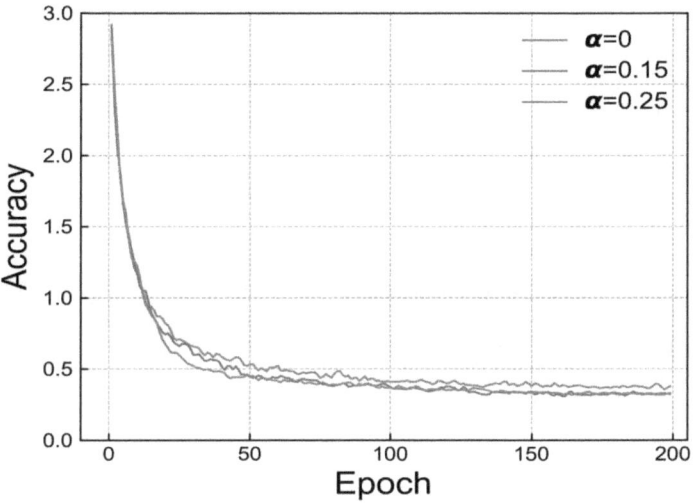

Fig. 9. Loss Under Different Data Sharing Ratio

5 Conclusions

This paper proposes a Semi-Asynchronous Federated Dynamic Mutual Distillation algorithm to enhance model training efficiency using the Semi-Asynchronous FL method. A dynamic mutual distillation approach is introduced, along with a design for dynamic mutual distillation intensity. Additionally, a data sharing mechanism based on differential privacy is explored to reduce model bias from Non-IID data. Simulation results demonstrate that SFMD improves model accuracy while significantly reducing communication overhead.

References

1. Huang, X., Wu, Y., Liang, C., Chen, Q., Zhang, J.: Distance-aware hierarchical federated learning in blockchain-enabled edge computing network. IEEE Internet Things J. (2023)
2. Chellapandi, V.P., Yuan, L.Q., Brinton, C.G., Żak, S.H., Wang, Z.: Federated learning for connected and automated vehicles: a survey of existing approaches and challenges. IEEE Trans. Intell. Veh. (2023)
3. McMahan, B., Moore, E., Ramage, D., Hampson, S., Arcas, B.A.: Communication-efficient learning of deep networks from decentralized data. In: Proceedings of the Artificial Intelligence and Statistics, pp. 1273–1282 (2017)
4. Xie, C., Koyejo, S., Gupta, I.: Asynchronous federated optimization. arXiv preprint arXiv:1903.03934 (2019)
5. Zhang, Y., et al.: CSAFL: a clustered semi-asynchronous federated learning framework. In: Proceedings of the 2021 International Joint Conference on Neural Networks (IJCNN), pp. 1–10 (2021)
6. Wu, W., He, L., Lin, W., Mao, R., Maple, C., Jarvis, S.: SAFA: a semi-asynchronous protocol for fast federated learning with low overhead. IEEE Trans. Comput. **70**(5), 655–668 (2020)

7. Jeong, E., Oh, S., Kim, H., Park, J., Bennis, M., Kim, S.-L.: Communication-efficient on-device machine learning: federated distillation and augmentation under non-IID private data. arXiv preprint arXiv:1811.11479 (2018)
8. Li, S., et al.: Distilling a powerful student model via online knowledge distillation. IEEE Trans. Neural Netw. Learn. Syst. (2022)
9. Do, T., Nguyen, B.X., Nguyen, H., Tjiputra, E., Tran, Q.D., Nguyen, A.: Addressing non-IID problem in federated autonomous driving with contrastive divergence loss. arXiv preprint arXiv:2303.06305 (2023)
10. Atapour, K., Seyedmohammadi, S.J., Abouei, J., Mohammadi, A., Plataniotis, K.N.: FedD2S: personalized data-free federated knowledge distillation. arXiv preprint arXiv:2402.10846 (2024)
11. Mu, X., et al.: Fedproc: prototypical contrastive federated learning on non-IID data. Future Gen. Comput. Syst. **143**, 93–104 (2023)
12. Li, T., Sahu, A.K., Zaheer, M., Sanjabi, M., Talwalkar, A., Smith, V.: Federated optimization in heterogeneous networks. In: Proceedings of Machine Learning and Systems, vol. 2, pp. 429–450 (2020)

Computation Offloading and Resource Allocation in Multi-constraint Edge Environments Using DRL

Junjie Zhang[1], Bing Xiong[1], Zhiqin Huang[1], Zhengxin Yu[2], Wang Miao[3], and Zheyi Chen[1(✉)]

[1] College of Computer and Data Science, Fuzhou University, Fuzhou, China
z.chen@fzu.edu.cn
[2] School of Computing and Communications, Lancaster University, Lancaster, UK
[3] College of Engineering, Computing and Mathematics, University of Plymouth, Plymouth, UK

Abstract. Through deploying computation and storage as ubiquitous resources at the network edge, Mobile Edge Computing (MEC) is a promising paradigm to obtain low-delay and high-reliability service experience. However, computation offloading and resource allocation in MEC environments are challenging due to dynamic system state and variable user demand. Existing solutions can not well adapt to such dynamic MEC environments with multiple constraints, because they depend on prior knowledge, which is difficult to obtain in highly dynamic and time-varying MEC systems. To solve this issue, we propose a novel Joint computation Offloading and resource Allocation empowered by deep Reinforcement Learning (JOA-RL) method. For multi-user sequential tasks, the JOA-RL can generate appropriate schemes according to current computational resources and network conditions, aiming to improve the success rate of task execution while reducing the task execution delay and energy consumption. Meanwhile, the JOA-RL introduces a preprocessing mechanism of task priority, which makes it able to make fast decisions to find appropriate computing modes for different tasks. Extensive experiments verify the effectiveness and superiority of the JOA-RL method. The results show that the JOA-RL achieves a higher success rate of task execution and a better balance between delay and energy consumption than other benchmark methods, and a higher success rate of task execution.

Keywords: Mobile edge computing · Computation offloading · Resource allocation · Multi-constraint optimization · Deep reinforcement learning

1 Introduction

With the rapid evolution of artificial intelligence and communication technologies, various new applications have been emerging such as virtual reality and face recognition. To better support high-quality smart services, these applications need to collect large amounts of sensing data generated by computation-intensive tasks, which pose a significant challenge to the hardware performance of mobile devices [1]. However, due to constraints within device size and manufacturing cost, mobile devices are typically equipped with small batteries. As a result, mobile devices executing these new applications regularly struggle to achieve high performance and sustainable processing simultaneously [2]. In response to this challenge, Cloud computing possesses sufficient computational and storage resources, which can help motile devices compensate for their limitations on hardware performance [3]. However, the vast separation between mobile devices and clouds leads to significant data transfer delay [4], which severely impacts the user experience and hinders its adoption to support delay-sensitive applications.

Distinguished from cloud computing, Mobile Edge Computing (MEC) in the vicinity of mobile devices deploys computational and storage resources at the network edge [5], where users' tasks can be offloaded from mobile devices to nearby MEC servers. Therefore, MEC can efficiently avoid network congestion and decrease the response time of network services. Due to the constraints of practical deployment environments, MEC servers are equipped with fewer resources and multiple MEC servers collaborate to achieve better service flexibility. This complicates resource allocation in resource-constrained MEC systems. Moreover, mobile devices are required to run continuously to support various applications. These devices are constrained by battery capacity, which further complicates the problem of resource management in MEC systems. Recently, the emergence of the integration of MEC and Wireless Power Transmission (WPT) has been a promising measure to boost the power of mobile devices [6]. Specifically, the Access Point (AP) and MEC servers are located at the edge of the network, allowing the AP to offer on-demand energy to the Center Processing Unit (CPU) and radio transceivers of the wireless devices in a completely controllable way through WPT, and the collected energy is fed into the battery of Mobile Devices (MDs). Using the collected energy, MDs can process tasks locally or offload them. However, the multiple constraints of energy and delay bring new challenges to computation offloading and resource allocation in edge environments [7].

To harvest the potential of MEC systems, tremendous research works have been made in the area of resource optimization. The majority of the current solutions are developed referring to rules [8], heuristics [9], and control theory [10]. They may work well in specific scenarios but cannot fully adapt to dynamic MEC environments with multiple constraints. For example, it is easy to apply rule-based tactics to meet transient demands, but they only consider the current state features and pursue short-term benefits. As a result, they are not flexible enough to meet dynamic demands from a long-term perspective, leading to redundant delays and energy consumption. Moreover, these classic solutions need many iterations to find a feasible solution, resulting in excessive computational complexity and resource overheads. Deep Reinforcement Learning (DRL) also has been applied in this challenging problem [11–14], which utilizes Deep Neural

Networks (DNN) to extract the essential features from high-dimensional state spaces. Most of DRL-based methods were developed based on value-based DRL. The training process is inefficient when handling a huge action space. The action space in the MEC can be quite huge and the value-based DRL cannot converge to the optimal result. To bridge these gaps, we propose a Joint computation Offloading and resource Allocation with deep Reinforcement Learning (JOA-RL) method. The main contributions of this work are summarized as follows.

- We design a unified computation offloading and resource allocation model for dynamic MEC environments with multiple constraints. Specifically, a pre-processing mechanism of task priority is developed to assign priorities to tasks according to their data size and the performance of MDs.
- We develop a novel JOA-RL method, aiming to efficiently approximate the optimum strategy for computation offloading and resource allocation in dynamic MEC environments. In JOA-RL, the critic's network adopts a value-function-based single-step update to assess the current policy, and the actor's network adopts the policy gradient to update the policy.
- Extensive simulation experiments validate the proposed JOA-RL approach's feasibility and effectiveness. The performance shows that JOA-RL achieves a better balance between delay and energy consumption than the widely deployed benchmark approach. In addition, JOA-RL achieves a higher mission execution success rate.

The rest of this paper is organized as follows. Section 2 reviews the related work. Section 3 describes the model and formulates the problem. Section 4 details the proposed method. The performance evaluations are presented in Sect. 5. Section 6 concludes this article.

2 Related Work

Classic Methods. Existing classic solutions for computation offloading and resource allocation are based on rules [8], heuristics [9], and control theory [10]. Mao et al. [15] developed a block coordinate descent-based method to save energy consumption. Xia et al. [16] proposed a offloading strategy with game theory, aiming to reduce the communication overhead and offloading latency. Mao et al. [17] has designed a differentially private offloading solution for DNNs to reduce communication costs while ensuring offloading privacy. However, these methods can not take well into account the dynamical task arrival in the MEC environment and the impact of multi-constraint conditions on task execution, which might result in excessive delay and energy consumption.

DRL-Based Methods. DRL selects actions based on system states in a dynamic situation, which is deemed as a feasible solution. Wu et al. [11] proposed a Deep Q-Networks (DQN)-based offloading and an optimization algorithm-based resource allocation strategy to save system costs. Su et al. [12] decoupled the multi-stage stochastic problems and designed a model-free DRL to improve the data processing capacity of MEC networks. Ho et al. [13] designed a DQN-based method for joint server selection and cooperative offloading to solve the formulated optimization problem to minimize computation delay. Yan et al. [18] proposed a efficient actor-critic framework which can quickly evaluate the energy-time performance of the offloading decisions. Most of these methods adopt value-based DRL methods. When the action space is numerous, these approaches make it difficult to guarantee optimum strategies. In particular, the value-based DRL has few discrete samples of actions if the action space is continuous. Therefore, the actions learned at each time step are inaccurate, causing unsatisfactory decision results.

3 System Model and Problem Formulation

As shown in Fig. 1, the proposed MEC system consists of a Base Station (BS), an MEC server, and N rechargeable MDs. The set of MDs is denoted as $MD = \{MD_1, MD_2, ..., MD_N\}$, which are equipped with Energy Harvest (EH) components and can be powered by Radio Frequency (RF) signals.

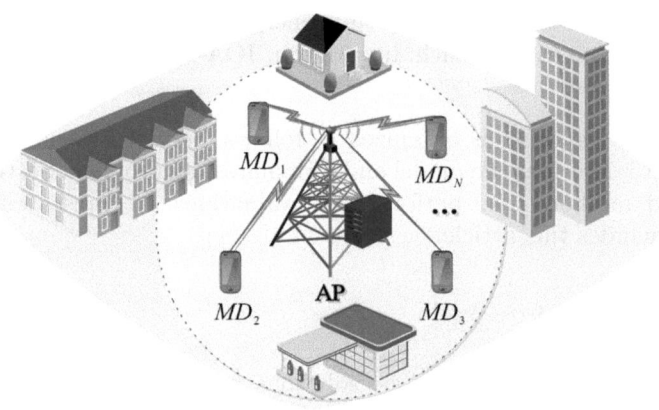

Fig. 1. Scenario of the proposed MEC system.

In a time slot T, MD_i generates a task, denoted by $Task_i^T = (D_i^T, C_i^T, T_d)$, where D_i^T is the data size, C_i^T is the required computational resources, and T_d is the maximum tolerable completion delay. MDs obtain power from the RF signal, and a task is expected to be completed within the maximum tolerable delay under the constraints of available battery power. Otherwise, the execution of the task is considered to be failed.

To avoid excessive delays or task failures caused by inappropriate coarse-grained decisions, time slots are divided into H sub-slots, where $t = 1, 2, ..., H$. In the MEC system, the MDs' tasks can be executed with the assistance of an MEC server. The corresponding communication, computing, and energy harvesting models are defined as follows.

3.1 Communication Model

Let $a_i^T \in \{0, 1\}$ denotes the offloading decision of MD_i in the time slot T. When $a_i^T = 1$, MD_i offloads the task to the MEC server for execution. In contrast, when $a_i^T = 0$, MD_i executes the task locally. If MD_i offloads the task into the MEC server, the task's data will be uploaded accordingly and the BS allocates bandwidth for the uploaded task. The signal-to-noise ratio of task uploading at the sub-time slot t is given as

$$SNR_i^t = \frac{h_i^t P_i}{\delta^2}, \tag{1}$$

where δ is the average power of Gaussian white noise. h_i^t and P_i represent the channel gain and the uploading power of MD_i within the sub-time slot t.

Thus, the uplink data rate of MD_i is

$$r_i^t = w_i^t B_{free}^t \log_2(1 + SNR_i^t), \tag{2}$$

where B_{free}^t is the available bandwidth of the MEC server within the current sub-time slot t, and w_i^t is the percentage of bandwidth allocated to MD_i.

3.2 Computing Model

When a task is generated by an MD, it is first added to a buffer queue of the MD. The subsequent tasks can be executed only after the former tasks are completed. Since both MDs and the MEC server can provide computing services, two computing modes are defined as follows.

Local Computing Mode. Different MDs may offer different computational capabilities (i.e., CPU frequency), and thus the delay and energy consumption of local computing mode is as

$$LocT_i^T = \frac{C_i^T}{f_i}, \ LocE_i^T = kC_i^T f_i^2, \tag{3}$$

where f_i is the CPU frequency of MD_i, C_i^T denotes the computational resources required by $Task_i^T$, and k is the capacitance factor.

Edge Computing Mode. When MDs offload tasks to the MEC server, the server allocates available resources to process tasks and feedback results to MDs once the tasks are completed. Since the data size of results is small, the overhead of downloading results is negligible. Thus, the delay and energy consumption of edge computing mode is

$$EdgT_i^T = \frac{D_i^T}{r_i^t} + \frac{C_i^T}{p_i^t f_{free}^t}, \ EdgE_i^T = P_i \frac{D_i^T}{r_i^t} + \frac{P_e C_i^T}{p_i^t f_{free}^t}, \tag{4}$$

where P_i represents the uploading power of MD_i within the sub-time slot t, f_{free}^t is the available computational resources of the MEC server in the sub-time slot t, p_i^t is the percentage of the computational resources allocated to MD_i and P_e is the power allocated to the task by the MEC server.

Thus, the delay and energy consumption of executing $Task_i^T$ is defined as

$$TC_i^T = \begin{cases} LocT_i^T, \alpha_i^T = 0 \\ EdgT_i^T, \alpha_i^T = 1 \end{cases}, \quad EC_i^T = \begin{cases} LocE_i^T, \alpha_i^T = 0 \\ EdgE_i^T, \alpha_i^T = 1 \end{cases}, \quad (5)$$

where α_i^T is the offloading decision for $Task_i^T$.

To efficiently find proper modes for task execution, a pre-processing mechanism of task priority is developed, which assigns priorities to tasks according to their data size and the performance of MDs. This mechanism measures the suitability of different tasks to be offloaded. The tasks with higher priority tend to be offloaded for execution, and the priority is defined as

$$pr_i^T = \frac{h_i^t}{D_i^T * f_i * P_i}, \quad (6)$$

where h_i^t is the transmission channel gain within the sub-time slot t, f_i is the computational power of MD_i, and P_i is the transmission power of MD_i.

3.3 Energy Harvesting Model

As aforementioned, each MD is equipped with a rechargeable battery with a maximum capacity of $B_{\max}$. The power of MD_i in the sub-time slot t is denoted as b_i^t. The size of the energy packet is denoted as e_t. For different states of task execution, the energy harvesting models are defined as follows.

1) If the task cannot be completed within the power support range of MD_i due to decision failure or no task within the sub-time slot t, the charging power of wireless components will be considered only. Thus, in the sub-time slot $t+1$, the charge level of MD_i is updated by

$$b_i^{t+1} = \min\{b_i^t + e_t, B_{\max}\}. \quad (7)$$

2) When the task of MD_i is executed locally within the sub-time slot t, the energy consumption is $LocE_i^T$, and the power of MD_i in the sub-time slot $t+1$ is

$$b_i^{t+1} = \min\{\max\{b_i^t + e_t - LocE_i^T, 0\}, B_{\max}\}. \quad (8)$$

3) When the task of MD_i is offloaded for execution, the energy consumption is $EdgE_i^T$, and the power of MD_i in the sub-time slot $t+1$ is

$$b_i^{t+1} = \min\{\max\{b_i^t + e_t - EdgE_i^T, 0\}, B_{\max}\}. \quad (9)$$

The aim of the proposed model is to make the weighted sum of delay and energy consumption for performing the time-series tasks generated by the MDs minimized, which is formulated as the optimization problem $P1$ as

$$\min_{\alpha_i^t, w_i^t, p_i^t} \sum_{t=1}^{T} \sum_{i=1}^{N} (q_1 TC_i^T + q_2 EC_i^T)$$
$$s.t. C1: \alpha_i^T \in [0,1], i \in N, t \in T$$
$$C2: E_i^T \leq b_i^t, i \in N, t \in T$$
$$C3: TC_i^T \leq T_d, i \in N \qquad , \qquad (10)$$
$$C4: \sum_{i=1}^{N} w_i^t = 1, i \in N, t \in T$$
$$C5: \sum_{i=1}^{N} p_i^t = 1, i \in N, t \in T$$

where q_1 and q_2 are the weights of delay and energy consumption during task execution. $C1$ represents that a task is only available for local execution or offloading to the MEC server. $C2$ means that the consumption of energy to perform the task cannot exceed the available power of MDs. $C3$ indicates that the time of execution of a task cannot exceed the maximal tolerable delay for that task, T_d. $C4$ is the constraint on the percentage of uploading bandwidth allocated to the offloaded tasks. $C5$ represents a constraint on the percent of resources allocated to the offloaded tasks.

4 The Proposed JOA-RL Method

To optimize $P1$, we propose JOA-RL to obtain optimal computation offloading and resource allocation strategies. In Fig. 2, the MEC system is regarded as the environment. The current system state s_t (considering task state and resource usage) is first fed into the DRL agent and the action a_t (computation offloading and resource allocation) under the policy μ is obtained. Next, the environment feedbacks a reward r_t and transfers to a new state s_{t+1}. This process can be described as an MDP process. Moreover, the state space, action space, and reward function of the JOA-RL method are defined as follows.

State space: The state space contains tasks $Task^t$ of all MDs within the time slot t, task priority pr^t, battery capacity b^t of MDs, and available computational resources of the MEC server f_{free}^t. Thus, the system state in the time slot t is

$$s_t = \{Task^t, pr^t, b^t, f_{free}^t\}, \qquad (11)$$

where $Task^t = \{Task_1^t, Task_2^t, ..., Task_N^t\}$, $pr^t = \{pr_1^t, pr_2^t, ..., pr_N^t\}$, and $b^t = \{b_1^t, b_2^t, ..., b_N^t\}$.

Action space: The DRL agent takes actions according to the current system state. The action space contains the offloading decision α^t, uploading bandwidth allocated to tasks w^t, and computational resources assigned to tasks p^t. Thus, the action in the time slot t is

$$a_t = \{\alpha^t, w^t, p^t\}, \qquad (12)$$

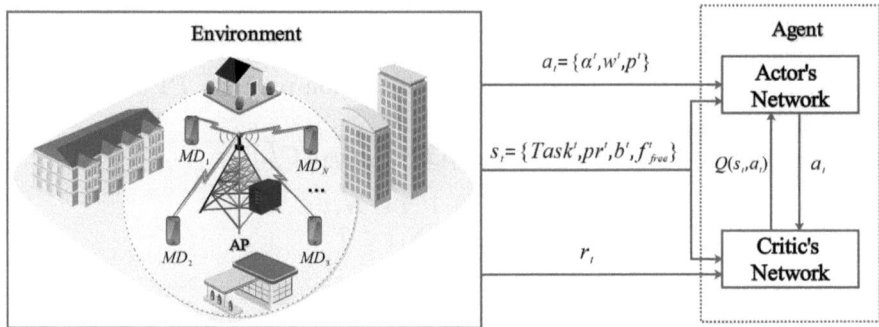

Fig. 2. Overview of the proposed JOA-RL method.

where $\alpha^t = \{\alpha_1^t, \alpha_2^t, ..., \alpha_N^t\}$, $w^t = \{w_1^t, w_2^t, ..., w_N^t\}$, $p^t = \{p_1^t, p_2^t, ..., p_N^t\}$.

Reward function: The goal of the proposed JOA-RL is minimization of the weighted sum of delay and energy consumption defined in $P1$. Thus, for the beginning of the time slot t, the immediate reward is

$$r_t = \begin{cases} -(q_1 F(EC_i^t) + q_2 F(TC_i^t)) * \frac{1}{pr_i^t}, \ succeed \\ -Pu^{C_i^t}, \ fail \ (C2 \ not \ satisfied) \\ -Pu^{C_i^t}, \ fail \ (C3 \ not \ satisfied) \end{cases}, \quad (13)$$

where F is the function that normalizes the delay and energy consumption to the same value range. Pu is the penalty coefficient for failed tasks.

In the process of computation offloading and resource allocation optimization in the multi-constraint MEC environment, the DRL agent selects an computation offloading and resource allocation action a_t under the current task state and resource usage s_t according to the policy μ. The environment feeds back a reward r_t according to an action a_t and transitions to a new system state s_{t+1}, which can be described as an MDP process.

The key steps of the JOA-RL method are listed in Algorithm 1. First, the main parameters are initialized (Lines 1~3). In particular, the independent target network is used in the JOA-RL to reduce the data correlation and enhance the robustness. In each training round, the JOA-RL inputs the state s_t into the actor's network, executes the action a_t, receives the output from the actor's network, and calculates the reward according to Eq. (13) (Lines 5~11).

Next, the environment feedbacks the reward r_t and the next state s_{t+1} (Line 12). The JOA-RL trains the critic's network θ^Q to fit $Q(s_t, a_t)$. When $Q(s_t, a_t)$ is determined, there must be a a_t that maximizes $Q(s_t, a_t)$ for a fixed s_t. However, the mapping between s_t and a_t is very complicated. To solve this problem, the actor-network θ^μ is used to fix this mapping, and $Q(s_t, a_t)$ is defined as

$$Q(s_t, a_t) = E[r(s_t, a_t) + \gamma Q(s_{t+1}, \mu(s_{t+1}))], \quad (14)$$

Algorithm 1: The proposed JOA-RL method

1. Initialize actor's network θ^μ and critic's network θ^Q
2. Initialize target network $\theta^{\mu'} \leftarrow \theta^\mu$ and $\theta^{Q'} \leftarrow \theta^Q$
3. Initialize replay buffer M, training round P, and time series length $T_{\max}$ per round
4. **for** epoch $n = 1, 2, ..., P$ **do**
5.   Initialize $s_1 = env.reset()$;
6.   **for** episode $t = 1, 2, ..., T_{\max}$ **do**
7.   Obtain action a_t according to s_t, where $\alpha_t = \mu(s_t|\theta^\mu) + N_t$;
8.   **if** $\alpha_i^t = 1$ **then**
9.   Offload tasks, allocate MEC resources according to w_i^t and p_i^t, and return reward (Eq. (13)), where $r_i^t = md.work\_edge(w_i^t, p_i^t)$;
10.   **else**
11.   Return reward after local execution (Eq. (13)), where $r_i^t = md.work\_edge(w_i^t, p_i^t)$;
12.   Get r_t and next state s_{t+1} after taking a_t, where $r_t, s_{t+1} = env.step(a_t)$;
13.   Store training samples in M, where $M.push(s_t, a_t, r_t, s_{t+1})$;
14.   Randomly take N samples from M, where $N * (s_t, a_t, r_t, s_{+1}) = M.sample(N)$;
15.   Calculate discounted rewards y_t, where $y_t = r_t + \gamma Q'(s_{t+1}, \mu'(s_{t+1}|\theta^{\mu'})|\theta^{Q'}$;
16.   Minimize critic's loss function L, where $L = \frac{1}{N}\sum_1^N \left(y_t - Q(s_t, a_t|\theta^Q)\right)^2$;
17.   Update actor's network, where $\nabla_{\theta^\mu} J = \frac{1}{N}\sum_1^N \nabla_{a_t} Q(s_t, a_t|\theta^Q)\nabla_{\theta^\mu}\mu(s_t|\theta^\mu)$;
18.   Update target networks, where $\theta^{\mu'} \leftarrow \tau\theta^\mu + (1-\tau)\theta^{\mu'}, \theta^{Q'} \leftarrow \tau\theta^Q + (1-\tau)\theta^{Q'}$;
19.   **end**
20. **end**

where the actor's network θ^μ outputs the action a_t with the maximum Q-value, and the process can be described as $a_t = \mu(s_t|\theta^\mu)$.

The objective of the actor's network is defined as

$$J(\theta^\mu) = E[r_1 + \gamma r2 + ...] = E[Q(s_t, \mu(s_t|\theta^\mu))|\theta^Q]. \tag{15}$$

In the replay buffer M, N records are randomly selected for training (Line 14). When optimizing the loss function, the performance of derivation is unstable, and the parameters may not be updated in the ideal changing direction of $\max(s_{t+1}, a_{t+1})$. To solve this problem, the JOA-RL introduces target actor's and critic's networks (i.e., $\theta^{\mu'}$ and $\theta^{Q'}$), where the critic's network calculates the current Q-value $Q(s_t, a_t)$ and defines the target Q-value y_t (Line 15). Then, the corresponding loss function is given (Line 16) and the gradient ascent method of minimizing the loss is applied. Next, the actor's network is updated (Line 18). At each episode, the target networks approach the online networks according to the updating step τ (Line 18). Distinguished from copying network parameters directly, this update manner makes the JOA-RL more stable.

5 Performance Evaluation

5.1 Experimental Setup

We conduct experiments based on Python, where MDs are spread stochastically and share the bandwidth under the coverage of the BS. The distribution of the computational capabilities of MDs is [1, 1.2] GHz/s and that of the MEC server is 20 GHz/s. Under the default settings, there are 10 MDs, the bandwidth is 10MHz, a time slot T is 1s, a sub-time slot t is 0.25 s, and there are 48 time slots in a training round. Pytorch is used to build and train the proposed JOA-RL, where the learning rate of the actor's and critic's networks are 0.0006 and 0.006, and the reward discount factor is 0.95. The other parameter settings are given in Table 1. Moreover, five benchmark methods are selected to evaluate the proposed JOA-RL, including 1) Local: all tasks are executed on MDs; 2) MEC: all tasks are offloaded to the MEC server for execution; 3) Random: all tasks are randomly executed on MDs or MEC server; 4) Greedy: when meeting the maximum tolerable delay, tasks are preferentially executed on MDs; 5) DQN [19]: a value-based DRL that allows learning determined policies by calculation of the likelihood of each action.

Table 1. Parameter settings

Parameter	Value	Parameter	Value	Parameter	Value
D_i^T	[0.5,1.5] MB	C_i^T	[1,2] GHz	T_d	1.5 s
h_i^t	10^{-3}	P_i	[400,600] mW	δ^2	10^{-9}
k	10^{-26}	B_{free}^t	10 MHz	P_e	100 mW
B_{max}	120 mJ	e_t	10 mJ	N	10

5.2 Simulation Results

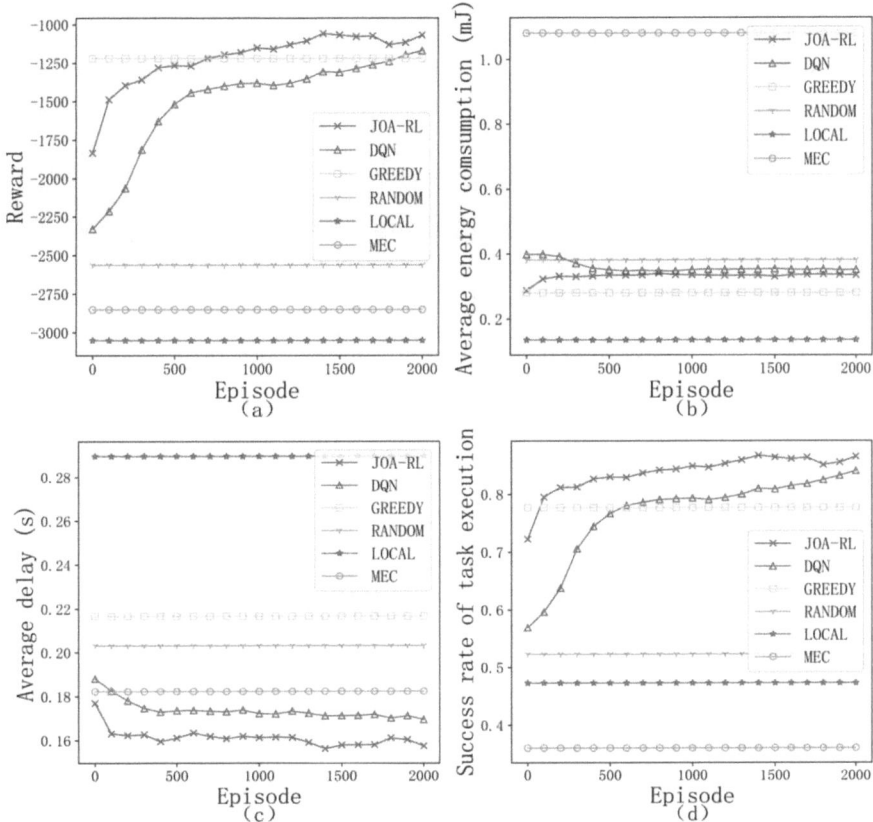

Fig. 3. Performance comparison between the JOA-RL and other methods.

As shown in Fig. 3, the proposed JOA-RL achieves better performance than the other five benchmark methods in terms of training reward, energy efficiency, average delay, and task execution success. To be specific, as shown in Fig. 3(a), the Local, MEC, and Random methods perform worse than the other three methods because they do not well consider the current system state and task characteristics, resulting in potential task execution exceeds the maximum tolerable delay and power constraints. Compared with the JOA-RL and DQN methods, the Greedy method focuses on the instant reward but does not consider the long-term one. Therefore, the Greedy method cannot keep better performance than the JOA-RL and DQN methods. The JOA-RL method integrates value and policy-based DRL, and thus it can handle the high-dimensional continuous space and converge faster, making it outperform the DQN method. In Fig. 3(b), the

MEC and the Local show the highest and lowest average task energy consumption, respectively. The Greedy method preferentially executes the task locally, and thus the energy consumption is only higher than the Local. Compared to the DQN method, the JOA-RL method provides better performance of energy efficiency after the training process is converged. In Fig. 3(c), the performance of the JOA-RL method outperforms the other five methods with respect to average task delay. In Fig. 3(d), the JOA-RL method achieves higher success rate of task execution than the other five methods.

Next, we evaluate the rewards obtained by different methods under various network bandwidths. As shown in Fig. 4, the changes in network bandwidth have no impact on the Local, because the tasks are not offloaded through the wireless network. In MEC systems, the lower bandwidth causes higher uploading delay, which results in high task failure rate because the constraint of the maximum tolerable delay cannot be satisfied. It is noted that the rewards are defined as the weighted sum of delay and energy consumption, and thus a better balance of delay and energy consumption leads to higher rewards. Compared with the DQN method, the JOA-RL method reaches a better balance between delay and energy consumption. This also shows the superiorities of the JOA-RL method in dynamic MEC environments.

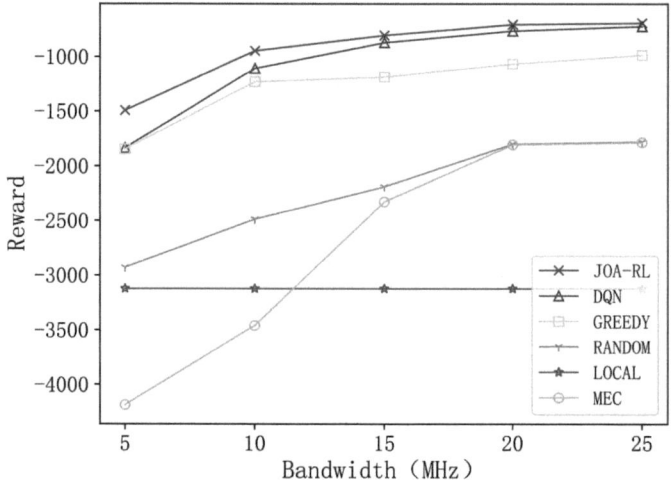

Fig. 4. Performance comparison of different methods with various network bandwidths.

6 Conclusions

In this paper, we first formulate the computation offloading and resource allocation in multi-constraint MEC environments as a model-free DRL problem. Next, we propose a novel JOA-RL method to improve the success rate of task execution and reduce the delay and energy consumption of task execution. Experimental results show that the proposed JOA-RL method outperforms other benchmark methods in improving task execution success rate and reducing task execution delay and energy consumption. Specifically, with dynamic network bandwidth and MEC server computation resources, the JOA-RL method always outperforms other methods. Meanwhile, compared to the advanced DQN method, the JOA-RL method also shows a better convergence effect.

Acknowledgment. This work was partly supported by the National Natural Science Foundation of China under Grant No. 62202103, the Natural Science Foundation of Fujian Province for Distinguished Young Scholars under Grant No. 2025J010020, and the Central Funds Guiding the Local Science and Technology Development under Grant No. 2022L3004.

References

1. Alsamhi, S.H., Almalki, F.A., Ma, O., Ansari, M.S., Lee, B.: Predictive estimation of optimal signal strength from drones over IoT frameworks in smart cities. IEEE Trans. Mob. Comput. (TMC) **22**(1), 402–416 (2023)
2. Jiang, W., Zhou, J., Cong, P., Zhang, G., Hu, S.: QoE and reliability-aware task scheduling for multi-user mobile-edge computing. In: Wang, L., Segal, M., Chen, J., Qiu, T. (eds.) WASA 2022. LNCS, vol. 13473, pp. 380–392. Springer, Cham (2022). https://doi.org/10.1007/978-3-031-19211-1_32
3. Chen, Z., Jia, H., Min, G., Luo, C., El-Ghazawi, T.: Adaptive and efficient resource allocation in cloud datacenters using actor-critic deep reinforcement learning. IEEE Trans. Parallel Distrib. Syst. (TPDS) **33**(8), 1911–1923 (2021)
4. Cong, P., Zhou, J., Li, L., Cao, K., Wei, T., Li, K.: A survey of hierarchical energy optimization for mobile edge computing: a perspective from end devices to the cloud. ACM Comput. Surv. (CSUR) **53**(2), 1–44 (2020)
5. Chen, Z., Zhang, J., Zheng, X., Min, G., Li, J., Rong, C.: Profit-aware cooperative offloading in UAV-enabled MEC systems using lightweight deep reinforcement learning. IEEE Internet Things (IoT) J. (2024)
6. Wang, X., et al.: Wireless powered mobile edge computing networks: a survey. ACM Comput. Surv. (CSUR) (2023)
7. Chen, Z., Xiong, B., Chen, X., Min, G., Li, J.: Joint computation offloading and resource allocation in multi-edge smart communities with personalized federated deep reinforcement learning. IEEE Trans. Mob. Comput. (TMC) (2024)
8. Ma, L., Wang, X., Wang, X., Wang, L., Shi, Y., Huang, M.: TCDA: truthful combinatorial double auctions for mobile edge computing in industrial internet of things. IEEE Trans. Mob. Comput. (TMC) **21**(11), 4125–4138 (2022)
9. Chen, Y., Zhang, N., Zhang, Y., Chen, X., Wu, W., Shen, X.S.: Toffee: task offloading and frequency scaling for energy efficiency of mobile devices in mobile edge computing. IEEE Trans. Cloud Comput. (TCC) **9**(4), 1634–1644 (2021)
10. Ning, Z., et al.: 5g-enabled UAV-to-community offloading: joint trajectory design and task scheduling. IEEE J. Sel. Areas Commun. (JSAC) **39**(11), 3306–3320 (2021)

11. Wu, Y.C., Dinh, T.Q., Fu, Y., Lin, C., Quek, T.Q.S.: A hybrid DQN and optimization approach for strategy and resource allocation in MEC networks. IEEE Trans. Wirel. Commun. (TWC) **20**(7), 4282–4295 (2021)
12. Bi, S., Huang, L., Wang, H., Zhang, Y.-J.A.: Lyapunov-guided deep reinforcement learning for stable online computation offloading in mobile-edge computing networks. IEEE Trans. Wirel. Commun. (TWC) **20**(11), 7519–7537 (2021)
13. Tai Manh Ho and KimKhoa Nguyen: Joint server selection, cooperative offloading and handover in multi-access edge computing wireless network: a deep reinforcement learning approach. IEEE Trans. Mob. Comput. (TMC) **21**(7), 2421–2435 (2022)
14. Chen, Z., Zhang, J., Huang, Z., Wang, P., Zhengxin, Yu., Miao, W.: Computation offloading in blockchain-enabled MCS systems: a scalable deep reinforcement learning approach. Future Gener. Comput. Syst. (FGCS) **153**, 301–311 (2024)
15. Mao, S., Leng, S., Zhang, Y.: Joint communication and computation resource optimization for noma-assisted mobile edge computing. In: IEEE International Conference on Communications (ICC), pp. 1–6. IEEE (2019)
16. Xia, S., Yao, Z., Li, Y., Mao, S.: Online distributed offloading and computing resource management with energy harvesting for heterogeneous MEC-enabled IoT. IEEE Trans. Wirel. Commun. (TWC) **20**(10), 6743–6757 (2021)
17. Mao, Y., Hong, W., Wang, H., Li, Q., Zhong, S.: Privacy-preserving computation offloading for parallel deep neural networks training. IEEE Trans. Parallel Distrib. Syst. (TPDS) **32**(7), 1777–1788 (2021)
18. Yan, J., Bi, S., Zhang, Y.J.A.: Offloading and resource allocation with general task graph in mobile edge computing: a deep reinforcement learning approach. IEEE Trans. Wirel. Commun. (TWC) **19**(8), 5404–5419 (2020)
19. Hsieh, L.T., Liu, H., Guo, Y., Gazda, R.: Deep reinforcement learning-based task assignment for cooperative mobile edge computing. IEEE Trans. Mob. Comput. (TMC), 1–15 (2023)

Anomaly Traffic Detection in Edge with Multi-scale Aggregated Transformer

Longxiang Xue, Junjie Zhang, Xiaowei Shi, Hongju Chen, and Zheyi Chen[✉]

College of Computer and Data Science, Fuzhou University, Fujian, China
z.chen@fzu.edu.cn

Abstract. Anomaly traffic detection is a key technology to ensure Quality-of-Service (QoS) and information security in edge computing. However, the huge volume and high dimension of edge traffic cause significant difficulty to anomaly detection. Meanwhile, the wide application of traffic encryption and the high dynamics of edge environments increase the complexity of detecting anomaly traffic. To address these important challenges, we propose a novel anomaly traffic detection method in edge with Multi-scale Aggregated Transformer (MA-Former), which can achieve accurate anomaly traffic detection only with characteristics of payload length and inter-arrival time of data packets. First, the MA - Former adopts a hierarchical architecture and multi-scale time-sequence representation to realize the mapping between feature sequences to reduce data dimension. Next, the mapping vector is encoded based on the multi-head self-attention mechanism. Finally, the feature vectors of each layer are aggregated, and the anomaly traffic detection is completed by pooling and the Softmax classifier. Using real-world datasets of edge traffic, extensive experiments are conducted to verify the effectiveness of the proposed MA-Former. The results show that the MA-Former achieves higher classification accuracy of anomaly traffic and superior generalization ability for different traffic than other benchmark methods.

Keyword: Edge computing · Anomaly traffic detection · Deep learning · Multi-scale representation · Self-attention mechanism

1 Introduction

The rapid development of the Internet-of-Things (IoT) plays an important role in many scenarios such as smart cities and industrial control [1]. By deploying computing and storage resources at the network edge, Mobile Edge Computing (MEC) can process the massive data generated by IoT devices more efficiently [2]. MEC reduces network latency and data transmission costs, becoming a key technology for realizing the decentralized intelligence for the IoT. With the popularity of the IoT, users are increasingly exposed to various types of anomaly traffic attacks (e.g., denial attacks of service, data leakage, and privacy infringement). To prevent these attacks, network traffic is usually encrypted to protect data confidentiality, integrity, and authentication to ensure edge network security [3]. Although traffic encryption can relieve security issues to some extent, it makes anomaly traffic difficult to detect, which seriously affects Quality-of-Service (QoS) and edge network security.

Through real-time monitoring and analysis, anomaly traffic detection can promptly detect and block anomaly traffic to ensure the security of edge networks. Most existing studies focus on cloud data centers, but they fail to fully consider the characteristics of edge environments. The data is transmitted and aggregated to data centers for processing in cloud computing [4], which causes high network latency and cannot meet the needs of applications with high real-time requirements. In contrast, MEC sinks computing and storage resources to edge nodes close to devices [5]. Therefore, deploying anomaly traffic detection modules on edge nodes can effectively avoid high latency in data transmission and reduce the pressure on the network bandwidth of cloud data centers. However, edge anomaly traffic detection still faces many challenges as follows.

- IoT devices and edge servers always generate huge high-dimensional data. Therefore, monitoring all traffic will seriously affect the real-time efficiency of detection, which will also lead to excessive detection costs.
- The application of traffic encryption increases the difficulty of detecting anomaly traffic, and thus it is necessary to select appropriate features for anomaly traffic detection. However, it remains challenging to fully consider the representativeness and separability of features during detection.
- The loads and requests of different devices in edge environments may change over time, and thus the edge anomaly traffic detection method should fit in such dynamics. Most existing studies use convolutional neural networks (CNN), recurrent neural networks (RNN), and their variants to detect anomaly traffic. However, they still cannot well capture long-distance dependencies, lack parallel processing capabilities, and require manual feature statistics.

To address these important challenges, we propose a novel anomaly traffic detection method in edge with Multi-scale Aggregated Transformer (MA-Former). The main contributions are summarized as follows.

- We propose an efficient edge anomaly traffic detection model. First, the data is preprocessed including deduplication and downsampling to optimize the data quality. Next, we extract key features from data packets and use these features to detect anomaly traffic.
- The proposed MA-Former first uses payload length and inter-arrival time of data packets as features and adopts a hierarchical architecture and multiscale representation to achieve mapping between feature sequences to reduce data dimensions. Next, the MA-Former uses a multi-head self-attention mechanism to encode mapping vectors. Finally, the feature vectors of each layer are aggregated, and the pooling and Softmax classifier are used to accurately detect anomaly traffic. Thus, the MA-Former can well solve the problem of anomaly traffic detection in an encrypted environment.
- Based on three real-world datasets of edge traffic, extensive experiments are conducted to verify the effectiveness of the proposed MA-Former. The experimental results show that the MA-Former can achieve higher anomaly traffic classification accuracy than other benchmark methods and show superior generalization ability for different traffic.

The rest of this paper is organized as follows. Section 2 reviews the related studies. Section 3 introduces the system model and problem definition. Section 4 describes the proposed MA-Former in detail. Section 5 evaluates and analyzes the performance. Section 6 concludes this paper.

2 Related Work

2.1 Anomaly Traffic Detection with Classic Machine Learning

Machine Learning (ML) based anomaly traffic detection methods mainly rely on statistical features. Liu et al. [6] designed a sequence of statistical features at the packet level and used a semi-supervised learning framework to classify encrypted services. Yamansavascilar et al. [7] selected more than 100 traffic features and used the k-nearest neighbor (K-NN) algorithm to classify traffic applications. Alshammari et al. [8] selected basic information features of traffic and used the C4.5 decision tree to improve the versatility of the model. Quan et al. [9] proposed a hierarchical classification structure with embedded features and used the random forest algorithm for classification. Aceto et al. [10] used payload length, direction, and inter-arrival time as abstract representations of packets in traffic and used Markov chains to model them. Fu et al. [11] proposed a malicious traffic detection method, encoding the packet sequence into a vector and then using unsupervised clustering to establish a traffic detection model.

2.2 Anomaly Traffic Detection with Deep Learning

Compared with ML, Deep Learning (DL) exhibits more powerful feature self- learning capabilities and can improve the accuracy and efficiency of anomaly traffic detection. Lotfollahi et al. [12] proposed a deep neural network-based payload detection, which combines SAE and CNN to extract byte patterns in packets. Hu et al. [13] combined CNN and long short-term memory (LSTM) networks to extract features from raw network traffic payloads. Ma et al. [14] constructed a three-channel image by sequentially storing the bytes of a data packet, and designed a traffic classification method based on incremental learning. Zheng et al. [15] proposed an end-to-end model that treats the packet sequence of a flow as a two-dimensional tensor and inputs it into a CNN for encrypted traffic classification. Chen et al. [16] took the information of the first 6 message segments of each flow as input and used LSTM to build a traffic classification model, thus achieving early classification of encrypted network traffic. As an emerging architecture in deep learning, Transformer [17] uses the self- attention mechanism to achieve efficient encoding and accurate decoding, which can mine the association between long and short sequences. Currently, few studies applied it to the problem of edge anomaly traffic detection. Lin et al. [18] proposed a Bidirectional Encoder Representations from Transformers (BERT) - based encrypted traffic classification model, which was pre-trained on large-scale unlabeled samples and then fine-tuned on a small amount of labeled data specific to the classification task.

However, the above studies ignored the long time series of traffic data under some situations, which may cause excessive calculation time. As for this problem, the multi-scale representation can effectively shorten the time-series length of the traffic data. In light of this idea, we propose the MA-Former that effectively combines Transformer with multi-scale representation, thereby improving the performance of anomaly traffic detection while reducing the model complexity.

3 System Model and Problem Definition

As shown in Fig. 1, the proposed model aims to improve the accuracy and efficiency of anomaly traffic detection, thereby ensuring the QoS and high reliability of edge systems.

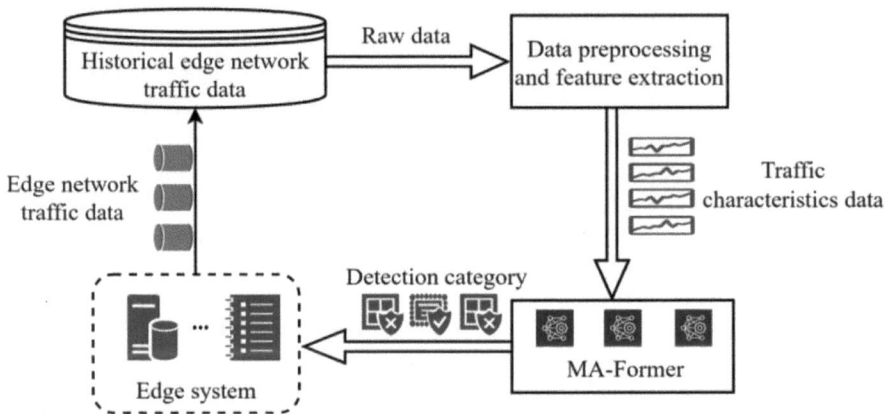

Fig. 1. The proposed model of anomaly traffic detection for edge systems.

Specifically, the raw traffic data is first split into independent sessions by five- tuple (i.e., source IP, destination IP, source port, destination port, and transport layer protocol). Next, the first t data packet is extracted for each session, where two features (i.e., payload length L and inter-arrival time T) are extracted from each data packet, and the first data packet T is set to 0. The i-th training traffic sample is defined as

$$X_i = \left[x_1^i, x_2^i, ..., x_t^i\right] \quad (1)$$

where t represents the time step. The sample corresponding to the j-th time step is x_j^i, which represents the feature data of the packet, denoted as $x_j^i = \left[L_j^i, T_j^i\right]$, where L_j^i and T_j^i represent the payload length of the j-th packet in the i-th sample and the arrival interval time with the $j-1$-th packet, respectively. The extracted features are arranged by time to obtain the training sample $X_i = [[L_1^i, T_1^i], ...[L_t^i, T_t^i]]$.

Therefore, the training sample set is defined as

$$D = \{(X_i, Y_i)\}_{i=1}^{N} \quad (2)$$

where N is the total number of training samples. Y_i is the label of the sample X_i and $Y_i \in \{1, 2, ..., K\}$, where K is the total number of anomaly traffic types.

The goal of anomaly traffic detection is building an efficient model on a given dataset D to maintain the consistency between the predicted label $Y_i{'}$ and the true label Y_i of the sample X_i. To evaluate the performance of the model, we use the evaluation metrics as follows.

$$accurary = \frac{TP + TN}{TP + TN + FP + FN} \quad (3)$$

$$precision = \frac{TP}{TP + FP} \quad (4)$$

$$recall = \frac{TP}{TP + FN} \quad (5)$$

$$F1\_score = \frac{2 * precision * recall}{precision + recall} \quad (6)$$

where TP (True Positive) indicates the number of samples predicted by the model as positive examples and whose actual labels are also positive examples. Similarly, TN, FP, and FN are defined accordingly.

4 The Proposed MA-Former

4.1 Overview

As shown in Fig. 2, the proposed MA-Former combines the multi-scale time sequence representation with the self-attention mechanism, which consists of four parts: input layer, encoding layer, classification layer, and output layer. First, the input layer extracts key feature information from the original traffic data. Next, the encoding layer adopts a hierarchical structure, where each encoding module contains a time sequence representation module and a Transformer encoding module, which work together to capture the changeable traffic patterns. Then, the outputs of all encoding modules are aggregated and a comprehensive feature vector is extracted via an average pooling layer. Finally, the vector is input into the Softmax classifier to obtain traffic detection results.

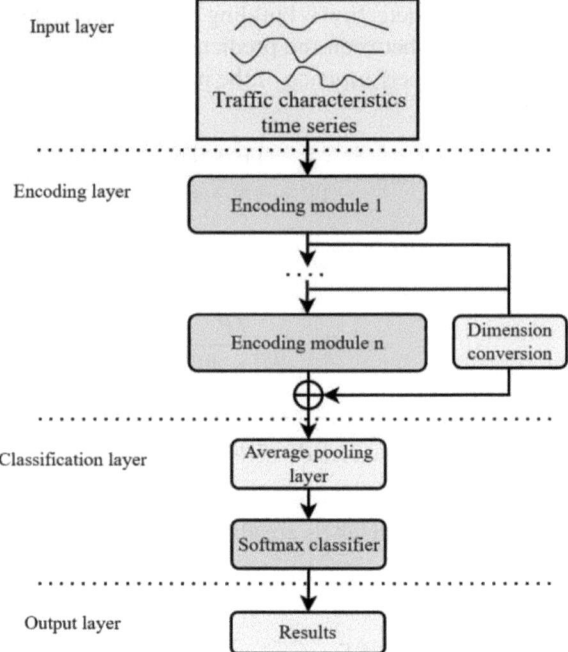

Fig. 2. Overview of the proposed MA-Former.

4.2 Encoding Layer

Considering that the classic Transformer has difficulty in processing long-time sequences efficiently, the encoding layer combines multi-scale time representation with a self-attention mechanism. For anomaly traffic detection, the time sequence information of the data packet is similar to the position encoding of the Transformer, which reflects the sequential nature of the data packet. Thus the encoding layer introduces position encoding in the time sequence representation module and adopts a hierarchical architecture for multi-scale temporal representation. This layer consists of multiple encoding modules, performs feature extraction at each layer, and aggregates the feature vectors of each layer to fully understand the characteristics of the input data.

The structure of the encoding module is shown in Fig. 3. First, the sequence representation module splits the packet feature time sequence $X \in \mathbb{R}^{t \times m}$ to shorten its length. Let the slice size be v, the input sequence contains m features, and the time dimension is t. After sequence segmentation, the length of the new sequence is $\frac{t}{v}$, and the size of each slice is $v \times m$. Then, these slices are projected onto a new dimension C and normalized. Finally, the normalized sequence is added to the position code to obtain the new time sequence $X\prime \in \mathbb{R}^{\frac{t}{m} \times C}$ Position encoding is a key step in Transformer, including absolute and relative position encoding. The encoding layer can fuse two-position encoding by representing the contextual information between adjacent time slices. Specifically, one-dimensional convolution is used to capture the positional relationship between adjacent time slices, where the convolution kernel size is set to k and $\frac{k}{2}$ zeros are used for padding to prevent the scale reduction problem.

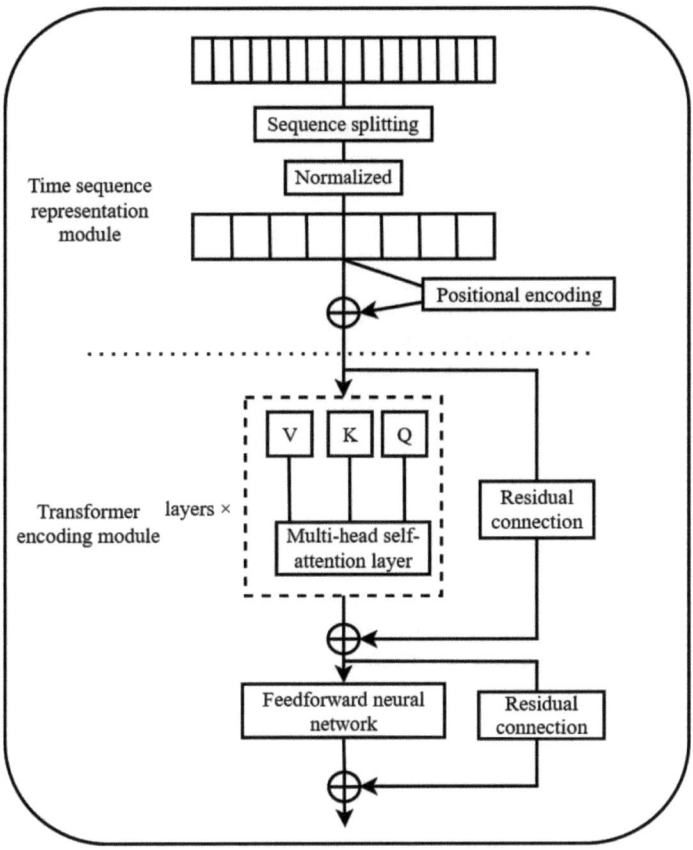

Fig. 3. Structure of encoding module.

Next, the new temporal representation is input into the multi-head self-attention layer with the query Q, key K, and value V as input, and the output matrix can be calculated by

$$Attention(Q, K, V) = softmax\left(\frac{QK^T}{\sqrt{d_k}}\right)V \qquad (7)$$

where d_k represents the dimension of the input query Q and key K.

For single-head self-attention, averaging suppresses the representation of sub-space information from different positions, while multi-head self-attention solves this problem well. The calculation process is defined as

$$MultiHead(Q, K, V) = Concat(head_1, ..., head_h)W^O \qquad (8)$$

where h is the number of attention heads and *Concat* represents the serial concatenation operation. The calculation process for each head is defined as

$$head_i = Attention\left(QW_i^Q, KW_i^K, VW_i^V\right) \qquad (9)$$

where the matrix $W_i^Q \in \mathbb{R}^{C_i \times d_{head}}$, $W_i^K \in \mathbb{R}^{C_i \times d_{head}}$, $W_i^V \in \mathbb{R}^{C_i \times d_{head}}$ are the linear projection parameters, and the dimension of each head is $d_{head} = \frac{C_i}{h}$.

After being processed by the multi-head self-attention layer, the result will be passed to the fully connected feedforward neural network (FNN), which will then extract features from multiple angles. The structure contains two linear transformations and embeds the ReLU activation function, which is defined as

$$FNN(X) = max(0, xW_1 + b_1)W_2 + b_2 \qquad (10)$$

Finally, the output of FNN is passed to the classification layer to complete anomaly traffic detection. To effectively avoid the gradient vanishing problem, residual connections are introduced in the multi-head self-attention module. Moreover, residual connections are introduced in the multi-head self-attention module thus the input tensor can be directly connected to the output tensor, allowing gradients to be passed to deeper networks.

4.3 Classification Layer

The results obtained by each encoding layer are averaged and aggregated and then input into the average pooling layer. Then, the feature vector processed by the pooling layer is sent to the Softmax classifier, and the probability distribution of each category is calculated. This process is defined as

$$p_i(x) = \frac{\exp(x_i)}{\sum_k^{K=1} \exp(x_k)}, \qquad (11)$$

where $p_i(x)$ represents the probability of the i-th category, x represents the model output, and K represents the number of categories of training samples. The Softmax function converts the model output into a probability distribution and selects the label with the highest probability as the predicted label.

4.4 Model Training

The training process of the MA-Former is shown in Algorithm 1. The input is edge traffic data Xi, training round N and training batch B. First, the parameters of the MA-Former are initialized (Line 1). In each training round and training batch, the sample is input into the time sequence representation module and the sequence is segmented to obtain the vector $\widehat{X}_i$ (Line 4). Then, the convolutional network is used to map the vector $\widehat{X}_i$ dimension to the new dimension C and obtain the new vector representation $\overline{X}_i$ (Line 5). Next, $\overline{X}_i$ is normalized to extract the position information of $\overline{X}_i$ and it is added to the normalized vector to obtain a vector $X_{i'}$ containing the position information (Line 6). Then, the vector $X_{i'}$ is input into the multi-head self-attention encoding module to obtain the vector ∂_i (Line 7), and the features are extracted through the FNN to obtain h_i (line 8). Next, h_i is average pooled, and the predicted label $Y_{i'}$ is obtained using the Softmax classifier (Lines 9-10). Finally, the cross entropy loss $loss_i$ is calculated based on the true label and the predicted label (Line 11), and the network parameters of the

MA-Former are updated through the AdamW optimizer to optimize the performance of anomaly traffic detection (Line 12).

Algorithm 1: The training of the proposed MA-Former

Input: edge traffic data $X_i = [x_1, x_2, \ldots, x_t]$, round N, batch B
Output: traffic category Y'_i
1 Initialize the network parameters for the MA-Former;
2 **for** *epoch* = 1, 2, ..., N **do**
3   **for** *i* = 1, 2, ..., B **do**
4   Segment feature data X_i: $\widehat{X}_i \leftarrow \psi(X_i)$;
5   Perform feature mapping on $\widehat{X}_i$: $\overline{X}_i \leftarrow \alpha(\widehat{X}_i)$;
6   Positional code addition: $\widehat{X}_i \leftarrow Norm(\overline{X}_i) + \theta(\overline{X}_i)$;
7   Multi-head self-attention encoding: $\partial_i \leftarrow MultiHead(\widehat{X}_i)$;
8   Feedforward neural network encoding: $h_i \leftarrow FNN(\partial_i)$;
9   Perform average pooling on h_i: $h'_i \leftarrow MeanPool(h_i)$;
10   Predict Y'_i using feature vector h'_i: $Y'_i \leftarrow softmax(h'_i)$;
11   Calculate the cross entropy loss of Y'_i: $loss_i \leftarrow CE(Y'_i)$;
12   Update the network parameters using the AdamW optimizer;
13   end
14 end

---

5 Performance Evaluation

5.1 Dataset and Experimental Setup

We conduct experiments on a workstation equipped with a GeForce RTX 3090 GPU, CUDA 11.4, and Ubuntu 22.04.2. Based on the deep learning framework PyTorch 1.11.0, we implement the proposed MA-Former and conduct experiments on the following three real-world datasets.

1. ACI-IoT-2023 [19]: An IoT network traffic dataset that contains various attack records within a week, covering multiple network attack types such as reconnaissance (Recon), denial of service (DoS) attacks, brute force cracking (Brute Force) and spoofing.
2. USTC-TFC-2016 [20]: An application network traffic dataset that includes normal traffic types such as Facetime, FTP, MySQL, and anomaly traffic types such as Neris, Nsis, and Virut.
3. CIC-IOT-2023 [21]: An IoT network traffic dataset, which is obtained by executing 105 attacks on an IoT topology with 33 devices.

In the datasets, the categories with too few samples are removed to ensure the stability of the model. As shown in Table 1, the ACI-IoT-2023 dataset contains 4 anomaly traffic types. The original USTC-TFC-2016 dataset contains 10 normal traffic types and 10 anomaly traffic types, where 6 anomaly traffic types are selected and the other with too few samples are removed. Meanwhile, the 10 normal traffic types are classified into 1 category. The original CIC-IOT-2023 dataset contains 7 anomaly traffic types, where distributed DoS and DoS are merged into 1 category and 3 categories with too few samples are removed.

Table 1. Detailed labels in datasets

Dataset	Benign traffic label	Anomaly traffic label
ACI-IoT-2023	Benign	Brute Force, DoS, Recon, Spoofing
USTC-TFC-2016	Benign	Cridex, Htbot, Miuref, Neris, Nsis, Virut
CIC-IOT-2023	Benign	DDoS/DoS, Mirai, Spoofing

For the MA-Former, we set the number of encoding modules to 3, the slice size of each module to 2, the training rounds to 50, the batch size to 64, the learning rate to 0.001, the self-attention heads to 4, and the self-attention head layers to 6. Furthermore, random sampling is introduced to balance the sample data. Specifically, 3000 samples are extracted from each category for the ACI-IoT- 2023 and 1000 samples are extracted from each category for the other datasets. Moreover, the ratio of the training, validation, and testing sets is 6:2:2.

To evaluate the performance of the proposed MA-Former, the following bench- mark methods are used for comparison.

4. 1D CNN [22]: One-dimensional CNN is used to process time sequence daa. It can extract key information from time sequence data and use it for classification tasks.
5. TSCRNN [23]: A sampling strategy is used to collect samples from longterm streams, which extracts abstract spatial features through CNN, and then introduces stacked bidirectional LSTM to learn temporal features.
6. Deep Packet [12]: A classification method extracts and analyzes the payload of raw network traffic packets by combining SAE and CNN.

5.2 Experimental Results and Analysis

Hyperparameter Selection. Figures 4(a) and (b) evaluate the effects of the number of packets and the size of the hidden layer of the encoding module on the classification accuracy and efficiency of the proposed MA-Former. When the number of packets is 8, the accuracy reaches a peak of 0.9992. As the hidden layer size increases, the accuracy also increases. When the hidden layer size is 128, the accuracy reaches a peak of 0.9993, but it leads to significant increase in training time. When the hidden layer size is 64, the accuracy drops slightly to 0.9992, but the training time is shortened by 10.52 seconds. Therefore, we choose 8 packets and a 64-unit hidden layer for the MA-Former.

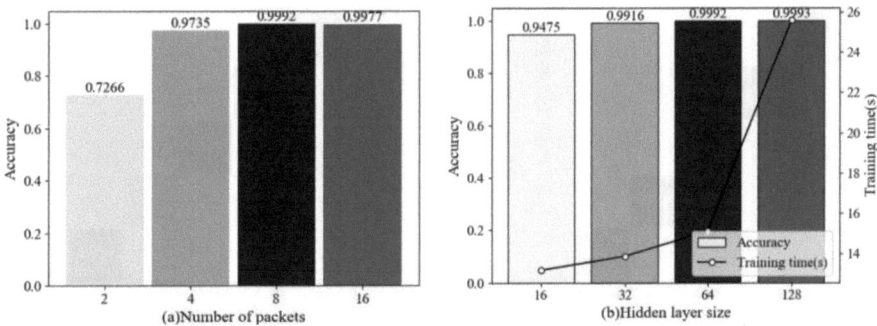

Fig. 4. Classification accuracy and efficiency of the MA-Former with different numbers of packets and hidden layer sizes.

Comparison with Benchmarks. Table 2 compares the anomaly traffic classification performance of different methods on the ACI-IoT-2023 dataset. The F1-score of the MA-Former reaches 0.9993, which is 9.89%, 6.51%, and 42.30% higher than other benchmark methods, respectively. Meanwhile, the MA-Former shows significant advantages in other performance matrices. This is because the MA-Former can accurately obtain the time sequence representation and introduces a multi-head self-attention mechanism, which enables it to automatically learn and extract key classification features. In contrast, the 1D CNN has limited ability to extract and learn time features. Although the TSCRNN uses bidirectional LSTM for feature learning, the learning effect is not good when it only relies on the packet payload length and the arrival interval. Deep Packet only relies on payload, making it ineffective for encrypted traffic.

Next, Figs. 5(a), (b), (c), and (d) use confusion matrices to evaluate the classification performance of different methods. The rows and columns represent the true label and predicted label of the sample, and the depth of the diagonal color intuitively reflects the degree of classification confusion of each category.

Table 2. Comparison with benchmark methods on ACI-IoT-2023

Method	Accuracy	Precision	Recall	F1 score
1D CNN	0.9140	0.9319	0.9046	0.9004
TSCRNN	0.9398	0.9461	0.9352	0.9342
Deep Packet	0.5764	0.5831	0.5759	0.5763
MA-Former	**0.9992**	**0.9993**	**0.9993**	**0.9993**

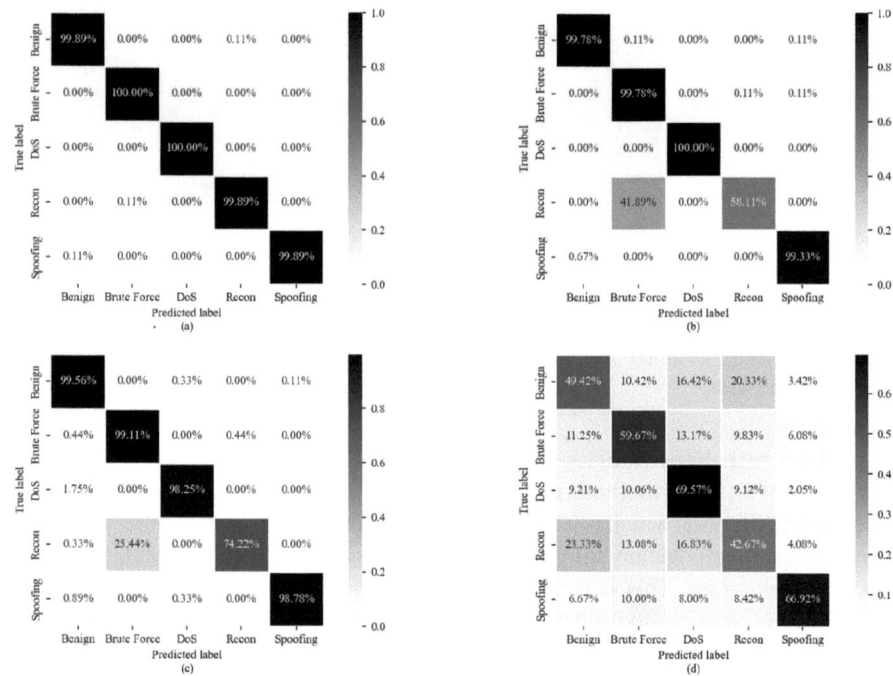

Fig. 5. Confusion matrices of different methods on ACI-IoT-2023: (a) MA-Former, (b) 1D CNN, (c) TSCRNN, (d) Deep Packet.

The experimental results show that the proposed MA-Former can achieve the best classification performance. For Brute Force and DoS attacks, the accuracy of the MA-Former reaches 100%. For Recon attacks, the accuracy of the MA- Former is also as high as 99.89%, while the classification accuracy of 1D CNN, TSCRNN, and Deep Packet is only 58.11%, 74.22%, and 42.67%, respectively. This is because both Recon and Brute Force attacks involve a large number of attempts and probes on the target system, making it easy to be false positives. In comparison, the MA-Former can effectively distinguish these two types of traffic based on their subtle differences. This is because the designed multi-head self-attention mechanism can capture the indistinguishable features of these two types of attacks. Experimental results verify the effectiveness and superiority of the proposed MA-Former.

Generalization Analysis. Figures 6(a) and (b) evaluate the generalization ability of the proposed MA-Former on different datasets through confusion matrices. As shown in Fig. 6(a), there is some confusion between the Neris attack and the Virut attack in USTC-TFC-2016 by MA-Former, resulting in 8% of the Neris attacks being misclassified as Virut attacks and 12% of the Virut attacks being misclassified as Neris attacks. This is due to their similar propagation modes and hidden techniques. However, the MA-Former maintains above 95% accuracy for other categories. As shown in Fig. 6(b), the MA-Former also shows excel- lent performance on the CIC-IOT-2023 dataset. Although there are some minor misclassifications (i.e., 0.54% of Mirai attacks being misclassified as DDoS/DoS attacks and Spoofing attacks, respectively), the overall classification effect is excellent. As shown in Table 3, the MA-Former achieves an accuracy of 0.9641 and an F1 score of 0.9550 on USTC-TFC-2016, and an accuracy of 0.9916 and an F1 score of 0.9909 on CIC-IOT-2023. The results validate the MA-Former's adaptability to various datasets and strong generalization ability.

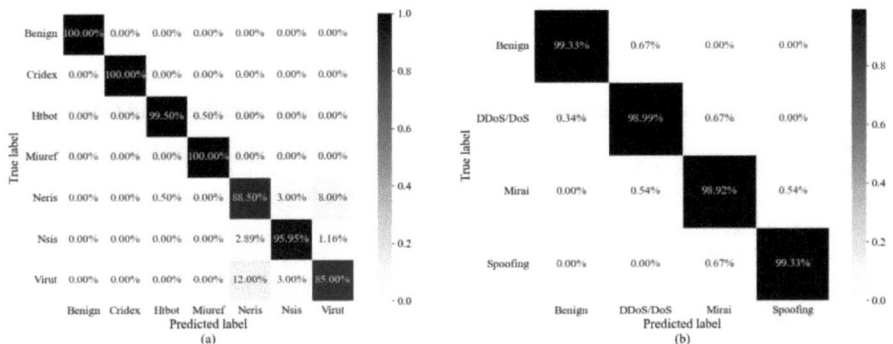

Fig. 6. Confusion matrices of the MA-Former on different datasets: (a) USTC-TFC- 2016, (b) CIC-IOT-2023.

Table 3. Performance of the MA-Former on different datasets

Dataset name	USTC-TFC-2016	CIC-IOT-2023
Accuracy	0.9641	0.9916
Precision	0.9547	0.9904
Recall	0.9556	0.9914
F1 score	0.9550	0.9909

6 Conclusions

In this paper, we propose a novel anomaly traffic detection method in edge with MA-Former, which combines the multi-scale time sequence representation and the self-attention mechanism. The MA-Former can accurately detect anomaly traffic with payload length and time interval. In MA-Former, the feature data is first segmented and mapped through the time-sequence representation module. Next, the mapping vector is encoded by the multi-head self-attention mechanism. Finally, the feature vectors of each layer are aggregated and input into the classifier to obtain anomaly traffic classification results. Based on real-world datasets of edge traffic, the effectiveness of the MA-Former is verified through extensive experiments. The experimental results show that the MA-Former can achieve higher anomaly traffic classification accuracy than other benchmark methods on different performance indicators, which also exhibit superior generalization ability for different traffic datasets.

Acknowledgment. This work was partly supported by the National Natural Science Foundation of China under Grant No. (62202103, 62372111), the Natural Science Foundation of Fujian Province for Distinguished Young Scholars under Grant No. 2025J010020, and the Central Funds Guiding the Local Science and Technology Development under Grant No. 2022L3004.

References

1. Mukhopadhyay, S.C., Suryadevara, N.K.: Internet of Things: Challenges and Opportunities. Springer (2014)
2. Chen, Z., Xiong, B., Chen, X., Min, G., Li, J.: Joint computation offloading and resource allocation in multi-edge smart communities with personalized federated deep reinforcement learning. IEEE Trans. Mobile Comput. (2024)
3. Velan, P., Čermák, M., Čeleda, P., Drašar, M.: A survey of methods for encrypted traffic classification and analysis 2015 Int. J. Netw. Manage. **25**(5), 355–374 (2015)
4. Chen, Z., Hu, J., Min, G., Zomaya, A.Y., El-Ghazawi, T.: Towards accurate prediction for high-dimensional and highly-variable cloud workloads with deep learning. IEEE Trans. Parallel Distrib. Syst. **31**(4), 923–934 (2019)
5. Chen, Z., Zhang, J., Zheng, X., Min, G., Li, J., Rong, C.-M.: Profit-aware cooperative offloading in UAV-enabled MEC systems using lightweight deep reinforcement learning. IEEE Internet Things J. (2024)
6. Liu, H., Wang, Z., Wang, Y.: Semi-supervised encrypted traffic classification using composite features set. J. Netw. **7**(8), 1195 (2012)
7. Yamansavascilar, B., Guvensan, M.A., Yavuz, A.G., Karsligil, M.E.: Application identification via network traffic classification. In 2017 International Conference on Computing, Networking and Communications, pp. 843–848. IEEE (2017)
8. Alshammari, R., Zincir-Heywood, A.N.: Can encrypted traffic be identified without port numbers, IP addresses and payload inspection? Comput. Netw. **55**(6), 1326–1350 (2011)
9. Quan, Y.-X., Dong, Y.-N., Xiang, Y., Chen, S.-S., Wang, Z.-J., Jin, J.: Fast online classification of network traffic using new feature-embedded hierarchical structure. Comput. Netw. **237**, 110106 (2023)
10. Aceto, G., Bovenzi, G., Ciuonzo, D., Montieri, A., Persico, V., Pescapè, A.: Characterization and prediction of mobile-app traffic using Markov modeling. IEEE Trans. Netw. Serv. Manag. **18**(1), 907–925 (2021)
11. Fu, C., Li, Q., Shen, M., Xu, K.: Realtime robust malicious traffic detection via frequency domain analysis. In: Proceedings of the 2021 ACM SIGSAC Conference on Computer and Communications Security, pp. 3431–3446 (2021)
12. Lotfollahi, M., Siavoshani, M.J., Zade, R.S.H., Saberian, M.: Deep packet: a novel approach for encrypted traffic classification using deep learning. Soft Comput. **24**(3), 1999–2012 (2020)
13. Xinyi, H., Chunxiang, G., Wei, F.: [retracted] CLD-net: a network combining CNN and LSTM for internet encrypted traffic classification. Secur. Commun. Netw. **2021**(1), 5518460 (2021)
14. Ma, X., Zhu, W., Wei, J., Jin, Y., Dongsheng, G., Wang, R.: EETC: an extended encrypted traffic classification algorithm based on variant resnet network. Comput. Secur. **128**, 103175 (2023)
15. Zheng, W., Gou, C., Yan, L., Mo, S.: Learning to classify: a flow-based relation network for encrypted traffic classification. In: Proceedings of the Web Conference, pp. 13–22 (2020)
16. Chen, W., Lyu, F., Wu, F., Yang, P., Xue, G., Li, M.: Sequential message characterization for early classification of encrypted internet traffic. IEEE Trans. Veh. Technol. **70**(4), 3746–3760 (2021)

17. Vaswani, A., et al.: Attention is all you need. Adv. Neural Inform. Process. Syst. **30** (2017)
18. Lin, X., Xiong, G., Gou, G., Li, Z., Shi, J., Yu, J.: ETBERT: a contextualized datagram representation with pre-training transformers for encrypted traffic classification. In: Proceedings of the ACM Web Conference, pp. 633–642 (2022)
19. ACI IoT network traffic dataset 2023. IEEE Dataport 20 (2023). https://doi.org/10.21227/qacj-3x32
20. Wang, W., Zhu, M., Zeng, X., Ye, X., Sheng, Y.: Malware traffic classification using convolutional neural network for representation learning. In: International Conference on Information Networking, pp. 712–717. IEEE (2017)
21. Neto, E.C.P., Dadkhah, S., Ferreira, R., Zohourian, A., Lu, R., Ghorbani, A.A.: Ciciot2023: a real-time dataset and benchmark for large-scale attacks in IoT environment. Sensors **23**(13), 5941 (2023)
22. Wang, W., Zhu, M., Wang, J., Zeng, X., Yang, Z.: End-to-end encrypted traffic classification with one-dimensional convolution neural networks. In: IEEE International Conference on Intelligence and Security Informatics, pp. 43–48. IEEE (2017)
23. Lin, K., Xiaolong, X., Gao, H.: TSCRNN: a novel classification scheme of encrypted traffic based on flow spatiotemporal features for efficient management of IIOT. Comput. Netw. **190**, 107974 (2021)

Communication Efficient Fuzzy Clustered Graph Federated Learning

Weishan Zhang[✉], Ziyu Wang, Hongwei Zhao, Zhicheng Bao, Yuru Liu, Haoyun Sun, Tao Chen, and Baoyu Zhang

Qingdao Institute of Software, College of Computer Science and Technology, China University of Petroleum (East China), Qingdao, China
zhangws@upc.edu.cn, {wangziyu,zhw,dongshou2015}@s.upc.edu.cn

Abstract. Federated learning enables collaborative training of multiple participants and aggregation to generate global models while protecting data privacy. However, this approach is challenged by the substantial communication overhead imposed by the transmission of model parameters from clients to the fusion server in the process of obtaining a global model. The accuracy of the global model may decrease on clients due to concept drift between client data. To resolve these problems, we propose a communication efficient Fuzzy Clustered Graph Federated Learning (FCGFL) approach, where a graph federated learning method based on a personalized decoupling idea is designed, with clients uploading shared layer parameters to reduce the number of transmitted model parameters to improve communication efficiency. A fuzzy clustered federated learning method based on multi-step matrix optimization is designed in FCGFL to improve the model accuracy of federated learning by optimizing the affiliation matrix of fuzzy clustering, and to enhance the convergence speed to reduce the number of communication rounds. FCGFL is evaluated on public datasets and also industrial defect scenarios, and the results show that FCGFL outperforms the existing federated learning algorithms, with a reduction in communication time per round of 5%, a reduction in the average number of rounds for convergence of about 40%, and an improvement in average model accuracy of 2%.

Keywords: graph federated learning · fuzzy clustering · local random walk · communication efficiency

1 Introduction

Deep learning and artificial intelligence are widely used in various fields, and data from multiple parties are usually pooled for unified training to obtain highly accurate complex network models. Due to the importance of data security and privacy, strict regulations have been proposed to govern the use of data [9]. Companies often do not agree to share image data for centralized training due to commercial data security and privacy concerns, leading to data silos. Federated learning can train models while protecting data privacy, and it does not require participants to upload raw data but aggregates client model parameters, which helps to solve data silo problems [32].

However, federated learning encounters several problems in practice. To achieve optimization of model parameters, frequent communication and coordination between clients and central server is required [23]. Clients have limited computational, storage, and communication resources, while the parameters of deep learning networks are usually large, which not only puts high computational resource requirements on the server but also leads to long training time. To solve these problems, researchers proposed clustered federated learning, which divides clients into different clusters with similar data distributions and aggregates models within clusters, reducing the number of rounds to reach convergence, improving communication efficiency and model generalization capability [24]. However, the problem of huge number of transmitted parameters brought by deep neural networks still affects the communication efficiency of clustered federated learning. Numerous clients send their model parameters to central server, which requires high communication cost, which is not conducive to the application of clustered federated learning in practical engineering field [30]. Arivazhagan et al. [2] set personalized layers for federated learning, which reduces the number of communication parameters from the client model and helps to reduce communication time. Based on this approach, this paper uses a personalized decoupled federated learning method, where the network is divided into personalized and shared layers at clients, and only the shared layers are federated for aggregation.

At the same time, in practical application scenarios, concept drift may be common. Concept drift is inevitable in practical scenarios, as clients collect data under different conditions [10]. Concept drift means that the same labels are characterized differently in different clients, leading to poor performance of global models obtained from classical federated learning training on clients. It leads to the situation that some clustered objects are in the fuzzy region between different clusters, while these clustered objects should belong to two or more clusters simultaneously. In classical clustering methods, they are classified into a certain cluster [17], and clients cannot obtain enough data for effective training, and the model performance is thus degraded. Fuzzy clustering can obtain overlapping clusters to form a more accurate cluster division, and its application to federated learning can fully utilize the data of overlapping nodes, which is more suitable for the above scenario [22]. Existing fuzzy clustered federated learning methods have poor clustering results and are deficient in accuracy and convergence speed. Graph federated learning uses the information of a graph to help identify potential relationships between clients and calculate the affiliation of clients more accurately. Fuzzy clustering uses affiliation to get faster and more accurate cluster partitioning results to improve the performance of federated learning.

To address the above challenges, in this paper, a fuzzy clustered graph federated learning method, named FCGFL, is proposed, which constructs a client relationship graph by a personalized decoupling method, represents client features with shared layer parameters, and reduces the number of communication parameters. Multi-step random walking is used to optimize local features of the graph, and a fuzzy clustering federated learning method based on multi-step matrix optimization is proposed to enhance the fuzzy clustering effectiveness and generate multiple personalized aggregated model parameters. The contributions of the paper are as follows:

1) A graph federated learning method based on personalized decoupling method is proposed to construct the node graph using the shared layer parameters while the personalization layers are not involved in the communication, which reduces the number of communication parameters and improves communication efficiency.
2) A fuzzy clustered federated learning method based on multi-step matrix optimization is proposed to improve the clustering accuracy and global model performance, which uses multi-step random walking to compute the local features of the graph and optimize the affiliation matrix for fuzzy clustering, improving the clustering accuracy and aggregation model performance.
3) Three datasets are used to evaluate the accuracy and communication efficiency of the method in image classification tasks.

The rest of the paper is organized as follows. Section 2 will present the related work on communication efficiency in federated learning, fuzzy clustered federated learning, and graph federated learning. Section 3 will present the details of the overall architecture and methodology of FCGFL. Section 4 will present the experiments and results of FCGFL. Section 5 will present the conclusion and future work.

2 Related Work

Federated learning, which can co-train multiple clients while protecting data privacy, has been rapidly developing in the context of increasing attention to data security. Model generalization and communication efficiency are important research directions in federated learning.

2.1 Communication Efficiency in Federated Learning

In federated learning, parameters are shared between the server and clients through the network, but the communication resources are often limited, and frequent communication will consume a lot of time and reduce the efficiency of federated learning. To solve the communication bottleneck, there are efforts on model compression, model aggregation algorithm optimization, and other aspects [1].

Pian et al. [20] introduced the use of output logits and compressed sketches methods in federated learning to reduce model size and decrease communication overhead. Su et al. [26] proposed a variable-length code compression method that can reduce the number of model parameters in the communication of federated learning. Khan et al. [11] proposed a compression pipeline composed of pruning and quantization-aware training for deep compression of client models. Liu et al. [16] proposed a quantized compressive sensing method to achieve dimensionality reduction of client models in federated learning. Oh et al. [18] used dimensionality reduction and vector quantization to compress the local model updates for each device, designed vector quantizers, optimized the key parameters for compression, and recovered the sparse signal at the server with model aggregation. However, there is a discrepancy between the compressed model and the original model, which can lead to a decrease in the accuracy of the model.

The accuracy of the local model may degrade the overall performance of the global model, making federated learning require more rounds of training to reach convergence and less efficient communication. To address this problem, researchers optimize federated learning from the perspective of model aggregation algorithms. Talasso et al. [27] proposed a method for clustering models based on their similarity to improve federated aggregation efficiency and reduce communication overhead. Gao et al. [6] used parameter decoupling to implement personalization layers for each client, and Arivazhagan et al. [2] proposed FedPer with personalization layers, where clients retain personalization layers while sharing the base layer globally.

2.2 Fuzzy Clustered Federated Learning

Clustering divides clients into clusters and classifies clients with similar features into the same cluster. Clients within each cluster are very similar, while clients between clusters are very different. Using clustering for federated model aggregation improves federated learning performance and communication efficiency by exploiting the similarity between clients.

One of the established federated clustering methods is to upload the data distribution and data volume of different clients as clustering metrics, which leads to leakage of information about the dataset in communication, which does not ensure data security [3,14]. Another clustering approach is based on model similarity, and some optimized federated algorithms have emerged based on the k-means clustering method. For example, Palihawadana et al. [19] used the k-means algorithm to establish similarity metrics between clients. Wang et al. [28] proposed a clustering method for weighted model aggregation that computes the cosine similarity of the gradients of the client models during training. Donald et al. [25] combined clustered federated learning with passive domain adaptation on a server using labeled data for pre-training and unlabeled data on the client, extending the application of clustering federated learning in unsupervised learning.

The data of overlapping nodes are composed of several parts with different cluster features. Traditional federated clustering uses the node for the optimization of one cluster, and cannot optimize other clusters with some data features of the node. Fuzzy clustering uses overlapping nodes to optimize multiple clusters according to affiliation, which effectively uses overlapping nodes. So introducing fuzzy clustering into federated learning can improve the clustering effect. Li et al. [12] proposed a federated soft clustering method, which achieves local training and federated clustering of the model. Ruan et al. [22] proposed FedSoft based on fuzzy clustered federated learning using the proximal term update to control the load of the client and proved the federated convergence of the fuzzy clustering strategy. Meanwhile, fuzzy clustering has been applied in various real-world environments, such as solar power prediction and electricity usage behavior analysis [29,31], showing good performance in real-world scenarios.

2.3 Graph Federated Learning

Fuzzy clustered federated learning for improving federated aggregation performance presupposes reasonably accurate client relationships. Using a graph to describe node relationships helps capture the correlations between clients and obtain deep knowledge of the relationships between client nodes. Meanwhile, using a graph to store the correlations between nodes facilitates further optimization to get accurate node relationships and helps fuzzy clustering for accurate cluster division.

Chen et al. [5] proposed a structured federated learning method, which stores the relational graphs in the server and then, based on the structure of the relational graph, performs client-centric model aggregation. Chen et al. [4] proposed FedGraph, where each client owns a subgraph, uses GNN to calculate the similarity between clients and performs federated model aggregation using the weighted average method. Using graphs to construct client associations, perform fuzzy clustering and model aggregation can reduce errors of cluster delineation and enhance the model effect within the clusters using data from overlapping clients.

3 Methodology

Given a set of clients with different datasets, FCGFL aims to obtain the relationships between clients, optimize data transmission to improve communication efficiency through personalized decoupling, aggregate model parameters and obtain better models through fuzzy clustering. We first introduce the overall architecture of FCGFL. Next, we illustrate the proposed graph federated learning based on personalized decoupling and fuzzy clustered federated learning based on multi-step matrix optimization, respectively.

3.1 Overall Architecture

The FCGFL federated learning framework consists of a server and clients $\{c_1, c_2, ..., c_N\}$, and Fig. 1 shows the overall architecture of FCGFL. Each client has its local dataset $\{D_1, D_2, ..., D_N\}$. The client is responsible for training a local model using a neural network to obtain $\{W_1, W_2, ..., W_N\}$ and uploading the model parameters to the server. The server is responsible for constructing the client relationships graph, performing fuzzy clustering and aggregating the model parameters, and sending the aggregated parameters to the client to update model parameters.

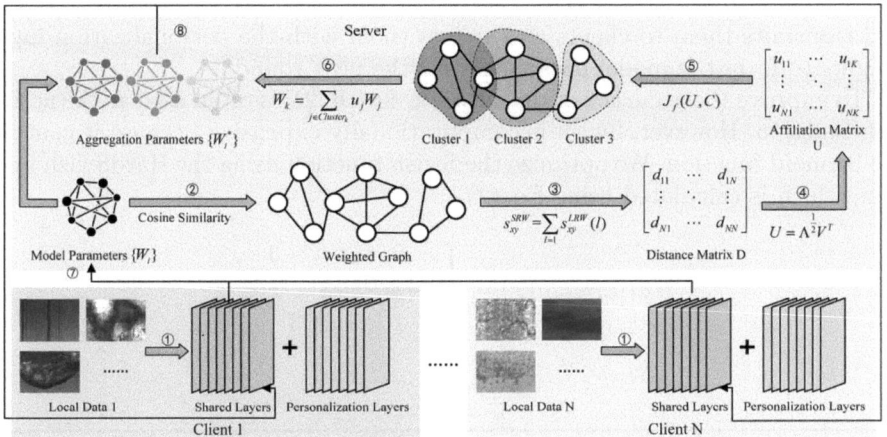

Fig. 1. The overall architecture of FCGFL

The overall FCGFL algorithm is shown in algorithm 1, which consists of two main parts: graph federated learning based on personalized decoupling and fuzzy clustered federated learning based on multi-step matrix optimization. Before training starts, the client $\{c_1, c_2, ..., c_N\}$ and the model parameters $\{W_1^0, W_2^0, ..., W_N^0\}$ are initialized. Each client uses its local dataset to train and update the model parameters. The cross-entropy loss function $Loss(w, D)$ is used to calculate the model loss in the image classification task of clients, which is calculated using Eq. (1).

$$Loss(w, D) = -\sum_{(x,y) \in D} y_a log p(w, x) \quad (1)$$

where D is the dataset, $p(w, x)$ is the predicted value of the model w based on the data sample x, y is the true label of x, and y_a is the a-th element of the true label.

After clients reach a certain number of training rounds, clients upload the model parameters. Through graph federated learning based on personalization decoupling, each client decouples the model parameters, divides the local network into personalization and shared layers, and transmits the shared layer parameters $W_{S_i}^j$ to the server. The server receives the shared layer parameters $\{W_{S_1}^j, W_{S_2}^j, ..., W_{S_N}^j\}$ to calculate the similarity between clients, and construct a federated nodes graph, and then build and update a similarity matrix A. Then, using fuzzy clustered federated learning based on multi-step matrix optimization, the affiliation matrix for fuzzy clustering is calculated U. Based on the fuzzy clustering results, the server aggregates the shared layer parameters of clients in the clusters. It obtains the aggregation parameters $\{W_{S_1}^j, W_{S_2}^j, \cdots, W_{S_K}^j\}$, and transmits them to clients and splices them with the personalization layers weights to form the model parameters for the next round.

To improve the accuracy of the network, Swish [21] is often used as the activation function. However, Swish is computationally expensive because it contains the Sigmoid function. We optimize the Swish function using the HardSwish function, which is calculated using Eq. (2).

$$HardSwish(x) = \begin{cases} 0 & x \leq -3 \\ \frac{x(x+3)}{6} & -3 < x < 3 \\ 1 & x \geq 3 \end{cases} \qquad (2)$$

Algorithm 1. FCGFL training process

Hyperparameter: number of clients N, number of training rounds R, number of local training epochs E, number of clusters K, local networks learning rate η.
Initializes clients $\{c_1, c_2, \ldots, c_N\}$ and model parameters $\{W_1^0, W_2^0, \ldots, W_N^0\}$.
1: **Clients** c_i:
2: **for** $j = 1, 2, ..., R$ **do**
3:   **for** $k = 1, 2, \ldots, E$ **do**
4:     $W_{i,k}^j \leftarrow W_{i,k-1}^j - \eta \nabla L(W_{i,k-1}^j)$
5:   **end for**
6:   $(W_{S_i}^j, W_{P_i}^j) \leftarrow W_{i,E}^j$
7:   send $W_{S_i}^j$ to Server, receive $W_{S_i}^{j*}$ from Server
8:   $W_{i,E}^{j+1} \leftarrow W_{S_i}^{j*} + W_{P_i}^j$
9: **end for**
10: **Server:**
11: **for** $j = 1, 2, \ldots, R$ **do**
12:   receive $\{W_{S_1}^j, W_{S_2}^j, ..., W_{S_N}^j\}$
13:   Compute A according to (3)
14:   Compute U according to (8) and (11)
15:   **for** l=1,2,...,K **do**
16:     $W_{S_l}^j \leftarrow \sum_{m \in cluster_l} u_m W_{S_m}$
17:     send $W_{S_l}^j$ to clients
18:   **end for**
19: **end for**

3.2 Graph Federated Learning Based on Personalized Decoupling

It has been proved to be effective in convolutional neural networks to construct personalized layers by parameter decoupling and improve the efficiency of federated aggregation [2]. To obtain a high accuracy of image classification, EfficientNet-b3 is used as the network for the local model of clients, which is split into two parts: the personalization layers and the shared layers. There is concept drift in the data of clients, which means that the same label has different image features in different clients. The difference between client networks mainly lies in how to process the obtained image features and get their labels accordingly. In the training, the feature extraction module of EfficientNet-b3 gets information needed by other clients, and the classifier of the network gets personalized labels suitable for local data. Therefore, the feature extraction module is used as the shared layers, while the personalization layers include the classifier layer and the last few basic layers.

During local training, train the whole network without decoupling. The model parameters are iteratively trained using the local dataset, with the model weights $W_i = W_{S_i} + W_{P_i}$ for client node i, where W_{S_i} is the shared layers weights, and W_{P_i} is the personalization layers weights, which include the classifier layer and the last basic blocks. Only W_{S_i} is uploaded during federated model aggregation to improve the efficiency of federated communication.

After receiving W_{S_i} from the clients, the server constructs a weighted undirected graph $G = \{V, E\}$ based on their similarity, describing the relationships between clients, where V represents clients and E represents the association between clients, and a_{bc} is the weight of the edges between clients b and c, which is computed based on node parameters. At epoch j, the similarity between clients b and c is calculated using Eq. (3).

$$a_{bc}^j = \frac{\Delta W_b^j \cdot \Delta W_c^j}{||\Delta W_b^j|| ||\Delta W_c^j||} \tag{3}$$

where ΔW_b^j denotes the changes in the uploaded parameters of client b compared to the previous round of communication, which is calculated using Eq. (4).

$$\Delta W_i^j = Flatten(W_{S_i}^j - W_{S_i}^{j-1}) \tag{4}$$

The relational information of the federated node graph is stored in a $N \times N$ matrix A, which is initially set to 0.

3.3 Fuzzy Clustered Federated Learning Based on Multi-Step Matrix Optimization

In this section, the relational information between clients in A is used for fuzzy clustered federated learning to accurately aggregate the shared layers weights of similar clients. The distances between points in the client relationships graph are computed first, and random walk is an effective and widely used method for distance calculation.

Random walk is a Markov chain that describes a sequence of nodes visited by a random walker in a network and is used to represent the distance between two nodes in the network. Random walk captures local features in the graph to optimize the similarity matrix with low computational complexity. The process can be described by a transfer probability matrix P, where P_{xy} denotes the probability that the random walker of node x will walk to y in the next step. $v_{xy}(t)$ denotes the probability that the random walker will be located at node y after t steps, which is calculated using Eq. (5).

$$\vec{v_x}(t) = P^T \vec{v_x}(t-1) \tag{5}$$

where $\vec{v_x}(0)$ is an $N \times 1$ vector and T is the matrix transpose. The local random walk exponent of a random walker starting from node x and located at node y after t steps is calculated using Eq. (6).

$$s_{xy}^{LRW}(t) = \frac{k_x}{\theta(x)} \cdot v_{xy}(t) + \frac{k_y}{\theta(y)} \cdot v_{yx}(t) \tag{6}$$

where k_x and k_y are the degrees of nodes x and y respectively, $v_{xy}(t)$ and $v_{yx}(t)$ denote the probability of transitioning from node x to y and from y to x at time step t, and $\theta(x)$ denotes the sum of the weight of the edges of node x concerning all of its neighbors, which is calculated using Eq. (7).

$$\theta(x) = \sum_{z \in N(x)} w(x, z) \tag{7}$$

where $N(x)$ denotes the set of neighbouring nodes of node x, $w(x,z)$ denotes the weights of the edges between nodes x and z, which are obtained from the matrix A.

Liu et al. [15] proposed a SRW index to reduce the influence of distant nodes in a graph on the computation. The method uses multi-step random walking to make the distance between nodes with high similarity smaller and the distance between nodes with low similarity larger in the graph with distance weight, the SRW index is calculated using Eq. (8).

$$s_{xy}^{SRW}(t) = \sum_{l=1}^{t} s_{xy}^{LRW}(l) \tag{8}$$

This yields a distance matrix $D = \{d_{xy}\}$ between the nodes of the graph, and the normalized distance d_{xy} between node x and node y is calculated using Eq. (9).

$$d_{xy}(t) = \begin{cases} 1 - s_{xy}^{SRW}(t) & x \neq y \\ 0 & x = y \end{cases} \tag{9}$$

Using multidimensional scaling to map each element in D to a lower dimensional space while maintaining the distance relationships between the original elements, multidimensional scaling finds a set of coordinates in the lower dimensional space that are as consistent as possible with the distances or similarities between the original elements and ultimately results in a lower dimensional representation of the matrix data. The distance matrix D of $N \times N$ is processed using multidimensional scaling, H is a centering matrix, which is calculated using Eq. (10).

$$H = I - \frac{1}{N}\vec{i}\vec{i}^T \tag{10}$$

where I is the unit matrix, and $\vec{i}$ is an N-dimensional column vector, the inner product matrix $\tilde{D}$ is calculated using Eq. (11).

$$\tilde{D} = -\frac{1}{2}H(D \circ D)H \tag{11}$$

where ∘ denotes the Hadamard product of the matrix. The singular value decomposition of the matrix is performed, the first p eigenvectors are selected as the axes of the low-dimensional space, and the approximate representation of the nodes in the p-dimensional space can be obtained by projecting D onto them. The optimized matrix U is obtained after the optimization of local features of the graph.

The optimized graph is processed by fuzzy clustering. Each point has a certain degree of affiliation and belongs to a different class. The degree of affiliation indicates the strength of the association between a node and a particular cluster. Fuzzy clustering aims to minimize the function J_f, which is calculated using Eq. (12).

$$J_f(U, C) = \sum_{i=1}^{N}\sum_{l=1}^{K} u_{il}^f \|x_i - c_l\|^2 \tag{12}$$

where u_{il} is the affiliation degree of the ith node to the lth cluster, $x_i - c_l$ is the distance between the ith node and the center of the lth cluster, and f is the fuzzy index. J_f is optimised iteratively by updating the degree of affiliation u_{il} and the centre of clustering c_l.

4 Experiment

We evaluate the accuracy and communication efficient of FCGFL using image classification datasets, and compare FCGFL with the federated learning baseline algorithms. The clustering division results of FCGFL is also evaluated.

4.1 Dataset and Evaluation Configuration

The datasets used for the experiments include CIFAR10 and also two datasets from industrial real-world scenarios, Northeast Hot Strip Steel (NEU) [8] and Kaggle Shevell Steel (KSS) [7]. The data was divided into training and validation sets with a ratio of 9:1.

To make the dataset conform to data distribution in federated learning, Dirichlet is used to partition data to clients based on data labels, with $\alpha = 1.0$.

The image-flipping method is used to initialize the cluster structure. N clients are partially overlapped into K clusters, and the image data in each cluster is rotated at different angles. For example, at K = 3, the data from 0 to 2 clients are rotated by 120°, the data from 3 to 5 clients are rotated by 240°, the data from the 6 to 8 clients remain unchanged, while the data from 9 client is partially rotated by 120° and partially unchanged. This setup ensures the clients' data distribution conforms to concept drift.

FCGFL is compared five federated algorithms to evaluate the accuracy. FedAvg is the fundamental algorithm of federated learning. Ditto [13] uses regularization terms to find personalized models between global and local models. FedPer [2] uses decoupling for personalization. ClusteredFL [24] uses hard clustering as the federated aggregation strategy. Fedsoft [22] introduces fuzzy clustering into federated learning.

Pytorch is used to set up the experimental environment, and experiments trained with 12 GB RAM and NVIDIA GeForce RTX3080. EfficientNet-b3 is used as the network for local models, which has a high accuracy in image classification.

Initialization sets the multi-step random walking iteration parameter to 3, the multidimensional mapping dimension parameter to 2, the learning rate to 0.001, the number of federated aggregation rounds to 100, and the number of clients training rounds to 3.

4.2 Communication Efficiency Comparisons

FCGFL can improve communication efficiency while ensuring accuracy. Firstly, FCGFL uses a graph federated learning method based on personalized decoupling, which transmits fewer parameters and reduces data transmission time. Secondly, the fuzzy clustered federated learning method based on multi-step matrix optimization used by FCGFL has lower computational complexity and faster fuzzy clustering speed. The communication efficiency of the baseline algorithms and FCGFL using the KSS dataset under K = 3 is compared experimentally.

Model performance is also evaluated by calculating the average accuracy of all clients. As shown in Table 1, N denotes the number of nodes in federated learning, *Params* denotes the number of parameters transmitted per communication, and *Communication* and *Total* denote the communication time and total training time, respectively. We can see that FCGFL has the highest accuracy compared to other federated algorithms while transmitting the least number of parameters per communication. The result shows that FCGFL has the shortest communication time and training time, which are at least 5% shorter than other algorithms.

Using the KSS dataset, the convergence speed of each algorithm under the condition of K = 3, N = 10 are compared. As shown in Fig. 2, the curves of different colors indicate the change of accuracy in the training of different algorithms, and the vertical dashed lines show the rounds of convergence of the algorithms, when the accuracy change of three consecutive rounds is less than 0.001, it is considered that the training is close to convergence. The figure shows that FCGFL

Table 1. Communication efficiency comparison experiments

Method	Accuracy		Params(MB)		Communication(s)		Total(s)	
	N = 5	N = 10	N = 5	N = 10	N = 5	N = 10	N = 5	N = 10
FedAvg	0.7696	0.7685	10.213	10.213	4031	7390	35018	38296
Ditto	0.9021	0.9009	10.213	10.213	4054	7401	34677	37943
FedPer	0.7583	0.7595	9.635	9.635	**3797**	6974	30604	34784
ClusteredFL	0.8679	0.8689	10.213	10.213	4056	7375	34496	37770
FedSoft	0.9012	0.9010	10.213	10.213	4039	7395	33528	36825
FCGFL	**0.9237**	**0.9209**	**9.635**	**9.635**	3803	**6972**	**29806**	**32981**

has the fastest convergence speed, converging at round 10, which is about 40% earlier on average compared to the other algorithm rounds, and it reduces the number of communication rounds to improve the communication efficiency in practical scenarios. Also its model has the highest average accuracy with better generalization ability and training efficiency.

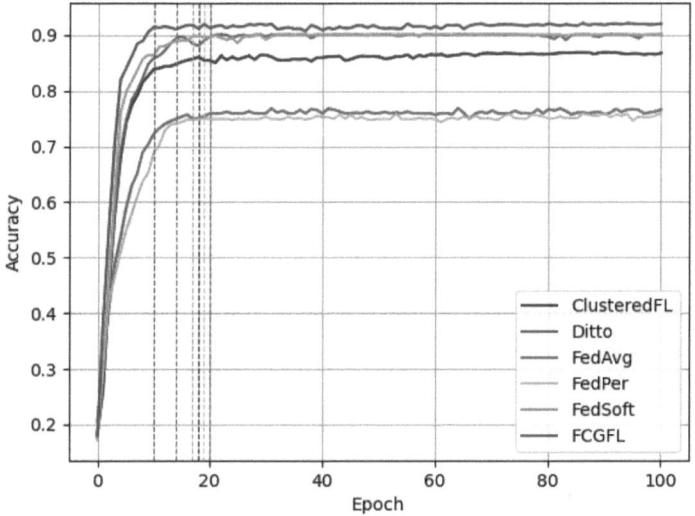

Fig. 2. Training accuracy curves of algorithms in K=3

4.3 Accuracy Comparisons

Accuracy comparison experiments are conducted using 10 clients. A locally trained comparison experiment for a total of 100 rounds of training was set up. The experiment compared the results of different algorithms with K = 2, 3, and 4 clusters.

The results are shown in Table 2. It can be observed that FCGFL has higher accuracy in different numbers of clusters and different datasets, which proves that graph federated learning based on fuzzy clustering can enhance the performance of federated learning. Compared with other algorithms, it can be seen that FCGFL consistently has the highest accuracy, and its accuracy is improved by about 2% over FedSoft. This shows that the FCGFL can make use of the relationships between clients to enhance the federated aggregation efficiency.

Table 2. Accuracy comparison experiments

Method	CIFAR10			NEU			KSS		
	K=2	K=3	K=4	K=2	K=3	K=4	K=2	K=3	K=4
Local	0.8194	0.8216	0.8173	0.9083	0.9046	0.9054	0.9034	0.9015	0.9007
FedAvg	0.8132	0.8107	0.8125	0.7904	0.7693	0.7426	0.7881	0.7685	0.7562
Ditto	0.8256	0.8352	0.8207	0.9072	0.9034	0.8952	0.9064	0.9009	0.8914
FedPer	0.8055	0.8061	0.8003	0.8032	0.7612	0.7553	0.8041	0.7595	0.7541
ClusteredFL	0.8096	0.8137	0.8109	0.8984	0.8703	0.8656	0.8951	0.8689	0.8512
FedSoft	0.8210	0.8228	0.8251	0.9095	0.9028	0.9012	0.9089	0.9010	0.9008
FCGFL	**0.8335**	**0.8358**	**0.8260**	**0.9293**	**0.9265**	**0.9260**	**0.9231**	**0.9209**	**0.9201**

4.4 Clustering Division Results

In the clustering algorithms, achieving correct cluster divisions is crucial, which affects the effectiveness of federated clustering. Using the KSS dataset, the division results of each federated clustering algorithm under the condition of K=3, N=10 are compared in experiments. Given clients 0–9, one client is an overlapping node with different clustering feature data, and the other clients are non-overlapping nodes. The results are shown in Table 3. The results show that shared layers do not affect the accuracy of cluster delineation, and FCGFL, can act as the fuzzy clustering algorithm, can delineate clusters correctly and earlier.

Table 3. Clustering results of algorithms

Method	Round	Delineation results
ClusteredFL	20	{{0,1,2,9},{3,4,5},{6,7,8}}
FedSoft	17	{{0,1,2,9},{3,4,5},{6,7,8,9}}
FCGFL	**10**	{{0,1,2,9},{3,4,5},{6,7,8,9}}

5 Conclusion

In this paper, a fuzzy clustered graph federated learning algorithm is proposed to provide a new solution for the improvement of communication efficiency and model accuracy in federated learning. FCGFL utilizes shared layer weight parameters to construct a graph for client relationships, which can reduce the communication overhead. A fuzzy clustered federated learning method based on multi-step matrix optimization is designed to enhance the clustering effect and thus improve the accuracy of federated learning. We evaluate the performance of FCGFL 3 datasets, and the results show that FCGFL has better accuracy and communication efficiency than existing federated learning algorithms.

In the future, we plan to apply FCGFL to complex visual tasks and multi-task learning to expand the application areas of FCGFL. We will also combine the foundation model to study the fuzzy clustered graph federated learning method for multimodal data processing.

References

1. Almanifi, O.R.A., Chow, C.O., Tham, M.L., Chuah, J.H., Kanesan, J.: Communication and computation efficiency in federated learning: a survey. Internet Things **22**, 100742 (2023). https://doi.org/10.1016/j.iot.2023.100742
2. Arivazhagan, M.G., Aggarwal, V., Singh, A.K., Choudhary, S.: Federated learning with personalization layers (2019)
3. Bao, W., Wang, H., Wu, J., He, J.: Optimizing the collaboration structure in cross-silo federated learning. In: Proceedings of the 40th International Conference on Machine Learning, pp. 1718–1736. PMLR (2023)
4. Chen, F., Li, P., Miyazaki, T., Wu, C.: Fedgraph: federated graph learning with intelligent sampling. IEEE Trans. Parallel Distrib. Syst. **33**(8), 1775–1786 (2022). https://doi.org/10.1109/TPDS.2021.3125565
5. Chen, F., Long, G., Wu, Z., Zhou, T., Jiang, J.: Personalized federated learning with graph (2022)
6. Gao, L., Fu, H., Li, L., Chen, Y., Xu, M., Xu, C.Z.: Feddc: federated learning with non-iid data via local drift decoupling and correction. In: 2022 IEEE/CVF Conference on Computer Vision and Pattern Recognition (CVPR), pp. 10102–10111 (2022). https://doi.org/10.1109/CVPR52688.2022.00987
7. Grishin, A.: BorisV, iBardintsev, inversion, Oleg: Severstal: Steel defect detection (2019). https://kaggle.com/competitions/severstal-steel-defect-detection
8. He, Y., Song, K., Meng, Q., Yan, Y.: An end-to-end steel surface defect detection approach via fusing multiple hierarchical features. IEEE Trans. Instrum. Meas. **69**(4), 1493–1504 (2020). https://doi.org/10.1109/TIM.2019.2915404
9. Huang, W., et al.: Federated learning for generalization, robustness, fairness: a survey and benchmark. IEEE Trans. Pattern Anal. Mach. Intell. 1–20 (2024). https://doi.org/10.1109/TPAMI.2024.3418862
10. Kang, M., Kim, S., Jin, K.H., Adeli, E., Pohl, K.M., Park, S.H.: Fednn: federated learning on concept drift data using weight and adaptive group normalizations. Pattern Recogn. **149**, 110230 (2024). https://doi.org/10.1016/j.patcog.2023.110230. https://www.sciencedirect.com/science/article/pii/S0031320323009275

11. Khan, F.M.A., Abou-Zeid, H., Hassan, S.A.: Deep compression for efficient and accelerated over-the-air federated learning. IEEE Internet Things J. **11**(15), 25802–25817 (2024). https://doi.org/10.1109/JIOT.2024.3373460
12. Li, C., Li, G., Varshney, P.K.: Federated learning with soft clustering. IEEE Internet Things J. **9**(10), 7773–7782 (2022). https://doi.org/10.1109/JIOT.2021.3113927
13. Li, T., Hu, S., Beirami, A., Smith, V.: Ditto: Fair and robust federated learning through personalization. In: Proceedings of the 38th International Conference on Machine Learning, pp. 6357–6368. PMLR (2021)
14. Li, Z., Chen, Z., Wei, X., Gao, S., Ren, C., Quek, T.Q.: Hpfl-cn: communication-efficient hierarchical personalized federated edge learning via complex network feature clustering. In: 2022 19th Annual IEEE International Conference on Sensing, Communication, and Networking (SECON), pp. 325–333 (2022). https://doi.org/10.1109/SECON55815.2022.9918588
15. Liu, W., Lü, L.: Link prediction based on local random walk. Europhys. Lett. **89**(5), 58007 (2010). https://doi.org/10.1209/0295-5075/89/58007
16. Liu, Z., Wang, H., Li, X.: Feduveqcs: universal vector quantized compressive sensing for communication-efficient federated learning. IEEE Internet Things J. (2024). https://doi.org/10.1109/JIOT.2024.3440959
17. Naghi, M.B., Kovács, L., Szilágyi, L.: A review on advanced c-means clustering models based on fuzzy logic. In: 2023 IEEE 21st World Symposium on Applied Machine Intelligence and Informatics (SAMI), pp. 000293–000298 (2023). https://doi.org/10.1109/SAMI58000.2023.10044530
18. Oh, Y., Lee, N., Jeon, Y.S., Poor, H.V.: Communication-efficient federated learning via quantized compressed sensing. IEEE Trans. Wirel. Commun. **22**(2), 1087–1100 (2023). https://doi.org/10.1109/TWC.2022.3201207
19. Palihawadana, C., Wiratunga, N., Wijekoon, A., Kalutarage, H.: Fedsim: similarity guided model aggregation for federated learning. Neurocomputing **483**, 432–445 (2022). https://doi.org/10.1016/j.neucom.2021.08.141
20. Qi, P., Chiaro, D., Guzzo, A., Ianni, M., Fortino, G., Piccialli, F.: Model aggregation techniques in federated learning: a comprehensive survey. Future Gener. Comput. Syst. **150**, 272–293 (2024). https://doi.org/10.1016/j.future.2023.09.008. https://www.sciencedirect.com/science/article/pii/S0167739X23003333
21. Ramachandran, P., Zoph, B., Le, Q.V.: Searching for activation functions. CoRR arxiv:1710.05941 (2017)
22. Ruan, Y., Joe-Wong, C.: Fedsoft: soft clustered federated learning with proximal local updating. In: Proceedings of the AAAI Conference on Artificial Intelligence, vol. 36, no. 7, pp. 8124–8131 (2022). https://doi.org/10.1609/aaai.v36i7.20785
23. Sabah, F., Chen, Y., Yang, Z., Azam, M., Ahmad, N., Sarwar, R.: Model optimization techniques in personalized federated learning: a survey. Expert Syst. Appl. **243**, 122874 (2024). https://doi.org/10.1016/j.eswa.2023.122874. https://www.sciencedirect.com/science/article/pii/S0957417423033766
24. Sattler, F., Müller, K.R., Samek, W.: Clustered federated learning: model-agnostic distributed multitask optimization under privacy constraints. IEEE Trans. Neural Netw. Learn. Syst. **32**(8), 3710–3722 (2021). https://doi.org/10.1109/TNNLS.2020.3015958
25. Shenaj, D., et al.: Learning across domains and devices: style-driven source-free domain adaptation in clustered federated learning. In: 2023 IEEE/CVF Winter Conference on Applications of Computer Vision (WACV), pp. 444–454 (2023). https://doi.org/10.1109/WACV56688.2023.00052

26. Su, X., Zhou, Y., Cui, L., Lui, J.C.S., Liu, J.: Fed-cvlc: compressing federated learning communications with variable-length codes. In: IEEE INFOCOM 2024 - IEEE Conference on Computer Communications, pp. 601–610 (2024). https://doi.org/10.1109/INFOCOM52122.2024.10621361
27. Talasso, G.U., de Souza, A.M., Bittencourt, L.F., Cerqueira, E., Loureiro, A.A.F., Villas, L.A.: Fedsccs: hierarchical clustering with multiple models for federated learning. In: ICC 2024 - IEEE International Conference on Communications, pp. 3280–3285 (2024). https://doi.org/10.1109/ICC51166.2024.10622346
28. Wang, D., Zhang, N., Tao, M.: Clustered federated learning with weighted model aggregation for imbalanced data. China Commun. **19**(8), 41–56 (2022). https://doi.org/10.23919/JCC.2022.08.004
29. Wang, Y., Ma, J., Gao, N., Wen, Q., Sun, L., Guo, H.: Federated fuzzy k-means for privacy-preserving behavior analysis in smart grids. Appl. Energy **331**, 120396 (2023). https://doi.org/10.1016/j.apenergy.2022.120396
30. Wen, J., Zhang, Z., Lan, Y., Cui, Z., Cai, J., Zhang, W.: A survey on federated learning: challenges and applications. Int. J. Mach. Learn. Cybern. **14**(2), 513–535 (2023). https://doi.org/10.1007/s13042-022-01647-y
31. Yoo, E., Ko, H., Pack, S.: Fuzzy clustered federated learning algorithm for solar power generation forecasting. IEEE Trans. Emerg. Top. Comput. **10**(4), 2092–2098 (2022). https://doi.org/10.1109/TETC.2022.3142886
32. Yuan, L., Wang, Z., Sun, L., Yu, P.S., Brinton, C.G.: Decentralized federated learning: a survey and perspective. IEEE Internet Things J. (2024). https://doi.org/10.1109/JIOT.2024.3407584

A Distributed Container-Based Internet of Things (IoT)-Enabled Autonomous E-Healthcare System for Development and Operations (DevOps)

Qinglong Dai[✉], Guangjun Qin, and Ran Li

Beijing Union University, Beijing, People's Republic of China
xxtqinglong@buu.edu.cn

Abstract. It is a trend for hospitals to shift healthcare applications to cloud computing because the cloud has a powerful computing ability. The valuable, sensitive patient data is stored in the remote cloud. This makes it necessary for a hospital to build an autonomous cloud. However, there is a conflict between limited IT department staff and prosperous e-healthcare applications. To solve this problem, a distributed container-based Internet of Things (IoT)-enabled e-healthcare system for Development and Operations (DevOps) is presented. Using container technology and orchestration, a traditional healthcare application is deconstructed into a series of containers and is reorganized according to the application logic that facilitates DevOps. The introducing of container technology makes it possible to automatically increase or decrease docker containers when the e-healthcare application scales up or down. The function and performance of the proposed system are proved through three cases, i.e., scalability, service, and continuous integration (CI)/continuous delivery (CD) pipeline.

Keywords: Cloud computing · container · scalability · orchestration · CI/CD

1 Introduction

The Internet of Things (IoT) has been widely used in the field of healthcare. More and more people pay attention to health and are willing to spend money on healthcare. According to IDC's report, global shipments in 2023 are poised to reach 442.7 million wearable devices this year, growing 6.3% year over year [1]. These wearable devices are able to collect patients' temperature, blood pressure,

---

Supported by Science and Technology General Projects of Beijing Education Commission (Research on Optical and Wireless converged Access Network Networking Technology in Smart Traffic, No. KM202111417010), China Computer Federation (CCF) Opening Project of Information System (Research on Massive Event Flow oriented Stream Computing Framework, No. CCFIS2019-01-01).

electrocardiogram (ECG), pulse, oximetry, and other parameters in real-time. For example, smart portable products can now be used to monitor different medical aspects to track human health via Bluetooth, and Long-rage Radio (LoRa). The collected data should be calculated, processed, and analyzed to obtain patients' status. The data processing has a high requirement on servers' computing ability and can be accomplished on local servers or the third-party remote cloud.

The concept of cloud computing is advancing and thus the innovation that can be utilized to build up a diverse set of systems to convalesce the framework [2]. Cloud computing can provide huge computing resources in an on-demand way. By emerging thousands of servers' storage space, CPU, and network, cloud computing could hold an application or a service using a pay-as-you-go model. To get low service latency, it is feasible to offload the computing entity from the remote cloud to user-near edge or gateways. Thus, edge computing and fog computing occur.

e-healthcare System is a system that employs information and communication technologies (ICT) to seek, identify, understand, solve, and evaluate health issues [3]. Cloud computing, IoT, Big data, artificial intelligence, and so on, are all in the field of ICT [4]. With the help of ICT, e-healthcare system can provide e-healthcare service at any time, from any location.

The information technology (IT) department in a healthcare (HC, i.e., hospital) plays an essential role in connecting engineers, administrators, doctors, and patients. Normally, the IT department is only responsible for the proper functioning of software. This means that the software of healthcare applications or services is developed and completed by a software company outside the hospital. The technical detail of healthcare applications or services is a black box.

Although it is a trend for hospitals to shift healthcare applications to cloud computing, the privacy issue of patient data can not be neglected. On the one hand, the patient data is sensitive [5]. In case of patient data (e.g. genetic data) leakage, hospitals have to bear legal risks and financial losses. On the other hand, completely relying on third-party cloud computing may lead to additional capital expense and operating expenses. Besides, patients' data, such as Electronic Medical Records (EMR), is valuable and may contain the hidden patterns of their behavior or habits. Thus, private cloud computing may be an optional solution.

The challenge of applying private cloud computing for e-healthcare originates from the conflict between limited IT department staff and prosperous e-healthcare applications. From the perspective of the IT department, its staff is not specialized in software development. It is their responsibility to make sure the software works. A newly emerged e-healthcare application means the learning, deployment, and maintenance costs. From the perspective of e-healthcare applications, every application requires a relatively separate development. For example, software A is developed by company B. Software C is developed by company D. The data generated by software A and that generated by software C are stored in two databases. Even the multiple software developed by the same company, their data is not stored in the same database. This leads to the resource waste. To the best of our knowledge, no system-level solution has provided easy, fast, flexible e-healthcare application management, operation, and maintenance.

The contributions of this paper are listed as follows:

1. A distributed container-based e-healthcare system is presented. Using the lightweight virtual machine technology, i.e., Docker and corresponding container orchestration, a traditional healthcare application is deconstructed into a series of containers and is reorganized according to the application logic that facilitates development and operations.
2. The scalability of the proposed system is highlighted. Docker and container orchestration make it possible to automatically increase or decrease docker when the e-Healthcare application scales up or scales down. An e-healthcare application can be continuously developed, tested, and operated.
3. Three cases about scalability, service, and continuous integration (CI) /continuous delivery (CD) pipeline, are displayed. The function and the performance of the proposed system are validated.

The rest of this paper is organized as follows. Section 2 reviews related work on e-healthcare system. Section 3 proposes a distributed container-based IoT-enabled autonomous e-Healthcare system. Three cases about scalability, service, and DevOps, are conducted in Sect. 4. Finally, Sect. 5 concludes the paper and looks to the future.

2 Related Work

Around the IoT-enabled e-healthcare system, plenty of work has been done, focusing on not only system design but also on specific application implementations.

A multi-function and portable health monitoring system was designed and implemented for daily medical inspections. The monitoring indicators included heart rate (HR), blood oxygen saturation level (SpO2), body temperature, photoplethysmography (PPG) signal, ECG signal, room temperature, and room humidity. The monitoring data was displayed on a sensor built-in screen and transmitted to either a mobile application via a local wireless network or the remote cloud [6].

To overcome the inconvenience of multiple IoT gateways and expand the coverage, an edge-based hybrid network system was presented by Wu et al. [7] This system consists of hybrid routers and an IoT gateway. The router supports two kinds of wireless protocols, Bluetooth low energy and LoRa. The minimal delay of processing data at the edge was lowered to 11.5 ms.

Misra et al. proposed an IoT-based Ambulatory vitals (i-AVR) monitoring and recommender system to assist the time-critical scenarios, such as ambulator patient transits [8]. Due to a portable healthcare unit and an android navigation unit, i-AVR was able to compute the criticality index of the en-route patient and recommend the nearest healthcare center.

A healthcare device interoperability (HeDI) system was developed for IoT-enabled in-home healthcare monitoring [9]. It had multiple sensors wirelessly connected to an edge device. This edge device acted as a wireless communication gateway to a remote server. An initial information handshaking mechanism between the sensor adapters and the edge device was used at the beginning of the system startup progress. The system was scalable and away from dependencies on a system's physical ports.

In some scenarios, the IoT-enabled e-healthcare system was used to hold a specific application.

In the scenario of fall detection, a wearable monitoring system based on cloud computing was presented [10]. With narrow-band IoT and a server-client architecture, it could achieve an accuracy of 94.88%.

To cope with the geographical dispersion and the dynamicity of the device, an intelligent end-edge-cloud architecture for visual healthcare IoT (HIoT) systems. On the basis of human-machine-things characteristics analyses and intelligence measurement, the proposed framework could optimize the efficiency of data processing and device deployment [11].

A computation offloading using reinforcement learning (CORL) scheme was put forward to minimize latency and energy consumption. A combined latency and energy cost minimization problem was formulated to find an optimal available resource node to offload task [12].

The model training needs a powerful computing ability for data processing. A proportionate data analytics (PDA) for heterogeneous healthcare data stream processing was introduced. An example of streamlined classification was given for segregating errors from the variations in different time intervals [13]. A machine learning (ML) classification algorithm was employed to predict heart disease in a medical IoT-based cloud-fog diagnostics environment [14]. Federated learning (FL) was used for resource-limited computation in an edge-based medical IoT circumstance [15].

Table 1. Related work summary

Work	IoT	Remote cloud	Edge computing	Monitering	Data processing
[6]	✓	✓		✓	
[7]	✓	✓	✓	✓	✓
[8]	✓				✓
[9]	✓	✓	✓		
[10]	✓	✓		✓	✓
[11]	✓	✓	✓	✓	✓
[12]	✓		✓		✓
[13]	✓	✓			✓
[14]	✓	✓	✓	✓	✓
[15]	✓		✓	✓	✓

To sum up, like Table 1, the e-Healthcare application is coupled with the system in existing works. A system is specialized for one application. This would significantly increase the workload of the IT department.

3 System Overview

In our proposed system, a software no longer merely supports only one application. By introducing the thinking of microservices, an e-Healthcare application becomes an aggregation of multiple microservices which are organized in an orchestration way.

Microservices in our system exist in the form of Docker. The existence of microservices changes the way of application development and operations.

3.1 Composition

Our proposed system consists of three layers, as shown in Fig. 1, i.e., physical infrastructure layer, middleware layer, and application layer.

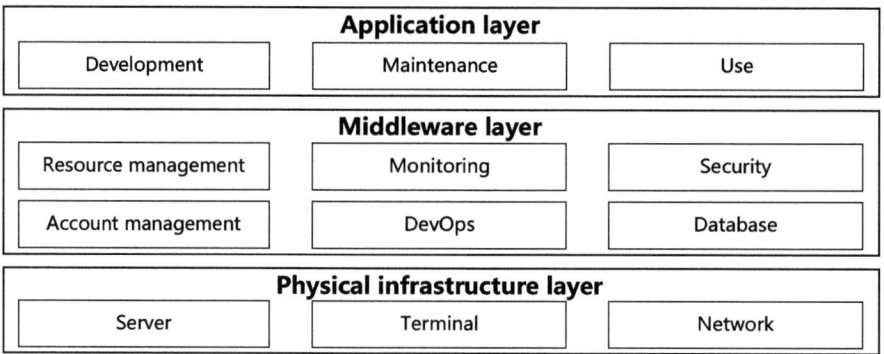

Fig. 1. system architecture

Pysical Infrastructure Layer. It is the tangible physical infrastructure, including servers, terminals, and networks. Servers can be rack-mounted servers and tower servers. Terminals come in a variety of forms, such as mobile phones, wearable devices, and so on. Terminals are essentially sensors. Networks include links (i.e., fiber links, copper cables, wireless links, etc.) and relay devices (i.e., switches, routers, etc.). Like a graph, servers and terminals are the nodes and networks connect different nodes.

Middleware Layer. It is the core of the proposed system and includes resource management, monitoring, security, account management, DevOps, and database. The storage, computing, and network capability of the physical infrastructure layer are treated as resources and under unified management, after resource abstraction. The total resources, used resources, and available resources are monitored in real-time which reflects the resource consumption of e-healcare applications. Figure 2 is a snapshot of resource usage in the proposed system. The security module provides protection for data and applications. Account management assigns different authorities to different level system users. For example, administrator users can allocate resources, and delete resources. Tenant users can apply resources, and build a development team. Development users can modify application source code. Individual users can only use the developed e-healthcare application. DevOps is able to orchestrate a series of containers (i.e., Docker) according to a certain e-healthcare application logic. The database is used to store system data, both the data of the system itself and the data generated by the e-healthcare application.

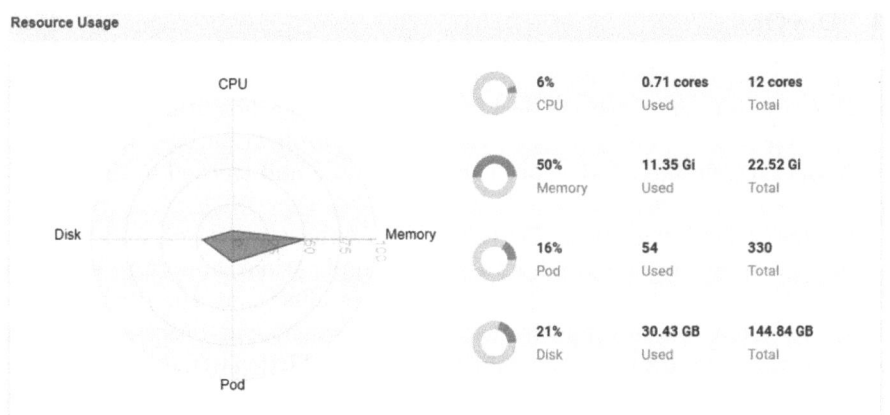

Fig. 2. Resource usage

Application Layer. It is the top layer of the proposed system. On the base of the physical infrastructure layer and middleware layer, the application layer can hold multiple e-healthcare applications rather than one single application. As long as the available resources allow and the application logic is clear, any e-healthcare application can run on top of the system.

If three layers are owned by a hospital, the e-Heathcare system is a private cloud computing platform and autonomous.

3.2 Microservices

The architecture change brings the change of application provision.

In the proposed system, the smallest unit of an application is a container, i.e., docker. One application is built by a set of Docker containers. Each docker is a set of capabilities and focuses on solving a specific problem. A container runs in its own process and communicates with other dockers through a lightweight application programming interface (API). Each container can be developed, deployed, operated, and scaled without affecting the functioning of other containers. A container is only responsible for one function point and does not need to share any of its code, or implementation with other containers. Microservices bring agility, flexible scaling, easy deployment, reusable code, and resilience.

Unlike the traditional application which completes a function by itself, the application for microservices is conducted by multiple containers. That is where microservices get their name. In practice, one or more Docker containers can be deployed with the sharing storage, network, and container running discipline. This way of container deployment is Pod. Containers are an isolation of resources, while Pods are wrappers of containers, a virtual level of abstraction.

3.3 DevOps

By introducing the thinking of microservices and applying containers in the proposed system, the work of the IT department in a hospital is simplified to DevOps. The service lifecycle of an e-healthcare application (i.e., develop, test, deploy, operate, update, and so on) can be executed and tracked in the proposed system.

DevOps is the integration of cultural philosophies, practices, and tools that increase an organization's ability to deliver applications and services at high velocity: evolving and improving products more effectively than organizations using traditional software and infrastructure management processes. In traditional software and infrastructure management, the IT department uses independent tools to accomplish tasks that would require the association of other teams, and this further lowers a team's efficiency. Meanwhile, in DevOps, development and operations are deeply emerging across the entire application and services lifecycle (i.e., design, develop, test, deploy, operation, update, etc.), rather than siloed.

DevOps brings continuous integration (CI), and continuous delivery (CD). CI is a software development practice where developers regularly merge their code changes into a central repository, after which automated builds and tests are run. CD is a software development practice where code changes are automatically built, tested, and prepared for a release to production.

Through CI and CD, the IT department of a hospital is able to find and fix software bugs quickly, improve the application quality, and reduce the time it takes from development to release. The disadvantage of the proposed system is that it requires the IT department of a hospital to have code development capability. This capability can be possessed by recruiting the hospital's own development team or by purchasing development services from a third-party software company.

4 Case Study

The performance of the proposed system is validated through three cases, i.e., scalability, service, and CI/CD pipeline.

4.1 Scalability

The proposed system can work well under an increasing or decreasing workload. To hold an e-healthcare application/service well, at least one pod should be established to run the basic service function, such as receiving the data from sensors, serving as an HTTP server, etc. In a real e-healthcare application, the workload of an application is dynamic. For example, users' access to the system is concentrated during working hours, while the number of users during non-working hours is low. When the workload of the application/service exceeds the capacity of the existing pod, the number of Docker containers in the pod should increase in time which is scale-up. When the workload of the application/service is much lower than the capacity of the existing pod, the number of Docker containers in the pod should decrease in time which is scale-down.

The life of a pod in the proposed system is displayed in Fig. 3. The unit of memory usage is Mi and equal to 1024*1024. From the beginning, there is no memory usage consumption. Once the e-healthcare application is deployed, the docker container starts. After the docker container is working properly, the monitoring of the docker container memory usage consumption starts. Because of the existence of the time from the docker container starting to working, the point of monitoring start is slightly behind that of the docker container start. With the increasing of application workload, the memory usage of the pod would increase. When the workload stabilizes, so does the memory usage. If there is a sudden growth or contraction in the application workload, the pods will be scaled up or down to fit the workload, and memory usage will increase or decrease accordingly. This is the memory usage fluctuation in the dotted box Fig. 3. When the e-Healthcare application stops, the memory usage which occupied by docker containers would gradually decrease until 0, and finally stop monitoring data.

The pod generation latencies of different docker containers are shown in Fig. 4. The pod generation latency is actually the time from docker start to monitoring data in Fig. 3. In the proposed system, httpd docker container is used as a web service server, MySQL docker container is used as a database, and CentOS docker container is used as an operation system environment.

The latency of the first time is greater than that of the non-first time for each docker container. Because the docker container is stored centrally in the remote docker repository. The first-time deployment of a docker container takes extra time to download from the remote docker repository. The latencies of different docker containers are positively proportional to the size of docker containers' size (httpd 61.68 Mb, MySQL 159.13 Mb, CentOS 79.65 Mb), whether it is the first time or the non-first time. By repeating the experiment several times, the latency error of the first time is larger than that of the non-first time. The

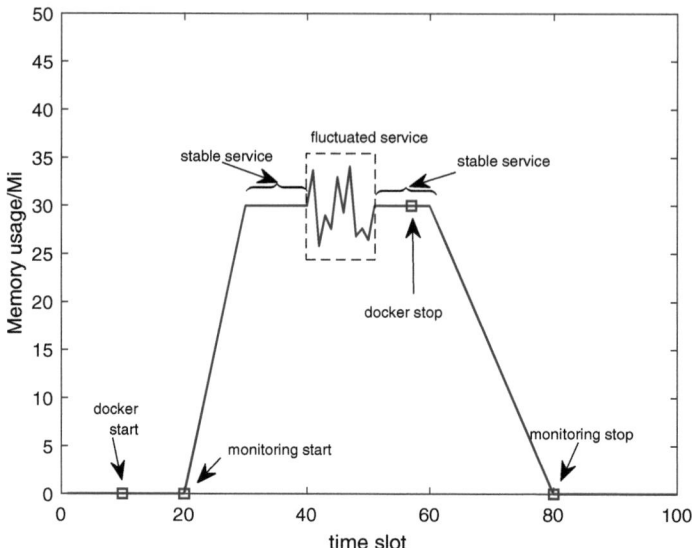

Fig. 3. The life of a pod

reductions of latency and latency error for the non-first time are both the result of downloading the remote docker container to the local docker repository.

The screenshot of memory usage for a web service in the proposed system is shown in Fig. 5. The name of the docker container is automatically generated according to the project name (i.e., httpd-v1), the pod id (i.e., 64fb47f56f) and the random string (i.e., the 5-letter length string after the last -). In the proposed system, once the docker container is down, a new one will be generated at once. At 16:39:37, two docker containers are all down, the proposed system immediately creates a new container with a suffix r2292. At 16:54:37, a new docker container with a suffix 4hsxq is created since the workload exceeds r2292 docker container's capacity. The memory usage of this docker container further increases with the increasing workload. At the same time that the 4hxsxq docker container is deleted (i.e., 19:19:37), a docker container with a suffix z9mnk is created and last to the end of the entire application.

4.2 Service

An IoT service of patient movement monitoring is shown in Fig. 6. For ease of explanation, the movement monitoring device under the experimental conditions is a Linux computer (i.e., Raspberry 4B+) with a 6-axis movement sensor (i.e., MPU6050), as shown in Fig. 6(a). In a realistic environment, the movement monitoring device is normally a wearable device like a watch, a bracelet, or a wrist belt. The movement data (i.e., Gx, Gy, Gz, Ax, Ay, Az) of a patient is collected by the devices in time, as shown in Fig. 6(b). Gx, Gy, Gz represent the velocity components of the device in the X-axis, Y-axis, and Z-axis. Ax, Ay, Az represent the

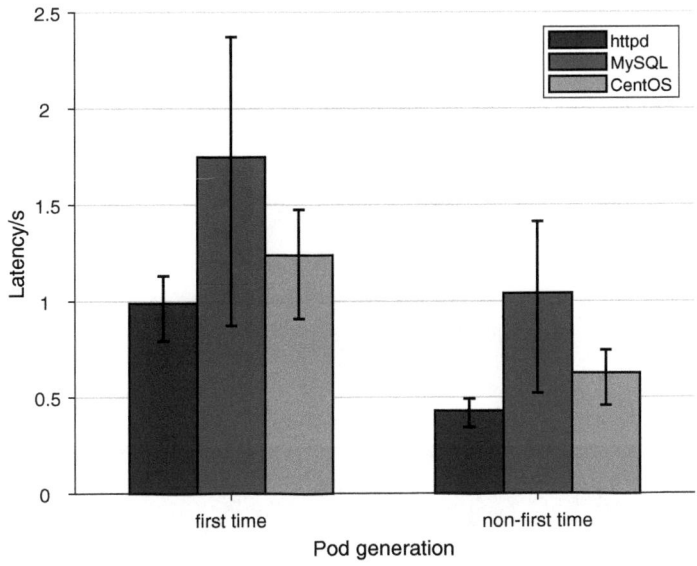

Fig. 4. Pod generation latency

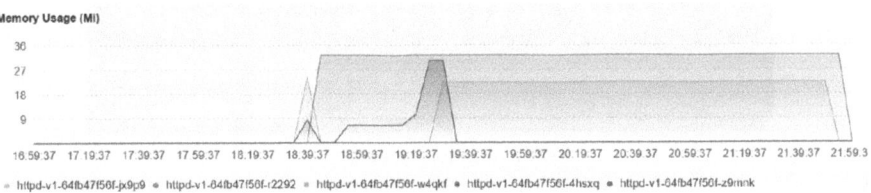

Fig. 5. A screenshot of memory usage for a web service

acceleration components of the device in the X-axis, Y-axis, and Z-axis. These 6 indicators of the device are updated every 500 milliseconds and can be used to reflect the patient's movement in a three-dimensional space.

On the base of collected patient movement data, the patient movement in a particular area can be visualized to show some trends directly. Figure 7(a) is the patient movement of Jinan (a city in Shandong Province, China). The radius of the circle is positively related to the number of monitoring patients who stay in the area of Jinan. The data of all the cities in Shandong province is shown in Fig. 7(b). The purple line means that some patients move from one city to another. Unfortunately, there are some downsides to data visualization. For example, the details and trajectory of the patient's movement cannot be displayed in detail.

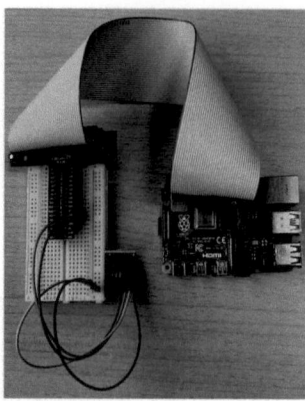

(a) Monitoring device

(b) Monitoring data

Fig. 6. An IoT service of patient movement monitoring

4.3 CI/CD Pipeline

The CI/CD pipeline provides a graphical application edit ability to automatically deploy applications. Figure 8 is the CI/CD pipeline of the patient monitoring service mentioned in section IV.B. The name of this CI/CD pipeline is test-pipeline. The pipeline is assembled by multiple stages, i.e., clone code, unit test, build&push, push latest, and deploy. The pipeline supports customized stages. The IT department staff is free to edit the e-healthcare application logic using sequential, branching, and looping structures in the stage.

In the clone code stage, the proposed system would automatically pull the latest from the code repository. The code repository is the place where the code developed by developers is stored. In the unit test stage, the proposed system would verify the sub-function according to the pre-defined test strategies. In the build&push stage, a basic docker container is built as the running environment for the developed application or code. The well-built docker container is used to hold the code artifact (i.e., .jar package). In the deploy stage, the docker container with the latest code is deployed in the real running environment. Note

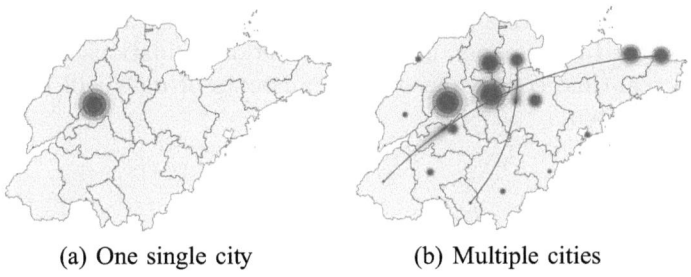

(a) One single city   (b) Multiple cities

Fig. 7. Patient movement data visualization

Fig. 8. The screenshot of a CI/CD pipeline

that the CI/CD pipeline makes it realistic for people who are not proficient in programming to operate an e-healthcare application well.

Once a source code change is updated to the code repository by developers, the proposed system can automate the testing of the new code, the building of docker containers, and the containerized deployment of the new code in the production environment, according to the pre-defined stage in the `test-pipeline` pipeline.

5 Conclusion and Future

This paper presented a distributed container-based IoT-enabled autonomous e-healthcare system for DevOps. A three-layer system design, microservices, and DevOps were used to solve the problem between limited IT department staff and prosperous e-healthcare applications. Through the proposed system, the IT department was able to provide CI/CD. The functionality and performance of the proposed system were proved via three cases.

In future work, more quantitative performance experiments and the resource scheduling of multiple container-based e-healthcare services will be carried out. Visualization of patient trajectories in a hospital campus strategies can also be a piece of work. A performance comparison between our work and the existing work is necessary. In this paper, only some function validations have been down. Besides, the real-time computing of huge amounts of data will be added as a module to the system.

References

1. Ubrani, R.L.J., Shirer, M.: Global shipments of wearable devices forecast to rebound in 2023, according to IDC tracker (2023)
2. Kohli, R., Garg, A., Phutela, S., Kumar, Y., Jain, S.: An improvised model for securing cloud-based e-healthcare systems. In: Marques, G., Bhoi, A.K., Albuquerque, V.H.C.d., K.S., H. (eds) IoT in Healthcare and Ambient Assisted Living, pp. 293–310 (2021)
3. Dhatterwal, J.S., Kaswan, K.S., Baliyan, A., Jain, V.: Integration of cloud and IoT for smart e-healthcare. In: Connected e-Health: Integrated IoT and Cloud Computing, pp. 1–31. Springer (2022)
4. Beltre, A., Saha, P., Govindaraju, M.: KubeSphere: an approach to multi-tenant fair scheduling for kubernetes clusters. In: 2019 IEEE Cloud Summit, pp. 14–20. IEEE (2019)
5. Komalasari, R.: Cloud computing's usage in healthcare. In: Recent Advancements in Smart Remote Patient Monitoring, Wearable Devices, and Diagnostics Systems, pp. 183–194. IGI Global (2023)
6. Siam, A.I.: Portable and real-time IoT-based healthcare monitoring system for daily medical applications. IEEE Trans. Comput. Soc. Syst. **10**(4), 1629–1641 (2023)
7. Wu, F., Qiu, C., Wu, T., Yuce, M.R.: Edge-based hybrid system implementation for long-range safety and healthcare IoT applications. IEEE Internet Things J. **8**(12), 9970–9980 (2021)
8. Misra, S., Pal, S., Pathak, N., Deb, P.K., Mukherjee, A., Roy, A.: I-AVR: IoT-based ambulatory vitals monitoring and recommender system. IEEE Internet Things J. **10**(12), 10318–10325 (2023)
9. Pathak, N., Misra, S., Mukherjee, A., Kumar, N.: HeDI: healthcare device interoperability for IoT-based e-health platforms. IEEE Internet Things J. **8**(23), 16845–16852 (2021)
10. Qian, Z., et al.: Development of a real-time wearable fall detection system in the context of internet of things. IEEE Internet Things J. **9**(21), 21999–22007 (2022)
11. Yang, Z., Liang, B., Ji, W.: An intelligent EndEdge-cloud architecture for visual IoT-assisted healthcare systems. IEEE Internet Things J. **8**(23), 16779–16786 (2021)
12. Yadav, R., et al.: Smart healthcare: RL-based task offloading scheme for edge-enable sensor networks. IEEE Sens. J. **21**(22), 24910–24918 (2021)
13. Kumar, P.M., et al.: Clouds proportionate medical data stream analytics for internet of things-based healthcare systems. IEEE J. Biomed. Health Inform. **26**(3), 973–982 (2022)
14. Chakraborty, C., Kishor, A.: Real-time cloud-based patient-centric monitoring using computational health systems. IEEE Trans. Comput. Soc. Syst. **9**(6), 1613–1623 (2022)
15. Gupta, A., Misra, S., Pathak, N., Das, D.: FedCare: federated learning for resource-constrained healthcare devices in IoMT system. IEEE Trans. Comput. Soc. Syst. **10**(4), 1587–1596 (2023)

Signal Processing and Optimization Algorithms

Weakly Supervised Multimodal Video Anomaly Detection Based on Knowledge Distillation

Lulu Yang[1](✉) 🆔, Xiaoyu Wu[1] 🆔, and Simin Li[2] 🆔

[1] Communication University of China, Beijing 10024, China
{yangll,wuxiaoyu}@cuc.edu.cn
[2] Institute of Electronic Engineering, Academy of Engineering Physics, Mianyang 621900, China
annelsm@163.com

Abstract. Weakly supervised video anomaly detection uses only video-level labels during the training process to detect frame-level anomalies, featuring low cost and high performance. However, weakly supervised hard labels contain limited information and are subject to certain noise. Additionally, in real-world scenarios, normal and anomalous events are very complex, making it difficult for a single modality of data to encompass sufficient fundamental information. Therefore, our proposes a weakly supervised multimodal video anomaly detection method based on knowledge distillation to address these issues. Specifically, we designed an audio-guided multimodal fusion method that reuses similarity matrices to enhance model performance with minimal additional parameters. Additionally, we proposed a method for generating supervisory signals based on soft labels. We use a general teacher network to generate soft labels and employ a Logits distillation approach to guide our student model in learning more data information. Soft labels can more accurately reflect the true distribution of samples and mimic the decision boundaries of the teacher model, effectively improving the detection performance of the student model. Extensive experiments demonstrate that our method achieves competitive results on two public benchmarks.

Keywords: Feature Aggregation · Soft Labels · Multimodal · Knowledge Distillation

1 Introduction

In recent years, with the rapid development of the internet and the advancement of smart cities and digital societies, the demand for social security levels has continuously increased. The widespread use of surveillance cameras is of significant practical importance in combating crime and maintaining social stability. Video anomaly detection has become a key technology aimed at identifying behaviors and events in videos that do not meet expectations and accurately locating the start and end times of these anomalies. It has broad applications in smart monitoring, industrial production, and traffic management [1, 2].

Weakly supervised methods have become a mainstream direction for video anomaly detection [3–5]. During the training phase, only video-level annotation information is required, significantly reducing the labor costs associated with frame-level annotations. These methods are characterized by low cost, high performance, and broad applicability. The main process consists of feature extraction and aggregation, as well as anomaly event detection.

Existing methods primarily utilize appearance features for modeling [4–8] and employ snippet-level temporal modeling to capture global and local video characteristics. In detecting anomalies, they adopt multi-instance learning to construct loss functions, scoring and ranking different snippets of each video while maximizing the score disparity between normal and anomalous video features [9–13]. Although these methods have achieved certain results, they often fall short in capturing sufficient fundamental information from unimodal anomaly data. Most existing approaches primarily use RGB features or simply concatenate the two modalities [14, 15], neglecting the temporal modeling of audio features or is not sufficiently concise [16]. Furthermore, under weak supervision, the video-level binary labels obtained during the training phase are simplistic hard labels. While easy to annotate, these hard labels lose distribution information between different snippets of the video and overlook some intra-class and inter-class relationships, introducing a certain level of noise (Fig. 1).

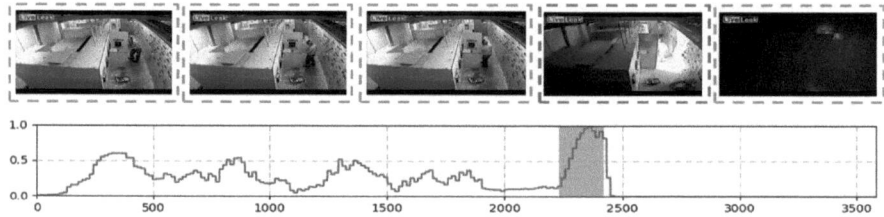

Fig. 1. Definition of Video Anomaly Detection

To address these issues, this paper proposes a weakly supervised multimodal video anomaly detection method based on knowledge distillation. It first designs an audio-guided multimodal fusion method, calculating the similarity matrix of audio and video features to generate an audio attention map, which is dynamically fused with the video RGB features. On the other hand, to mitigate the information insufficiency and noise problems caused by the singular supervisory signal under weak supervision, a soft label-based supervisory signal generation method is proposed. This method employs a generic teacher network to generate soft labels, guiding our student model to learn more data information based on logits distillation. Utilizing a two-stage approach, features from the frozen pre-trained teacher network are extracted, followed by fine-tuning with a multilayer perceptron to adapt to the variations in the anomaly detection task. Soft labels can more accurately reflect the true distribution of samples, enabling the student model not only to learn the standard classification task labels but also to mimic the decision boundaries of the teacher model. This effectively enhances the generalization ability and accuracy of the student model.

The main contributions of this paper are summarized as follows:

- We propose a weakly supervised multimodal video anomaly detection method based on knowledge distillation. Research [4] has demonstrated the effectiveness of using similarity matrices for temporal encoding. By reusing the similarity matrix and adding a minimal amount of parameters, we utilize audio features to guide the modeling of RGB features, enriching the modal characteristics, increasing the model's detection accuracy, and laying a solid foundation for subsequent anomaly detection.
- We introduce the use of knowledge distillation to output the logits distribution of the teacher model as a guide for the student to learn fine-grained soft labels between snippets. This approach addresses the issue of insufficient supervisory signals (with low information entropy) found in simple hard labels, enabling better localization of anomaly boundaries.
- Our model achieves competitive results on two datasets through a straightforward approach, and extensive experiments demonstrate the effectiveness of this method.

2 Related Work

2.1 Video Anomaly Detection

With the rapid development of deep learning in the field of computer vision, video anomaly detection methods based on deep neural networks have gradually become mainstream. One classification approach is based on the level of supervision, dividing methods into unsupervised, weakly supervised, and fully super-vised. Compared to unsupervised methods, which are not robust enough, and fully supervised methods, which are time-consuming and labor-intensive, weakly supervised video anomaly detection algorithms only require video-level annotation information during the training phase. By learning more discriminative feature representations based on video-level positive and negative sample labels, these algorithms can achieve frame-level anomaly event localization during the testing phase. This significantly reduces the human cost associated with frame-level annotations and features low cost, high performance, and broad applicability.

In weakly supervised video anomaly detection, it is common to construct loss functions for training using video-level labels. Existing methods primarily utilize Multiple-Instance Learning (MIL) to build the loss function. Sultani et al. [9] first proposed a multi-instance ranking loss. Wu et al. [27] designed a loss function to cluster normal features, using an attention mechanism to separate the foreground and background of anomalous samples. However, research has found that MIL has some potential drawbacks, as the information it contains is limited and introduces some label noise. Some researchers have employed various methods to guide the generation of anomaly scores in hopes of acquiring more supervisory information and mitigating the negative impact of noise. Zhou et al. [7] learned the distribution of normal features and treated anomalies as samples outside that distribution. By introducing uncertainty learning into the video anomaly detection task, they increased the distance between potential normal and abnormal samples, but this did not address the issue of low entropy in weakly supervised label information. Wei et al. [28] input their features into a multi-layer perceptron to generate soft labels, calculating the cross-entropy loss between predicted scores and soft labels to supervise the feature fusion network, allowing it to learn more useful information. However, due to the sparsity of abnormal features, soft labels generated solely by a simple multi-layer perceptron may struggle to accurately represent anomalies. Our method employs a two-stage approach, selecting a teacher network for logits distillation to enrich the intra-class and inter-class information contained in the supervisory signal, effectively guiding the student network for localization in a simple and effective manner. Additionally, some methods leverage external semantic information of anomalies to achieve joint optimization of internal and external anomaly semantics, such as knowledge graphs or learnable tokens [5, 29]. This research enhances the semantic expressiveness of visual features and the ability to discriminate anomalous events by incorporating external video anomaly knowledge into the original video input through prompt learning.

2.2 Feature Extraction and Temporal Aggregation

In the field of video anomaly detection, feature networks [5, 17–19] are commonly used to extract appearance features for modeling. For anomalous events such as shootings and explosions, audio information can also serve as an effective feature representation [20, 21]. After obtaining the features, it is necessary to perform temporal modeling to capture the complete contextual relationships.

Abnormal events exhibit a certain continuity. For instance, fighting, assault, and theft cannot be semantically perceived and inferred accurately based solely on a specific snippet of video, which may lead to deviations in the localization area. Therefore, it is essential to perform temporal modeling on video snippets to capture complete contextual information. Currently, mainstream temporal context modeling methods typically use GCN [22, 23] or Transformer self-attention mechanisms [24]for temporal modeling. Peng et al. [25] designed a novel framework that incorporates audiovisual fused features into a hyperbolic manifold, creating a full graph convolutional network in hyperbolic space to explore feature similarities and temporal relationships between snippets. Another study [26] introduced a Dynamic Erasure Network (DE-Net) to learn multiscale temporal features. This network applies multiple one-dimensional convolutional layers with different stride lengths and kernel sizes to learn local features and uses the self-attention mechanism in Transformers to learn global temporal representations, enabling it to extract features at different temporal scales from snippets of varying lengths. Reusing the similarity matrix as a temporal modeling network allows us to achieve a high-performance detection model with fewer parameters. Therefore, we not only compute the similarity matrix between video features but also calculate the similarity matrix between audio and video, performing adaptive dynamic fusion to obtain features enriched with more information guided by audio.

3 Method

3.1 Overview

The overall framework is shown in Fig. 2. Our model mainly consists of two parts: the student network and the teacher network. The student network includes a global-local feature aggregation module for audio and video feature learning, as well as a cross-modal semantic alignment module to enrich visual representations, enhancing the model's ability to recognize anomalous scenes. The teacher network generates soft labels through knowledge distillation, serving as the supervisory signal for the student network. In the following sections, we will first introduce the feature extraction process, then elaborate on the aforementioned components, and present the objective function.

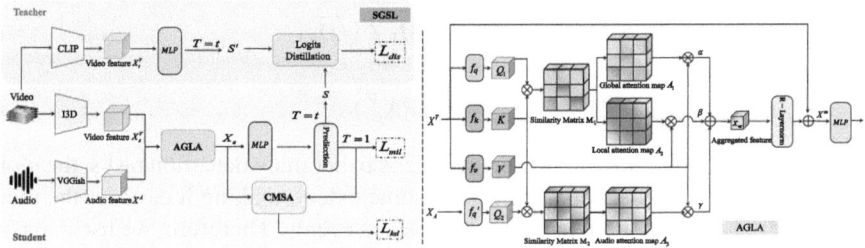

Fig. 2. The proposed overall architecture. Our method mainly consists of four parts: feature extraction, temporal feature aggregation (AGLA), cross-modal semantic enrichment for anomaly alignment (CMSA), and Supervised Signal Generation Module Based on Soft Labels (SGSL). Ultimately, it is optimized through multi-task joint learning.

3.2 Audio-Visual Feature Extraction

For the student network, given an untrimmed video V, we first use a sliding window to divide it into non-overlapping snippets v_i. The sliding window size is set to 16 frames, and if the video ends with fewer than 16 frames, those frames are discarded. Subsequently, these snippets are fed into a frozen pre-trained network to extract RGB features, denoted as $X_s^V \in R^{N \times D}$, where D is the feature dimension and N is the sequence length.

Since the durations of different videos vary, to ensure parallel computation during the training phase and improve computational efficiency, this paper follows the temporal sampling approach [17, 20, 29]. A fixed threshold Γ is set for truncation operations. Additionally, to compensate for the traditional reliance on spatiotemporal features, the teacher network employs a vision-language pre-trained model for feature extraction, enhancing video content through rich semantic understanding, effectively bridging the gap between simple pixel-based data and more human-like interpretations of video content [30] to obtain frame-level features $X_t^V \in R^{N \times d}$, where d is the feature dimension.

For the audio data, we divide it into overlapping snippets of 960 ms, with each snippet aligned to the end of the video clip, and then feed it into the feature extraction network to obtain $X^A \in R^{N \times D'}$.

3.3 Audio-Visual Global-Local Feature Aggregation (ALGA)

Research [4] indicates that reusing similarity matrices has fewer parameters and lower computational costs. We utilize an attention mechanism to model the time series and apply global-local temporal modeling to the RGB features. Firstly, the RGB features are mapped to corresponding vectors through different linear layers, and the similarity matrix M_1 is computed using the query and key vectors. Subsequently, global and local attention maps are generated based on the similarity matrix, where the global attention map captures the global dependencies of the sequence features, and the local attention map uses a mask to obtain the local receptive field within the neighborhood. The calculation process of X^g is as follows:

$$M_1 = f_q(X_s^V) \cdot (f_k(X_s^V))^T \tag{1}$$

$$A_1 = \text{softmax}(M_1 / \sqrt{D_h}) \tag{2}$$

$$X^g = A_1 f_v(X_s^V) \tag{3}$$

Due to the long duration of untrimmed videos in anomaly detection tasks, the global receptive field can introduce distant noise to some extent, making it easy for the model to inaccurately locate the boundaries of anomalous events. Therefore, we use a masked similarity matrix to construct local attention maps, capturing the local relationships between adjacent frames. The formula is as follows:

$$M'_{ij} = \begin{cases} M_{ij}, & \text{if } j \in \left[\max(0, i - \lfloor w/2 \rfloor), \min(i + \lfloor w/2 \rfloor, N)\right] \\ -\infty, & \text{others} \end{cases} \tag{4}$$

$$A_2 = \text{softmax}(M' / \sqrt{D_h}) \tag{5}$$

$$X^l = A_2 f_v(X_s^V) \tag{6}$$

Where w is the window size of the local neighborhood. The similarity scores outside the neighborhood window are set to negative infinity, and after Softmax normalization, these weights become 0, effectively achieving explicit masking of distant positions.

Inspired by the methods, audio information is used to generate a similarity matrix in a similar manner. Given an audio feature X^A, calculate the inner product of the query vector for each snippet with the K vector to obtain the similarity matrix M_2. By multiplying these two similarity matrices with the value vector of the RGB features, we achieve features X^a guided by audio, as shown in the following formula.

$$M_2 = f'_q(X^A) \cdot (f_k(X_s^V))^T \tag{7}$$

$$A_3 = \text{softmax}(M_2 / \sqrt{\tilde{D}_h}) \tag{8}$$

$$X^a = A_3 f_v(X_s^V) \tag{9}$$

After obtaining the aforementioned features, we dynamically fuse the three using learnable weights.

$$X_{ag} = \alpha \cdot X^g + \beta \cdot X^l + \gamma \cdot X^a, \quad \alpha, \beta, \gamma \in (0, 1) \tag{10}$$

$$X^m = \text{Norm}(X^V + f_h(X_{ag})) \tag{11}$$

The weights are dynamically adjusted as the network parameters are updated, achieving multi-scale aggregation of context through adaptive weighted summation. This process calibrates the local context representation while suppressing distant noise, thereby enhancing the discriminability of the video snippets. The aggregated features X_{ag} are mapped back to the original feature space through a linear mapping layer f_h, while applying a residual connection and layer normalization. Finally, the fused multimodal features are passed through a multi-layer perceptron to obtain a higher-level feature representation X_e. The calculation process is as follows:

$$X_e = MLP(X^m) \tag{12}$$

$$MLP = \text{Dropout}(GELU(Conv1D(\cdot))) \tag{13}$$

3.4 Supervised Signal Generation Module Based on Soft Labels (SGSL)

The features X_e obtained from the ALGA module are passed through another identical MLP to obtain more complex nonlinear features. Finally, the prediction scores are derived from causal convolution, where the difference between Conv1D and conv is that the stride of conv is greater than 1.

$$Logi = MLP(X_e) \tag{14}$$

$$S = \sigma(conv(Logi)) \tag{15}$$

Following [4], we apply the MIL-based loss as the fundamental objective function. First, sort the scores of s in descending order, and take the average of the top-k snippet scores as the anomaly score for the video.

$$p_i = \frac{1}{k} \sum_{i=1}^{k} Ranking(S) \tag{16}$$

For abnormal videos, $k = \lceil N/q + 1 \rceil$. q is the scale coefficient sampled and for normal videos, $k = 1$.

Video abnormal detection under the weak supervision task contains only video-level hard labels, and not all fragments in abnormal videos include abnormalities. We hope that a label containing more information can guide the network for training. Logits distillation is first proposed in [31], which pointed out that the smooth distribution of teachers predicted is more suitable for students to learn than Dirac.

We first input the video frame to the frozen CLIP model to get the sequence features, and generate soft labels S' using the Softmax function with temperature T.

$$S' = \frac{\exp\{L(X_t^V)/T\}}{\sum \exp\{L(X_t^V)/T\}} \tag{17}$$

$$L(\cdot) = R\{FC(\cdot)\} \tag{18}$$

R is the activation function and FC is the linear layer.

During training, a larger temperature T results in smaller inter-class differences in the Logits Distillation prediction scores compared to when $T = 1$. This allows the network to focus more on smaller initial prediction values, enabling it to learn the relationship between abnormal categories and normal videos. Meanwhile, the student network also generates prediction scores S' at the same temperature and distills them with the teacher network.

For the student network, binary cross-entropy is used to construct the loss function for MIL:

$$L_{mil} = \sum_{n=1}^{N} -y_i \log(p_i) \qquad (19)$$

For the knowledge distillation component, the loss is constructed using KL divergence:

$$L_{dis} = KL(S'\|S) = \sum -S' \log(\frac{S}{S'}) \qquad (20)$$

3.5 Cross-Modal Semantic Alignment (CMSA)

The concept of anomalies is complex and diverse. Therefore, similar to [4], we utilize the ConceptNet [33] knowledge base to obtain anomaly cues. The specific process is as follows:

First, select 12 common relations from ConceptNet. For the anomaly category C_i, traverse all semantic relationships and count the number of edges in each relation group. Then, select the top 5 most frequent relations for retrieval, establishing all edges with the category as either the head or tail node to obtain relevant concepts and their corresponding relevance scores. Next, filter the corresponding concepts with scores above the average to expand the original anomaly category. Finally, feed the expanded concept labels into the CLIP model, and compute the average of the resulting features as the final text features T.

In real-world scenarios, anomalies often occur for a short duration, with much of the content being normal or background information. Therefore, the visual information corresponding to the anomaly label primarily consists of the anomalous foreground. It is necessary to separate the potential anomalous foreground from the background in continuous video snippets. The formula is as follows:

$$V^f = \frac{\exp(\zeta S) - 1}{\sum_k (\exp(\zeta S) - 1)} \cdot X_e \qquad (21)$$

$$V^b = \frac{\exp(\zeta (1 - S)) - 1}{\sum_k (\exp(\zeta (1 - S)) - 1)} \cdot X_e \qquad (22)$$

S represents the anomaly scores outputted by the classifier and k indicates the number of the snippet. ζ is a predefined scaling factor. $1 - S$ represents the normal confidence level of the current segment. $\exp(\cdot) - 1$ is an enhanced score that takes values between 0 and

1. For anomalous videos, the goal is to minimize the distance between the foreground and the anomalous semantics, as well as the distance between the background and the normal semantics. In contrast, for normal videos, only the distance between the visual foreground and the normal semantics is considered. A one-way alignment design strategy is employed to map visual representations to textual representations, measuring the semantic similarity between the two using cosine distance, as shown in Eqs. (23) and (24).

$$S(V, \mathcal{T}) = \frac{V \cdot \mathcal{T}^T}{\|V\| \|\mathcal{T}\|} \tag{23}$$

$$p_i^{v2t}(V) = \frac{\exp(S(V, \mathcal{T}_i)/\tau)}{\sum_{k=1}^{C+1} \exp(S(V, \mathcal{T}_k)/\tau)} \tag{24}$$

$C + 1$ denotes abnormal and normal classes, and τ is a temperature coefficient. The cross-modal semantic alignment loss is constructed using KL divergence, and its calculation formula is as follows:

$$L_{kd} = E_{p \sim p(V)} \left[\log p^{v2t}(V) - \log q^{v2t}(V) \right] \tag{25}$$

Where p represents the semantic similarity score from video to text, and q denotes the semantic consistency label from video to text. If the two form a positive sample pair, then $q = 1$. Conversely, $q = 0$.

3.6 Multi-task Learning

The overall loss function is shown in the formula:

$$L = \lambda L_{mil} + \mu L_{kd} + \varphi L_{dis} \tag{26}$$

λ, μ, φ represent the weight coefficients for different losses. With the combined effect of these three components, the model can learn discriminative representations for both positive and negative samples while effectively mining the anomalous semantics of different categories. This, in turn, enhances the model's generalization ability and detection accuracy in complex scenarios.

4 Experiments

4.1 Datasets and Evaluation Metric

We perform experiments on two challenging anomaly benchmarks, i.e., UCF-Crime [9] and XD-Violence [17] datasets. Details are given as follows:

UCF-Crime. It is collected from surveillance cameras in real-world scenarios and contains 1,900 untrimmed long videos, totaling 128 h of footage at a frame rate of 30 fps. The training set includes 810 anomalous videos and 800 normal videos, while the test set comprises 140 anomalous videos and 150 normal videos. the dataset includes 13 categories of anomalous events, such as abuse, arrest, and arson.

XD-Violence. It is currently the largest existing dataset for violent videos, consisting of 4,754 untrimmed long videos with a total duration of 217 h. The training set includes 1,905 violent videos and 2,049 non-violent videos, while the test set contains 500 violent videos and 300 non-violent videos. This dataset is collected from 91 movies and YouTube videos, covering various scenarios such as television, sports, and gaming, resulting in a richer variety of anomalous event types

Evaluation Metrics. For the UCF-crime dataset, we use the Area Under the ROC Curve (AUC) to evaluate model performance. For the XD-Violence dataset, Average Precision (AP) is adopted as the evaluation metric. generally speaking, a higher ROC or AP value indicates better model performance. Additionally, considering that anomalous events are much rarer than normal events in real-world scenarios, we use the False Alarm Rate (FAR) to measure the probability of the model misclassifying normal events as anomalous, with a lower FAR being preferable.

4.2 Implementation Details

Data Pre-Processing. Consistent with existing methods [4, 27], for the student network, we encode videos features using the RGB flow I3D video encoder pre-trained on the Kinetics [33] dataset. For audio features, we utilize the VGGish [34] audio encoder pre-trained on the AudioSet [35] dataset. For the teacher network, based on existing research [5], we employ the visual encoder ViT from the CLIP (ViT-B/16) pre-trained model to extract features, processing one frame for every 16 frames of video to obtain frame-level features.

Hyperparameter Settings. For the XD-Violence dataset, the dimensionality of the appearance features extracted by the I3D network is $D = 1024$, while the dimensionality of the appearance features extracted by the CLIP network is $d = 512$. The audio features extracted by the VGGish network have a dimensionality of 128. In the AGLA module, with a local window size w of 9. The fusion weights for local and global feature vectors α, β, γ are initialized to 0.5. In the student network's MLP, the two 1D convolution layers have 128 and 300 nodes, respectively, while the causal convolution layer has a time step set to 6. In the teacher network's MLP, the mapping dimension of the hidden layer is 256, and the distillation temperature T is set to 7. $\lambda \mu \varphi$ are 1, 0.7, and 0.5.

For the UCF-Crime dataset, the observation time step length in the causal convolution of the classifier is set to 9, and the distillation temperature T is set to 5. The other settings remain consistent with those in the XD-Violence dataset.

Training and Test Details. During the training process, this paper uses the Adam optimizer to update network parameters. $\Gamma = 200$ and the scaling factor q is set to 16. The initial learning rate for both datasets is set to 0.0005, employing a cosine decay strategy, with a dropout value of 0.1. The batch size is set to 128, and the model is trained for a total of 30 epochs. The model is built on the PyTorch deep learning framework, and the experimental platform runs on Ubuntu 20.04. The CPU model is Intel Xeon Gold 6240, and the GPU model is a single NVIDIA Tesla A40.

4.3 Comparison with State-of-The-Art Methods

We report the state-of-the-art results on the two benchmarks in Tables 1 and 2. All methods are weakly supervised.

Table 1. Performance comparison of state-of-the-art methods on the XD-Violence dataset.

Method	Feature	AP(%)↑	FAR (%)↓
HL-Net[17]	I3D + VGGish	78.64	-
ACF[28]	I3D + VGGish	80.13	1.12
MSAF[14]	I3D + VGGish	80.51	-
CLIP-TSA[19]	CLIP	82.17	-
MACIL-SD[36]	I3D + VGGish	83.40	-
CMA-LA[37]	I3D + VGGish	83.54	-
TPWNG[38]	CLIP	83.68	-
VadCLIP[5]	CLIP	84.51	-
WS-VAD[39]	I3D + VGGish	84.24	-
BN-WVAD[40]	I3D + VGGish	85.26	-
HyperVD[25]	I3D + VGGish	85.67	-
CFA[41]	I3D + VGGish	**86.34**	-
PEL4VAD[4]	I3D RGB	85.59	0.57
OURS	I3D + VGGish	**86.58**	0.1

As shown in Table 1, recent research methods often utilize I3D and CLIP as feature extraction networks, commonly employing RGB features extracted by I3D and audio for multimodal fusion. HyperVD [25] and CFA [41] model features in hyperbolic space, capturing the hierarchical relationships between normal and anomalous representations through spatial and temporal feature learning. Methods such as CLIP-TSA [19], TPWNG [38], and VadCLIP [5] leverage the powerful semantic understanding of the CLIP model, enhancing model performance through contrastive learning with various forms of text and visual inputs. Other models reduce the semantic gap between unimodal and multimodal features using different audio-video fusion methods. Our method achieves better performance than most recent models and compared to our previous work[4], the best detection performance improved by 0.99%, while the anomalous false alarm rate decreased by 0.47%.

Table 2. Performance comparison of state-of-the-art methods on the UCF-Crime dataset.

Method	Feature	AUC(%)↑	FAR (%)↓
CR-UNet[42]	I3D RGB	85.24	-
MLAD[43]	I3D RGB	85.47	-
NL-MIL[11]	I3D RGB	85.63	-
S3R [6]	I3D RGB	85.99	-
WS-VAD [39]	I3D RGB	86.19	-
MGFN [44]	I3D RGB	86.98	-
BN-WVAD [40]	I3D RGB	87.24	-
CLIP-TSA[19]	CLIP	87.58	-
TPWNG[38]	CLIP	87.79	-
VadCLIP [5]	CLIP	**88.02**	-
PEL4VAD[4]	I3D RGB	86.76	0.47
OURS	I3D RGB	87.21	**0.06**

As shown in Table 2, our model achieves comparable performance to BN-WVAD [40]. Additionally, among recent anomaly detection methods, those based on the CLIP network have yielded more advanced results. This is attributed to the fact that the UCF-Crime dataset consists of anomalous videos in surveillance scenarios, which often feature blurred images, unclear subjects, and considerable background redundancy. The powerful semantic alignment capability of the CLIP model allows for more effective representation of anomalous scenes, compensating for the deficiencies in visual information. Compared to our previous work [4], the best detection performance improved by 0.45%, while the anomalous false alarm rate decreased by 0.41%.

4.4 Ablation Studies

Effect of Proposed Module. We conducted an ablation study on the proposed module using the XD-Violence dataset, as shown in Table 3. The Baseline refers to the combination of RGB feature aggregation and the CMSA module. The experimental results indicate that the Average Precision (AP) improved by 0.99%, and it can be seen that the AGLA module contributed an additional 0.2% increase in AP, with a significant reduction in the FAR. This suggests that the inclusion of audio features complements the visual features and reduces misclassification of normal events. The SGSL improved by 0.79%, and the anomalous FAR decreased by 0.47%, indicating that the CLIP model, as the teacher in the knowledge distillation process, effectively transmits learned representations and decision-making processes to the student.

Contribution of Components of the TCA Module. Table 4 resents the results of the AGLA module on the XD-violence dataset. When only audio features are used, the performance is poor due to the significant amount of noise, which prevents the network from learning effective knowledge. In contrast, when using fused features, the Average Precision (AP) significantly increases. Furthermore, the increase in the number of parameters for the multimodal features is minimal.

Table 3. Contribution of Each Component on the XD-Violence Dataset.

Baseline	AGLA	SGSL	AP (%)↑	FAR (%)↓
✓			85.59	0.57
✓	✓		85.79	0.00
✓		✓	86.33	0.38
✓	✓	✓	86.58	0.1

Table 4. Results of the AGLA Module on the XD-Violence Dataset.

Feature Modality	Parameters(M)	AP (%)↑	FAR (%)↓
Audio	0.287	67.74	0.41
Baseline(RGB)	1.21	85.59	0.57
AGLA(RGB + Audio)	1.223	**85.79**	**0.00**

Ablation of Different Weights in AGLA. Table 5 explores the impact of different weight settings on the model during audio-video feature fusion. It can be seen that the best performance is achieved when $\beta = 1 - \alpha$, indicating that the global and local features of the visual data are complementary, while audio features provide a certain supplementary effect when visual features are learned adequately. The poor performance of the last two methods can be attributed to the following reasons: in the second row of the table, the presence of noise in the audio information affects the learning of visual features, while in the third row, the lack of mutual constraints on the weights leads to feature redundancy, impairing model performance. Additionally, our model achieved a certain performance improvement with only a small increase in parameters.

Table 5. Different Weights in AGLA on the XD-Violence Dataset.

Fusion Parameters	AP (%)↑	FAR (%)↓
$\alpha, \beta=1-\alpha, \gamma$	**85.79**	**0.00**
$\alpha, \beta, \gamma=1-\alpha-\beta$	85.28	0.18
α, β, γ	85.3	0.07

Ablation of Different Temperatures in SGSL. As shown in Fig. 3, for the XD-Violence dataset, as the temperature increases from 1 to 7, the model performance shows an upward trend, achieving optimal results at T = 7 and then gradually declines. This indicates that as the temperature rises, the gap between the soft labels of the teacher network becomes smoother, increasing the information entropy. This allows the student model to learn more distributional information, aiding in boundary determination. However, when the temperature becomes too high, the positive and negative samples become too similar, which is detrimental to learning anomalous features, effectively introducing noise and leading to a decrease in model performance.

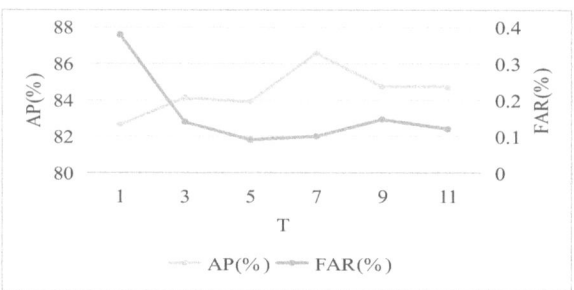

Fig. 3. Experimental Results of Different Temperatures on the XD-Violence Dataset

4.5 Qualitative Results

We present the qualitative results of our method on the XD-Violence test videos in Fig. 4. The orange boxes indicate the snippets where anomalous events occur. The Y-axis represents the anomaly scores, while the X-axis represents the frame numbers. The top section shows the results of our model, and the bottom section displays the baseline results.

It can be observed that our model achieves more precise anomaly localization compared to the baseline, particularly in cases of continuous and short-duration anomalies, where our model is more sensitive to boundaries. This is attributed to the richer anomaly characteristics provided by the multimodal audio, along with the distilled soft labels that contain more information. These soft labels can guide the student model in boundary localization through the teacher model.

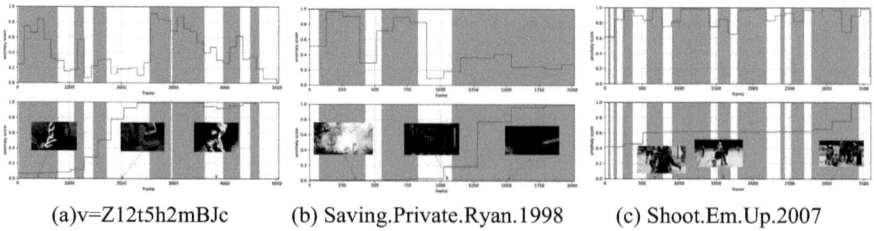

(a)v=Z12t5h2mBJc (b) Saving.Private.Ryan.1998 (c) Shoot.Em.Up.2007

Fig. 4. Qualitative results on the XD-Violence.

5 Conclusions

In this paper, we primarily investigate multimodal feature aggregation and soft label-based signal generation in weakly supervised video anomaly detection. We propose a video anomaly detection algorithm based on knowledge distillation for audio-video global-local feature aggregation, and we validate the effectiveness of this framework on two public datasets, achieving competitive results while significantly reducing the false alarm rate. This demonstrates that our method effectively alleviates the issues of incomplete representation in unimodal data and the limited information content of weakly supervised labels. Future work will explore how to obtain better normal modality representations and implement anomaly detection in open domains.

Acknowledgement. This work was supported by the state key development program in 14th Five-Year under Grant No. 2021YFF0900701 and 2021YFF0602103, and in part by Natural Science Foundation of China (No. 61801441). We also thank the research funds under the High-quality and Cutting-edge Disciplines Construction Project for Universities in Beijing (Internet Information, Communication University of China).

References

1. Liu, W., Lian, D., Luo, W., Gao, S.: Future frame prediction for anomaly detection – a new baseline. In: 2018 IEEE Conference on Computer Vision and Pattern Recognition (CVPR), pp. 1–13. IEEE, Salt Lake City (2018)
2. Bogdoll, D., Nitsche, M., Marius Zollner, J.: Anomaly detection in autonomous driving: a survey. In Proceedings of the IEEE/CVF Conference on Computer Vision and Pattern Recognition, pp. 4488–4499. IEEE, Louisiana (2022)
3. Zhang, C., et al.: Exploiting completeness and uncertainty of pseudo labels for weakly supervised video anomaly detection. In: 2023 IEEE/CVF Conference on Computer Vision and Pattern Recognition (CVPR), pp. 16271–16280. IEEE, Vancouver, BC (2023)
4. Pu, Y., Wu, X., Yang, L., Wang, S.: Learning prompt-enhanced context features for weakly-supervised video anomaly detection. IEEE Trans. Image Process. **33**, 4923–4936 (2024)
5. Wu, P., et al.: VadCLIP: adapting vision-language models for weakly supervised video anomaly detection. In: Proceedings of the AAAI Conference on Artificial Intelligence, vol. 38, no. 6, pp. 1–10 (2024)
6. Wu, J.C., Hsieh, H.Y., Chen, D.J., Fuh, C.S., Liu, T.L.: Self-supervised sparse representation for video anomaly detection. In: Avidan, S., Brostow, G., Cissé, M., Farinella, G.M., Hassner, T. (eds.) Computer Vision – ECCV 2022. ECCV 2022. Lecture Notes in Computer Science, vol. 13673. Springer, Cham (2022). https://doi.org/10.1007/978-3-031-19778-9_42
7. Zhou, H., Yu, J., Yang, W.: Dual memory units with uncertainty regulation for weakly supervised video anomaly detection. In: Proceedings of the AAAI Conference on Artificial Intelligence, pp. 3769–3777 (2023)
8. Cho, M., et al.: Look around for anomalies: weakly-supervised anomaly detection via context-motion relational learning. In: Proceedings of the IEEE/CVF Conference on Computer Vision and Pattern Recognition (CVPR), pp. 1–10 (2023)
9. Sultani, W., Chen, C., Shah, M.: Real-world anomaly detection in surveillance videos. In: Proceedings of the IEEE Conference on Computer Vision and Pattern Recognition (CVPR), pp. 6479–6488 (2018)

10. Li, S., Liu, F., Jiao, L.: Self-training multi-sequence learning with transformer for weakly supervised video anomaly detection. In: Proceedings of the AAAI Conference on Artificial Intelligence, vol. 36, no. 2, pp. 1395–1403 (2022)
11. Park, S., Kim, H., Kim, M., et al.: Normality guided multiple instance learning for weakly supervised video anomaly detection. In: Proceedings of the IEEE/CVF Winter Conference on Applications of Computer Vision, pp. 2665–2674 (2023)
12. Wei, D.L., Liu, C.G., Liu, Y., et al.: Look, listen and pay more attention: fusing multi-modal information for video violence detection. In: 2022 IEEE International Conference on Acoustics, Speech and Signal Processing, pp. 1980–1984 (2022)
13. Ristea, N.C., Croitoru, F.A., Dascalescu, D., et al.: Lightning fast video anomaly detection via adversarial knowledge distillation. arXiv preprint arXiv:2211.15597 (2022)
14. Wei, D., Liu, Y., Zhu, X., et al.: MSAF: multimodal supervise-attention enhanced fusion for video anomaly detection. IEEE Sig. Process. Lett. **29**, 2178–2182 (2022)
15. Gu, C., Wu, X., Wang, S.: Violent video detection based on semantic correspondence. IEEE Access **8**, 85958–85967 (2020)
16. Wu, X., Pu, Y., Wang, S., Liu, Z.: Special video recognition based on semantic embedding learning. Acta Electonica Sinica **51**, 3225–3237 (2023)
17. Wu, P., et al.: Not only look, but also listen: learning multimodal violence detection under weak supervision. In: Vedaldi, A., Bischof, H., Brox, T., Frahm, JM. (eds.) Computer Vision – ECCV 2020. ECCV 2020. Lecture Notes in Computer Science(), vol. 12375. Springer, Cham (2020). https://doi.org/10.1007/978-3-030-58577-8_20
18. Radford, A., et al.: Learning ransferable visual models from natural language supervision. In: International Conference on Machine Learning, PMLR, pp. 8748–8763 (2021)
19. Joo, H.K., et al.: Clip-TSA: clip-assisted temporal self-attention for weakly-supervised video anomaly detection. In: 2023 IEEE International Conference on Image Processing (ICIP), pp. 1–10. IEEE (2023)
20. Liu, X., Lu, H., Yuan, J., et al.: CAT: causal audio transformer for audio classification. In: 2023 IEEE International Conference on Acoustics, Speech and Signal Processing, pp. 1–5 (2023)
21. Zhu, W., Omar, M.: Multiscale audio spectrogram transformer for efficient audio classification. In: 2023 IEEE International Conference on Acoustics, Speech and Signal Processing, pp. 1–5 (2023)
22. Dengxiong, X., Bao, W., Kong, Y.: Multiple instance relational learning for video anomaly detection. In: 2021 International Joint Conference on Neural Networks, pp. 1–8 (2021)
23. Cao, C., Zhang, X., Zhang, S., et al.: Adaptive graph convolutional networks for weakly supervised anomaly detection in videos. IEEE Sig. Process. Lett. **29**, 2497–2501 (2022)
24. Sun, S., Gong, X.: Long-short temporal co-teaching for weakly supervised video anomaly detection. In: 2023 IEEE International Conference on Multimedia and Expo, pp. 2711–2716 (2023)
25. Peng, X., et al.: Learning weakly supervised audio-visual violence detection in hyperbolic space. arXiv preprint arXiv:2305.18797 (2023)
26. Zhang, C., Li, G., Qi, Y., et al.: Dynamic erasing network based on multi-scale temporal features for weakly supervised video anomaly detection. arXiv preprint arXiv:2312.01764 (2023)
27. Wu, P., Liu, J.: Learning causal temporal relation and feature discrimination for anomaly detection. IEEE Trans. Image Process. **30**, 3513–3527 (2021)
28. Nesen, A., Bhargava, B.: Knowledge graphs for semantic-aware anomaly detection in video. In: 2020 IEEE Third International Conference on Artificial Intelligence and Knowledge Engineering (AIKE), pp. 65–70. IEEE (2020)

29. Zhen, Y., Guo, Y., Wei, J., et al.: Multi-scale background suppression anomaly detection in surveillance videos. In: 2021 IEEE International Conference on Image Processing (ICIP), pp. 1114–1118. IEEE (2021)
30. Radford, A., et al.: Learning transferable visual models from natural language supervision. In: International Conference on Machine Learning, PMLR, pp. 8748–8763 (2021)
31. Hinton, G., Vinyals, O., Dean, J.: Distilling the knowledge in a neural network. arXiv preprint arXiv:1503.02531 (2015)
32. Speer, R., Chin, J., Havasi, C.: ConceptNet 5.5: an open multilingual graph of general knowledge. In: Proceedings of the AAAI Conference on Artificial Intelligence, vol. 31, no. 1, pp. 4444–4451, February 2017
33. Kay, W., et al.: The Kinetics human action video dataset. arXiv preprint arXiv:1705.06950 (2017)
34. Hershey, S., et al.: CNN architectures for large-scale audio classification. In: 2017 IEEE International Conference on Acoustics, Speech and Signal Processing (ICASSP), New Orleans, Louisiana, pp. 131–135 (2017)
35. Gemmeke, J.F., et al.: Audio set: an ontology and human-labeled dataset for audio events. In: 2017 IEEE International Conference on Acoustics, Speech and Signal Processing (ICASSP), New Orleans, Louisiana, pp. 1–5 (2017)
36. Yu, J., Liu, J., Cheng, Y., et al.: Modality-aware contrastive instance learning with self-distillation for weakly-supervised audio-visual violence detection. In: Proceedings of the 30th ACM International Conference on Multimedia, pp. 6278–6287 (2022)
37. Pu, Y., Wu, X.: Audio-guided attention network for weakly supervised violence detection. In: 2022 2nd International Conference on Consumer Electronics and Computer Engineering (ICCECE), pp. 219–223. IEEE (2022)
38. Yang, Z., Liu, J., Wu, P.: Text prompt with normality guidance for weakly supervised video anomaly detection. In: Proceedings of the IEEE/CVF Conference on Computer Vision and Pattern Recognition (CVPR), pp. 18899–18908 (2024)
39. Fan, Y., et al.: Weakly-supervised video anomaly detection with snippet anomalous attention. IEEE Trans. Circ. Syst. Video Technol. (2024)
40. Zhou, Y., Qu, Y., Xu, X., et al.: BatchNorm-based weakly supervised video anomaly detection. arXiv preprint arXiv:2311.15367 (2023)
41. Ghadiya, A., Kar, P., Chudasama, V., et al.: Cross-modal fusion and attention mechanism for weakly supervised video anomaly detection. In: Proceedings of the IEEE/CVF Conference on Computer Vision and Pattern Recognition, pp. 1965–1974 (2024)
42. Gan, K.Y., Cheng, Y.T., Tan, H.K., et al.: Title of the paper. IEEE Access **11**, 36658–36671 (2023)
43. Zhang, C., Li, G., Xu, Q., et al.: Weakly supervised anomaly detection in videos considering the openness of events. IEEE Trans. Intell. Transp. Syst. **23**(11), 21687–21699 (2022)
44. Chen, Y., Liu, Z., Zhang, B., et al.: MGFN: magnitude-contrastive glance-and-focus network for weakly-supervised video anomaly detection. In: Proceedings of the AAAI Conference on Artificial Intelligence, vol. 37, no. 1, pp. 387–395 (2023)

A Combined Phase Optimisation and Clipping Reduction PAPR Technique for LCSS System

LuShuang Liao[1], Lin Zheng[1], and Chao Yang[1,2]($\boxtimes$)

[1] Key Laboratory of Cognitive Radio and Information Processing, Ministry of Education, Guilin University of Electronic Technology, Guilin 541000, China
[2] National Key Laboratory of Wireless Communications, Chengdu, Chengdu 611731, China
ycguet@gmail.com

Abstract. LoRa is a pivotal technology in low power wide area networks, characterized by its low power consumption and long-range communication capabilities. However, it suffers from the drawback of low spectral efficiency. Currently, various spectrally efficient CSS modulation techniques have been proposed to address this issue. Among them, the LCSS system offers additional degrees of freedom through the number of layers (L), enabling a wider range of achievable spectral efficiency. Nevertheless, the LCSS system faces an important challenge due to its multi-layer chirp modulation, namely high peak-to-average power ratio (PAPR). This paper analyzes the influencing factor of PAPR in the LCSS system based on signal correlation, pointing out its PAPR related to intial phases among different layers. Furthermore, a searching method is given for the phase optimization PAPR suppression, and a combination way using phase optimization and clipping method is present for PAPR suppression. Additionally, complementary cumulative distribution function (CCDF) and bit error rate (BER) analysis are provided for PAPR evaluation. Simulation experimental results demonstrate that these proposed methods effectively mitigate PAPR and avoid the loss of BER.

Keywords: LoRa · Chirp Spread Spectrum · Peak to Average Power Ratio

1 Introduction

Low Power Wide Area Networks (LPWANs) have recently emerged as a promising communication solution for many Internet of Things (IoT) applications [1]. The Long Range (LoRa) technology is a crucial component of the LPWANs,

---

This work is supported in part by the National Nature Science Foundation (62461016) and National Key Laboratory of Wireless Communications Foundation (IFN20230209), as well as Fund of Key Laboratory of Cognitive Radio and Information Processing, Ministry of Education CRKL200102.

offering the ability to balance sensitivity and data rate through the utilization of different spread spectrum factors (SF) [2]. However, it still has relatively low realizable spectral efficiency (SE), still lacking the capability to support video and other multimedia services [3].

Consequently, recent studies have proposed various modulation techniques similar to LoRa, such as IQ-TDM-CSS [4], Dual-mode (DM)-TDM-CSS [5], LCSS [6], and LDMCSS [6], aiming to enhance spectral efficiency. The IQ-TDM-CSS technique multiplexes two chirps with different slopes in the time domain and utilizes the IQ component of non-chirped symbols, thereby enabling a fourfold increase in spectral efficiency compared to LoRa. However, due to the use of both in-phase and quadrature domains, non-coherent detection cannot be performed, and it is very sensitive to phase and frequency offset. On the other hand, DM-TDM-CSS rectifies the limitation of IQ-TDM-CSS, which can transmit $4*SF-4$ bits per Ts. Therefore, for $SF = [7,12]$, it can achieve a limited number of SEs. The LCSS and LDMCSS techniques both employ time domain multiplexing methods to combine symbols with different chirp rates [6], thereby offering additional degrees of freedom through the number of layers L and achieving a wider range of achievable spectral efficiency (SE). Additionally, LCSS exhibits relative robustness against frequency and phase offsets, supports coherent and incoherent detection, demonstrates slightly superior performance compared to LDMCSS, and can achieve higher SE than LDMCSS. However, the LCSS waveform lacks a constant envelope, resulting in high peak-to-average power ratio (PAPR). Furthermore, as the number of layers increases, PAPR also increases.

On the other hand, the PAPR problem is also encountered in the development of 3G and 4G communication waveforms, and numerous strategies have been proposed to effectively mitigate PAPR, including clipping [7], filtering [8], coding [9], Selected mapping (SLM) [10] and Partial transmit sequence (PTS) [11]. [7–9] are gains that achieve PAPR reduction at the cost of in-band signal distortion or transmission rate loss. [10,11] reduce the probability of occurrence of large peak power signals by weighting the transmitted symbols using different phase sequences (scrambled phase sequences) so that the peaks of the sub-signals do not reach phase coherence at the same moment in the time domain, but require simultaneous transmission of sideband information at the expense of part of the transmit bandwidth [12].

Given that LCSS systems have an unused phase dimension available for effective utilization, they are well-suited for such phase weighting methods. In this paper, phase optimization and clipping technology are appiled on LCSS for PAPR reduction. Firstly, we analyze the relaitonship between intial phases and PAPR in LCSS signals, then give a search way for phase optimization PAPR suppression. To further improve the suppression effect, we use a combination of phase optimization and clipping methods. Finally, PAPR suppression performances of this method and power spectral density are analyzed by simulations.

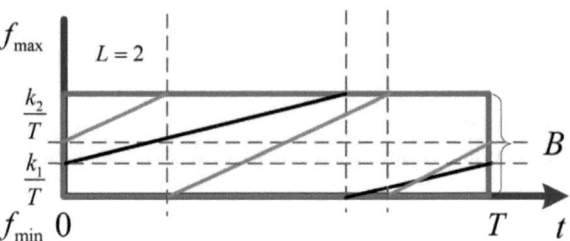

Fig. 1. LCSS system model.

2 LCSS Signal Model

The conventional LoRa technology employs Chirp Spread Spectrum (CSS) modulation to convert data information into chirp symbols [1]. The frequency range and data rate of LoRa modulation are determined by the bandwidth B and the spreading factor $SF \in \{6, 7, 8, ...12\}$. The discrete-time chirp symbol $x(n)$, where $n \in (0, M-1)$ and M represents the number of samples with duration Ts, can be expressed in its complex baseband equivalent form when sampled at the Nyquist sampling rate $fs = M/Ts = B$ [5].

$$x(n) = \exp\left(j\pi \frac{2kn}{M}\right) \exp\left(j\frac{\pi}{M}n^2\right) = f(n)c(n) \quad (1)$$

where, k is the modulation information, $k \in [0, M-1]$. The LoRa signal in [6] is represented as the product of a chirp symbol (spread symbol) $c(n) = \exp\left(j\frac{\pi}{M}n^2\right)$ and a non-chirp symbol $f(n) = \exp\left(j\pi\frac{2kn}{M}\right)$, where $f(n)$ can have one (such as LoRa) or multiple (such as DM-CSS) activated frequency shifts (FSs). The outcome of spreading its spectrum involves an internal mapping of FSs to cyclic time shifts. The spread symbol $c(n)$ can have different slopes [6]. Specifically, the chirp rate of LoRa is defined as $a = B/Ts$, and the signal spans B Hz in Ts seconds [6]. In the LCSS system, the chirp rate is summarized as $a = lB/Ts$. So $c(n)$ can be written as follows.

$$c_l(n) = \exp(j\frac{\pi}{M}ln^2) \quad (2)$$

The spreading symbol corresponds to an up-chirp when $l = 1$, and conversely, it corresponds to a down-chirp when $l = -1$. The LCSS system employs positive chirp rate transmission and designates the number of layers as L, with $l \in [1, L]$. The notation for the initial level is presented below. The notation for layer l is expressed in the following:

$$x_l(n) = \exp(j\frac{\pi}{M}(2k_l n + ln^2)) \quad (3)$$

Then, the symbols of the L-layer are superimposed to obtain the composite signal, called LCSS:

$$s(n) = \sum_{l=1}^{L} x_l(n) = \sum_{l=1}^{L} \exp(j\frac{\pi}{M}(2k_l n + ln^2)) \quad (4)$$

The LCSS system allows each layer to transmit SF bits, enabling each LCSS symbol to transmit $L*SF$ bits, resulting in an achievable SE of $L*SF/M$ bit/s/Hz. The LCSS system model is shown in Fig. 1

The large peak power signal in an OFDM system is attributed to the superposition of multiple continuous subcarrier signals with a certain symmetric phase(identical phases or constant phase jumps) [13]. This phenomenon also accounts for the significant peak power signal observed in the LCSS signal. Furthermore, as the number of LCSS layers increases, both PAPR and nonlinear distortion become more pronounced.

3 PAPR Analysis of LCSS Signals

The Peak-to-Average Power Ratio (PAPR) is defined as the ratio of the peak power to the average power of a signal, denoted by ρ. The specific expression can be stated as follows.

$$\rho = \frac{\max_n |s(n)|^2}{\frac{1}{M}\sum_{n=0}^{M-1}|s(n)|^2} \quad (5)$$

where $s(n)$ is the LCSS signal. The high PAPR occurs because of the composition of multiple statistically independent subcarrier signals, and when their envelope values are superimposed with the same phase, the synthetic signal envelope varies drastically, and in the extreme case, the peak power of the LCSS signal containing L subcarriers is L times the average power.

For convenience of discussion and analysis, assuming that the amplitudes of $s(n)$ are all 1, the instantaneous power value of $s(n)$ is expressed as

$$|s(n)|^2 = \sum_{l\in L}\sum_{p\in L} x_l(n)x_p(n)^* = L + 2\sum_{l=1}^{L-1}\sum_{p=l+1}^{L} x_l(n)x_p(n)^* \quad (6)$$

where,

$$\sum_{l=1}^{L-1}\sum_{p=l+1}^{L} x_l(n)x_p(n)^* = \sum_{l=1}^{L-1}\sum_{p=l+1}^{L} \exp(j\frac{\pi}{M}(2(k_l-k_p)n + (l-p)n^2))$$
$$= \sum_{l=1}^{L-1}\sum_{p=l+1}^{L} e^{j\theta(\Delta l, \Delta k)} \quad (7)$$

The average power of $s(n)$ can be expressed as:

$$\frac{1}{M}\sum_{n=0}^{M-1}|s(n)|^2 = \frac{1}{M}\sum_{l\in L}\sum_{p\in L}\sum_{n=0}^{M-1} x_l(n)x_p(n)^*$$
$$= \frac{1}{M}(LM + 2\sum_{l=1}^{L-1}\sum_{p=l+1}^{L} I_{(\Delta l,\Delta k)} e^{j\theta(\Delta l,\Delta k)}) \quad (8)$$

where I is the value of correlation between signals with different slopes.

The PAPR of the LCSS signal can be expressed as:

$$\rho_{LCSS} = \frac{\max_n |s(n)|^2}{\frac{1}{M}\sum_{n=0}^{M-1}|s(n)|^2} = \max_n \left[\frac{L + 2\sum_{l=1}^{L-1}\sum_{p=l+1}^{L} e^{j\theta_{(\Delta l, \Delta k)}}}{L + \frac{2}{M}\sum_{l=1}^{L-1}\sum_{p=l+1}^{L} I_{(\Delta l, \Delta k)} e^{j\theta_{(\Delta l, \Delta k)}}} \right] \quad (9)$$

From the above equation, it can be seen that the PAPR of the LCSS system is closely related to the inter-correlation value I between the subcarriers (signals with different slopes) as well as the phases, which can be adjusted by weighting a set of phases to adjust $\theta_{(\Delta l, \Delta k)}$ or to break the symmetry of such phases, and by continuously searching, from which a set of optimal sets of phases that minimise the PAPR is found to be weighted on the signals used for data transmission, and then the large peak power can be significantly reduced probability of the signal appearing.

4 Combined Techniques for PAPR Reduction

According to the relationship between PAPR and phase and mutual interference analyzed above, a phase search optimization scheme is designed in this section: a set of phase sequences are randomly generated and weighted to each subsignal, and the PAPR value of the superimposed signal LCSS is used as the target condition to find the best phase sequence group within the set search value range. This method does not require a large amount of computation, only requires storage space.

Therefore, the LCSS signal after adding the phase factor is:

$$s(n) = \sum_{l=1}^{L} x_l(n) = \sum_{l=1}^{L} \exp(j\frac{\pi}{M}(2k_l n + ln^2)) \exp(j\theta_l) \quad (10)$$

where $\theta_l \in \{\theta_l | l = 1, ..., L\}$ is a randomly generated set of phases.

The integrated PAPR value is:

$$\rho_{LCSS} = \frac{\max_n |s(n)|^2}{\frac{1}{M}\sum_{n=0}^{M-1}|s(n)|^2} = \max_n \left[\frac{L + 2\sum_{l=1}^{L-1}\sum_{p=l+1}^{L} e^{j\theta}}{L + \frac{2}{M}\sum_{l=1}^{L-1}\sum_{p=l+1}^{L} I_{(\Delta l, \Delta k)} e^{j\theta}} \right] \quad (11)$$

where θ is the composite phase under the influence of $\theta_{(\Delta l, \Delta k)}$ and θ_l

Therefore, the PAPR value of the LCSS signal is used as the optimisation objective, and the phase iterative optimisation method aims to find the optimal θ corresponding to $\{\theta_1, \theta_2, ..., \theta_L\}$ that minimises the PAPR value, viz:

$$\min_{\tilde{\theta}} \{\rho_{LCSS}\} \quad \tilde{\theta} = \theta_1, \theta_2, ..., \theta_L \quad (12)$$

The iterative search process of the phase iterative optimisation method with a single LCSS symbol as an example:

Step 1: A set of L random phases $\{\theta_1, \theta_2, ..., \theta_L\}$ are randomly generated and then weighted to the signals with different slopes to compute and save the PAPR values of the LCSS signals;

Step 2: Repeat Step 1, compare the calculated PAPR value with the previous PAPR value, take the smaller value and save its corresponding phase combination, iterate G times, the phase combination corresponding to the smallest PAPR value is the best phase combination.

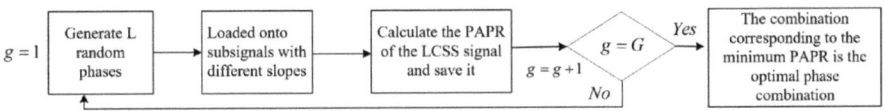

Fig. 2. The search process for phase optimization.

In a frame of data, the phase combination searches between symbols are independent of each other, and multiple objectives are optimised at the same time to maximise the PPAR suppression of this scheme. However, it should be noted that this method can only obtain sub-optimal results, and it is necessary to continuously increase the number of search iterations and improve the phase search accuracy in order to approximate the optimal solution, the block diagram of the phase-weighted search process, as shown in Fig. 2.

The amplitude clipping process is specified by the clipping ratio (CR) and is a nonlinear process. The clipping of the time domain signal arises the problem of in-band distortion and out-of-band spectral growth, leading to performance degradation [14]. Considering the limitations of this scheme's suppression effect, we integrate phase weighting and clipping techniques to enhance PAPR reduction while also considering BER performance and Out of band leakage. This approach initially applies a weight to the signal's phase and subsequently trims it by a small amount based on a threshold, further reducing the signal's PAPR. Additionally, we compare the PAPR reduction capabilities and BER performance of the phase optimization method, clipping method, and their combined implementation.

5 Simulation and Numerical Results

The simulation results are presented in this section to illustrate the proposed method for suppressing PAPR effects in the LCSS system, along with a comparison of BER performance in an AWGN channel. To better illustrate PAPR, the complementary cumulative distribution function (CCDF) is used, which shows the probability that ρ exceeds a specified threshold, ρ_0, i.e., $Pr(\rho > \rho_0)$ [6]. The simulation parameters can be found in Table 1.

Table 1. Simulation parameters.

Time-bandwidth product M	$2^8, 2^{10}$
Bandwidth B	5MHz
Symbol duration T	M/B
Layers L	6, 8
Number of searches G	1000
Clipping rate CR	1.46

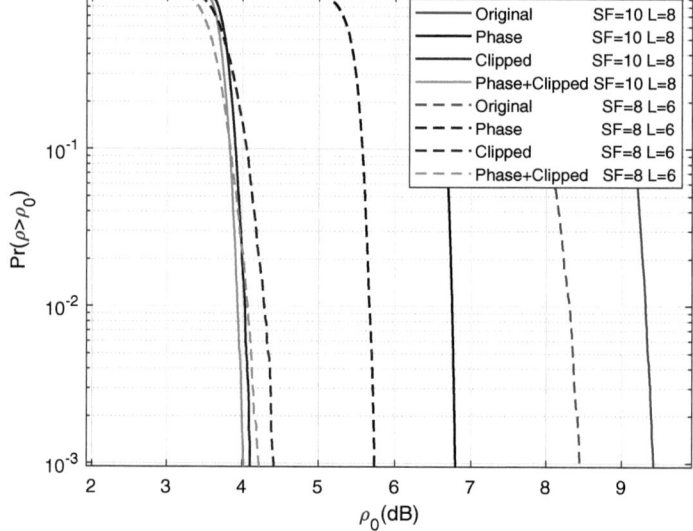

Fig. 3. PAPR CCDF curves for LCSS with different reduction techniques, when SF=8,10 and L=6,8, CR=1.46.

Figure 3 The CCDF curves of the PAPR of the original LCSS signal and the LCSS signal applied with different PAPR reduction techniques when SF=8 and SF=10. The solid and dashed lines represent the CCDF curves of PAPR for SF=10 (L=8) and SF=8 (L=6) signals, respectively. In this figure, red denotes the original LCSS signal, black represents the application of phase optimization technique, blue signifies the use of clipping technique, while green indicates a combination of phase optimization and clipping technique. It is evident that both phase optimization and clipping techniques effectively reduce the PAPR value of the signal. Furthermore, it can be observed that combining these two techniques further decreases the PAPR value. For instance, in a signal with SF=10 and L=8 configuration, it is possible to achieve a reduction in PAPR value by approximately 4 dB with an amplitude decrease close to 5.4 dB.

Figure 4 compares the BER performance of LCSS applying different PAPR reduction techniques over AWGN channels. The unmarked curve and the pent-

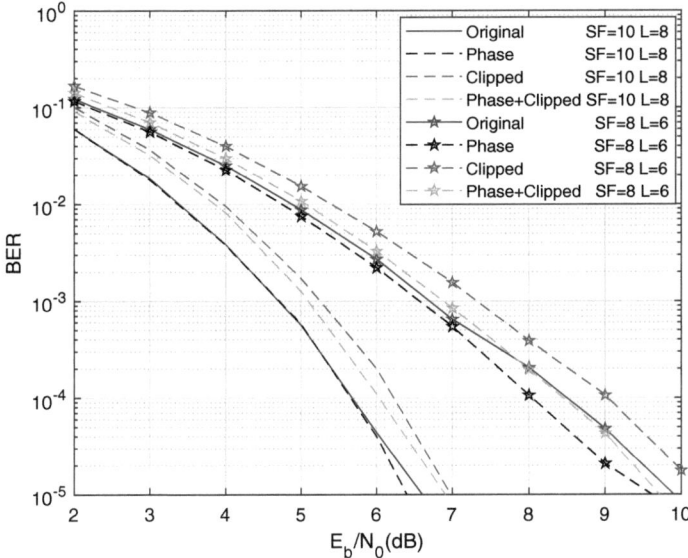

Fig. 4. BER performance comparison of different techniques in AWGN channel (M = 256 , M = 1024).

pointed star curve represent SF=10, L=8 and SF=8, L=6 signals respectively. In this representation, the original LCSS signal is depicted in red, the application of phase optimization technique is shown in black, the application of clipping technique is represented by blue, and the combination of phase optimization and clipping technique is denoted by green. It can be observed that solely applying phase optimization improves the BER performance due to its impact on mutual interference between sub-signals; loading the phase reduces mutual interference and enhances BER performance accordingly. However, using only clipping technology significantly degrades BER performance. On the other hand, combining phase optimization with clipping technology further reduces PAPR while mitigating the impact of clipping and improving signal BER performance.

Figures 5 compare the power spectral density (PSD) of the LCSS signal before and after phase optimization and phase optimization combined with clipping, respectively. Both signals were generated using identical parameters: SF = 10, L =8, BW = 125 kHz, a=8 (oversampling factor), CR=1.46 (clipping rate), and the same set of random data symbols. Loading the phase can effectively address the issue of inter-symbol phase discontinuity in the LCSS signal itself, resulting in improved out-of-band leakage shown in Fig. 5(a); there is approximately a 10 dB difference measured at a frequency offset of 500 kHz from the carrier frequency. However, applying clipping technology introduces spectrum leakage; hence combining both technologies helps mitigate spectrum leakage while still presenting an overall improvement in out-of-band suppression.

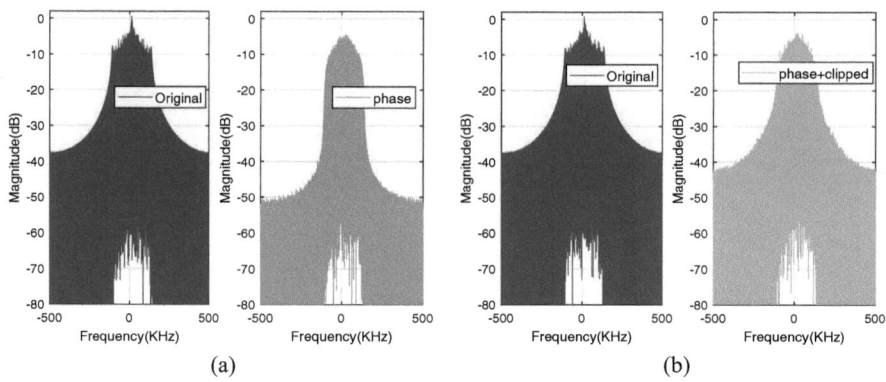

Fig. 5. PSD of LCSS signals processed by phase optimization and combining techniques, CR=1.46.

6 Conclusion

In this paper, we introduce the model of the LCSS system and analyse the PAPR of the system based on signal correlation theory, and propose a PAPR suppression technique that combines phase optimisation and clipping. This technology can effectively reduce PAPR of the system, and BER almost no loss. In addition, this technology reduces the PAPR while maintaining the high data rate of the LCSS system, which can be applied to the video service needs of IoT applications that require high speed and low power consumption, such as fixed surveillance, mobile law enforcement instrumentation, and drone inspections.

References

1. Nguyen, T.T., Nguyen, H.H., Barton, R., Grossetete, P.: Efficient design of chirp spread spectrum modulation for low-power wide-area networks. IEEE Internet Things J. **6**(6), 9503–9515 (2019)
2. LoRaWAN 1.1 Specification, Technical Report, LoRa Alliance Tech. Committee, Fremont, CA, USA (2017)
3. Jiang, Z.W., Yao, S.B., Pan, T.: Research on application and strategy of internet of things in 5G-A era. Designing Tech. Posts Telecommun. **7**, 30–35 (2024)
4. An, S., Wang, H., Sun, Y., Lu, Z., Yu, Q.: Time domain multiplexed LoRa modulation waveform design for IoT communication. IEEE Commun. Lett. **26**(4), 838–842 (2022)
5. Azim, A.W., Bazzi, A., Fatima, M., Shubair, R., Chafii, M.: Dual-mode time domain multiplexed chirp spread spectrum. IEEE Trans. Veh. Technol. **72**(12), 16086–16097 (2023)
6. Azim, A.W., Bazzi, A., Bomfin, R., Shubair, R., Chafii, M.: Layered chirp spread spectrum modulations for LPWANs. IEEE Trans. Commun. **72**(3), 1671–1687 (2024)
7. Armstrong, J.: Peak-to-average power reduction for OFDM by repeated clipping and frequency domain filtering. Electron. Lett. **38**(5), 246–247 (2002)

8. Wang, L.Q., Tellambura, C.: A simplified clipping and filtering technique for PAR reduction in OFDM systems. IEEE Sig. Process. Lett. **12**(6), 453–456 (2005)
9. Jones, A.E., Wilkinson, T.A., Barton, S.K.: Block coding scheme for reduction of peak to mean envelop power ratio of multicarrier transmission schemes. Electron. Lett. **30**(25), 2098–2099 (1994)
10. Han, S.H., Lee, J.H.: Modified selected mapping technique for PAPR reduction of coded OFDM signal. IEEE Trans. Broadcast. **50**(3), 335–341 (2004)
11. Ho, W.S., Madhukumar, A.S., Chin, F.: Peak-to-average power reduction using partial transmit sequences: a suboptimal approach based on dual layered phase sequencing. IEEE Trans. Broadcast. **49**(2), 225–231 (2003)
12. Hou, J., Ge, J., Li, J.: Peak-to-average power ratio reduction of OFDM signals using PTS scheme with low computational complexity. IEEE Trans. Broadcast. **57**(1), 143–148 (2011)
13. Hanif, M., Nguyen, H.H.: Frequency-shift chirp spread spectrum communications with index modulation. IEEE Internet Things J. **8**(24), 17611–17621 (2021)
14. Sahu, K., Veeramanju, K.T.: PAPR reduction in OFDM system using iterative clipping and filtering technique along with convolutional code. In: 2015 Fifth International Conference on Communication Systems and Network Technologies, Gwalior, India, pp. 412–415 (2015)

A Structure of MWC Based on Overlapping Window Method for Wideband LFM

Juejia Liang[1], Chao Yang[1,2], and Lin Zheng[1(✉)]

[1] Key Laboratory of Cognitive Radio and Information Processing, Ministry of Education, Guilin University of Electronic Technology, Guilin 541000, China
gwzheng@gmail.com
[2] National Key Laboratory of Wireless Communications, Chengdu 611731, China

Abstract. In response to the issues of high sampling rate and large reconstruction computation for Ultra-Wideband LFM signal in existing MWC systems, a novel MWC sampling structure based on overlapping windows is proposed, which can turn a wideband LFM into multiple small bandwidth signals with frequency sparsity. In the designing of overlapping window, the symmetry of LFM's time-frequency windowing is utilized for suppressing energy leakage and ensuring the sparsity in the frequency domain. This structure overcomes the traditional limitations on sampling rate and does not require prior knowledge of the chirp rate. Simulations and tests on real-world signals confirm the effectiveness of the proposed structure for LFM signal processing. Experimental results show that this approach not only reduces the required sampling rate but also enables efficient and stable signal reconstruction under various SNR conditions. Compared to traditional compressed sampling and rectangular window segmentation methods, the proposed structure demonstrates significant advantages in both reconstruction accuracy and sampling efficiency.

Keywords: Overlapping Windows · MWC Sampling Structure · Compressed Sampling · Wideband LFM Signal

1 Introduction

Ultra-Wideband LFM signals exhibit excellent anti-multipath ability and high range resolution, making them highly promising for applications in communication [1] and radar systems [2]. According to the Nyquist sampling theorem, the sampling rate must be at least twice the highest frequency of the signal to ensure accurate reconstruction. However, since the signal typically span a wide spectral range, traditional analog-to-digital converters (ADCs) must operate at extremely high sampling rates to prevent information loss. To address this challenge, some studies have focused on leveraging compressed sensing theory to reduce the sampling rate requirements for wideband chirp signals.

This work is supported in part by the National Nature Science Foundation (62461016) and National Key Laboratory of Wireless Communications Foundation (IFN20230209), as well as, Fund of Key Laboratory of Cognitive Radio and Information Processing, Ministry of Education CRKL200102.

Since wideband LFM signals are not sparse in the frequency domain, and sparsity is the key objective of compressed sampling, researchers have focused primarily on how to effectively reduce the bandwidth when integrating LFM signals with compressed sampling. Xiaomin Li et al. proposed an Modulated wideband converter(MWC) structure based on the fractional Fourier transform [3], which converts the wideband LFM into a single tone for achieving frequency sparsity, thereby achieving sparsity in the frequency domain. However, it requires prior knowledge of the chirp rate of the LFM signal. Similarly, Yang EP et al. proposed a method that first estimates the chirp rate using short-time Fourier transform (STFT) [4], followed by de-chirping and compressed sampling via the MWC framework. However, this approach is ineffective when multiple types of LFM signals are present. Additionally, although [5] mentions the combination of MWC and STFT, the essence of the method lies in performing sub-band down-conversion of wideband LFM signals within the MWC framework, followed by using STFT-DPT to estimate the chirp parameters, which does not reduce the sampling rate requirements for LFM signals in the MWC framework.

Gabor compressed sensing [6] was first proposed by Matusiak et al., but it was not used in LFM signals. Considering the advantage of Gabor compressed sensing structure over signals with the time-frequency sparsity, [7] applied it to the sampling and reconstruction of wideband LFM signals. However, unlike the support set in MWC which is towards sub-bands, Gabor's support set is for frequency points. This results in a larger search set compared to MWC, making the search process more prone to errors. In fact, continuous time-domain windowing for a wideband LFM signals can turn a wideband signals into multiple narrowband signals, but small rectangular windowing used for wideband LFM will cause spectrum spreading, further deteriorating signal's frequency sparsity. In this paper, a MWC structure with a overlapping window is proposed for wideband LFM, where a overlapping window is designed by the symmetry of LFM's time-frequency windowing. Through reconstructing of multiple time overlapping window, original signal can be recovered by adding up signals reconstructed from all time overlapping window.

This structure is not only simple but also significantly reduces the required sampling rate. Simulation results demonstrate that, compared with Gabor compressed sampling [7] and rectangular window MWC structures, the proposed method excels in terms of sampling rate and reconstruction performance. Furthermore, the performance patterns under different window lengths and signal-to-noise ratios (SNRs) are thoroughly explored.

2 Theoretical Analysis

The system mainly uses LFM signal to explain, and the signal model is shown in Eq. 1

$$x(t) = Ae^{j2\pi(f_0 t + k_f t^2)}, \qquad (1)$$

where k_f is the chirp rate and f_0 is the signal carrier frequency.

2.1 MWC Structure

The Modulated Wideband Converter (MWC) is an structure based on the theory of Compressed Sensing (CS). Originally proposed by Y. C. Eldar et al. [8], its goal is to significantly reduce the sampling rate of wideband signals, lowering it far below the traditional Nyquist rate. The core concept of MWC is to modulate and mix the wideband signal using random sequences, causing all of its information to be aliased into the lower frequency range, then the wideband signal can be sampled in a lower frequency range. These low-frequency samples retain the key information of the original signal, and the original wideband signal is then recovered using compressed sensing algorithms, achieving a balance between reduced sampling rates and signal fidelity.

The MWC structure is a multi-channels compressed sampling structure, as shown in Fig. 1.

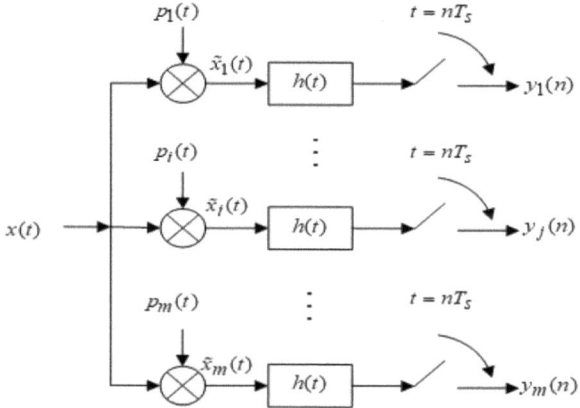

Fig. 1. Modulated wideband converter

The time-frequency domain analysis of the signal's transmission through a single channel of the MWC system is shown as follows.

In the MWC structure, the signal is first multiplied by a random sequence to obtain $\tilde{x}_i(t)$, The expression for $\tilde{x}_i(t)$ is shown in Eq. (2), where c_{il} represents the sparse domain coefficients of the random sequence, which in this paper are expressed as the Fourier coefficients of the random sequence.

$$\tilde{x}_i(t) = p_i(t)x(t)$$
$$= \sum_{l=-\infty}^{\infty} (c_{il} e^{j\frac{2\pi}{T_p}lt}) x(t) \cdot \quad (2)$$

The random sequence $p_i(t)$ is a pseudo-random periodic sequence, which effectively performs a frequency shifting operation on the original signal. Consequently, in the frequency domain, the high-frequency components of the signal are aliased into the low-frequency region, as shown in Eq. (3). $X(f)$ represents the spectrum of the original signal.

$$\begin{aligned}
\tilde{X}_i(f) &= \int_{-\infty}^{\infty} \tilde{x}_i(t) e^{-j2\pi ft} dt \\
&= \int_{-\infty}^{\infty} x(t) \left(\sum_{l=-\infty}^{\infty} c_{il} e^{j\frac{2\pi}{T_p} lt} \right) e^{-j2\pi ft} dt \\
&= \sum_{l=-\infty}^{\infty} c_{il} \int_{-\infty}^{\infty} x(t) e^{-j2\pi (f - \frac{l}{T_p})t} dt \\
&= \sum_{l=-\infty}^{\infty} c_{il} X(f - lf_p).
\end{aligned} \quad (3)$$

Finally, the aliased signal is sampled at a low rate to obtain the sampling sequence $y_i(t)$, and its frequency domain expression is given as follows:

$$\begin{aligned}
Y_i(e^{j2\pi fT_s}) &= \sum_{n=-\infty}^{\infty} y_i[n] e^{-j2\pi fnT_s} \\
&= \sum_{l=-L_0}^{L_0} c_{il} X(f - lf_p), f \in F_s.
\end{aligned} \quad (4)$$

From the frequency domain expression of $y_i(t)$, it can be observed that all spectral components of the original signal are captured, although they are aliased together with different coefficients. However, when there are enough channels, the uncorrelated nature of these channels makes it possible to unaliasing the results, which is the fundamental idea behind compressed sampling reconstruction.

How is the sampling rate of MWC structure selected, E. Candès, R. G. Baraniuk, and others proposed that to reconstruct the original signal with a high probability, the number of sampling channels in the MWC must satisfy the condition [9] shown in Eq. (5)

$$\begin{aligned}
M &\geq cK \log(N/K), \\
K &= B/f_s,
\end{aligned} \quad (5)$$

where N is the number of frequency bands divided by the perception bandwidth, c is a constant affected by the observation matrix and K is the signal sparsity, B is the bandwidth of the signal and f_s indicates the sampling rate of MWC single channel.

Terence Tao also pointed out that in a compressed sensing system, to successfully reconstruct the original signal, the sampling rate must be at least twice the signal bandwidth [10]. However, for wideband LFM signals, achieving such a sampling rate presents a significant challenge for hardware.

2.2 MWC Structure with Overlapping Windows

A. Time-frequency consistency of windowed LFM signals

As can be seen from Eq. (5), the compressed sampling rate is primarily determined by the signal's sparsity in the frequency domain. However, wideband signals tend to exhibit poor frequency domain sparsity, which directs our focus towards reducing the bandwidth of wideband LFM signals. The target signal is an LFM signal, and to ensure that wideband LFM signals maintain frequency domain sparsity in MWC reconstruction, segmented reconstruction can be considered. The rectangular window is a simple and commonly used time-domain segmentation function, and its mathematical expression is as follows:

$$r(t) = \begin{cases} 1, & 0 \leq t \leq T \\ 0, & otherwise \end{cases} \tag{6}$$

Here, T represents the time-domain window length. In this scenario, only a small portion of the target signal is present within a single time segment. By converting the wideband LFM signal into smaller bandwidth LFM signals for reconstruction, the signal's frequency domain sparsity K in Eq. (5) can be significantly reduced. However, the rectangular window introduces frequency domain energy leakage, which to some extent reduces frequency domain sparsity. This issue can lead to substantial search challenges and reconstruction errors in the MWC sampling system.

Therefore, we can consider utilizing the time-frequency symmetry of windowing LFM signals, where the suppression of high or low-frequency components in the time domain is similarly reflected as the attenuation of these frequency components in the frequency domain, thus demonstrating the symmetry of time-frequency characteristics. When applying a time-domain window to an LFM signal, restricting the time range allows selective suppression of specific frequency components. For instance, selecting a time-domain window to suppress high-frequency components results in the attenuation of the signal's high-frequency parts; similarly, a window that suppresses low-frequency components will reduce the contribution of low-frequency parts. This correspondence between time-domain and frequency-domain components can be clearly observed in the frequency domain.

The time-frequency symmetry diagram of LFM signal windowing is shown in Fig. 2.

The solid orange line in the Fig. 2 represents a single time-domain window, while the dashed orange line represents the adjacent overlapping window. The solid orange part can be regarded as the time-domain representation of a window that suppresses the LFM signal. This time-domain window divides the LFM signal into two parts: low-frequency suppression and high-frequency suppression, attenuating the signal energy in both regions. The signal after suppression, denoted as $q(t)$, can be expressed as follows.

$$q(t) = x(t)w(t), \tag{7}$$

Where $x(t)$ is the original LFM signal and $w(t)$ is the time window. Meanwhile, the frequency domain of $q(t)$, which is the blue part in Fig. 2 can be expressed as

$$Q(f) = X(f) * W(f) \tag{8}$$

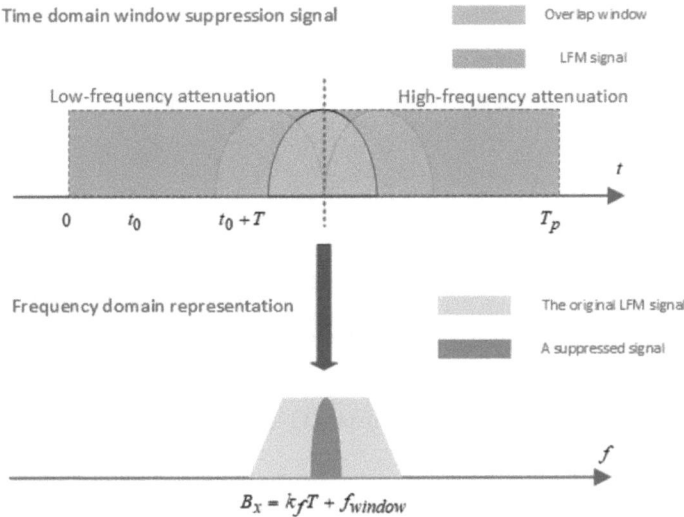

Fig. 2. Time-frequency symmetry of LFM windowing

The above formula can be regarded as the convolution of the original signal and the time-domain window spectrum, so the segmented signal frequency domain bandwidth

$$B_x \approx k_f T + f_{window}. \tag{9}$$

At this point, the LFM signal is suppressed by the time-domain window. Due to its time-frequency consistency, the bandwidth in the frequency domain is also reduced accordingly.

In conclusion, we can choose the Hanning window as an example, which effectively suppresses spectral leakage, as the time-domain segmentation function. The mathematical expression of the Hanning window is as Eq. (10):

$$w(t) = 0.5 \times (1 - \cos(2\pi \frac{t}{T})) \, t \in [0, T] \tag{10}$$

The bandwidth differences resulting from the segmentation of the LFM signal using these two types of time-domain windows are shown in Fig. 3.

After windowing, the wideband LFM signal is converted into a narrowband LFM signal with bandwidth B_x, which exhibits improved frequency domain sparsity.

B. The proposed system structure

As mentioned in the previous section, using the Hanning window not only reduces the bandwidth of the LFM signal but also alleviates the spectral leakage caused by the rectangular window, enabling segmented compressed sensing for wideband LFM signals. However, when reconstructing the signal segments, it is necessary to overlap and combine adjacent segments to recover the original signal. Therefore, the time-domain window must have overlapping regions. To ensure there is neither insufficient nor excessive overlap during signal reconstruction, the overlapping windows used for time-domain

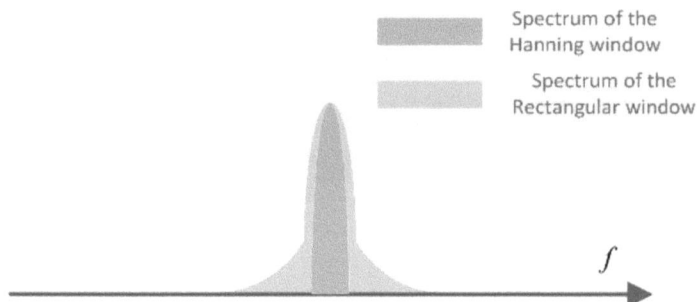

Fig. 3. Split bandwidth for different Windows

segmentation must satisfy the COLA (Constant Overlap-Add) condition. The expression for the COLA condition is shown below:

$$\sum_k w(t - k\Delta t) = C. \qquad (11)$$

This means that after applying windowing to the segmented signal, the overlapping window regions can smoothly transition during the stitching process, ensuring that the signal is neither amplified nor attenuated. This guarantees that the reconstructed x_j from the algorithm can accurately reconstruct the original signal x.

The mathematical expression for overlapping Hanning Windows is as Eq. (12):

$$w_k(t) = \begin{cases} 0.5 \times (1 - \cos(2\pi \frac{t}{T})) & t \in [(k-1)\Delta t, (k-1)\Delta t + \mu T] \\ 1 & t \leq ((k-1)\Delta t + \mu T, k\Delta t) \\ 0.5 \times (1 - \cos(2\pi \frac{t}{T})) & t \in [k\Delta t, k\Delta t + \mu T] \end{cases} \qquad (12)$$

The Hanning window has a shift interval of $\Delta t = (1 - \mu)T$, and the overlap ratio between two adjacent time-domain windows is $\mu \in [0, 1]$. For ease of analysis and implementation, the system uses Hanning windows with 50% overlap. The main lobe width of this Hanning window [11] can be approximated as

$$f_{hann} = \frac{4}{T}. \qquad (13)$$

At this point, by combining Eqs. (5), (9), and (13), the sampling rate of the MWC structure based on the overlapping windowing method can be derived

$$M \geq cK' \log(N/K'),$$
$$K' = (k_f T + \frac{4}{T})/f_s. \qquad (14)$$

In the MWC structure based on the overlapping windowing method, the signal is processed by a Hanning window of length T, which suppresses both low and high-frequency components, resulting in signal segments x_j. During this process, the bandwidth of the wideband LFM signal is significantly reduced, allowing it to be compressed and sampled by the MWC system. The observation result after compressed sampling is $Y_j(n)$, and its expression is as follows:

$$Y_j = \begin{bmatrix} y_{j1} \\ \vdots \\ y_{ji} \\ \vdots \\ y_{jm} \end{bmatrix} = \begin{bmatrix} [w(t - j\Delta t)x(t)p_0(t)] * h(t) \\ \vdots \\ [w(t - j\Delta t)x(t)p_i(t)] * h(t) \\ \vdots \\ [w(t - j\Delta t)x(t)p_m(t)] * h(t) \end{bmatrix} \qquad (15)$$

After applying the compressed sensing reconstruction algorithm, the reconstruction result x_j for the signal segment is obtained. The reconstructed x_j is then overlapped and combined with the adjacent signal segments to complete the reconstruction of the corresponding segment region.

The MWC structure based on the overlapping windowing method is shown in Fig. 4.

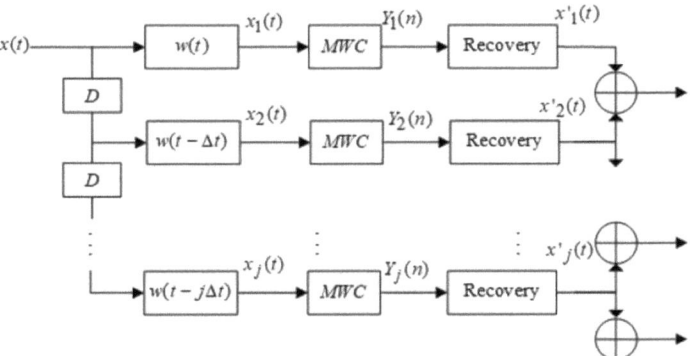

Fig. 4. The MWC structure with overlapping windows

3 Simulation Experiment

3.1 Signal Model

To validate the effectiveness of the proposed structure, an LFM signal with time-frequency symmetry is used as the experimental signal model. The expression for the LFM signal used in the simulation is:

$$x(t) = Ae^{j2\pi(f_0 t + k_f t^2)}, \qquad (16)$$

where signal bandwidth $B = 380MHz/3\mu s$, spectrum sensing range $f_{nyq} \in [0, 3GHz]$, pulse width $T_p = 3\mu s$, signal carrier frequency $f_0 = 2300MHz$. The signal diagram is shown in Fig. 5.

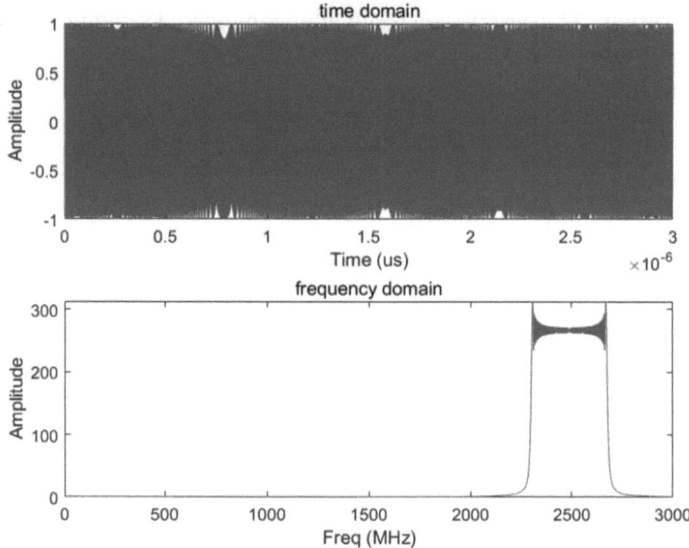

Fig. 5. LFM signal waveform diagram

3.2 Design of Overlapping Windows

For the LFM signal model mentioned above, the overlapping windowed MWC sampling structure is used to sample the signal. To achieve higher reconstruction accuracy, the system employs a Hanning window as the time-domain overlapping window, with a rectangular window introduced as a control group. $w(t)$ represents the Hanning window function, and the window length is $T = 0.2\mu s$. The overlap ratio between adjacent time-domain windows in this system is $\mu = 0.5$, so two adjacent signal subsegment enter the system with a time interval of $\Delta t = (1 - \mu)T = 0.1\mu s$. The overlapping Hanning window satisfies the COLA condition, as shown in Fig. 6.

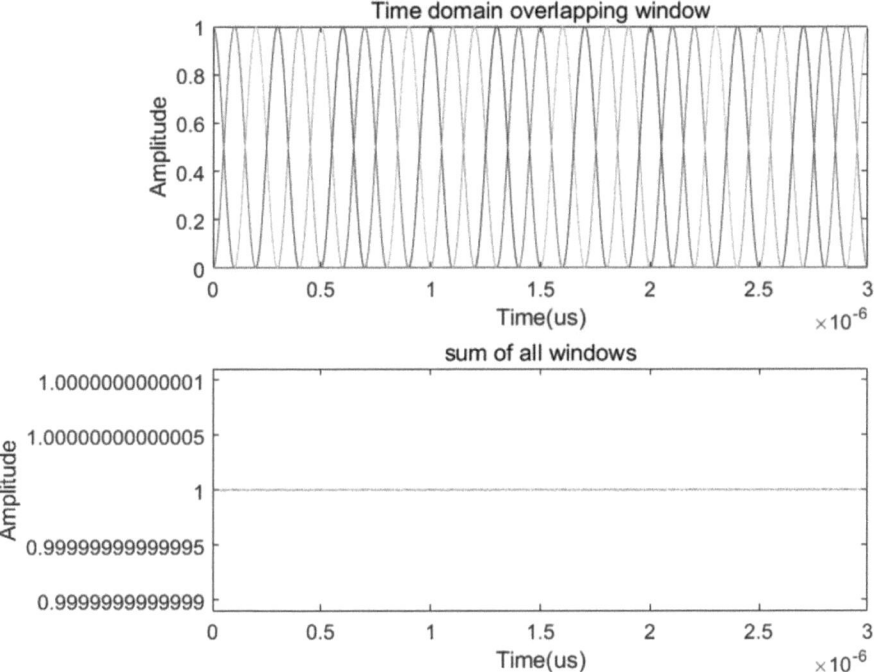

Fig. 6. Overlapping Windows and their addition values

Since applying a Hanning window to the LFM signal in the time domain is equivalent to convolving the signal's spectrum with the window's spectrum in the frequency domain, the bandwidth of the signal after passing through a Hanning window of length $T = 0.2\mu s$ can be approximately expressed as:

$$B_x \approx k_f T + \frac{4}{T} = \frac{380}{3} \times 0.2 + \frac{4}{0.2} = 45.3 MHz. \tag{17}$$

Figure 7 illustrates the frequency band suppression effects of the rectangular window and Hanning window, respectively. Compared to the original signal spectrum shown in Fig. 5, both window functions effectively reduce the signal bandwidth, but the rectangular window introduces spectral leakage, resulting in much lower sparsity compared to the Hanning window.

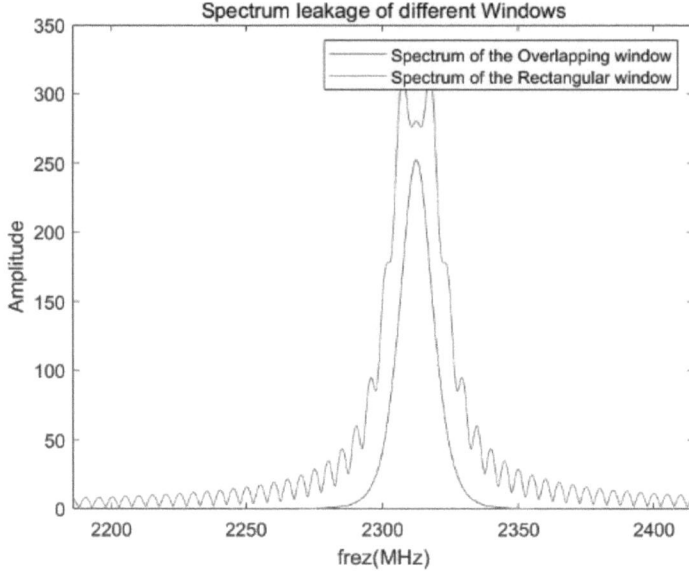

Fig. 7. Bandwidth after cutting LFM signals in different Windows

From Eqs. (14), (17), we know that the bandwidth suppressed by the Hanning window is closely related to the window length. Therefore, by changing the length of the time window, different signal bandwidths can be obtained to meet the acceptable sampling rate for capturing the signal.

3.3 Reconstruction Efficacy Comparison of LFM Signals

To validate the effectiveness of the proposed scheme, comparative experiments were conducted on the compressed sampling and reconstruction of LFM signals using different sampling structures. The sampling structures used for comparison include the Gabor compressed sampling structure and the rectangular window MWC sampling structure. To quantify the reconstruction performance of different structures, the relative error (RE) is introduced as a metric for reconstruction error. The expression for RE is as follows:

$$RE = \frac{|x' - x|_2^2}{|x|_2^2}, \tag{18}$$

Here, x' represents the reconstructed signal. Each set of parameters undergoes 100 Monte Carlo experiments, and when the reconstruction error is below a certain threshold, the reconstruction is considered successful. The simulation is divided into two parts. First, under high signal-to-noise ratio (SNR) conditions, the reconstruction accuracy of different structures is observed. A reconstruction is considered successful when the relative reconstruction error is less than 0.05. However, as noise interference is inevitable during the operation of the sampling system, this section also conducts experiments under various SNR conditions to observe the impact of SNR on the proposed structure. Due to the presence of noise folding in noisy environments, reconstruction is considered successful when the relative reconstruction error is less than 0.25.

The simulation was first conducted in a high signal-to-noise ratio environment with $snr = 100$. The system parameters used in the simulation are shown in Table 1, and the simulation results are presented in Fig. 8.

Table 1. Simulation parameter

Parameters	Symbols	Values
Signal-to-noise ratio	*SNR*	100
The length of window	T	0.2 μs
Window time shift	Δt	0.1 μs
Number of Windows	n	31

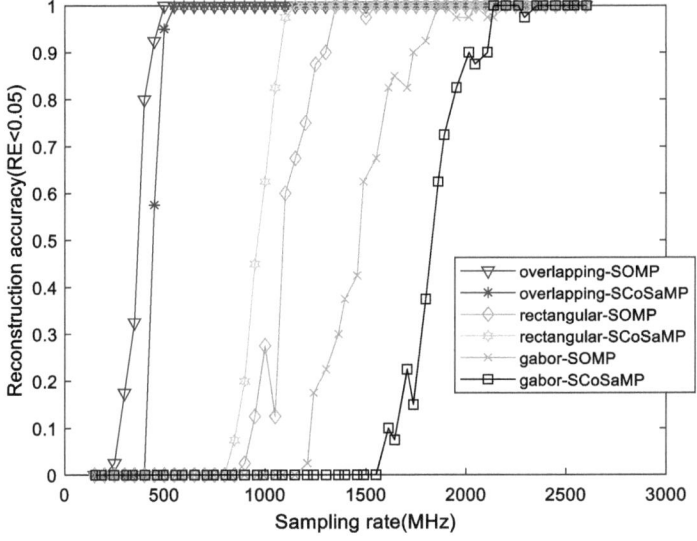

Fig. 8. Reconstruction accuracy of different structures

From the simulation results under high SNR conditions, it can be observed that compared to Gabor compressed sampling, the windowed MWC sampling structure achieves correct reconstruction at a lower sampling rate. In contrast, Gabor compressed sensing requires a significantly higher sampling rate. This is mainly due to the fact that in Gabor compressed sensing, the search targets are individual frequency points, resulting in a larger search space and higher search complexity. Additionally, comparing the two different windowing methods reveals that the overlapping window method achieves correct reconstruction at a lower sampling rate than the rectangular window segmentation method, which is attributed to the Hanning window's ability to suppress spectral leakage.

Next, simulations were conducted under different SNR conditions. The system parameters used in these simulations are shown in Table 2, and the simulation results are presented in Fig. 9.

Table 2. Simulation parameter

Parameters	Symbols	Values
The length of window	T	$0.2\ \mu s$
Window time shift	Δt	$0.1\ \mu s$
Number of Windows	n	31

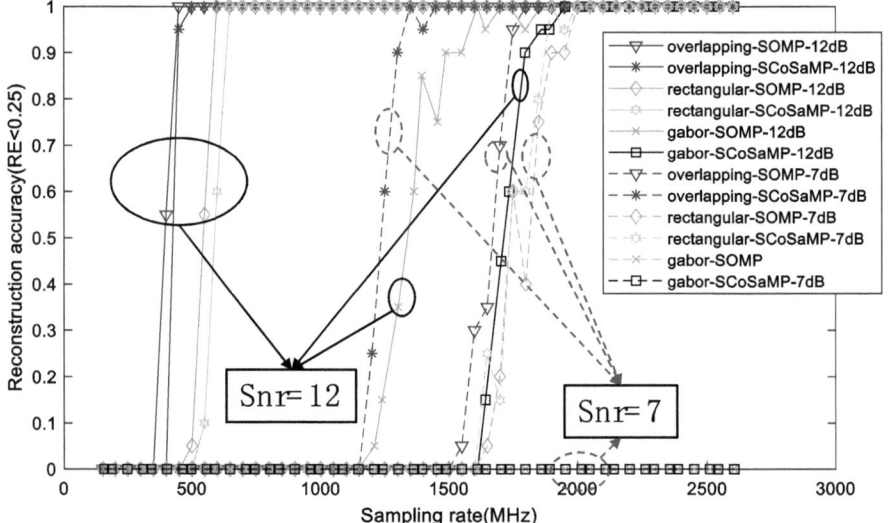

Fig. 9. Reconstruction accuracy of different SNR

The experimental results show that when SNR = 12dB, the sampling rate required for correct reconstruction in the windowed MWC structure is significantly lower than that of Gabor compressed sensing. Additionally, the overlapping window method achieves correct reconstruction faster than the rectangular window segmentation method.

At SNR = 7dB, Gabor compressed sensing fails to reconstruct the original signal due to difficulties in searching for the support set caused by high noise levels. However, the overlapping window-based MWC structure can still correctly reconstruct the signal with the lowest sampling rate among the three methods. This simulation demonstrates that, regardless of the noise environment, the overlapping window-based MWC sampling structure offers the most efficient compressed sampling performance.

Based on Eq. (14), the efficiency of this structure in reducing the sampling rate can be derived. As pointed out in [9], when the observation matrix is a Gaussian random matrix and the system operates in a noiseless environment, the constant c in Eq. (14),

(5) is typically set to 2. Therefore, it can be inferred that to satisfy the requirement for accurate reconstruction, the number of sampling channels in this system must meet the following conditions:

$$M \geq cK' \log(N/K') \approx 47,$$
$$K' = (k_f T + \frac{4}{T})/f_s \approx 6. \tag{19}$$

therefore, the sampling rate required for accurate reconstruction in this system is approximately 470 MHz. This conclusion is validated by the results in Fig. 8, where both the SCoSaMP and SOMP algorithms achieve a reconstruction accuracy of over 95% when the sampling rate reaches 500 MHz. Similarly, for the original LFM signal used in this paper, the number of sampling channels required for the traditional MWC sampling system to achieve a reconstruction accuracy(RE < 0.05) of over 95% is:

$$M \geq cK \log(N/K) \approx 180,$$
$$K = B/f_s \approx 50. \tag{20}$$

the required sampling rate is approximately 2000 MHz, whereas the MWC structure with overlapping windows requires only 470 MHz, which is one-fourth of the sampling rate required by the traditional MWC structure while maintaining the same reconstruction accuracy.

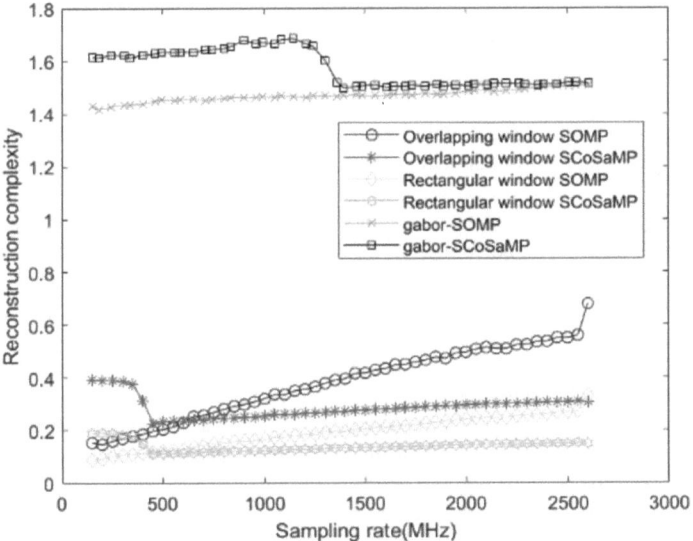

Fig. 10. The reconstruction complexity of different algorithms

In addition, this paper analyzes the differences in reconstruction complexity among different algorithms. As shown in Fig. 10, the reconstruction complexity of Gabor compressed sensing is significantly higher than that of the windowed MWC structure. This is because, in Gabor compressed sensing, the search is conducted over frequency points rather than frequency bands, resulting in a larger search space, which is consistent with the aforementioned viewpoint. However, the reconstruction complexity of the rectangular windowed MWC structure is slightly lower than that of the overlapping windowed MWC structure. This is due to the overlapping regions in the time windows of the overlapping windowed MWC structure, which require more windows to fully segment the entire signal, leading to increased reconstruction complexity from more segmented parts.

4 Conclusion

This paper investigates the compressed sampling and reconstruction of wideband LFM signals. In response to issues such as sampling system incompatibility and large reconstruction search space in existing compressed sampling systems for LFM signals, a novel MWC sampling structure based on overlapping windows is proposed. This method overcomes the traditional compressed sampling rate limitations for LFM signals and does not require prior knowledge of the chirp rate, offering broader applicability. Simulations and tests on real-world signals confirm the effectiveness of the proposed compressed sampling structure for LFM signals. Experimental results show that the proposed method reduces the sampling rate requirements while ensuring accurate reconstruction of the original LFM signal, and it also improves the system's operational stability.

References

1. Wen, Z., Liu, M., Chen, Y., Zhao, N., Nallanathan, A., Yang, X.: Multi-component LFM signal parameter estimation for symbiotic Chirp-UWB radio systems. IEEE Trans. Cogn. Commun. Netw. **10**(5), 1608–1619 (2024)
2. Wei, Z., Fu, N., Jiang, S., Li, X., Qiao, L.: Parameter measurement of LFM signal with FRI sampling and nuclear norm denoising. IEEE Trans. Instrum. Measur. **71**, 1–17 (2022). Art no. 2002417
3. Li, X., Wang, H., Luo, H.: Intra-pulse modulation recognition for fractional bandlimited signals based on a modified MWC-based digital receiver. IEEE Access **8**, 85067–85082 (2020)
4. Enpin, Y., Xiao, Y., Kaiyu, Q.: A novel compressive sampling system for chirp signal. IEICE Elec. Express **14**(8), 1–12 (2017)
5. Shou, M., Chen, M., Cheng, W.: A method for LFM signal parameter estimation based on MWC system and STFT-DPT. AIP Adv. **13**(5), 1–13 (2023)
6. Matusiak, E., Eldar, Y.C.: Sub-Nyquist sampling of short pulses. In: 2011 IEEE International Conference on Acoustics, Speech and Signal Processing (ICASSP), Prague, Czech Republic, pp. 3944–3947 (2011)
7. Chen, M., Qiang, W., Cheng, W., Yining, L.: Compressive sampling and reconstruction of linear frequency modulation signal based on Gabor frame. Xi Tong Gong Cheng Yu Dian Zi Ji Shu/Syst. Eng. Elec. **43**(4), 883–893 (2021)
8. Mishali, M., Eldar, Y.C.: From theory to practice: sub-Nyquist sampling of sparse wideband Analog signals. IEEE J. Sel. Top. Sig. Process. **4**(2), 375–391 (2010)
9. Candes, E.J., Romberg, J., Tao, T.: Robust uncertainty principles: exact signal reconstruction from highly incomplete frequency information. IEEE Trans. Inf. Theory **52**(2), 489–509 (2006)

10. Candes, E.J., Tao, T.: Near-optimal signal recovery from random projections: universal encoding strategies? IEEE Trans. Inf. Theory **52**(12), 5406–5425 (2006)
11. Oppenheim, A.V.: Discrete-time signal processing. Pearson Education India (1999)

STFT Spectrograms and Statistical Features Fusion for Emitter Identification Based on Deep Learning

Qi Cheng[1], Hongyujie Xiao[2(✉)], Julei Ye[2], Heng Liu[2], and Liu Yang[2]

[1] Key Lab of Information Coding and Transmission, Southwest Jiaotong University, Chengdu, China
 2022340312cq@my.swjtu.edu.cn
[2] Research Institute of National Defense Advanced Technology Sichuan Jiuzhou Electrical Group Co. Ltd., Mianyang, China
{xhyj,jourierye}@my.swjtu.edu.cn, {hengliu,yangliu}@swjtu.edu.cn

Abstract. Specific Emitter Identification (SEI) is a critical technology used to uniquely identify radio emitters based on their Radio Frequency Fingerprint (RFF) extracted from received signals. Deep learning (DL), which has proven effective in many recognition tasks, is believed to benefit SEI by strengthening wireless security authentication through RFFs. In this paper, we present a new approach for emitter identification that employs a feature late fusion strategy. Specifically, in order to identify eight LoRa transceivers of same model, a residual neural network-based DL model is presented which integrates the short-time Fourier transform (STFT) spectrograms with statistical features extracted from the in-phase and quadrature (IQ) signals, achieving a fusion of these two feature sets. The experimental results show that the proposed fusion strategy significantly improves recognition accuracy compared to using either STFT spectrograms or statistical features alone.

Keywords: SEI · STFT · statistical features · ResNet · feature fusion

1 Introduction

In wireless networks, IP or MAC addresses are always applied as the identification marks for device authentication. Due to the fact that IP and MAC addresses are easy to be forged and tampered, these traditional authentication schemes face huge security risks. Part of identification is to verify the identity of devices, which can be implemented by SEI [2–4]. SEI designates the individual emitter by extracting the RFF from the transmitted signals [1], which is caused by errors between component parameters and nominal values during the production of communication equipment. And is inherent and unique to each transmitter. RFF carries the hardware characteristics of the radiation source to be identified which is inherent and difficult to be counterfeited or tampered. Therefore, SEI based on RFF is believed to be more reliable than the traditional identification schemes based on IP or MAC addresses.

Based on the types of collected signals for identification, SEI can be divided into two categories [5]. One is based on the transient signals, which is usually generated when the transmitter is turned on or off. The other is with the steady-state signals, which are less challenging to be captured than the transient signals. SEI based on steady-state signal is the main research direction at present.

Traditional SEI is mostly achieved by comparing the predetermined features of the received signal with the known samples in the pre-designing signal feature database.[6]. However, these methods are particularly limited for non-stationary and non-linear problems. In comparison, SEI based on DL approaches are more robust and can extract more effective features from signals, hence leading to higher accuracy [7]. Actually, DL has been widely used in computer vision, natural language processing, intelligent control and other fields due to its excellent performance. In emitter identification area, the application of DL not only improves the identification accuracy, but also introduces a new framework in the SEI task. Therefore, a lot of recent works start to study the emitter identification issues by using DL techniques with RFF. [8] proposes an automatic recognition algorithm for the quasi-LFM radar signals based on fractional Fourier transform and time-frequency analysis. A spectrum computation scheme is proposed for the signal feature analysis by using STFT and k-means clustering [9]. Same as [8], the different emitter signals used in [9] for performance evaluation are not the real captured signals, but the simulated signals. A reasonable environmental cognition model for multifunctional phased array radar based on time-frequency analysis and high-order spectral analysis is proposed in [10] in which the WVD-Hough transform and Bispectrum estimation are applied to acquire the key parameters of radar signal such as modulated rate, width and modulated law. All above works assume that the different emitters adopt different modulation in their experiments, resulting in great difference in signal waveforms. In the case that the same modulation scheme is applied by different radiation sources, it undoubtedly becomes more challenging for the emitter identification.

To recognize the emitters with the same modulation, whose waveform has subtle distinction, this paper studies the fingerprint extraction and fusion strategy, in which the STFT spectrograms and statistical features are fused to construct the RFF of each emitter. The ResNet network, which is one of the typical DL structures, is applied to identify eight LoRa transmitters, which emit the signals with the same modulation scheme. The experimental results show that with our proposed feature fusion strategy the classifier can achieve a higher recognition success rate for the eight emitters identification task.

The remainder of this paper is organized as follows. In Sect. 2, the feature extraction is described. In Sect. 3, the dataset used in this paper is introduced. The proposed model is presented in detail in Sect. 4 and the experimental results are shown in Sect. 5. Section 6 concludes the paper.

2 Feature Representation

2.1 Time-Frequency Representation

Traditionally, RFF for SEI is mainly extracted from either the time-domain or frequency-domain of a RF signal. However, as the electromagnetic environment becomes more and more complicated, it is far from enough to accurately identify the RF emitter in a single domain. The time-frequency domain transformation can reflect the distribution of signal energy on the time-frequency plane, which simultaneously reveals the characteristics of instantaneous frequency and amplitude. Therefore, the time-frequency domain transformation is appropriate for comprehensively describing the varying properties of the signals [11].

Commonly used time-frequency domain transformations are STFT, wavelet transform (WT), and Wigner-Ville Distibution (WVD), etc. The calculated cost of STFT mainly comes from the combination of linear transforms, which is much lower than that of other time-frequency transforms. Furthermore, STFT and WT only show cross terms in their overlapping regions, while WVD may be disturbed by the cross term in more regions [11]. Hence, STFT is chosen in this paper as the time-frequency representation scheme to generate the signal spectrogram. The STFT for the discretized intra-pulse sequence is given by

$$STFT(n, k) = \sum_{m=-(N-1)/2}^{(N-1)/2} z(m)w^*(m-n)e^{-j2\pi km} \quad (1)$$

where $z(m)$ is the analytic form of signal and $w(m)$ is the Hamming window function of length N. As illustration, the STFT Spectrograms of signals captured from four LoRa emitters are plotted in Fig. 1.

2.2 Statistical Features

It can be seen from Fig. 1 that the STFT spectrograms from different emitters show subtle distinctions in images. To further increase the distinguishability of each emitter, time-domain statistical features are also extracted as listed in Table 1, which are fused with the STFT spectrograms to form the RFF of the emitters.

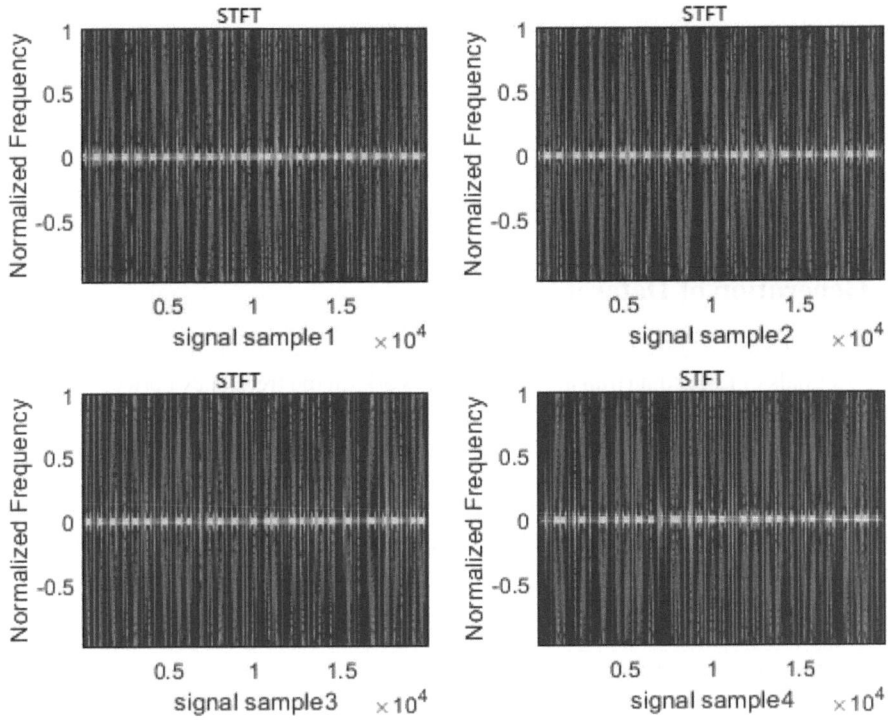

Fig. 1. The STFT Spectrograms of signals captured from 4 LoRa emitters.

Table 1. Extra Statistical Features Based on Time-Domain Signals

Feature	The Calculation Formula
Mean	$Xmean = \frac{1}{N_s} \sum_{n=1}^{N_s} A(n)$
Variance	$X_{\text{var}} = \frac{1}{N_s} \sum_{n=1}^{N_s} [A(n) - X_{mean}]^2$
Standard deviation	$\sigma = \sqrt{\frac{1}{N_s} \sum_{n=1}^{N_s} [A(n) - X_{mean}]^2}$
Skewness	$\beta = \dfrac{\frac{1}{N_s} \sum_{n=1}^{N_s} [A(n) - X_{mean}]^3}{X_{\text{var}}^{1.5}}$
Third origin moment	$Xmean_3 = \frac{1}{N_s} \sum_{n=1}^{N_s} A^3(n)$
Third center moment	$X_{\text{var}_3} = \frac{1}{N_s} \sum_{n=1}^{N_s} [A(n) - X_{mean}]^3$

(continued)

Table 1. (*continued*)

Feature	The Calculation Formula
Kurtosis	$\mu = \dfrac{\frac{1}{N_s}\sum_{n=1}^{N_s}[A(n)-X_{mean}]^4}{X_{var}^2} - 3$

3 Generation of Dataset

A Universal Software Radio Peripheral (USRP) based platform is developed to capture the IQ signals of LoRa data transmitters, which works at the frequency between 410 MHz and 441 MHz. The structure of the platform is shown in Fig. 2.

The NI USRP-2942R, with high-speed analog-to-digital converters and digital-to-analog converters to stream baseband I/Q signals to a host PC over 1/10 Gigabit Ethernet, is selected as a tunable RF transceiver. It offers frequency ranges up to 4.4 GHz with up to 20 MHz of instantaneous bandwidth. Meanwhile, MATLAB software provides a toolbox to support USRP device to achieve the acquisition of RF IQ signals received by USRP through MATLAB program.

The serial port assistant is used on the source PC to transmit the analog data to the LoRa data transmitter through the serial line, and the LoRa transmitter transmits the data through the antenna in the form of LoRa RF signals. Meanwhile, a NI USRP-2942R is connected with a PC in which the MATLAB controls acquisition of LoRa signals before the IQ signals are preprocessed and saved.

In this paper, the RF IQ signals are captured from eight LoRa data transmitters of the same model. In MATLAB, the USRP receiver bandwidth is set to 2 MHz and the center frequency is set to 433 MHz, which is the same as the transmission frequency of LoRa data transmitter. The time-domain captured RF IQ signals are plotted in Fig. 3, as well as their constellations are shown in Fig. 4. The eight LoRa data transmitters are configured to automatically retransmit data at an interval of 1 ms. For each LoRa transmitter, a 100-s signal is captured with the data size 0.1 GB, which is further segmented into 1000 MAT files. Therefore, the total signal data size of eight LoRa transmitters is about 0.8 GB.

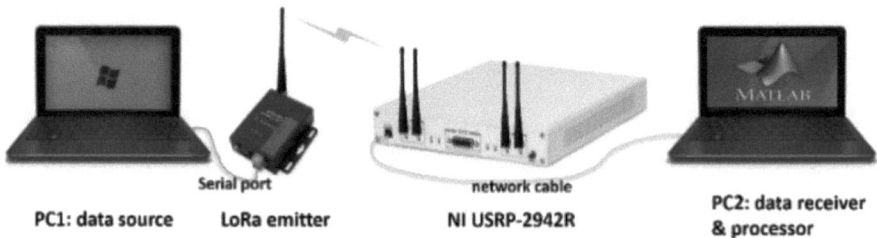

Fig. 2. The Data acquisition platform.

Furthermore, based on the feature extraction strategy in Sect. 2, the STFT spectrograms and statistical features of the captured LoRa signal are extracted respectively. The

STFT spectrograms data size of each LoRa emitter is about 150 MB, including 1000 STFT spectrograms with a resolution of 875 × 656. The statistical features of the eight LoRa emitters are all stored in a CSV file with a size of only 1.92 MB.

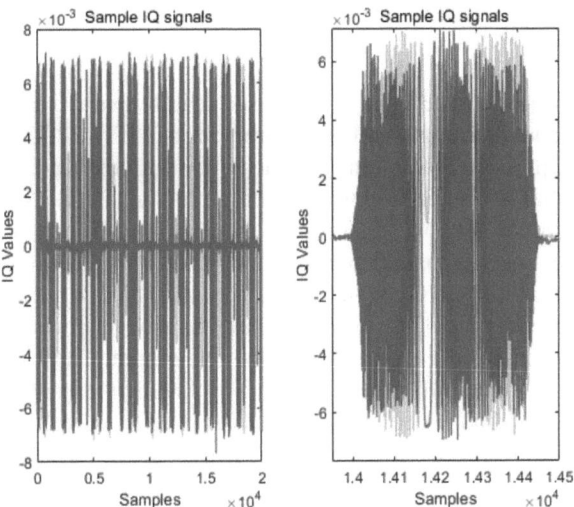

Fig. 3. RF IQ Captured Data from LoRa..

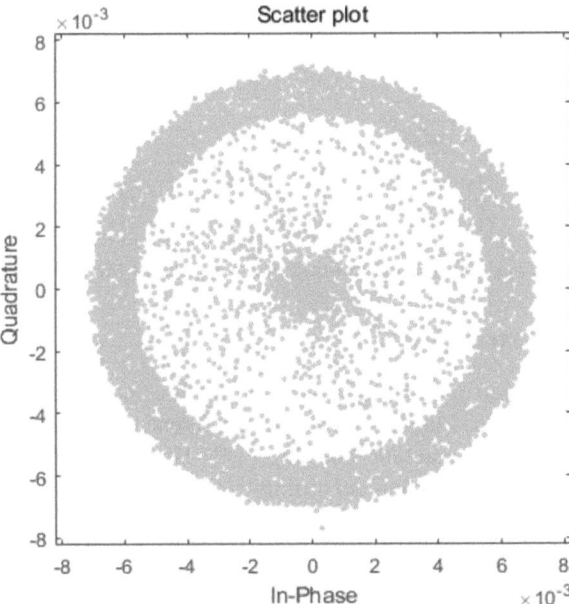

Fig. 4. The constellation of the acquired signal.

4 Proposed Feature Fusion Model Based on dl

With the statistical features and STFT spectrograms extracted from each emitter, DL model is built based on ResNet with the late feature fusion strategy.

4.1 ResNet

Deep residual networks are the most widely used feature extraction networks. ResNet introduces the residual learning to solve the problem which is difficult to be optimized in deep network[12]. ResNet maintains high accuracy with reduced information redundancy in data and has a deeper structure than the previous network model. The basic structure of the residual network is shown in the Fig. 5(a), from which it is seen that there is a shortcut connection path between input x and $F(x) + x$. For the deep network, it can be simplified to the structure which consists of one shallow network. Additionally, for each shallow network, there is an identity mapping between its input and output. The shortcut connection passes the input x directly to the output. Thus, the output result is $H(x) = F(x) + x$. In the case of $F(x) = 0$, $H(x) = x$, which refers to the identity mapping. The so-called residual is derived as $F(x) = H(x) - x$, where $F(x)$ is the learning goal of network. Ultimately the goal of ResNet is to make the residual result approach to 0.

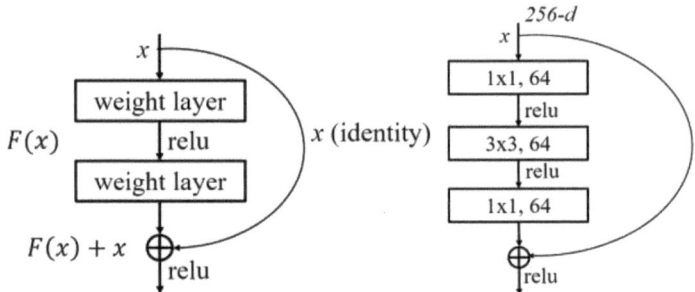

Fig. 5. (a)Residual learning: a building block. (b)one of the residual structures.

4.2 Feature Fusion Strategy

In this paper, STFT spectrograms and statistical features are fused, which is a type of multimodal feature fusion. Fusion methods of different modalities have always been a challenge in multimodal machine learning [13]. These approaches can be broadly classified into early and late fusion according to the fusion location in the processing chain [14].

Early fusion [15] is considered to have better performance because it fuses different features at the beginning of processing. The multiple features are fused by concatenating data into a joint representation. The joint representation must ensure that the features are properly aligned for further joint processing. Late fusion [15], on the other hand, is the simpler and more commonly used fusion strategy, which merges the features after the processing in different unimodal streams separately and respectively. In this paper, the scales of the two features differ greatly and it is difficult to make them aligned. Therefore, the late fusion strategy is adopted in this paper with the fusion strategy of the STFT spectrograms and statistical features shown in Fig. 6.

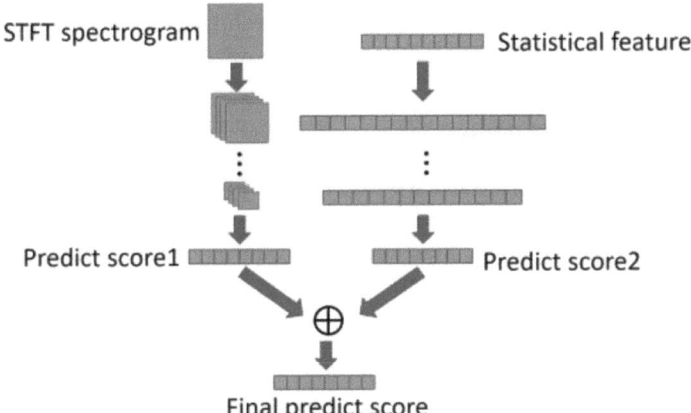

Fig. 6. Late fusion strategy for STFT spectrograms and statistical features.

4.3 Proposed Model Structure

Late fusion is applied in this paper and ResNet50 model is utilized to learn the complex feature representations from the input signal STFT spectrograms. Additionally, a proposed network structure is integrated to the ResNet50 model, which is mainly composed of a convolution layer, a maximum pooling layer and 4 full connection layers to learn the statistics of IQ signals. Finally, the features learned from STFT spectrograms and statistical features are merged to obtain the final output. The final model structure and the key parameters are shown in Fig. 7.

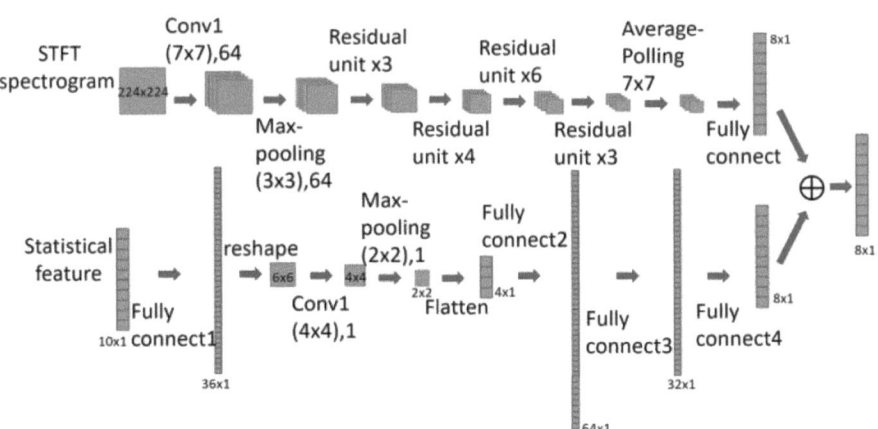

Fig. 7. Deep learning model structure.

5 Experiments

5.1 Proposed Model Structure

The experiment is conducted based on the dataset presented in Sect. 3. The dataset is randomly shuffled before learning. The training set, validation set and test set are splitted according to proportion of 6:2:2.

5.2 Proposed Model Structure

The recognition accuracy with and without feature fusion are compared in Fig. 8. In the experiment, the models are trained for 60 epochs using the Adam optimizer and the cross-entropy is used as the loss function. It is seen from Fig. 8 that the best accuracy results for STFT spectrograms and statistical features are 89.75% and 81.88%, with the learning rates of 0.003 and 0.01 respectively. On the contrary, the best accuracy result for the feature fusion strategy is 93.44%, which is higher than only STFT spectrograms or statistical features are applied.

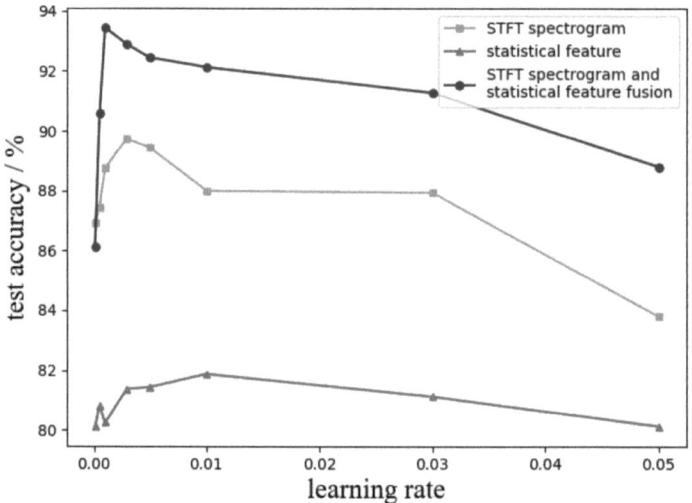

Fig. 8. Recognition Accuracy With and Without Feature Fusion.

The variation of accuracy and loss value of the model on the training set and validation set with epoch is shown in Fig. 9, from which it is seen that the accuracy and loss value tend to converge when epoch = 40.

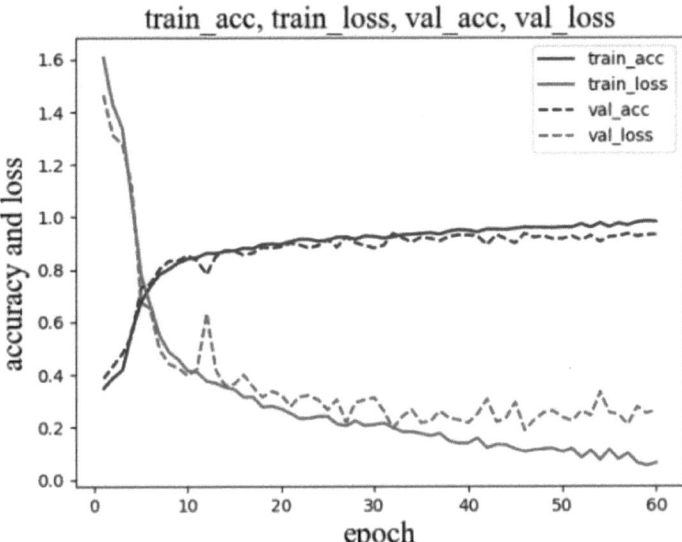

Fig. 9. The variation trend of model accuracy and loss.

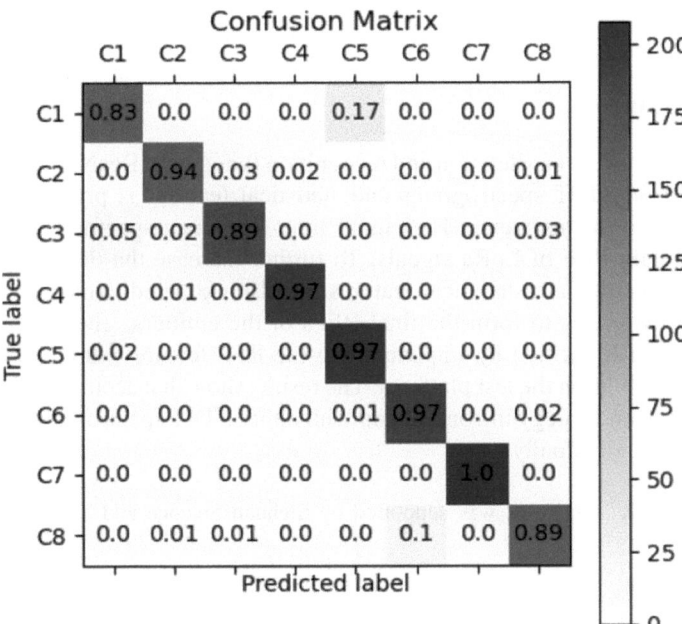

Fig. 10. Confusion matrix.

The classification confusion matrix of eight Lora emitters on the test set is shown in Fig. 10, in which it is seen that the classification prediction accuracy for the 3 devices are lower than 90%. Additionally, the classification accuracy for the rest 5 devices are almost close to 100%, resulting in an overall accuracy of 93.44%.

To further test the performance of the proposed classifier under the severe conditions, additive noises are added to the captured signals artificially with different signal-to-noise ratios (SNR) levels. Table II shows the accuracy of the proposed classifier under different SNR with the proposed classifier with learning rate of 0.001. It can be seen from Table 2 that when SNR is greater than 20dB, the accuracy is above 75%. If the SNR further increases to 30dB, the accuracy reaches 92%.

Table 2. The Accuracy under Different SNR Signals

SNR	Test Accuracy
−20 dB	34.25%
−10 dB	36.50%
0 dB	40.06%
10 dB	48.38%
20 dB	77.06%
30 dB	92.06%
40 dB	92.38%
50 dB	93.31%

6 Conclusion

Based on the powerful classification and recognition function of ResNet, a feature fusion strategy based on STFT spectrograms and statistical features is proposed to identify emitter individual in this paper. The signal time-frequency spectrum is obtained by STFT as the main RFF of LoRa signals. To further increase the distinguishability of each emitter, time-domain statistical features are also extracted, which are fused with the STFT spectrograms to form the final RFFs of the emitters. The feasibility of the proposed method is verified by implementing the RFF feature extraction and feature fusion DL algorithms on the test platform. The results show that accuracy improves with the proposed fusion strategy in comparison with either STFT spectrograms or statistical features applied individually.

Acknowledgement. This work was supported by Sichuan Science and Technology Program 2023YFG0100.

References

1. Zha, X., Qiu, Z., Feng, Y., Cun, C., Shen, Z.: Deep ensemble learning with reconstruction cancellation for specific emitter identification. In: Proceedings of the 2021 IEEE 21st International Conference on Communication Technology (ICCT), pp. 79–82 (2021). https://doi.org/10.1109/ICCT52962.2021.9657886

2. León, O., Hernández-Serrano, J., Soriano, M.: Securing cognitive radio networks. Int. J. Commun. Syst. **23**(5), 633–652 (2010)
3. Knox, D.A., Kunz, T.: RF fingerprints for secure authentication in single-hop WSN. In: International Conference on Wireless and Mobile Computing, Networking and Communications, Avignon, France, pp. 567–573, October 2008
4. Zhang, J., Li, G., Marshall, A., Hu, A., Hanzo, L.: A new frontier for IoT security emerging from three decades of key generation relying on wireless channels. IEEE Access **8**, 138406–138446 (2020)
5. Lin, Y., Jia, J., Wang, S., Ge, B., Mao, S.: Wireless device identification based on radio frequency fingerprint features. In: IEEE International Conference on Communications (ICC), Dublin, Ireland, pp. 1–6, June 2020
6. Zhong, Y., Zhang, L., Pu, W.: Multimodal deep learning model for specific emitter identification. In: Proceedings of the 2021 IEEE 6th International Conference on Signal and Image Processing (ICSIP), pp. 857–860 (2021). https://doi.org/10.1109/ICSIP52628.2021.9688616
7. Riyaz, S., Sankhe, K., Ioannidis, S., Chowdhury, K.: Deep learning convolutional neural networks for radio identification. IEEE Commun. Mag. **56**(9), 146–152 (2018). https://doi.org/10.1109/MCOM.2018.1800153
8. Cunxiang, X., Limin, Z., Zhaogen, Z.: Quasi-LFM radar waveform recognition based on fractional Fourier transform and time-frequency analysis. J. Syst. Eng. Electron. **32**(5), 1130–1142 (2021). https://doi.org/10.23919/JSEE.2021.000097
9. Xiao, Z., Yan, Z.: Radar emitter identification based on novel time-frequency spectrum and convolutional neural network. IEEE Commun. Lett. **25**(8), 2634–2638 (2021). https://doi.org/10.1109/LCOMM.2021.3084043
10. Ren, M., Tian, Y.: Radar signal cognition based time-frequency transform and high order spectra analysis. In: Proceedings of the 2017 IEEE International Conference on Signal Processing, Communications and Computing (ICSPCC), pp. 1–4 (2017). https://doi.org/10.1109/ICSPCC.2017.8242457
11. Wu, J., Zhong, Y., Chen, A.: Radio modulation classification using STFT spectrogram and CNN. In: Proceedings of the 2021 7th International Conference on Computer and Communications (ICCC), pp. 178–182 (2021). https://doi.org/10.1109/ICCC54389.2021.9674714
12. He, K., Zhang, X., Ren, S., et al.: Deep residual learning for image recognition. In: Proceedings of the IEEE Conference on Computer Vision and Pattern Recognition, pp. 770–777 (2016)
13. Baltrušaitis, T., Ahuja, C., Morency, L.: Multimodal machine learning: a survey and taxonomy. IEEE Trans. Pattern Anal. Mach. Intell. **41**(2), 423–443 (2019). https://doi.org/10.1109/TPAMI.2018.2798607
14. D'mello, S.K., Kory, J.: A review and meta-analysis of multimodal affect detection systems. ACM Comput. Surv. **47**(3), Article 43 (2015). 36 p. https://doi.org/10.1145/2682899
15. Snoek, C.G.M., Worring, M., Smeulders, A.W.M.: Early versus late fusion in semantic video analysis. In Proceedings of the 13th Annual ACM International Conference on Multimedia (MULTIMEDIA 2005), pp. 399–402. Association for Computing Machinery, New York (2005). https://doi.org/10.1145/1101149.1101236

A Fast Rivet Detection Algorithm Based on VanillaNet Network and Computer Vision

Juntian Zheng[1] and Peiyan Yuan[1,2(✉)]

[1] School of Software, Henan Normal University, Xinxiang 453000, China
peiyan@htu.cn
[2] Engineering Laboratory of Intellectual Business and Internet of Things Technologies, Xinxiang 453000, Henan, China

Abstract. Riveting is the main connection method in aircraft assembly, and its detection is crucial to ensure flight safety. In view of the problem that traditional manual visual inspection methods are difficult to meet the needs of large-scale and high-precision detection, a fast rivet detection algorithm based on the VanillaNet network is proposed. First, by using the VanillaNet network architecture, the complex backbone part in the traditional YOLO series algorithm is replaced, effectively reducing the complexity of the model. Secondly, the Bi-FPN (Bidirectional Feature Pyramid Network) and the RFA (Receptive-Field Attention) detection head combined with the spatial attention mechanism are introduced to improve the multi-scale detection performance and difficult sample feature extraction capabilities of the model respectively. In addition, an industrial-grade dataset containing a variety of rivet models and defect classifications is constructed, and the generalization ability of the model is improved through a variety of data enhancement techniques. Experimental results show that compared with the YOLOv8 baseline model, the fast rivet detection algorithm has a 6.7% increase in average accuracy and a 126% increase in detection speed. The fast rivet recognition algorithm provides a new solution for automated detection in the aviation manufacturing industry and has broad application prospects.

Keywords: VanillaNet · Bi-FPN · RFAconv · Rivet Identification · Computer Vision

1 Introduction

The global aviation manufacturing industry continues to grow, with the market size exceeding one trillion dollars. According to statistics, the global aviation equipment market has been growing at a compound annual growth rate (CAGR) of about 5% over the past few years [1]. Fortune Business Insights predicts that the global commercial aviation equipment market will grow at a rate of 3.7% in the next five years, reaching a market size of $1.1769 trillion by 2027. As of September 2022, the global fleet size reached 28,848 aircraft, of which 23,904 were in service and 4,944 were grounded. According to a report released by China Commercial Aircraft Corporation, the world will need 42,428 commercial aircraft worth $6.4 trillion in the next 20 years. By then, the global commercial aircraft fleet will reach 47,531, with an average annual growth rate of 6.56%, and the average annual market size will exceed $300 billion [2].

With the rapid development of the global aviation manufacturing industry, the assembly of large aircraft is characterized by numerous components, large part sizes, complex structures, and high installation precision requirements. On average, the assembly cost of an aircraft accounts for 40% of its total cost, and the assembly cycle accounts for 40–50% of the total manufacturing cycle [3].

Riveting is the most common method for connecting components in aircraft assembly. It offers stable connection performance, is resistant to deformation, easy to inspect and maintain, and convenient to install and replace. Typically, riveting accounts for 60–80% of all aircraft connection methods [4], and the number of rivets can range from tens of thousands to millions [5]. Whether in the assembly or maintenance stages, the inspection of rivets incurs significant labor costs and time. Traditional manual visual inspections cannot cope with the large workload and high precision requirements of this task [6]. According to the "Civil Aircraft Airworthiness Directive," visual assessment by workers is still the basic step in determining whether an aircraft is airworthy. Statistics show that 70% of aircraft fatigue failures are caused by fatigue failure at the connection points of structural components, with 80% of fatigue cracks occurring at the connection holes [7]. This indicates that the assembly quality of aircraft component connections has a significant impact on aircraft safety performance.

To pursue faster, cheaper, and more accurate inspection methods, various modern equipment and sensors have been tried to replace traditional manual visual inspection methods. Some researchers have used 3D printers and point cloud technology to quickly model the 3D information of aircraft skins, transforming the rivet detection problem into a 3D point cloud fitting problem. Xie et al. proposed using a mobile 3D scanning system to automatically capture the 3D point cloud of the aircraft skin and use point cloud processing technology to measure the flatness of the rivets [8]. In March of the same year, they also proposed a multi-structure fitting algorithm based on 3D point clouds to perform rivet detection, reducing fitting variability [9]. Huang et al. proposed a rivet flatness detection method based on the normal vector-density clustering algorithm. Firstly, the initial point cloud data is sampled based on normal vector [10]. Then, density clustering algorithm is used to cluster the rivet head point cloud. Then, the random sample consistency algorithm is used to fit the contour of the rivet head point cloud, and the rivet head model parameters are obtained. However, these studies did not address the inherent disadvantages of point cloud technology in engineering applications:

- Point cloud information requires a large amount of storage space and computing resources, leading to slow processing speeds.
- The sampling of large-scale aircraft components poses challenges. Whether the sampling is uniform and whether there is noise interference directly affects data accuracy.
- Different spacecraft have different models and components, leading to inconsistent modeling information, and different point cloud processing algorithms are needed for different point clouds, which complicates the process and increases costs.

Some scholars have used Pulsed Eddy Current (PEC) technology to detect multistructure riveting components. This technology uses electromagnetic induction to generate transient electromagnetic field pulses, inducing eddy currents on the surface of the metal components under test. These currents are then measured and analyzed to determine surface or near-surface defects. Shao et al. used a flow sensing system that includes an EC sensor array and a multi-channel electromagnetic instrument to inspect simulated samples of riveted joints with defects [11]. They processed the collected data using Hough Circle Transform (HCT) and texture analysis, allowing for the detection and localization of fatigue cracks on the samples. The Karpenko Physico-Mechanical Institute of the National Academy of Sciences of Ukraine, in collaboration with several foreign aircraft companies, developed the Leotest VD 3.03 high-frequency EC flaw detector based on self-generating modes and micro single-coil EC probes for detecting surface-breaking fatigue cracks [12]. They invented and studied an original scheme for intermittent oscillation in a dual-loop self-generating setup.

It is evident that pulse eddy current technology performs well in non-destructive testing. However, due to the inherent mechanisms of the technology, any factors that can interfere with electromagnetic induction will affect the detection results. For instance, the reliance on the material's conductivity, the changes in conductivity due to corrosion and oxidation layers on the surface of rivets, and poor handling effects on deformed rivets can impact detection accuracy and reliability, especially for poorly processed or uneven workpieces. Environmental factors such as temperature and humidity can also influence detection outcomes, necessitating controlled conditions that increase production costs.

In summary, many scholars and research institutions have provided viable solutions to these problems using modern technology, but unavoidable deficiencies remain. Since the landmark breakthrough of deep learning [13] in image recognition, more scholars have attempted to utilize deep learning methods to address rivet identification issues [14, 15]. Yang et al. [16] trained feature parameter samples of rivet heads using Support Vector Machine algorithms, exploring the correlation between the feature parameters of rivet heads and mathematical models, while verifying model accuracy. Ling et al. [17] proposed using ResNet deep neural networks to detect defects such as missing pins, bolts, and rivets in freight vehicles. Leandro et al. [18] applied convolutional neural network-based machine learning techniques for the classification and detection of large fasteners, demonstrating that this neural network paradigm in industrial environments can reliably estimate mechanical parameters, thus enhancing the performance and flexibility of advanced manufacturing processes for large structural components. Zhang et al. proposed a defect detection method for saw chain assembly based on residual networks and knowledge encoding, achieving part segmentation and assembly defect recognition, which holds significant reference value for detecting other types of simple assemblies in the industry [19]. Li proposed an effective defect detection network for aircraft skin fasteners called YOLO-FDD [20] based on the YOLO (You Only Look Once) [21] framework, achieving a mean Average Precision (mAP) of 83.08% and a detection speed of 30.44 FPS, showcasing the enormous application potential of the YOLO framework in detecting defects in aircraft skin fasteners.

Despite the good performance brought by increasingly complex and sufficiently deep models in the field of industrial inspection, their requirements for hardware computing power and network environments have become more stringent [22, 23]. For instance, ResNets consume a significant amount of external chip memory bandwidth when merging features from different layers [24, 25]. Similarly, YOLOv8, while improving accuracy compared to earlier versions of YOLO, also experiences a dramatic increase in training costs. For many military-industrial complexes and production facilities that require confidentiality and can only provide local area networks, it is challenging to offer the necessary network environment and hardware support at a reasonable cost. Therefore, the conflict between the need for high-performance computing hardware and massive network bandwidth support, and the requirement for cost reduction in uncertain network environments for detection, presents a significant challenge.

In summary, this paper thoroughly studies the YOLO algorithm framework and its adaptability to rivet features on aircraft skins. A new fast rivet identification algorithm is proposed based on the latest VanillaNet network, replacing the backbone part of the YOLO neural network. This allows for the rapid and accurate detection of various rivet states on aircraft skin using only a regular camera without additional hardware or environmental requirements, significantly improving detection performance and reducing training costs. The main contributions of this paper are as follows:

(1) In the process of rivet detection, hardware equipment is often incomplete, and the working environment is complex. To avoid deployment difficulties caused by deep convolutional layers and complex network structures, this paper proposes using the VanillaNet network to replace the backbone part of the YOLO (such as YOLOv5, YOLOv8) series algorithms. This is a novel and simplified network architecture that avoids the excessive depth, residuals, and complex operations of the YOLO series. It consists of only six convolutional layers while retaining excellent performance, making it suitable for mainstream modern devices in various work environments.
(2) To improve the model's performance in multi-scale environments and better adapt to resource-constrained environments, this paper adopts the Bi-FPN (Bidirectional Feature Pyramid Network) to replace the Path Aggregation Feature Pyramid Network (PAFPN) in YOLOv8.
(3) Inspired by RFAConv [26] convolution, this paper proposes an RFAhead detection head that combines spatial attention mechanisms with convolution to enhance the model's ability to extract features from challenging samples.
(4) A classification standard for rivet status using visualization methods was established. Through real-world sampling and data augmentation techniques like random rectangular occlusion, inversion, translation transformation, random noise generation, and motion blur, a large and accurate rivet status dataset was created.

2 Related Work

The emergence of deep learning algorithms has improved the performance of small target detection model. In 2016, Chen et al. put detection objects on small targets, built a benchmark data set for small target detection and enhanced the then most advanced R-CNN algorithm to improve the performance of small target detection [27]. This research path later became a classic approach in the field of deep learning applications in computer vision. In the same year, Redmon et al. proposed the YOLO Convolutional neural network at CVPR 2016, which redefines detection as a single regression problem. By predicting multiple bounding boxes and class probabilities simultaneously through a single convolutional network, the ultra-fast recognition rate makes it possible to process streaming video in real time. To further improve the defects of YOLO in small target detection, Redmon et al. introduced Anchor Boxes and more convolutional layers, and proposed YOLOv2 and YOLO9000 to improve the accuracy of target location and feature extraction capability [28]. In 2018, YOLOv3 continued to launch the context information module and feature pyramid network, and proposed a new basic network Darknet [29]. So far, YOLO algorithms and YOLO-like algorithms have been updated endlessly. In 2023, Ultralytics Company proposed a SOTA model named YOLOv8, which replaced the C3 structure of YOLOv5 with C2f structure, and proposed a new backbone network and a new loss function [30]. Although the performance of these models has been significantly improved under the efforts of many researchers, there is always a path that relies on the complexity of volume networks and more expensive hardware costs to complete the deployment, which will lead to the application of the model is increasingly impractical. In 2019, J. Miranda et al. utilized several cameras and deep learning to classify defects in images of aircraft fuselages [31]. In 2024, O'Gorman, D et al. validated the classification and recognition of rivet states using YOLOv8 on a small, unpublished micro dataset [32]. However, the size of this dataset is insufficient to validate the quality of the model.

3 Methods

The Fast Rive Detection Algorithm is a robust and rapid identification algorithm specifically designed for rivet recognition. It consists of the VanillaNet network, Bi-FPN, and a three-channel detection head called FRAhead. This section will provide a detailed explanation of its components and principles, with the specific network architecture illustrated in Fig. 1.

3.1 The Minimalist VanillaNet Network

VanillaNet is a deep learning neural network architecture that emphasizes minimalism. Unlike the trend in the past few decades of enhancing model performance by increasing network complexity, VanillaNet adopts a carefully designed simple yet powerful framework. It avoids high depth, shortcuts, and complex operations such as self-attention by pruning nonlinear activation functions after training to restore the original architecture, thereby overcoming the challenges posed by network complexity.

Taking the six-layer structure of Vanillanet used in this article as an example, as shown in Fig. 2, the initial part of the network employs a convolutional layer with a size of 4×4, a depth of 3 (corresponding to the number of input image channels), and C (a user-defined number of output channels), with a stride set to 4. The network then progressively deepens and expands its feature extraction capability through three stages (Stage 1, 2, and 3). In each stage, a max pooling layer with a stride of 2 is applied, which not only reduces the spatial dimensions of the feature maps but also lowers the computational load by retaining significant features. Additionally, to enhance the feature

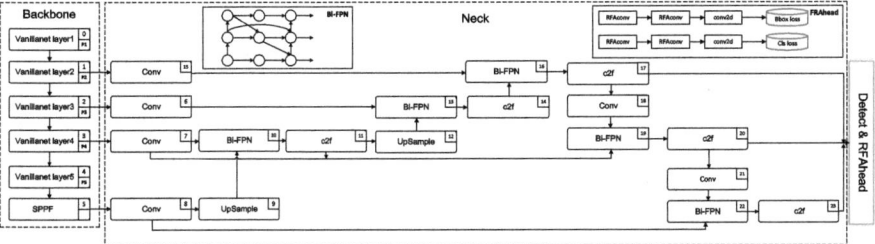

Fig. 1. The framework of the Fast Rivet Detection Algorithm

representation capability of the network, the number of channels in the feature maps is doubled after each stage, meaning that the number of channels increases to twice that of the previous stage after each stage. In Stage 4, unlike the previous stages, the number of channels in the feature maps is no longer increased; instead, an average pooling layer is utilized. This average pooling layer further reduces the spatial dimensions of the feature maps while smoothing the feature responses, preparing for subsequent classification tasks. Finally, the network concludes with a fully connected layer, which maps the high-level features extracted from the previous stages to the final classification results. This layer is responsible for classifying the input image based on the learned feature representations and outputs the predicted probabilities for each category.

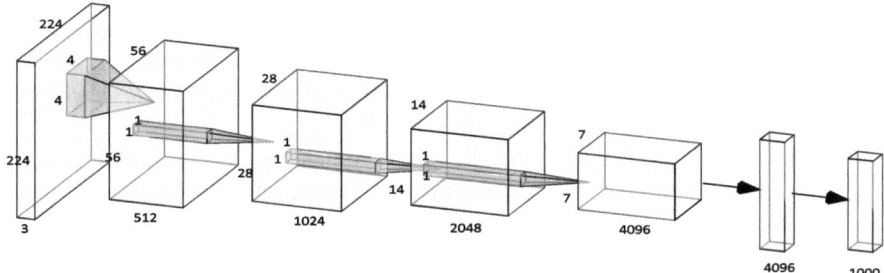

Fig. 2. The framework of the Vanillane

3.2 Bidirectional Feature Pyramid Network (Bi-FPN)

The Bi-FPN was proposed by the Google Brain research team, as part of the new architecture EfficientDet, specifically appearing in the neck section. The core idea of Bi-FPN is structural feature fusion, which involves performing feature fusion simultaneously along both top-down and bottom-up paths. This structural feature fusion allows for better integration of feature maps from different images, enhancing the network's capability to express multi-scale information.

The feature fusion module in Bi-FPN includes several key operations:

- Feature Fusion: Different scale feature maps are fused through a weighted summation approach. Bidirectional fusion allows feature maps to complement each other in different directions.

- Feature Balancing: This involves balancing the feature maps of different scales to ensure that each scale contributes reasonably to the final fusion result.
- Feature Transformation: Convolution operations are applied to the feature maps to adjust the number of channels and spatial dimensions, ensuring that the fused feature maps are suitable for subsequent processing.

Based on these concepts, this paper proposes a Bi-FPN network structure suitable for Ultralytics, as shown in Fig. 2. By modifying the yaml file, it now supports three detection heads. Although Bi-FPN was not specifically designed for lightweight applications, its bidirectional feature pyramid network structure effectively addresses issues such as information bottlenecks and feature distortion present in feature pyramid networks through adaptive feature fusion and selection. This efficient feature fusion approach can reduce unnecessary feature redundancy, thereby indirectly decreasing computational load while maintaining or improving detection accuracy.

3.3 The Receptive-Field Attention Detection Head

The detection head in object detection models with architectures similar to YOLO refers to the part of the network responsible for generating detection results. It handles object classification, localization, and bounding box regression simultaneously during image processing. The RFA (Receptive-Field Attention) convolution can be regarded as a lightweight, plug-and-play module that integrates a receptive-field attention mechanism into the convolutional layer. This mechanism provides an effective weighting to the convolution kernels by comprehensively considering the spatial features within the receptive field and the importance of each feature, addressing the issue of shared parameters in convolution kernels. It is designed to improve the model's performance with almost negligible computational cost and parameter increments.

To better understand the concept of the receptive field, as illustrated in Fig. 4, take a 3 × 3 convolution kernel as an example. Spatial Feature refers to the original feature map. The Receptive-Field Spatial Feature is a feature map derived from spatial features, represented by a set of non-overlapping sliding windows. Each 3 × 3 window in the Receptive-Field Spatial Feature represents a receptive-field slider (Fig. 3).

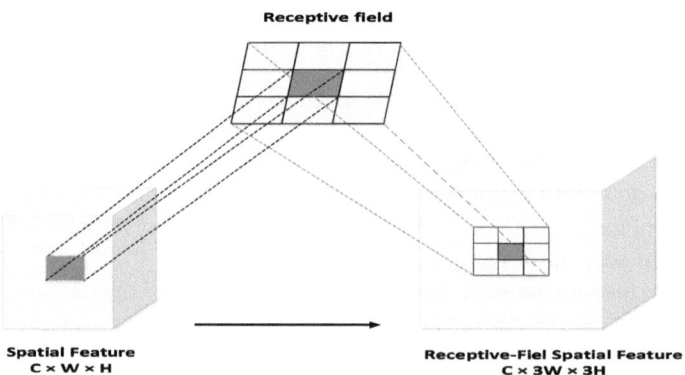

Fig. 3. The receptive-field spatial features are obtained by transforming the spatial features.

According to convention, this paper uses softmax to represent the importance of each spatial feature within the receptive field, as shown in the following formula:

$$F = softmax\left(g^{i \times i}(AugPool(X))\right) \times ReLU\left(Norm\left(g^{k \times k}(X)\right)\right) = A_{rf} \times F_{rf} \quad (1)$$

Here, $g^{i \times i}$ represents the grouping convolution of the size of i, k represents the size of the convolution kernel, Norm represents normalization, X represents the input feature map, and F is obtained by multiplying the attention graph A_{rf} with the transformed receiving field space feature F_{rf}. RFA convolution can solve the problem that standard convolution is insensitive to the shared parameter information caused by the change of detection position by emphasizing the importance of different features in the receptive field slider, thus bringing good benefits.

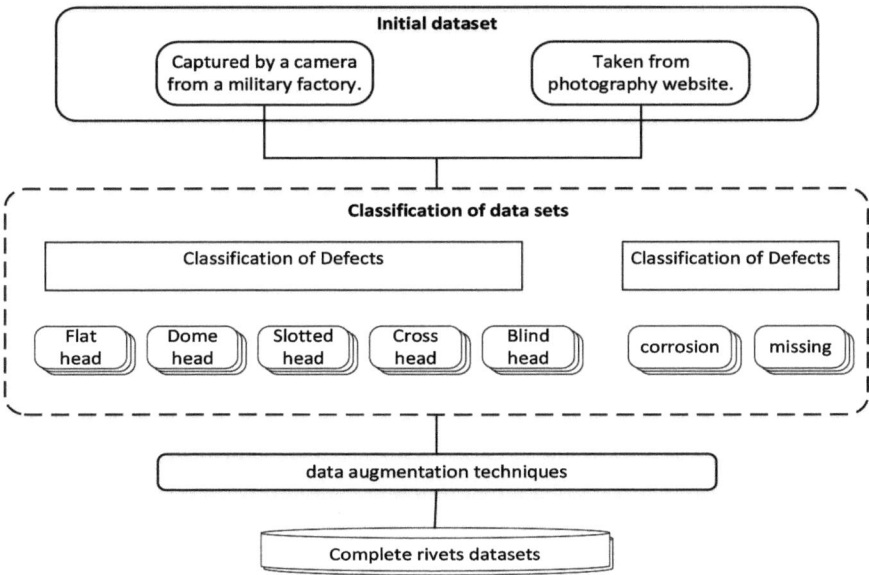

Fig. 4. The framework of the data set

4 Datasets

As a deep learning-based rivet recognition algorithm, the dataset is a crucial component of the model training process. Currently, there is no publicly available dataset suitable for industrial-grade detection of rivets on aircraft skin. This is evident in several ways: the relevant datasets are too small; the images are blurry with unclear details; and there is a lack of theoretical research on the states of rivets during the flight of the aircraft.

We conducted a classification study on different states of rivets, creating a large dataset comprising five types of rivets: slottedhead rivets, flathead rivets, domehead rivets, crosshead rivets, and blindhead rivets, along with two defect categories: rivet loss and rivet corrosion. In total, the dataset contains 10,745 images. This section introduces how to establish such an applicable industrial-grade dataset, including the sources of the dataset, the classification research based on the states of aircraft rivets, and the image enhancement techniques used. The specific framework is illustrated in Fig. 4. The dataset is currently open-sourced at https://github.com/skyjuntian/rivet-dataset.

4.1 Establishment and Classification of the Dataset

The initial dataset primarily consists of two parts: real-life images taken at aircraft manufacturing plants and collections from well-known photography websites. Rivets, as the most used fasteners on aircraft, include five general types: slottedhead rivets, flathead rivets, domehead rivets, crosshead rivets, and blindhead rivets. Extreme events leading to rivet deformation mainly stem from environmental corrosion and rivet loosening, which can result in rivet loss.

During the collection of the initial dataset, careful attention was paid to various factors such as angle, distance, lighting, and weather to ensure the dataset's diversity. For this purpose, we utilized a camera module equipped with a Sony IMX800 sensor, which features an aperture of f/1.6 and a 50-megapixel optical sensor. Combined with materials collected online, we developed an initial dataset that includes classifications for the five types of rivets and two defect categories: rivet loss and rivet corrosion. The initial dataset comprises a total of 1,535 images.

4.2 Data Augmentation

Data augmentation is a technique that expands a dataset by transforming or processing existing data to generate new samples, which helps improve the performance and generalization ability of machine learning models. To make this model more suitable for real-world application scenarios, we applied data augmentation techniques to the dataset. This included common methods such as horizontal rotation, inversion, and random noise generation, as well as more novel approaches like randomly generating rectangular occlusions and simulating motion blur caused by camera movement.

When objects in a scene move, the imagery of that scene will inevitably capture the complete combination of all positions of those objects during the exposure time (which depends on the shutter speed) and the perspective of the camera. In such scenarios, any object moving in the direction relative to the camera will appear blurred or shaken; this phenomenon of blur caused by object motion is called motion blur. If we only consider using the simplest hardware for detection tasks, the effect of motion blur will certainly permeate the entire detection process. To mitigate the negative impact of this phenomenon on model performance, we introduced blur into the training data. This aims to help the model learn to better handle motion blur situations, thereby enhancing its recognition and generalization capabilities in dynamic scenes.

The mathematical model is as follows: Suppose there is a moving object with a velocity v and a direction of motion θ (relative to the camera's direction of motion). Over a time t interval, the object moves from position (x, y) to position $(x + cosvt(\theta), y + cosvt(\theta)$. The motion blur present in the captured image can be represented by Eq. 2.

$$B(x, y) = \int_0^T (I(x - cosvt(\theta), y - sinvt(\theta))dt \qquad (2)$$

In this model, the blur kernel $B(x, y)$ function represents the dynamic blur effect applied to the image I at the position (x, y). It is the accumulated result of the pixel values of the input image I at position $(x - cosvt(\theta), y - sinvt(\theta))$ over the time t interval. During the training of this model, we selected a 15×15 kernel to perform a weighted average on the input image at an angle of 45 or -45 degrees (randomly chosen) along the direction θ, thereby producing the effect of motion blur. Through these data augmentation techniques, we expanded the initial dataset of 1,535 images to a total of 10,745 images, with specific classification details shown in Table 1.

Table 1. Results of classification of rivets

	Flathead	Slotted head	Missing	Dome head	Cross head	Blind head	Corrosion	Total
Train	510	450	345	4035	835	440	1395	7675
Test	204	180	138	1614	334	176	558	3070
total	714	630	483	5649	1169	616	1953	10745

5 Experiment

5.1 Model Evaluation

To comprehensively evaluate the network performance of the fast rivet recognition algorithm, this experiment employed the following six evaluation metrics to describe the model's performance during training: p (Precision), r (Recall), mAP (Mean Average Precision), $mAP_{0.5-0.95}$ (Average Precision with a threshold between 0.5 and 0.95), T_{tarin} (training duration), and FPS frame count.

Calculation of Metrics Related to Model Recognition Accuracy

p, r, mAP are conventional metrics for evaluating model detection performance. p refers to the proportion of true positive samples among the predicted positive samples, reflecting the accuracy of the model predictions—how many of the predicted positives are actual positives. r refers to the proportion of predicted positive samples among the actual positive samples, reflecting the comprehensiveness of the model's target detection—how many actual positives the model can identify. Mean Average Precision (mAP) is the average of the precision across multiple categories and is a crucial metric used in this experiment to evaluate model detection performance. It combines precision and recall and provides a comprehensive assessment of the model's performance in multi-category target detection tasks. Below are the formulas for these metrics.

$$p = \frac{T_P}{T_P + F_P} \quad (3)$$

$$r = \frac{T_P}{T_P + F_N} \quad (4)$$

$$AP = \int_0^1 p(r)dr \tag{5}$$

$$mAP = \frac{1}{n}\sum_{k=1}^{n} AP_k \tag{6}$$

AP estimates the average precision value for recall values ranging from 0 to1. P(r) represents the precision-recall curve, and n denotes the type of rivet. AP_k is the average precision for the k-th class. IOU is a commonly used metric for evaluating the localization accuracy of object detectors, calculated as the intersection area divided by the union area (between the predicted and ground truth bounding boxes). mAP refers to the mean average precision across IOU thresholds ranging from 0.5 to 0.95.

Calculation of Metrics for Evaluating Model Detection Speed
FPS is a commonly used metric when evaluating model detection speed. It refers to the number of images that can be detected per second. In the film industry, the standard 24 frames per second (fps) is often used to shoot films. At this frame rate, the human eye perceives a continuous and smooth sequence of images. With films shot at 24 fps, each frame has an exposure time of 0.042 s, which captures all changes within one second. If the frame rate is lower than this, human vision will notice a distinct "stuttering" effect. The fast rivet recognition algorithm aims to achieve a response time that exceeds human visual standards, making frame rate a key evaluation metric. The higher the frame rate, the smoother the perception for the human eye, and the faster and more efficient the computer is at recognizing images. The following is the formula for calculating FPS in this model.

$$FPS = \frac{1}{S} \tag{7}$$

$$S = S_{\text{Preprocess}} + S_{\text{Inference}} + S_{\text{Postprocess}} \tag{8}$$

In the above, S represents the time required for the model to detect a single image. It is the algebraic sum of three components: the time required in the preprocessing phase to convert the raw image into a format acceptable by the model, the time in the inference phase for the model to process the input data and generate detection results, and the time in the post-processing phase to convert the model's output (such as bounding boxes, confidence scores, etc.) into final interpretable results (such as marking objects on the image).

5.2 Experimental Environment and Setup

The model was trained on a computer equipped with an i5-11400H CPU and a GeForce RTX 3060Ti GPU, and tested on a Windows 10 operating system. The experimental environment was set up with Pytorch 1.12.1 and CUDA 11.6. After fine-tuning, the batch size was set to 4, and the training was conducted for 100 epochs. The input image size was 640 × 640, and the network took approximately 23 h to complete the training for all 100 epochs.

5.3 Ablation Study

To verify the optimization effects of various modules in the fast rivet recognition algorithm, we chose YOLOv8 from the Ultralytics framework as the baseline to compare the overall performance, detection speed, and recognition ability of each category between the two. Experiments show that the fast rivet recognition algorithm outperforms the baseline in the vast majority of metrics.

A Comparison of Accuracy and Duration Under Ablation Experiments

To demonstrate the necessity of each module in the fast rivet recognition algorithm, we take YOLOv8 from the Ultralytics framework as the baseline and gradually add and modify modules, observing the changes in model performance. Table 2 clearly shows that every module of the fast rivet recognition algorithm significantly improves the baseline. After modifying the Vanillanet backbone, the model's mAP increased by 2.6%, and $mAP_{0.5-0.95}$ improved by 3%. Subsequently, after modifying the BI-FPN module and the RFA detection head, compared to the baseline, the model's mAP improved by 5.4% and 6.7%, respectively. At the same time, the total training time of the model was reduced by 50.1%, significantly lowering the training cost shown in Fig. 5, this is the convergence result of the model's loss function and various network parameters over 100 epochs. It can be observed that around epoch 90, the model converges to a satisfactory outcome.

Table 2. Parameter evaluation of the model under ablation experiments

	mAP	p	r	$mAP_{0.5-0.95}$	T_{train}
Yolov8	0.855	0.958	0.733	0.728	49.95h
Vanillanet	0.881	0.827	0.841	0.758	22.80h
Vanillanet&BIFPN	0.909	0.965	0.819	0.813	22.39h
Vanillaet&BIFPN&RFA	0.922	0.958	0.853	0.821	24.91h

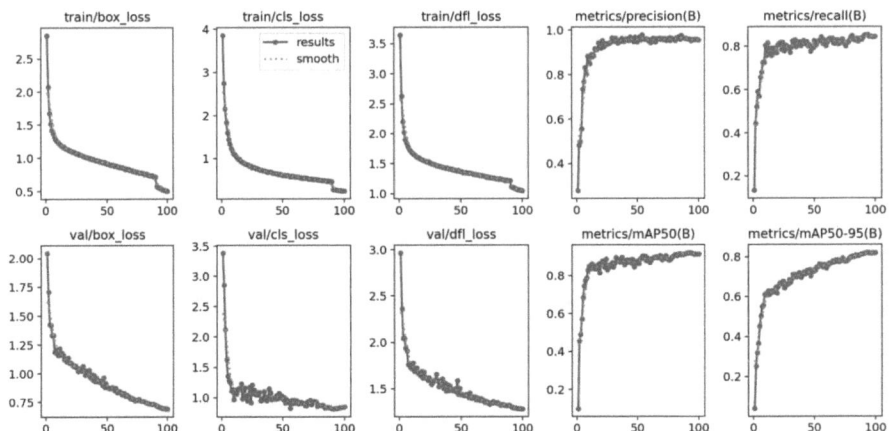

Fig. 5. Distribution of loss recall and precision mAP during training

A Comparison of Detection Rates Under Ablation Experiments

FPS is the most intuitive metric for measuring the detection speed of a model. For an image recognition model to visually achieve the smooth standard of dynamic objects perceptible to humans, it must reach at least 24 fps. As shown in Table 3, the original baseline performed poorly in terms of frame rate. Vanillanet's minimalist yet powerful network structure brought a significant improvement in the model's detection speed, reducing the time to recognize a single image by 25.5 ms. The efficient feature fusion scheme of Bi-FPN further reduced the model's inference time, cutting it by an additional 3.9 ms. The FRA detection head, being more diverse and complex compared to the original standard convolutional detection head, caused a slight increase in inference time. All the above results align with the hypotheses based on the model's principles. Overall, the final model reduced the time compared to the baseline by 27.6 ms and increased FPS by 126%.

Table 3. A comparison of detection rates under ablation experiments.

	$S_{Preprocess}$	$S_{Inference}$	$S_{Postprocess}$	S (ms)	FPS (fps)
Yolov8	0.855	0.958	0.733	0.728	49.95h
Vanillanet	0.881	0.827	0.841	0.758	22.80h
Vanillanet&BIFPN	0.909	0.965	0.819	0.813	22.39h
Vanillaet&BIFPN&RFA	0.922	0.958	0.853	0.821	24.91h

A Comparison of Detection Capabilities Across Different Rivet Categories

Table 4 shows that, compared to the baseline, the model's recognition ability in each category is significantly better, with the vast majority of categories achieving over 91%. Notably, for the worst-performing flat-head rivets, the model improved by 15.7% over the baseline. For dome-head rivets, which also had relatively weaker detection performance, the model still showed a 2.3% improvement. The weaker recognition of dome-head rivets may be related to the model's distance judgment of the detection target. In the next step, we will focus on the extraction of depth-of-field features.

Table 4. A comparison of different rivet categories under ablation experiments.

	Flathead	Slotedhead	Missing	Domehead	Cross head	Blind head	Corrosion
Yolov8	0.779	0.874	0.906	0.828	0.858	0.89	0.869
Vanillanet	0.953	0.913	0.889	0.841	0.889	0.839	0.845
Vanillanet&BIFPN	0.839	0.958	0.924	0.856	0.931	0.925	0.932
Vanillanet&BIFPN&RFA	0.936	0.965	0.925	0.851	0.927	0.913	0.938

6 Conclusion

This paper proposes a fast rivet recognition algorithm based on the VanillaNet network and computer vision, characterized by efficiency, precision, and low resource consumption. Through an innovative network architecture, it successfully achieves fast and accurate identification of rivets on aircraft skin, offering a new solution for automated inspection in the aerospace manufacturing industry. In this study, the minimalist VanillaNet network is used to replace the backbone in the Ultralytics framework to reduce model complexity and enhance detection efficiency. Additionally, Bi-FPN and the FRA detection head were utilized to improve the model's robustness and sampling capability, further boosting its performance. Experiments show that the model performs exceptionally well in detecting various types of rivets and defects. Compared to the baseline model, the fast rivet recognition algorithm achieved improvements in precision, recall, and average accuracy, with a 126% increase in detection speed and a 6.7% improvement in mAP. Future work could further optimize the model's structure, enhancing its ability to extract features such as depth of field to better adapt to more complex detection scenarios.

Acknowledgments. This work was supported in part by the National Natural Science Foundation of China under Grant No. 62072159 and No. 61902112, the Science and Technology Research Project of Henan province under Grant No. 222102210011 and No. 232102211061.

References

1. Tsinghua University Institute for Internet Industry. https://www.iii.tsinghua.edu.cn/info/1165/3947.htm. Accessed 21 Nov 2023
2. China Commercial Aircraft Market Forecast Annual Report (2022–2041). http://www.comac.cc/fujian/2022-2041nianbao_cn.pdf. Accessed 9 May 2024
3. Fan, Y.: Overview of aircraft digital assembly technology—a revolutionary change in aircraft manufacturing. Aviat. Manuf. Technol. (10), 42–48 (2016)
4. Wang, F., Hei, D., Zhao, S.: Research on fastener connection design based on aircraft structure assembly. Sci. Technol. Inf. **17**(22), 65–66 (2019)
5. Zhuang, Z.: Research on rivet detection and delivery technology based on robot vision. Nanjing Univ. Aeronaut. Astronaut. (2023)
6. Meng, D., Boer, W.U., Juan, X.U., et al.: Visual inspection of aircraft skin: automated pixel-level defect detection by instance segmentation. Chin. J. Aeronaut. **35**(10), 254–264 (2022)
7. Du, Z., Yao, Y., Wang, J.: Research status and development trends of robotic drilling and riveting systems. Aviat. Manufact. Technol. (04), 26–31 (2015)
8. Xie, Q., Lu, D., Du, K., et al.: RRCNet: Rivet Region Classification Network for rivet flush measurement based on 3-D point cloud. IEEE Transactions on Instrumentation and Measurement, vol. 70, pp. 1–12. IEEE, New York (2021)
9. Xie, Q., Lu, D., Du, K., et al.: Aircraft skin rivet detection based on 3D point cloud via multiple structures fitting. Comput. Aided Des. **120**, 102805 (2020)
10. Huang, L., Huang, X.: Research on aircraft skin rivet detection technology based on the normal vector-density clustering algorithm. Rev. Sci. Instrum. **95**(3), 035112 (2024)
11. Shao, Y., Meng, T., Yu, K., et al.: Automatic detection and imaging of rivet hole defects for aircraft structures with optimized sensor array using eddy current method and image analysis. IEEE Sens. J. **23**(5), 4597–4606 (2022)

12. Uchanin, V.: Enhanced eddy current techniques for detection of surface-breaking cracks in aircraft structures. Trans. Aerosp. Res. **2021**(1), 1–14 (2021)
13. Krizhevsky, A., Sutskever, I., Hinton, G.E.: ImageNet classification with deep convolutional neural networks. Adv. Neural. Inf. Process. Syst. **25**, 84 (2012)
14. Chang, B., Wang, Y., Zhao, X., et al.: A general-purpose edge-feature guidance module to enhance vision transformers for plant disease identification. Expert Syst. Appl. **237**(Part C), 121638 (2024)
15. Yuan, P., Han, Z., Zhao, X.: Integrating the edge intelligence technology into image composition: a case study. Peer-to-Peer Netw. Appl. **16**(4), 1641–1651 (2023)
16. Yang, J.F., Jiang, G., Chen, J.F.: Research of riveting structure identification and characteristic parameter analysis based on SVM. Adv. Mater. Res. **1049**, 1554–1557 (2014)
17. Xiao, L., Wu, B., Hu, Y.: Missing small fastener detection using deep learning. IEEE Trans. Instrum. Meas. **70**, 1–9 (2016)
18. Ruiz, L., Torres, M., Gómez, A., et al.: Detection and classification of aircraft fixation elements during manufacturing processes using a convolutional neural network. Appl. Sci. **10**(19), 6856 (2020)
19. Zhang, F., Wu, T., Liu, S., et al.: Real-time defect detection of saw chains on automatic assembly lines based on residual networks and knowledge coding. Eng. Appl. Artif. Intell. **128**, 107507 (2024)
20. Li, H., Wang, C., Liu, Y.: YOLO-FDD: efficient defect detection network of aircraft skin fastener. SIViP **18**(4), 3197–3211 (2024)
21. Redmon, J., Divvala, S., Girshick, R., et al.: You only look once: unified, real-time object detection. In: Proceedings of the IEEE Conference on Computer Vision and Pattern Recognition, pp. 779–788. IEEE, New York (2016)
22. Li, G., Zhang, J., Wang, Y., Liu, C., et al.: Residual distillation: towards portable deep neural networks without shortcuts. Adv. Neural. Inf. Process. Syst. **33**, 8935–8946 (2020)
23. Yuan, P., Huang, R., Zhang, J., et al.: Accuracy rate maximization in edge federated learning with delay and energy constraints. IEEE Syst. J. **17**(2), 2053–2064 (2023)
24. Yuan, P., Huang, R.: Integrating the device-to-device communication technology into edge computing: a case study. Peer-to-Peer Netw. Appl. **14**(2), 599–608 (2021)
25. Chen, H., Wang, Y., Guo, J., et al.: VanillaNet: the power of minimalism in deep learning. Adv. Neural Inf. Process. Syst. **36** (2024)
26. Zhang, X., Liu, C., Yang, D., et al.: RFAConv: innovating spatial attention and standard convolutional operation. arXiv preprint arXiv:2304.03198 (2023)
27. Chen, C., Liu, MY., Tuzel, O., Xiao, J.: R-CNN for small object detection. In: Lai, SH., Lepetit, V., Nishino, K., Sato, Y. (eds.) Computer Vision – ACCV 2016. ACCV 2016. Lecture Notes in Computer Science, vol. 10115, pp. 214–230. Springer, Cham (2017). https://doi.org/10.1007/978-3-319-54193-8_14
28. Redmon, J., Farhadi, A.: Yolo9000: better, faster, stronger. In: Proceedings of the IEEE Conference on Computer Vision and Pattern Recognition, pp. 7263–7271. IEEE, New York (2017)
29. Redmon, J., Farhadi, A.: Yolov3: an incremental improvement. arXiv preprint arXiv:1804.02767 (2018)
30. Howard, A., Sandler, M., Chu, G., et al.: Searching for MobileNetV3. In: Proceedings of the IEEE/CVF International Conference on Computer Vision, pp. 1314–1324. IEEE, New York (2019)
31. Miranda, J., Veith, J., Larnier, S., et al.: Machine learning approaches for defect classification on aircraft fuselage images acquired by a UAV. In: Proceedings of the SPIE, vol. 11172, pp. 49–56. SPIE, France (2019)
32. O'Gorman, D., Tobin, E.F.: Deep-learning-based defect detection for light aircraft with unmanned aircraft systems. IEEE Access **12**, 83876–83886 (2024)

A Cepstral Domain Radio Frequency Fingerprint Extraction Method for LTE-V2X

Ying Chen[1](✉), Aiqun Hu[2], and Yang Yang[3]

[1] School of Cyberspace Security, Southeast University, Nanjing, China
220224738@seu.edu.cn
[2] Purple Mountain Laboratories, School of Information Science and Engineering, Southeast University, Nanjing, China
aqhu@edu.cn
[3] Purple Mountain Laboratories, Nanjing, China

Abstract. Long-Term Evolution Vehicle-to-Everything (LTE-V2X) is a comprehensive communication solution tailored for vehicle-road collaboration to fulfill the diverse requirements of the Internet of Vehicles. To bolster the security performance of LTE-V2X, the hardware characteristics of transmitters, known as radio frequency (RF) fingerprints, can serve as unique identity IDs for LTE-V2X device authentication. In this paper, we present a scheme to extract RF fingerprints by recovered standard Demodulation Reference Signal (DMRS) sequences from received LTE-V2X signals. Building upon this, we propose a cepstrum domain cross-correlation method to enhance the fingerprint features and mitigate the impact of the channel on RF fingerprints. Subsequently, we select 10 On-Board Units (OBUs) to collect LTE signals in three scenarios (device direct connection scene, moving scene, and stationary scene) for experimentation. Results reveal that the recognition accuracy can achieve 94.3% at a signal-to-noise ratio (SNR) of 25dB and improves from 76.4% to 80.9% in the fingerprint cross-test of moving and stationary scenes after channel suppression.

Keywords: LTE-V2X · Cepstral Domain · RF Fingerprinting · Feature Enhancement

1 Introduction

Long-Term Evolution Vehicle-to-Everything (LTE-V2X), specifically designed for collaborative interactions between vehicles and the road infrastructure, offers capabilities for low-latency, high-reliability, high-speed, and secure communication in dynamic vehicular environments, catering to diverse applications within the Internet of Vehicles [1]. Despite these advantages, the inherent openness of

---

Supported by the National Natural Science Foundation of China under Grant 62171120.

wireless networks and the broadcast nature of wireless channels expose LTE-V2X to various security challenges, with spoofing attacks posing a particularly significant threat. Spoofing attacks occur when an adversary impersonates legitimate devices by falsifying their identity, which can lead to unauthorized access, disruption of services, or malicious interference in vehicular communication systems. To address these concerns, researchers have delved into the study and analysis of hardware circuit characteristics at the physical layer. They have recognized the unique hardware features of devices, defining them as a distinctive identity known as the "radio frequency fingerprint (RFF)".

The physical basis of RF fingerprinting lies in the deviation between the actual and nominal values of electronic devices [2], resulting in distinctions among transmitters using identical electronic components and establishing individual characteristics. Extracted features from device-emitted signals serve as unique identifiers for device identity, enabling accurate differentiation between emissions from different sources [3]. This capability is beneficial for addressing security concerns related to identity authentication. Prevalent RF fingerprint extraction methods can be mainly categorized into two types: one is feature extraction based on signal parameters [4–15], and the other is feature extraction based on signal transformation domain [16–20].

Despite these methods, there is a lack of research on RF fingerprint extraction for LTE-V2X, particularly in separating channel and fingerprint during air signal extraction. In this study, we introduce an innovative method for extracting RF fingerprints in LTE-V2X using standard demodulation reference signal (DMRS) sequences in the cepstral domain. Our method leverages cross-correlation to mitigate channel characteristic interference within the fingerprints. We experimentally evaluate the method in both the line-of-sight (LOS) dynamic scenario and the non-line-of-sight (NLOS) stationary scenario. The main contributions of our work can be outlined as follows:

- We propose a RF fingerprint extraction method utilizing DMRS sequences in the cepstrum domain.
- We enhance fingerprint features and mitigate channel characteristic interference within the fingerprints by applying cross-correlation.
- We gather datasets of Physical Sidelink Control Channel (PSCCH) and Physical Sidelink Shared Channel (PSSCH) across diverse scenarios and conduct extensive experiments in them to assess the effectiveness of the RF fingerprint extraction and channel suppression schemes.

2 A RF Fingerprint Technology for LTE-V2X

We utilized the Universal Software Radio Peripheral (USRP) to receive signals transmitted by the OBU. Figure 1 illustrates the main workflow of our work, where $DMRS_{tx}$ represents the received DMRS sequence of PSCCH/PSSCH, $DMRS_{Rx}$ corresponds to the standard DMRS sequence, STO denotes the Sampling Timing Offset and Channel State Information (CSI) represents the response of the channel state information.

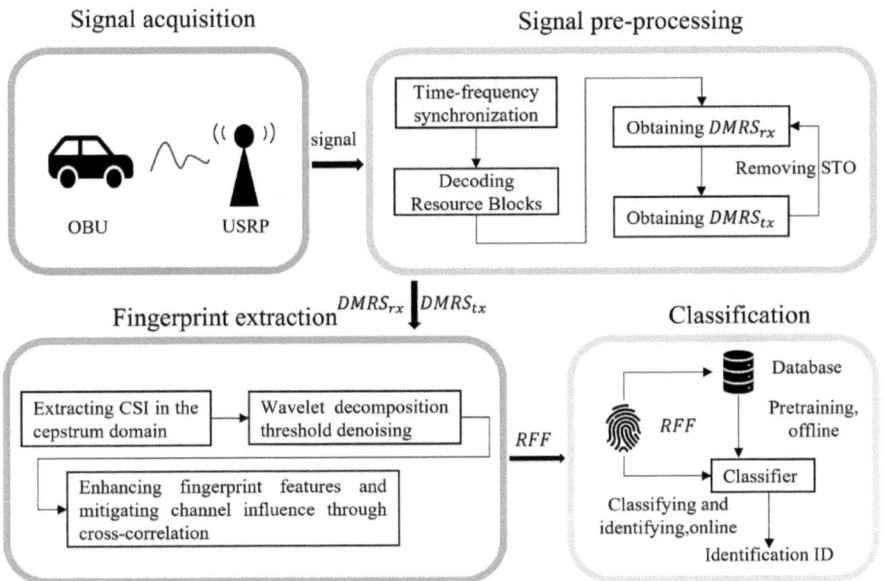

Fig. 1. The process of fingerprint extraction and identification for LTE-V2X.

2.1 Overview of LTE-V2X Direct Communication Signals

LTE-V technology operates in two modes: cellular mode (LTE-V-cell) and pass-through mode (LTE-V-direct), with the pass-through mode being the primary communication mode for LTE-V2X. The sidelink comprises three physical channels: PSSCH, PSCCH, and the Physical Sidelink Broadcast Channel (PSBCH). The PSSCH and PSSCH are transmitted in the same subframe, and they can be adjacent or non-adjacent in the frequency domain, with variable transmission intervals. The PSBCH signal occupies 72 subcarriers at the center of the sidelink bandwidth and has a fixed transmission interval of 160 ms. In practical applications, considering that multiple devices may access LTE-V2X simultaneously, using the PSBCH signal for fingerprint extraction for verification purposes takes longer due to its longer transmission intervals. Therefore, this paper chooses the PSCCH/PSSCH signals, which have more transmission frames and shorter transmission intervals, for RF fingerprint extraction.

2.2 RF Fingerprint Extraction Using DMRS Sequences

DMRS Sequences. The PSCCH is used to indicate the transmission information of the associated PSSCH, including the frequency-domain resource location and modulation mode. The PSCCH is transmitted in the same subframe as the associated PSSCH via frequency division multiplexing. Figure 2 illustrates the frame structure of PSCCH/PSSCH. A subframe consists of 14 SC-FDMA symbols, with the last symbol serving as a guard interval without data transmission.

Both PSCCH and PSSCH subframes contain four demodulation reference signals (DMRS) located at the same positions in the time domain, occupying the 3rd, 9th, 9th, and 12th symbols of the subframe.

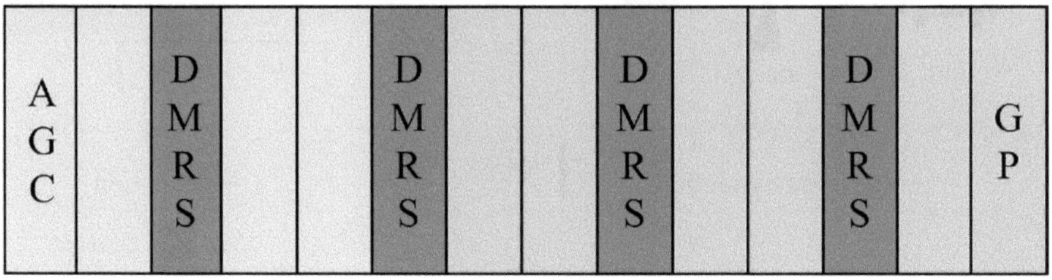

Fig. 2. Distribution of symbols in PSCCH/PSSCH subframes.

In LTE-V2X, the DMRS sequence is a form of Zero Correlation Zone (ZC) sequence characterized by a constant envelope with an amplitude of 1. The conveying of effective information is achieved through phase modulation.

Radio Frequency Fingerprint Extraction Method. Following the depicted preprocessing steps of the received signal (subframe) in Fig. 1, we can derive $DMRS_{rx}$ from the recived $DMRS_{rx}$, and the details are not discussed here. STO in Orthogonal Frequency Division Multiplexing (OFDM) systems occurs due to the misalignment between the receiver's symbol timing and the actual start of the OFDM symbols in the transmitted signal [21]. An STO with δ in the time domain causes a phase shift in the k-th subcarrier $k2\pi\delta/L$ in the frequency domain, where L is the number of sampling points. After obtaining $DMRS_{tx}$, the phase offset between $DMRS_{rx}$ and the standard sequence is calculated. As depicted in Fig. 3, a linear relationship exists between the phase offset and subcarrier position due to the STO.

Conducting a first-order polynomial fitting yields the STO values for each subcarrier, represented as $B = b_1, b_2, ..., b_N$. This process facilitates the elimination of the STO from the $DMRS_{rx}$ sequence:

$$DMRS_{rx} = DMRS_{rx} \cdot exp(B \cdot (-1j)) \quad (1)$$

The frequency domain relationship between $DMRS_{rx}$ and $DMRS_{tx}$ can be expressed as:

$$DMRS_{rx} = DMRS_{tx} \cdot RFF \cdot H + N \quad (2)$$

where H is the channel response and N is the noise. CSI can be represented as $CSI = RFF \cdot H$, then:

$$DMRS_{rx} = DMRS_{tx} \cdot CSI + N \quad (3)$$

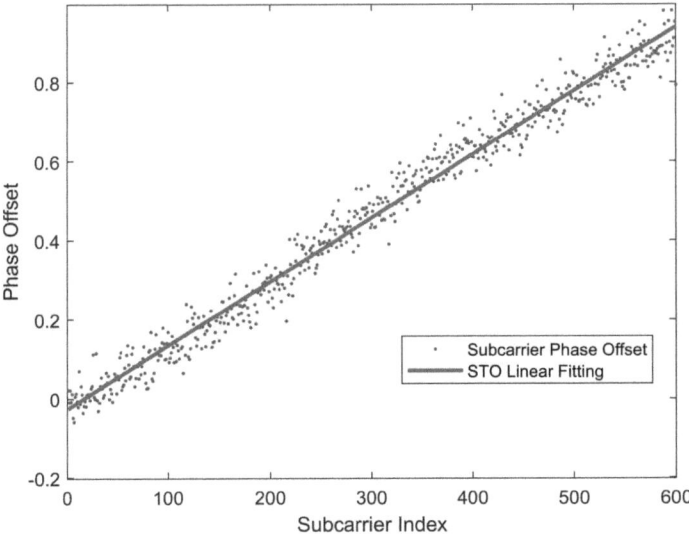

Fig. 3. Subcarrier phase deviation and linear fitting.

In the cepstral domain, the relationship is expressed as follows:

$$\log(DMRS_{rx}) = \log(DMRS_{tx}) + \log(CSI) + \log\left(\frac{N}{1 + DMRS_{tx} \cdot CSI}\right) \quad (4)$$

By rearranging Eq. 4, we derive:

$$\log(CSI) + \log\left(\frac{N}{1 + DMRS_{tx} \cdot CSI}\right) = \log(DMRS_{rx}) - \log(DMRS_{tx}) \quad (5)$$

where $\log\left(\frac{N}{1+DMRS_{tx} \cdot CSI}\right)$ represents the high-frequency component caused by noise, which can be removed using wavelet decomposition with soft thresholding, as illustrated in Fig. 4.

As per Eq. 5, $\log(CSI)$ is calculated for the four DMRS symbols in each subframe. The channel responses of different DMRS symbols within the same subframe exhibit a notable similarity. Hence, the average of $\log(CSI)$ obtained from the four DMRS symbols can serve as the extracted feature of the frame, and it facilitates the subsequent removal of residual random noise.

2.3 Fingerprint Enhancement Method in the Cepstrum Domain

In the cepstral domain, the relationship for the received wireless signal is expressed as:

$$\log(CSI) = \log(RFF) + \log(H) \quad (6)$$

This suggests an additive relationship between the RF fingerprint and the channel response characteristics. If the device and receiver are directly connected,

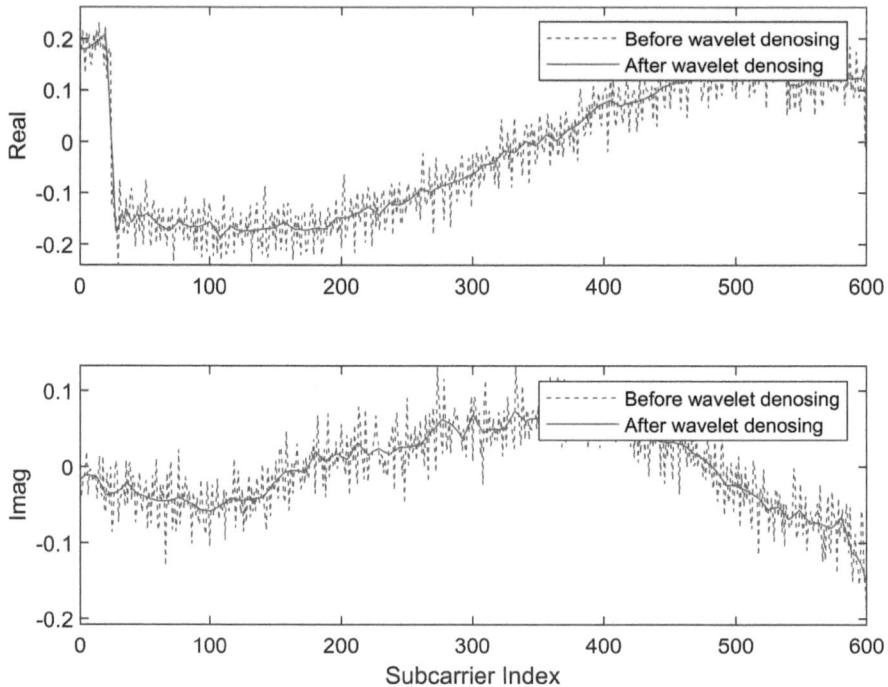

Fig. 4. CSI with high-frequency noise removed in the cepstral domain.

the transmitted signal does not pass through the air channel. In the cepstrum domain, the relationship is described as:

$$\log(CSI_{dl}) + \log\left(\frac{N}{1 + DMRS_{tx} \cdot CSI_{dl}}\right) = \log(DMRS_{rx}) - \log(DMRS_{tx}) \tag{7}$$

where CSI_{dl} represents the fingerprint and physical channel carried in the signal. We continue to employ wavelet decomposition to eliminate high-frequency noise. Due to the absence of interference from the air channel in this scenario, we can approximate the relationship between the resulting CSI_{dl} and the RFF obtained from the airborne signal as follows:

$$\log(RFF) \approx \log(CSI_{dl}) \tag{8}$$

Cross-correlation is a metric used to quantify the similarity between two signals. For two sequences $p(n)$ and $q(n)$, the cross-correlation $R_{p,q}(m)$ can be computed as:

$$R_{p,q}(m) = \sum_{n=-\infty}^{\infty} p(n)\, q(n-m) \tag{9}$$

where m is the value of the lag, which indicates how many units have been swiped to the right in $q(n)$. Let xcorr(p, q) be the result of the cross-correlation between

$p(n)$ and $q(n)$. If the sequences are not correlated with each other, theoretically there is:
$$\text{xcorr}(p, q) = 0 \tag{10}$$

Let $r_1(n)$, $r_2(n)$ and $r_3(n)$ be uncorrelated sequences. $\text{xcorr}(r_1+r_2, r_1+r_3)$ can be expressed as:

$$\begin{aligned} R_{r_1+r_2,r_1+r_3}(m) &= \sum_{n=-\infty}^{\infty}(r_1(n)+r_2(n))(r_1(n-m)+r_3(n-m)) \\ &= \sum_{n=-\infty}^{\infty} r_1(n)r_1(n-m) + \sum_{n=-\infty}^{\infty} r_1(n)r_3(n-m) \\ &+ \sum_{n=-\infty}^{\infty} r_2(n)r_1(n-m) + \sum_{n=-\infty}^{\infty} r_2(n)r_3(n-m) \\ &= R_{r_1,r_2}(m) + R_{r_1,r_3}(m) + R_{r_2,r_1}(m) + R_{r_2,r_3}(m) \end{aligned} \tag{11}$$

Since the length of the signal sequence acquired in reality is often limited, the calculated $\text{xcorr}(p, q)$ may not be zero even if the two sequences are not related. According to Eq. 15, we can further derive:

$$\text{xcorr}(r_1 + r_2, r_1 + r_3) = \text{xcorr}(r_1, r_1) + \text{xcorr}(r_1, r_2) + \text{xcorr}(r_2, r_1) + \text{xcorr}(r_2, r_3)$$
$$\approx \text{xcorr}(r_1, r_1) \tag{12}$$

In theory, the channel response and RF fingerprint are considered uncorrelated, and the RF fingerprints of different devices are also uncorrelated. Hence, it is plausible to consider suppressing the channel in $\log(RFF)$ using the cross-correlation method. Let the total number of connected devices be $device_{all}$, and denote the $\log CSI_{dl}$ and $\log CSI$ of device i as $\log CSI_{dl}^{i}$ and $\log CSI^{i}$ respectively. The final obtained RF fingerprint is denoted as rff_i. According to Eq. 16, it can be expressed as:

$$\begin{aligned} rff_i = \text{xcorr}\left(\sum_{k=1}^{device_{all}} \log CSI_{dl}^{k}, \log CSI^{i}\right) \\ = \text{xcorr}(\log CSI_{dl}^{i}, \log CSI_{dl}^{i} CSI^{i}) + other \end{aligned} \tag{13}$$

where $other$ is the cross-correlation result of independent RF fingerprints and channel responses, which accounts for a relatively small proportion of the rff_i. In the subsequent classification identification authentication, both the real part and the imaginary part of the rff_i are used together as features. Figure 5 illustrates the variations in fingerprints of different OBUs acquired under similar channel conditions, following cross-correlation processing.

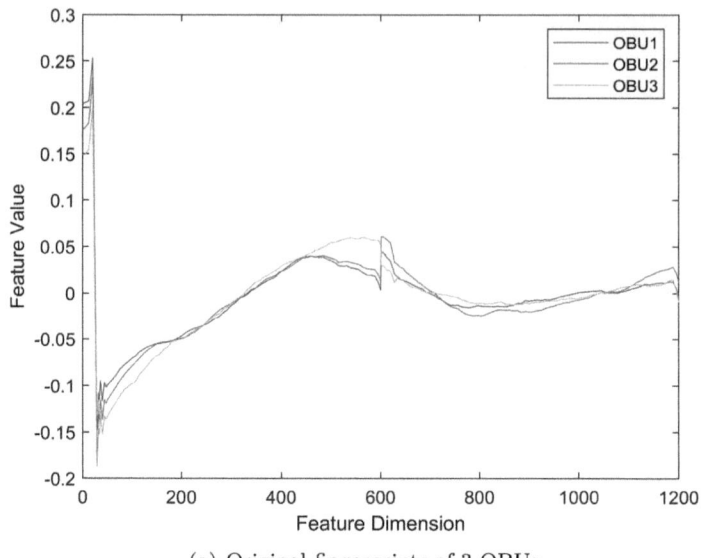

(a) Original fingerprints of 3 OBUs.

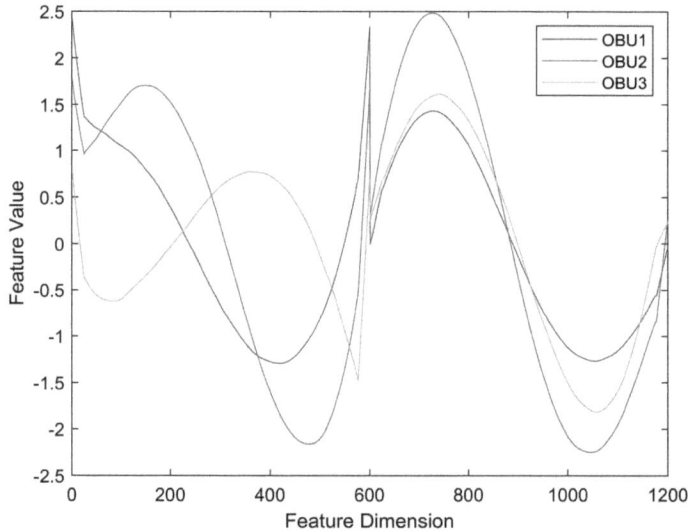

(b) Fingerprints of 3 OBUs calculated through cross-correlation.

Fig. 5. Comparison of fingerprints before and after cross-correlation of fingerprints

3 Experimental Testing and Result Analysis

3.1 Experimental Setup

We collected PSCCH/PSSCH data from 10 OBUs using a stationary USRP in a variety of scenarios, with each device transmitting data at a maximum bandwidth (10 MHz).

Table 1 illustrates the three scenarios evaluated in the study. In the Directly-connected scenario, the OBU is directly connected to the USRP without transmitting over the air channel. In the Stationary scenario, both the OBU and the USRP remain stationary indoors, separated by a wall. In the Moving scenario, the USRP is positioned on the roadside, while the OBU is mounted on a vehicle that moves back and forth along the road. We acquire 1000 PSCCH/PSSCH subframes across these scenarios for each OBU. The dataset is partitioned into training, validation, and test sets in a 3:1:1 ratio for the classification test.

Table 1. Experimental setup.

Scenarios	Distance from USRP	Description
Directly-connected	0 m	The signal frame is not transmitted over the air channel
Stationary	10 m	NLOS.
Moving	5-50 m	OBU moves at a speed of 30 km/h (LOS).

3.2 The Experimental Tests

In the direct connection setup, we evaluate the classification performance of fingerprints before and after applying wavelet denoising. The classification algorithms chosen for this assessment are cubic Support Vector Machine (SVM) and subspace discrimination. Figure 6 depicts the recognition accuracy of devices with and without denoising across different SNRs.

It is observed that the classification accuracy of RF fingerprints improves significantly after wavelet denoising compared to directly extracted fingerprints without denoising. The enhancement in fingerprint extraction accuracy is particularly notable at lower SNRs. This demonstrates that the wavelet denoising method exhibits a more pronounced noise reduction capability under low SNR conditions.

Subsequently, we conduct fingerprint extraction and classification on the gathered PSCCH/PSSCH data in both stationary and moving scenarios. The classifiers chosen for this analysis continue to be cubic SVM and subspace discriminant methods, with a maintained SNR level of approximately 35 dB. The average accuracy is presented in Table 2.

Table 2 demonstrates that in both stationary and mobile scenarios, subspace discriminant consistently outperforms cubic SVM, particularly in the mobile condition. For instance, with cross-correlation applied, the classification accuracy

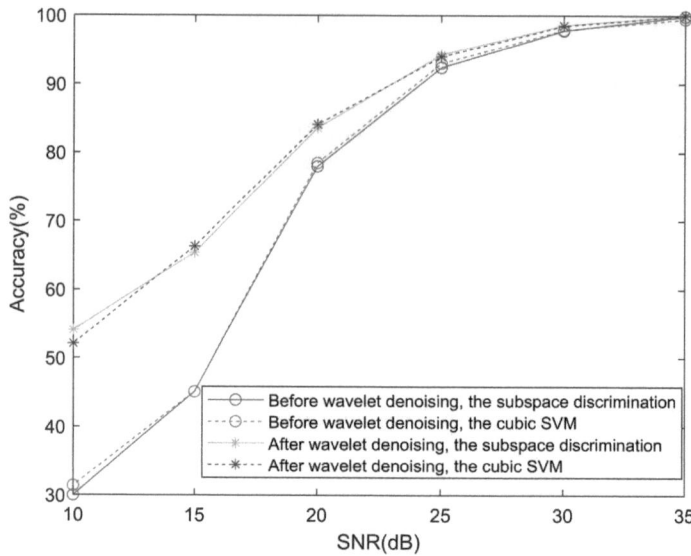

Fig. 6. Classification accuracy of fingerprints before and after wavelet decomposition threshold denoising at different SNRs in the direct connection setup.

Table 2. Classification Accuracy for Different Scenarios with and without Cross-correlation

Scenario	Cross-corr.	Method	Accuracy
Stationary	Yes	Cubic SVM	99.1%
Stationary	Yes	Subspace Discr.	99.3%
Stationary	No	Cubic SVM	96.5%
Stationary	No	Subspace Discr.	98.1%
Moving	Yes	Cubic SVM	54.3%
Moving	Yes	Subspace Discr.	93.3%
Moving	No	Cubic SVM	51.4%
Moving	No	Subspace Discr.	90.6%

of subspace discriminant in the moving scenario reaches 93.3%, whereas cubic SVM achieves only 54.3%. This substantial gap highlights the greater robustness of subspace discriminant to dynamic channel variations. Furthermore, cross-correlation plays a significant role in enhancing fingerprint feature extraction by reducing the impact of fluctuating channels. This effect is most evident in the mobile scenario, where the absence of cross-correlation leads to a decline in classification accuracy for both classifiers. Subspace discriminant drops to 90.6%, and cubic SVM decreases further to 51.4%. In contrast, the stationary scenario shows less sensitivity to cross-correlation, as channel conditions remain relatively stable, leading to smaller differences in performance. These results confirm that cross-correlation effectively mitigates channel-induced interference, especially in environments with high variability, thereby improving overall classification reliability.

Further, we conducted a cross-test using fingerprints from both the moving and stationary scenarios. The training set consisted of fingerprints extracted from PSCCH/PSSCH data collected in the moving scenario, while the test set was derived from PSCCH/PSSCH data collected in the stationary scenario, with an SNR of approximately 35 dB. We employed the subspace discriminant method as the classifier. Figure 7 presents the device classification results from the cross-test, with an average recognition accuracy of 76.4%.

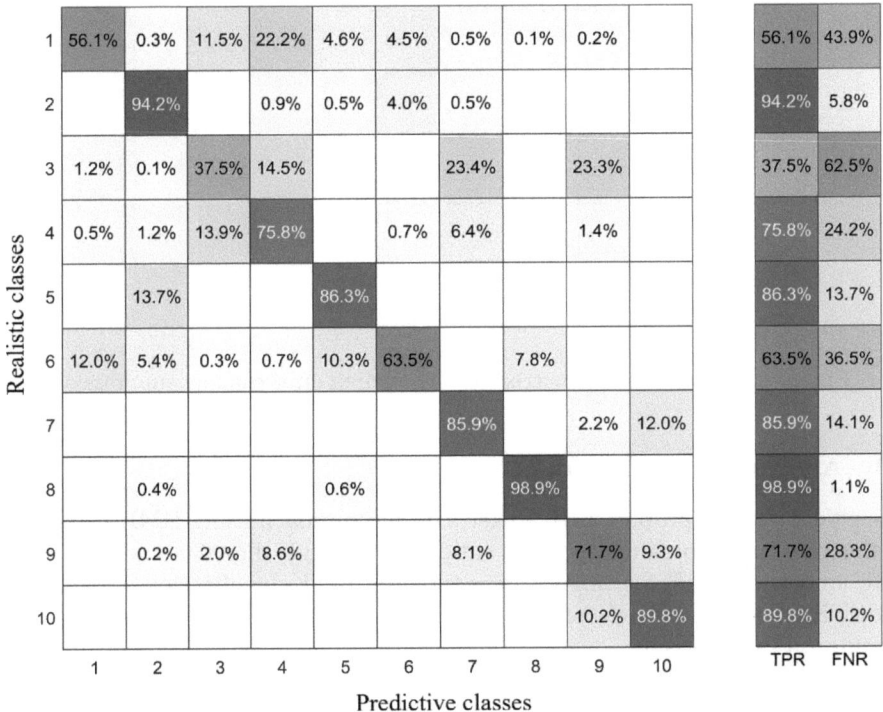

Fig. 7. The confusion matrix for cross-testing without channel suppression.

Subsequently, we applied cross-correlation between the previously extracted fingerprints and those obtained from the directly-connected scenario, and conducted another cross-test. Figure 8 shows the device-specific recognition accuracies. As can be observed, after enhancing the fingerprint features and reducing channel interference through the use of cross-correlation, the recognition accuracy of each device improved to varying extents, resulting in an increase in the overall average recognition accuracy to 80.9%.

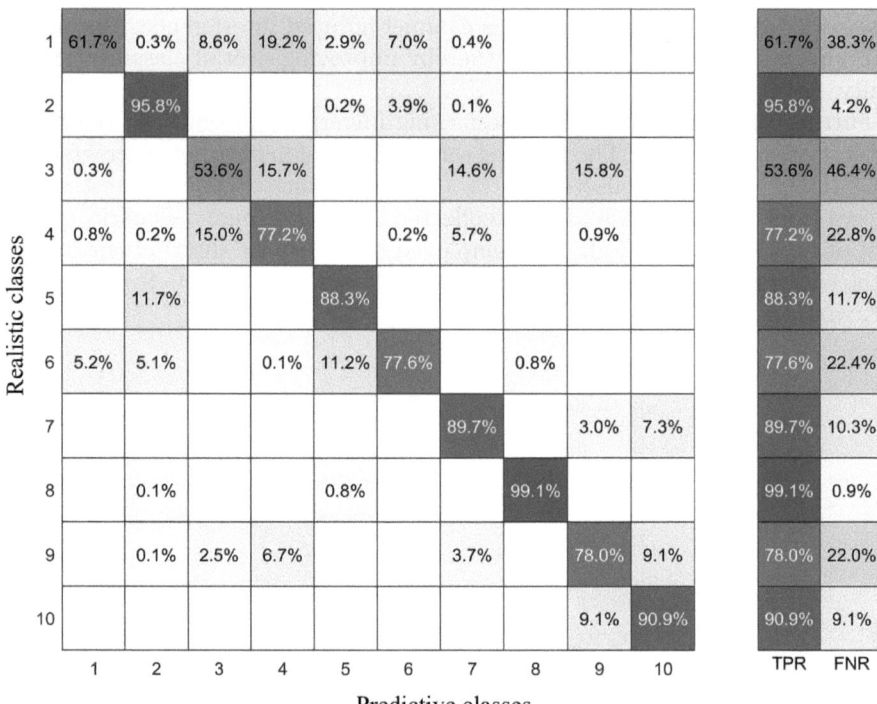

Fig. 8. The cross-testing matrix for fingerprints after channel suppression.

3.3 Analysis of the Results

The efficacy of the proposed RF fingerprinting approach using DMRS sequences in the cepstrum domain has been validated through direct connection of the OBU and the USRP for fingerprint extraction and classification. However, at low SNR levels (15 dB), recognition accuracy diminishes, necessitating wavelet decomposition denoising.

Fingerprint classification accuracy is lower for airborne signals compared to direct signals, highlighting the impact of channel characteristics. Rapid channel changes can degrade classification performance.

In the cepstrum domain, cross-correlation between the direct signal fingerprint and the airborne signal fingerprint improves recognition accuracy, demonstrating that fingerprint features are enhanced and channel interference is reduced.

4 Conclusion

In this paper, we propose a RF fingerprint extraction method in the cepstrum domain based on the differences between standard DMRS sequences and received DMRS sequences, using wavelet decomposition threshold denoising to eliminate high-frequency components caused by noise. Additionally, to mitigate the interference of channel characteristics on fingerprint features, we introduce a fingerprint feature enhancement method through cross-correlation with direct fingerprints. We collect PSCCH/PSSCH data in three different scenarios for experimental evaluation. The experimental results demonstrate the feasibility of the proposed RF fingerprint extraction and enhancement methods in LTE-V2X.

Acknowledgment. This research was supported by the Purple Mountain Laboratories for Network and Communication Security.

References

1. China Academy of Information and Communications Technology. White Paper on Connected Vehicles [R] (2017)
2. Yu, J., Li, G., Hu, A.: Time-domain baseband modeling of RF fingerprint for zero intermediate frequency digital communication transmitter. J. Terahertz Sci. Electron. Inf. (4) (2021). https://doi.org/10.11805/TKYDA2021139
3. Li, G., Yu, J., Hu, A.: Physical layer security methods based on device and channel characteristics. J. Cryptol. Res. **7**(02), 224–248 (2020)
4. Reising, D.R., Temple, M.A., Mendenhall, M.J.: Improved wireless security for GMSK-based devices using RF fingerprints. Int. J. Electron. Secur. Digit. Forensics **3**(1), 41–59 (2010)
5. Williams, M.D., Temple, M.A., Reising, D.R.: Augmenting Bit-Level Network Security Using Physical Layer RF-DNA Fingerprinting, pp. 1–6. IEEE Globecom, Miami (2010)
6. Williams, M.D., Munns, S.A., Temple, M.A., et al.: RF-DNA fingerprinting for airport WiMax communications security. In: IEEE International Conference Network and System Security, Melbourne, pp. 32–39 (2010)
7. Dubendorfer, C., Ramsey, B., Temple, M.: ZigBee device verification for securing industrial control and building automation systems. In: Butts, J., Shenoi, S. (eds) Critical Infrastructure Protection, pp. 47–62. Springer, Berlin, Heidelberg (2013)
8. Dubendorfer, C.K., Ramsey, B.W., Temple, M.A.: An RF-DNA verification process for ZigBee networks. In: IEEE Military Communication Conference, Orlando, pp. 1–6 (2012)
9. Li, C., Wang, J.: RF fingerprint classification and recognition of UAV based on short-time fourier transform. Commun. Technol. **55**(09), 1202–1207 (2022)
10. Xu, S., Huang, B., Huang, Y., Xu, Z.: Identification of individual radio transmitters based on selected surrounding-line integral bispectra. In: The 9th International Conference on Advanced Communication Technology, Gangwon, Korea (South), pp. 1147–1150 (2007). https://doi.org/10.1109/ICACT.2007.358561
11. Jia, J., Qi, L.: RF fingerprint extraction method based on bispectrum. J. Terahertz Sci. Electron. Inf. **19**(01), 107–111 (2021)
12. Chandran, V., Elgar, S.L.: Pattern recognition using invariants defined from higher order spectra to one-dimensional inputs. IEEE Trans. Signal Process. **41**(1), 205–212 (1993)
13. Tugnait, J.K.: Detection of non-gaussian signals using integrated polyspectrum. IEEE Trans. Signal Process. **42**(12), 3137–3149 (1994)

14. Cai, Z.: Individual identification of communication radiation sources based on bispectrum. J. Commun. **28**(2), 75–79 (2007)
15. Zhang, X., Shi, Y., Bao, Z.: A new feature vector using selected bispectra for signal classification with application in radar target recognition. IEEE Trans. Signal Process. **49**(9), 1875–1885 (2001)
16. Toonstra, J., Kinsner, W.: Transient analysis and genetic algorithms for classification. In: IEEE WESCANEX 95. Communications, Power, and Computing. Conference Proceedings, Winnipeg, MB, Canada, vol. 2, pp. 432–437 (1995). https://doi.org/10.1109/WESCAN.1995.494069.
17. Li, Y., Feiyi, X., Songlin, C., et al.: Feature extraction and recognition of RF fingerprint signals suitable for terminals. Commun. Technol. **051**(001), 63–66 (2018)
18. Huang, N.E., Shen, Z., Long, S.R.: The empirical mode decomposition and the Hilbert spectrum for nonlinear and non-stationary – time series analysis. Proc. R. Soc. Lond. A **1998**(454), 903–995 (1997)
19. Yuan, Y., Huang, Z., Wu, H., Wang, X.: Specific emitter identification based on Hilbert–Huang transform-based time–frequency–energy distribution features. IET Commun. **8**, 2404–2412 (2014). https://doi.org/10.1049/iet-com.2013.0865
20. Zhang, Y.: Research on extraction and recognition methods of RF fingerprints for wireless communication devices [Dissertation]. Xi'an University of Technology (2023). https://doi.org/10.27398/d.cnki.gxalu.2023.000593
21. Guo, Y., Ge, J., Liu, G., et al.: Efficient timing and frequency offset estimation scheme for OFDM systems. Trans. Tianjin Univ. **15**(1), 27–31 (2009)

SEQ-Track: Detecting Web Tracking with Sequences of Packet Lengths and Time Intervals

Yong Yuan, Ziling Wei[✉], Lin Liu, Shuhui Chen, and Jinshu Su

National University of Defense Technology, Changsha, China
{yuanyong,weiziling,liulin18,shchen,sjs}@nudt.edu.cn

Abstract. In recent years, web tracking has raised concerns about privacy during web browsing. This paper introduces SEQ-Track, a novel method for detecting web tracking behaviors by leveraging length and time information in encrypted traffic. SEQ-Track extracts the packet length sequences and time interval sequences of packets from network traffic flows and utilizes feature extractors based on the Convolutional Neural Network (CNN) and Transformer to perform web tracking detection. Our experimental results demonstrate that SEQ-Track performs well with over 90% accuracy across key evaluation metrics. The ablation study underscores the importance of the two sequences in the detection process. It also reveals that introducing statistical features results in minimal performance improvement while increasing computational complexity, highlighting the importance of careful feature selection, rather than simply increasing the number of features.

Keywords: web tracking · deep learning · traffic analysis · Transformer

1 Introduction

Web tracking is an online analytical behavior that collects personal browsing data across multiple websites. This data is often used for targeted advertising and personalized content recommendations. In recent years, more tracking technologies have been disclosed, raising concerns about privacy violations. Despite the existence of legal regulations, such as the General Data Protection Regulation (GDPR) [21], which aim to restrict the misuse of personal information, the covert nature of web tracking makes effective regulation of personal information challenging. Consequently, there is a growing need for robust detection methods to identify and mitigate web tracking activities to avoid illegal misuse of personal information.

Existing methods for web tracking detection can be broadly categorized into URL-based methods and other methods based on web page code or traffic analysis. However, URL-based methods can be easily circumvented by changing domain names, reducing their effectiveness against more complex trackers. Methods based on web page code [12,16,17,28] involve analyzing static code or dynamic execution of code on web pages and require modifications to the browser, which limits their applicability and widespread use. Most current traffic-based detection methods [13,20,22,28,29] extract features from plaintext network traffic for tracking detection. These methods require browser plugins or man-in-the-middle setups, which not only hinder widespread application but also pose potential privacy risks.

In this paper, we introduce SEQ-Track, a novel approach for detecting web tracking behaviors by analyzing encrypted traffic. In SEQ-Track, we extract length and time information from traffic flows, using sequences of packet lengths and time intervals to train a deep learning model for tracking detection. Requests involving tracking, such as loading advertisements and tracking script execution, often exhibit distinct traffic patterns in packet length and time intervals. To capture these patterns, we employ Transformer-based and Convolutional Neural Network (CNN)-based feature extractors in SEQ-Track. Additionally, the ability of SEQ-Track in analyzing encrypted traffic enhances its robustness in identifying tracking behaviors, eliminating the need for complex client-side configurations and reducing the risk of information leakage. This capability also allows for large-scale detection when deployed at network nodes.

We evaluate SEQ-Track with a dataset collected from the top 5k websites in the Tranco list. The results show that SEQ-Track achieves remarkable detection performance, with over 90% across key evaluation metrics, demonstrating its efficacy in identifying tracking behaviors. Furthermore, our ablation study shows the contributions of packet length sequence and packet time interval sequence in web tracking detection and illustrates the importance of correct feature selection by introducing statistical features.

The remainder of this paper is structured as follows. In Sect. 2, it describes the related work. Section 3 provides the details of SEQ-Track. Further, we present the evaluation part to demonstrate the performance and ablation study of SEQ-Track in Sect. 4. We discuss the limitations and future work in Sect. 5. The whole paper is concluded in Sect. 6.

2 Related Work

In this section, we briefly describe existing work on web tracking detection and analysis.

2.1 URL-Based Tracking Detection

URL-based tracking detection is the most widely used method for identifying tracking activity on the web. This approach relies heavily on the lists of URLs known to be associated with tracking activity, such as EasyList [3], EasyPrivacy [4], and Disconnect [2], which are maintained by communities and specialized organizations. Most browsers and ads-blocking extensions [1,14] use these lists to filter web requests on pages, reducing the probability of users being tracked. To alleviate the labor cost of updating filter lists, researchers [8,10,13,18,24] have explored ways to automatically generate filter lists. Furthermore, some studies [12,16,27] employed their own identification outcomes as a supplement to filter lists.

However, URL-based tracking detection is faced with challenges. Blocking tracking behavior via URLs can be easily evaded by changing domain names or using Content Delivery Networks (CDNs). Furthermore, filtered lists are not always effective, with false positives (false alarms) and false negatives (missed alarms) occurring [7].

2.2 Tracking Analysis on Web Code

Code on web pages often serves as an implementation for online tracking. Therefore, some researchers focused on detecting tracking by analyzing web page code through static and dynamic methods.

Ikaram et al. [15] employed machine learning classifiers to statically check the web page code for tracking behaviors. The classifiers were trained on syntactic and semantic features extracted from JavaScript programs. Ismael et al. investigated the correlation between tracking resources and proposed TrackSign based on code fingerprinting [11] and Astrack based on abstract syntax trees [9]. Additionally, Iqbal et al. [17] generated web page code structures into graphs and combined them with machine learning methods to block tracking.

Static analysis of web code is often limited by the complexity and diversity of the code, with obfuscation and compression techniques (such as webpack [6]) exacerbating these challenges. To more accurately uncover tracking behaviors, researchers have proposed dynamic analysis methods based on code behavior. Wu et al. [27] and Chen et al. [12] dynamically analyzed web codes and extracted features to apply machine learning methods for web tracking detection. Siby et al. [23] noted that AdGraph [17] is susceptible to adversarial evasion tactics deployed in the real world. They enhanced the robustness against such evasive maneuvers by employing a graph-based machine learning approach that focuses on the behavior of trackers.

2.3 Network Traffic Tracking Analysis

Traffic analysis is the study of monitoring and analyzing network traffic to detect traffic patterns, anomalies, and potential security threats. As a form of online behavior, web tracking inherently exhibits its unique characteristics in network traffic. Therefore, traffic analysis methods can be applied to the detection of web tracking. Recent studies have shown favorable results in web tracking detection through traffic analysis. Gugelmann et al. [13] and Shuba et al. [22] extracted features from HTTP request payloads to train machine learning classifiers for tracking detection. Metwallwy et al. [20] and Yu et al. [29] analyzed request fields for unique user identifiers. Yang et al. [28] transformed web page network requests into graphs and trained graph neural network models on them. These methods mainly rely on plain text traffic analysis, which may raise privacy concerns. Taking this into consideration, Lee et al. [19] first proposed using side-channel information from encrypted traffic for tracking classification.

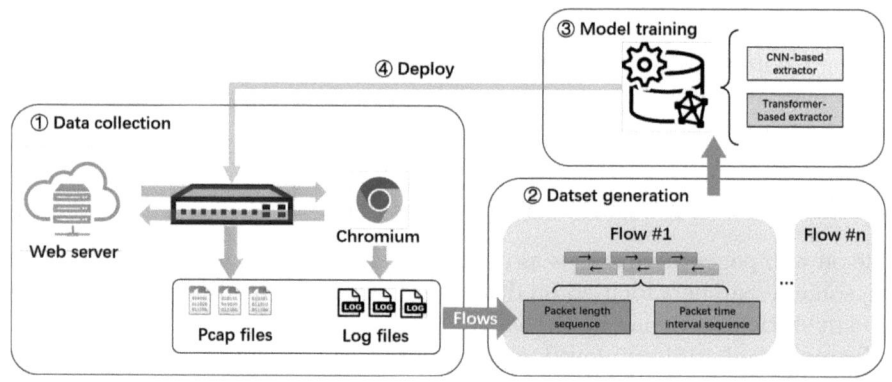

Fig. 1. The workflow of SEQ-Track

3 Design of SEQ-Track

This section presents the overall design of SEQ-Track, including flow collection, sequence process, and model design. Figure 1 illustrates the workflow of SEQ-Track. Under the SEQ-Track framework, a middle network node is placed between the browser and the web servers on the Internet. The workflow begins with the data collection phase, where this middle node captures the encrypted network traffic between a Chromium [25] browser and the visited websites. Each collected flow is then processed to extract the packet length sequence and the time interval sequence. These sequences are used to train deep learning models.

In the model, a Transformer-based feature extractor is applied to the packet length sequences, and a CNN-based feature extractor is applied to the time interval sequence. After the model training is complete, the model is deployed back onto the middle network node to distinguish whether the traffic generated by web page visits contains tracking behavior.

3.1 Flow Collection

Flow collection is achieved by automated control of the Chromium browser [25]. The browser accesses the target websites under the control of an automation program. During the browsing process, the program waits for the web pages to fully load, then performs several random scrolls, and closes the browser after a random waiting period to simulate real user behavior. Real-world traffic is collected through the middle network node and the logs are recorded by Chromium. By analyzing logs and collected traffic, we obtain the flows (often represented as groups of five tuples) and the URLs of resources requested by these flows. It is worth noting that modern web accesses often contain multiple flows from different sites, as web pages are loaded with a large number of third-party resources, including tracking resources.

We label each flow as either tracking or benign based on the URLs requested by the flow. It should be noted that, despite the well-known limitations, using filter lists as a source of ground truth is a common practice in related work because of the significant time and manpower required for manual labeling. Therefore, we employ the widely adopted EasyList [3] and EasyPrivacy [4] to label each flow for SEQ-Track. If any URL within a flow is identified as tracking by these filter lists, we label the flow as a tracking flow. However, if none of the URLs in a flow is identified as tracking, we label the flow as benign.

3.2 Sequence Process

This part describes how to process the flows obtained through data collection. By analyzing web tracking behaviors, we find that flow sequence data can effectively reflect the behavior patterns of web tracking. After fully considering effectiveness and robustness, we selected two types of sequence information from network traffic, namely packet length sequence and packet time interval sequence.

Packet Length Sequence. The packet length sequence is defined as the sequence of packet sizes at the IP layer. To distinguish between uplink (client to server) and downlink (server to client) packets, we assign positive values to uplink packet sizes and negative values to downlink packet sizes, creating a signed length sequence for each flow. The sequence is normalized to a fixed length of 1000. Sequences longer than 1000 are truncated, and shorter sequences are padded with zeros to ensure uniformity in length.

The analysis of the packet length sequence is based on the observation that requests for resources associated with tracking behavior often result in smaller packet sizes, leading to distinctive interaction patterns between tracking and benign flows. The reason for this phenomenon is that certain tracking resources (such as tracking pixels) are designed to avoid affecting normal user browsing or being detected. Additionally, certain tracking codes may be intentionally minimal, focusing solely on tracking without incorporating full functionality, resulting in smaller sizes. Furthermore, the packet length sequence can partially reflect the execution of web page code, subtly indicating tracking behavior patterns.

Packet Time Interval Sequence. We also consider the sequence of time intervals between packets. The time interval sequence is defined as $\Delta t_i = t_{i+1} - t_i$, where t_{i+1} and t_i denote the timestamps of consecutive packets. It is normalized to the same length of 1000 as the packet length sequence.

Due to the large variations in time intervals between packets, which can range from several seconds to microseconds, the raw data could potentially mislead the model. To mitigate this, we process each value in the sequence using the *tanh* function to reduce the impact of extreme values. The *tanh* function is defined as

$$\tanh(x) = \frac{e^x - e^{-x}}{e^x + e^{-x}}, \tag{1}$$

where x represents each time interval in the sequence. This transformation helps to normalize the data, preventing extreme values from disproportionately influencing the model.

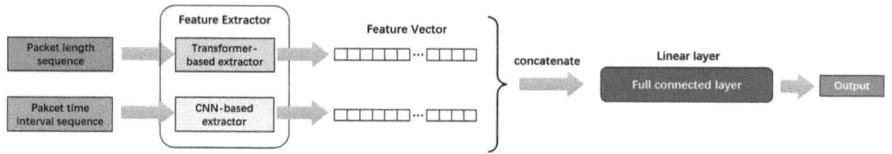

Fig. 2. The structure of the model

The analysis of packet time interval sequences is based on the observations that many tracking behaviors rely on JavaScript code executed on the web page. The code takes time to gather information and send it to tracking servers. For example, certain tracking scripts spend time collecting specific browser or hardware information to create fingerprints that are sent to servers to update browsing histories. This process results in time interval sequences distinct from typical web resource accesses, indirectly reflecting the execution of code and network requests on web pages, which can be used to detect tracking behaviors.

3.3 Model Design

The model structure is depicted in Fig. 2. For each flow, the packet length sequence is processed by a Transformer-based feature extractor, while the packet time interval sequence is processed by a CNN-based feature extractor. The Transformer-based extractor can simultaneously consider information from all positions in the sequence. It can establish long-distance dependencies within the sequence to extract global features in the packet length sequences. The CNN-based extractor uses convolutional operations to capture local features. In packet time interval sequences, it can identify and extract patterns and changes within continuous time intervals. These two feature extractors respectively process packet length sequences and packet time interval sequences into abstract feature vectors of the same dimension. The feature vectors are then concatenated and processed through a linear layer. The linear layer combines the feature vectors linearly to generate a new feature representation, resulting in a final output of length 1, determining whether the flow is tracking or benign. Details of the feature extractors are provided below.

Transformer-Based Feature Extractor. The Transformer-based feature extractor first uses a CNN layer for embedding the initial input sequence, where each channel corresponds to an embedding dimension. The embedded data is then input into a Transformer [26] encoder layer to extract high-dimensional features. Finally, global max pooling is applied to obtain the feature vector. The self-attention mechanism of the Transformer can focus on important parts and extract features in the sequence, especially those local features that may indicate tracking behavior. This makes the Transformer particularly suitable for processing packet length sequences, as it can effectively capture global dependencies and patterns within the sequences.

CNN-Based Feature Extractor. The CNN-based feature extractor uses a two-layer CNN model to extract features. This extractor leverages the ability of CNN to focus on local information to identify features in the sequence that can reveal tracking behavior. The main body of the model consists of two CNN layers. After processing through these layers, a feature vector of a specified length is generated. The choice of CNN for processing time interval sequences is driven by the need to capture short-term dependencies and local patterns in the sequences. Since the sequence often involves short time spans, the local temporal patterns are more indicative of tracking behavior.

4 Evaluation

This section presents the evaluation of SEQ-Track. We evaluate the performance impact of different feature extractors on the packet length sequence and the packet time interval sequence and examine the effectiveness of the sequences in the classification task. We also illustrate the importance of selecting appropriate features by experimenting with the inclusion of statistical features.

To evaluate SEQ-Track, we select the top 5k websites from the Tranco list [5] and apply the data collection method described in Sect. 3.1 by visiting their homepages. As a result, we collected a total of 43,910 flows for the following experiments, out of which 18,685 flows are labeled as tracking, and 25,225 flows are labeled as benign.

4.1 Feature Extractor Selection

In SEQ-Track, it is important to select appropriate feature extractors, as each extractor excels in processing different types of information. To validate the effectiveness of our chosen feature extractors, we conduct experiments to assess their detection performance under different extractor configurations. Specifically, we apply CNN-based and Transformer-based feature extractors to packet length sequence and packet time interval sequence respectively, resulting in the following four different experimental configurations.

1. Packet length sequence with Transformer-based feature extractor, packet time interval sequence with Transformer-based feature extractor

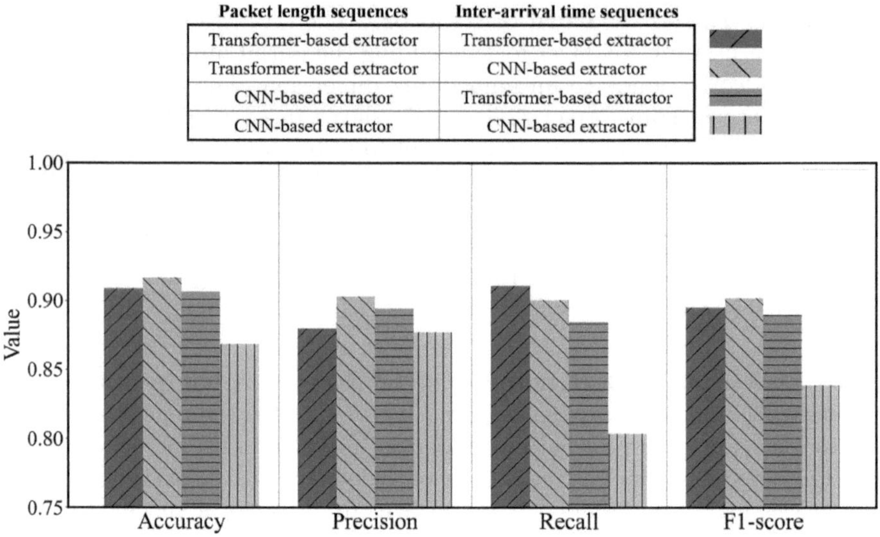

Fig. 3. Tracking performance comparison of SEQ-Track with different feature extractor combinations

2. Packet length sequence with Transformer-based feature extractor, packet time interval sequence with CNN-based feature extractor
3. Packet length sequence with CNN-based feature extractor, packet time interval sequence with Transformer-based feature extractor
4. Packet length sequence with CNN-based feature extractor, packet time interval sequence with CNN-based feature extractor

These configurations are compared based on their detection performances. We analyze and compare them using accuracy, precision, recall, and F1-score as our metrics, which are defined as follows.

$$Accuracy = \frac{TruePositives + TrueNegatives}{SampleNum} \quad (2)$$

$$Precision = \frac{TruePositives}{TruePositives + FalsePositives} \quad (3)$$

$$Recall = \frac{TruePositives}{TruePositives + FalseNegatives} \quad (4)$$

$$F1\text{-}score = 2 \times \frac{Precision \times Recall}{Precision + Recall} \quad (5)$$

In these equations, *TruePositives* (TP) refer to correctly identified flows of web tracking, *FalsePositives* (FP) are cases where non-tracking flows are incorrectly identified as tracking, *TrueNegatives* (TN) represent correctly identified non-tracking flows, and *FalseNegatives* (FN) occur when tracking flow is missed by SEQ-Track.

Figure 3 illustrates the impact of different configurations on model detection performance. Overall, SEQ-Track performs best when using the Transformer-based feature extractor for the packet length sequence and the CNN-based feature extractor for the packet time interval sequence. When both sequences use the Transformer-based feature extractor, although there is a minimal improvement in recall, the precision is significantly lower than the best configuration.

In web tracking detection, precision is more important than recall because false positives can disrupt the normal functionality of web pages. Minimizing false positives (high precision) is more crucial than identifying as many tracking behaviors as possible (high recall). Consequently, we choose the configuration with the Transformer-based extractor for the packet length sequence and the CNN-based extractor for the time interval sequence in SEQ-Track.

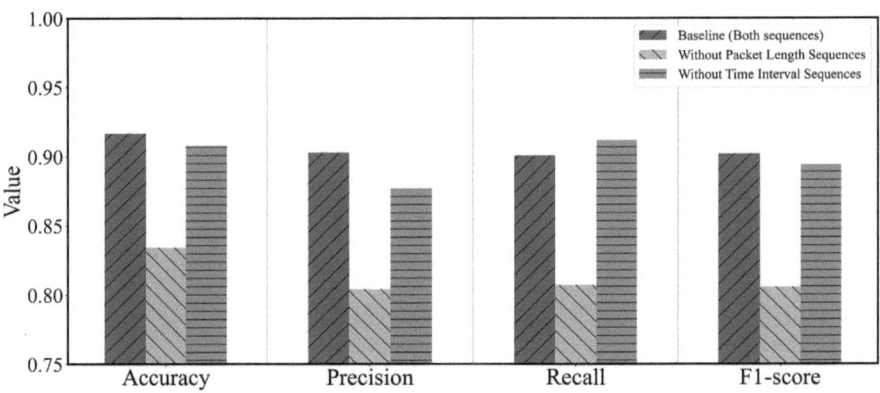

Fig. 4. Detection performance of SEQ-Track excluding different sequences

4.2 Ablation Study

In this part, we conduct an ablation study to evaluate the contribution of the packet length sequence and the packet time interval sequence to the overall performance of SEQ-Track. By removing the sequences separately and assessing their impact on detection performance, we determine their importance in the web tracking detection task. We evaluate the detection performance of SEQ-Track under different configurations: Baseline (i.e. using packet length sequence and packet time interval sequence), Without Packet Length Sequence, and Without Time Interval Sequence.

The experimental results are shown in Fig. 4. The experiment proves that the packet length sequence contributes more to SEQ-Track than the time interval sequence. Removing the packet time interval sequence has a minor impact on detection performance, with precision dropping slightly from 90.30% to 87.70%. In contrast, removing the packet length sequence significantly impacts detection performance, with the F1 score dropping from 90.19% to around 80.54%. This is because the time interval data within the flow is susceptible to network fluctuations. Transmission delays can cause variations in the time intervals, introducing unreasonable disturbances to the dataset. In contrast, packet length sequences are relatively stable and only exhibit issues, such as retransmitting packets, in particularly unstable network conditions, which did not occur during our data collection.

4.3 Statistical Features Analysis

In traffic analysis, a variety of features are commonly employed. Different traffic analysis tasks have their own set of features that are most suitable. As a general category of features, statistical features have demonstrated significant efficacy in prior research. In this experiment, we explore the benefit statistical features might bring to the performance of SEQ-Track. We compare SEQ-Track's performance before and after adding the statistical features, in terms of detection performance and the time required for training and inference.

Table 1. Performance Comparison of SEQ-Track before (Baseline) and after adding statistical features

Metric	Baseline	Adding features
Precision (%)	91.66	91.53
Recall (%)	90.30	90.01
Accuracy (%)	90.07	90.10
F1-Score (%)	90.19	90.05
Training Time/Epoch (second)	90.67	**106.03 (+16.94%)**
Inference Time/Sample (millisecond)	0.1975	**0.2552 (+29.21%)**

The statistical features are derived from the work of Lee et al. [19], including 62 related statistics of uplink packets, downlink packets, and all packets. Since statistical features are independent individual features without sequential information, we employed a feature enhancement method. This method utilizes several linear layers assigned to each feature to extract high-dimensional features. Subsequently, all these high-dimensional features pass through a global pooling layer, transforming the statistical features into feature vectors of the same dimensions as those extracted by the feature extractors mentioned in Sect. 3.3. Ultimately, the feature vector of statistical features will be concatenated with the feature vectors of the packet length sequence and the packet time interval sequence. They will then pass through a linear layer similar to that in Sect. 3.3 to determine whether the flow includes tracking behaviors.

Table 1 shows the details of our evaluation results. We can observe that SEQ-Track performs similarly before and after adding statistical features in tracking detection, but with a longer time to train and infer. To be more specific, the training time per epoch increases by 16.94%, from 90.67 s to 106.03 s, and the inference time per sample increases by 29.21%, from 0.1975 ms to 0.2552 ms. The results show that introducing statistical features results in a negligible improvement in detection accuracy in SEQ-Track. Instead, it increases the model parameters, leading to longer training and inference times. This indicates that feature selection is more critical than simply increasing the number of features.

5 Discussion and Future Work

This section discusses the limitations and potential improvements of SEQ-Track. Although it has shown good performance in web tracking detection, some aspects with limitations could still be investigated and improved in the future.

Sequence Extractors and Model Design. One potential improvement for SEQ-Track is the exploration of more effective sequence extractors and model designs. By leveraging advances in deep learning and sequence modeling, it is possible to develop more sophisticated extractors that can capture intricate patterns in sequences, thereby increasing detection performance.

More Effective Sequences. Another avenue for improvement involves exploring additional sequences that could aid in tracking detection. However, as discussed in Sect. 4.2, it is crucial to evaluate the actual effectiveness of new sequences in tracking detection rather than blindly adding them. The goal is to ensure that any new features introduced truly contribute to improved performance without unnecessarily increasing the complexity and training time of the model.

Real-Time Detection. Currently, SEQ-Track performs tracking detection on a complete traffic flow, which may not be optimal for preventing tracking behaviors in real time. Future work could investigate real-time detection mechanisms that operate on incomplete flows. Real-time detection capabilities would enable more immediate responses to tracking behaviors, potentially stopping them before they fully manifest and compromise user privacy.

6 Conclusion

In this paper, we introduce SEQ-Track, a novel method for detecting tracking behaviors with sequences of packet lengths and time intervals. Our approach extracts packet length sequences and packet time interval sequences from network traffic flows and processes them using Transformer-based and CNN-based feature extractors, respectively, for web tracking detection. In our experiments, SEQ-Track demonstrated outstanding performance, achieving over 90% in all key evaluation metrics. The experiments also validated the rationality of the chosen feature extractors and sequences, highlighting the importance of careful feature selection over merely increasing the number of features. Our future work aims to explore better feature extractors and sequences to further improve tracking detection performance, and to develop real-time detection capabilities to enable more timely responses to tracking behaviors.

References

1. Adblock plus. https://adblockplus.org/. Accessed 4 July 2024
2. Disconnect. https://disconnect.me/. Accessed 4 July 2024
3. Easylist. https://easylist.to/easylist/easylist.txt. Accessed 4 July 2024
4. Easyprivacy. https://easylist.to/easylist/easyprivacy.txt. Accessed 4 July 2024
5. Tranco list. https://tranco-list.eu/list/W9359/1000000. Accessed 4 July 2024
6. Webpack. https://webpack.js.org/. Accessed 4 July 2024
7. Alrizah, M., Zhu, S., Xing, X., Wang, G.: Errors, misunderstandings, and attacks: analyzing the crowdsourcing process of ad-blocking systems. In: Proceedings of the Internet Measurement Conference, pp. 230–244 (2019)
8. Bhagavatula, S., Dunn, C., Kanich, C., Gupta, M., Ziebart, B.: Leveraging machine learning to improve unwanted resource filtering. In: Proceedings of the 2014 Workshop on Artificial Intelligent and Security Workshop. AISec 2014, pp. 95–102. Association for Computing Machinery, New York (2014). https://doi.org/10.1145/2666652.2666662
9. Castell-Uroz, I., Fukuda, K., Barlet-Ros, P.: ASTrack: automatic detection and removal of web tracking code with minimal functionality loss. In: IEEE INFOCOM 2023-IEEE Conference on Computer Communications, pp. 1–10. IEEE (2023)
10. Castell-Uroz, I., Poissonnier, T., Manneback, P., Barlet-Ros, P.: URL-based web tracking detection using deep learning. In: 2020 16th International Conference on Network and Service Management (CNSM), pp. 1–5 (2020). https://doi.org/10.23919/CNSM50824.2020.9269065
11. Castell-Uroz, I., Solé-Pareta, J., Barlet-Ros, P.: TrackSign: guided web tracking discovery. In: IEEE INFOCOM 2021-IEEE Conference on Computer Communications, pp. 1–10. IEEE (2021)
12. Chen, Q., Snyder, P., Livshits, B., Kapravelos, A.: Detecting filter list evasion with event-loop-turn granularity Javascript signatures. In: 2021 IEEE Symposium on Security and Privacy (SP), pp. 1715–1729. IEEE (2021)
13. Gugelmann, D., Happe, M., Ager, B., Lenders, V.: An automated approach for complementing ad blockers' blacklists. In: Proceedings on Privacy Enhancing Technologies (2015)
14. Hill, R.: uBlock origin. https://github.com/gorhill/uBlock. Accessed 4 July 2024
15. Ikram, M., Asghar, H.J., Kaafar, M.A., Krishnamurthy, B., Mahanti, A.: Towards seamless tracking-free web: Improved detection of trackers via one-class learning. arXiv preprint arXiv:1603.06289 (2016)
16. Iqbal, U., Englehardt, S., Shafiq, Z.: Fingerprinting the fingerprinters: learning to detect browser fingerprinting behaviors. In: 2021 IEEE Symposium on Security and Privacy (SP), pp. 1143–1161. IEEE (2021)
17. Iqbal, U., Snyder, P., Zhu, S., Livshits, B., Qian, Z., Shafiq, Z.: ADGRAPH: a graph-based approach to ad and tracker blocking. In: 2020 IEEE Symposium on security and privacy (SP), pp. 763–776. IEEE (2020)

18. Le, H., et al.: {AutoFR}: automated filter rule generation for adblocking. In: 32nd USENIX Security Symposium (USENIX Security 2023), pp. 7535–7552 (2023)
19. Lee, D., Joo, M., Lee, W.: Net-track: generic web tracking detection using packet metadata. In: Proceedings of the ACM Web Conference 2023, pp. 2230–2240 (2023)
20. Metwalley, H., Traverso, S., Mellia, M.: Unsupervised detection of web trackers. In: 2015 IEEE Global Communications Conference (GLOBECOM), pp. 1–6. IEEE (2015)
21. The European parliament: The Council of the European Union: Regulation (EU) 2016/679 of the European parliament and of the council of 27 April 2016 on the protection of natural persons with regard to the processing of personal data and on the free movement of such data, and repealing directive 95/46/EC (general data protection regulation). Official Journal of the European Union (2016)
22. Shuba, A., Markopoulou, A., Shafiq, Z.: NoMoAds: effective and efficient cross-app mobile ad-blocking (the Andreas Pfitzmann best student paper award). In: Proceedings of the Privacy Enhancing Technologies Symposium (PETS), vol. 2018 (2018)
23. Siby, S., Iqbal, U., Englehardt, S., Shafiq, Z., Troncoso, C.: {WebGraph}: capturing advertising and tracking information flows for robust blocking. In: 31st USENIX Security Symposium (USENIX Security 2022), pp. 2875–2892 (2022)
24. Sjösten, A., Snyder, P., Pastor, A., Papadopoulos, P., Livshits, B.: Filter list generation for underserved regions. In: Proceedings of The Web Conference 2020, WWW 2020, pp. 1682–1692. Association for Computing Machinery, New York (2020). https://doi.org/10.1145/3366423.3380239
25. The Chromium Projects: Chromium. https://www.chromium.org/. Accessed 4 July 2024
26. Vaswani, A., et al.: Attention is all you need. Adv. Neural Inf. Process. Syst. **30** (2017)
27. Wu, Q., Liu, Q., Zhang, Y., Liu, P., Wen, G.: A machine learning approach for detecting third-party trackers on the web. In: Askoxylakis, I., Ioannidis, S., Katsikas, S., Meadows, C. (eds.) ESORICS 2016, Part I. LNCS, vol. 9878, pp. 238–258. Springer, Cham (2016). https://doi.org/10.1007/978-3-319-45744-4_12
28. Yang, Z., Pei, W., Chen, M., Yue, C.: WTAGRAPH: web tracking and advertising detection using graph neural networks. In: 2022 IEEE Symposium on Security and Privacy (SP), pp. 1540–1557. IEEE (2022)
29. Yu, Z., Macbeth, S., Modi, K., Pujol, J.M.: Tracking the trackers. In: Proceedings of the 25th International Conference on World Wide Web, pp. 121–132 (2016)

Enhanced Feature-Based Approach to Identify and Classify Android Encrypted Malware Traffic

Jiaqi Gao, Yaru He, Mingrui Fan, Yueming Lu, and Yaojun Qiao[✉]

Beijing University of Posts and Telecommunications, Beijing, China
{gaojiaqi,heyaru,fanmingrui,ymlu,qiao}@bupt.edu.cn

Abstract. Android mobile devices are ubiquitous and vulnerable to malware threats. Existing research mainly focuses on static malware detection methods, which are limited in detecting dynamically manifested or obfuscated malicious activities. Dynamic malware detection based on traffic analysis is crucial for improving network service quality and ensuring effective security monitoring. However, the widespread use of encryption protocols, especially the Transport Layer Security (TLS) protocol, poses a significant challenge in identifying and classifying encrypted malware traffic. This paper proposes a novel approach that leverages enhanced features and ensemble learning to identify and classify encrypted malware traffic for Android devices effectively. By analyzing the TLS protocol, an enhanced feature set is proposed, combining TLS protocol-related features with session-based statistical features to extract robust fingerprints from mobile device traffic. Then, an ensemble learning strategy is employed to construct a voting classifier that integrates the prediction results of multiple base classifiers, thus improving the classification accuracy. Extensive experiments using the CICAndMal2017 dataset demonstrate that our approach consistently outperforms other classifiers in all six tasks, achieving the highest weighted F1-Scores and improving balanced accuracy by up to 47.46% compared to the baseline method.

Keywords: Encrypted malware traffic · Android malware · Traffic analysis · Intrusion detection

1 Introduction

The widespread adoption of Android mobile devices in today's world is undeniable. According to the International Data Corporation, worldwide smartphone shipments are forecast to grow 4.0% year over year in 2024 to 1.21 billion, with Android maintaining its leading market share at 70.7% in the first quarter of 2024 [1,2]. As the number of Android applications increases and users increasingly rely on third-party app stores, the risk of malware infiltration into both official and unofficial markets rises [3]. Neglecting updates and failing to authenticate downloaded apps expose mobile devices to significant threats, compromising sensitive information such as bank passwords, text messages, contacts, and device data. Thus, effective malware detection solutions are crucial for safeguarding personal information on Android devices.

Android malware detection methods can be divided into two categories: static-based and dynamic-based. Static analysis examines an application file before execution, considering factors such as permissions, hardware, and software components, Application Programming Interface information, and intents [4,5]. However, static methods fall short when malicious activities are dynamically manifested or malware employs code modification and obfuscation techniques [6]. In contrast, dynamic analysis observes the behavior characteristics or patterns of malware during execution, making it particularly suitable for identifying dynamically changing malware. Network traffic analysis, a subset of dynamic analysis, holds great promise as it can be implemented at network gateways or other nodes, alleviating the resource constraints on mobile devices. Malware typically requires communication with remote servers over the internet for malicious activities, offering an opportunity to detect their activities through network traffic analysis [7,8].

Several studies have explored Android malware detection based on network traffic. For example, Chen et al. extracted 15 features from malicious Android traffic, including packet features and time-dependent flow features, and experimented with three classes of Android malware [9]. Gohari et al. utilized CICFlowMeter [10] to extract 86 network flow characteristics from each flow in the dataset [11]. However, the widespread use of encryption, especially Transport Layer Security (TLS), has given rise to a new challenge. Many variants of malware now use encrypted channels to communicate with command and control servers to download payloads, accept commands, and carry out malicious activities, as well as data exfiltration, making monitoring and detecting their activities difficult. More than 80% attacks now occur over encrypted channels, up from 57% [12,13]. Notably, none of the existing studies address the detection of Android malware in the presence of encrypted traffic.

Our approach enhances the feature set by incorporating TLS protocol-based features extracted from encrypted traffic into session-based features. Then, we propose a filter-based feature selection method using mutual information to optimize model performance while reducing the number of features. To accurately identify and classify Android malware, a voting classifier-based ensemble learning approach is proposed. We evaluated the performance of our method using raw Pcap data on the CICAndMal2017 dataset in three different scenarios: detecting malware, classifying malware categories, and identifying variations in malware families. Experimental results show that our proposal outperformed other classifiers in all six tasks, achieving exceptional weighted F1-Scores and significantly improving accuracy compared to the baseline techniques.

The rest of this paper is organized as follows: Sect. 2 presents the system architecture and our proposed Android malware detection method. In Sect. 3, we describe the datasets, configurations, and other information used in the experiments and present the experimental evaluation. Section 4 discusses and concludes.

2 Proposed Method

2.1 System Architecture

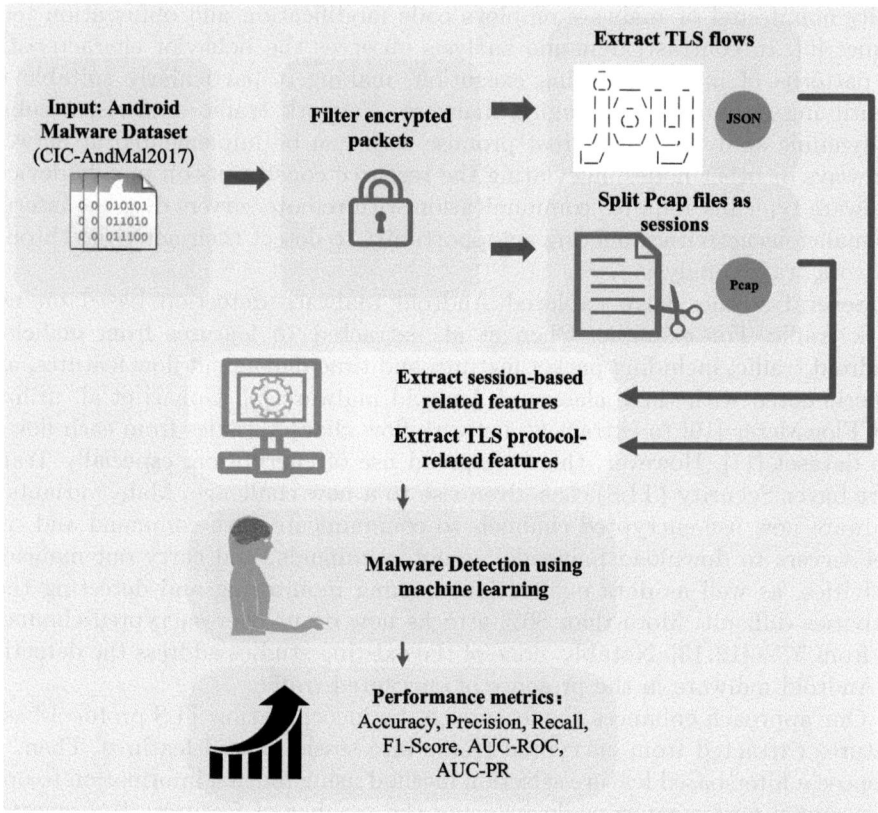

Fig. 1. An overall architecture of the proposed detection system for Android encrypted malware traffic.

Figure 1 provides the overall architecture of the proposed detection system. We begin our process with raw network traffic data in packet capture files (Pcap files). These Pcap files undergo a TLS protocol filter, allowing us to extract packets relevant to the TLS protocol selectively. To facilitate the feature extraction process, we utilize the Joy open source packet analysis tool [14], which extracts TLS flows and generates Json files. Simultaneously, we employ the SplitCap tool [15] to segment the Pcap file into session-based Pcap files. From these two distinct data sources, we extract two categories of features: TLS protocol-related features and session-based features. The TLS protocol-related features are then expanded to supplement session-based features, resulting in an enhanced feature set. This enhanced feature set serves as input for malware detection, leveraging a combination of mutual information-based feature selection and an ensemble learning strategy based on voting classifiers. During the detection phase, each test sample is assigned a predictive label. The effectiveness of our approach is evaluated using a set of performance metrics.

2.2 Extract Session-Based Related Features

First, we filter all packets associated with the TLS protocol. As the TLS protocol operates over TCP sessions, we segment the raw Pcap packet data by sessions. A session is the combination of all bidirectional flows between the communicating nodes. Subsequently, we extract the required features, as detailed in Table 1. Session-based features are classified into four categories: 4-tuple, packet count-related, packet size-related, and packet arrival time-related. Each category includes both basic and statistical features of the bidirectional flow, such as mean, standard deviation, mean absolute variance, median, maximum, and minimum.

Table 1. Session-based related features

Categories	Features	Dimensions
4-tuple	Src_IP,Src_Port,Dst_IP,Dst_Port	4
packet count-related	pktsCount_o,pktsCount_i,pktsCount_SR_ratio, pktsCount,packetcount_per_second, packetcount_per_second_o,packetcount_per_second_i	7
packet size-related	packetSizeSum_o,packetSizeMean_o,packetSizeStd_o, packetSizeMAD_o,packetSizeVar_o,pktSizeMedium_o, pktSize25_o,pktSize75_o, packetSizeMax_o, packetSizeMin_o,packetSizeRange_o,packetSizeSum_i, packetSizeMean_i,packetSizeStd_i,packetSizeMAD_i, packetSizeVar_i, pktSizeMedium_i,pktSize25_i, pktSize75_i,packetSizeMax_i,packetSizeMin_i, packetSizeRange_i,packetSizeSum,packetSizeSum_SR_ratio, packetSizeMean,packetSizeStd,packetSizeMAD, packetSizeVar,pktSizeMedium,pktSize25,pktSize75, packetSizeMax,packetSizeMin,packetSizeRange, packetsizeMarkov_i(i=0~24),packetsizedistribution_i(i=0~4)	64
packet arrival time-related	timeIntervalSum_o,timeIntervalMean_o,timeIntervalStd_o, timeIntervalMAD_o,timeIntervalVar_o,timeIntervalMedium_o, timeInterval25_o,timeInterval75_o,timeIntervalMax_o, timeIntervalMin_o,timeIntervalSum_i,timeIntervalMean_i, timeIntervalStd_i,timeIntervalMAD_i,timeIntervalVar_i, timeIntervalMedium_i, timeInterval25_i,timeInterval75_i, timeIntervalMax_i,timeIntervalMin_i,timeIntervalMean, timeIntervalStd,timeIntervalMAD,timeIntervalVar,timeIntervalMedium, timeInterval25,timeInterval75,timeIntervalMax,timeIntervalMin, flowDuration,flowDuration_o,flowDuration_i, timeIntervalMarkov_i(i=0~15),timeIntervaldistribution_i(i=0~3)	52
sum		127

2.3 Extract TLS Protocol-Related Features

The TLS protocol is the most commonly used encryption protocol, mainly employed to secure HTTP traffic through the HTTPS protocol. According to recent statistics, 99.9% of the surveyed websites support TLS 1.2. Therefore, we use the Joy tool to extract flows related to TLS 1.2.

Figure 2 illustrates the process of establishing a TLS 1.2 session connection. Following the completion of three TCP handshakes, the connection initiation over TLS begins with the client sending a Client Hello message to the server. This message includes information such as the TLS version, a list of offered Cipher Suites, and supported TLS extensions. In response, the server sends a Server Hello message, selecting the Cipher Suite and TLS extensions. In addition, the server issues a certificate message containing its certificate. The Server Key Exchange is required when certain key exchange methods are used and the server does not have a certificate and contains information that allows the Client to communicate the pre-master key. Subsequently, the client transmits a ClientKeyExchange message, providing the information necessary for the server to generate the final symmetric session key. After the ChangeCipherSpec, all subsequent messages are encrypted using the session key. Thus, substantial plaintext

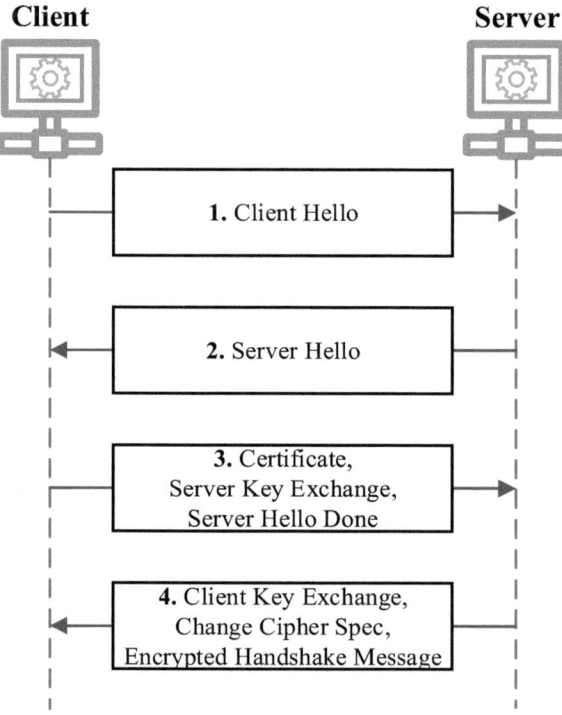

Fig. 2. TLS 1.2 establishes the connection process.

information is exchanged during the TLS 1.2 handshake phase, which is critical for our analysis.

This paper [16] discusses the development of Joy, a software tool designed to extract features from Pcap files and export the extracted TLS flow information to Json format. We utilize the Joy tool to obtain the Json document containing all relevant data and then employ Python for further feature extraction. During this process, we exclude TLS flows with incomplete handshakes, those with fewer than three packets in each direction, and flows missing key features. The extracted TLS protocol-related features include basic features; offered Cipher Suites, supported extensions list, client-supported elliptic curve (EC) point formats, and groups supported by EC; the number of offered cipher suite items, and the length of the supported extensions list. Specific TLS protocol-related features are detailed in Table 2.

Table 2. TLS Protocol-related Features

Features	Dimensions
Src_IP	1
Src_Port	1
Dst_IP	1
Dst_Port	1
Bytes_in	1
Bytes_out	1
Pkts_in	1
Pkts_out	1
Entropy	1
Total_entropy	1
Byte_dist_std	1
Byte_dist_mn	1
Duration	1
Client_key_length	1
Num_of_ciphersuits	1
Num_of_exts	1
Items of ciphersuits	348
Items of extensions	53
Items of supported_groups	22
Items of ec_point_formats	2
Sum	**441**

2.4 Malware Detection Using Machine Learning

During data preprocessing, we extract two types of features: session-based and TLS protocol-related. These features are then merged based on source IP, source port, destination IP, and destination port to cover the correlation information of network traffic data effectively. Then, we remove duplicate rows to maintain data uniqueness, exclude features with missing values to prevent model disruption, and remove feature columns containing only zeros since they add complexity without contributing to malware detection. Finally, columns with IP information are omitted to protect user privacy and sensitive network details.

In the malware detection phase, a feature selection method is employed to identify and retain the most representative features, thereby enhancing model training efficiency. Specifically, we employ Information Gain (IG) as the feature selection method, which considers the correlation between features and target class, as well as the correlation among features. Algorithm1 employs IG to rank features based on their information contribution towards classification. Features are ranked in descending order of their contribution. The K best features selected not solely based on the sum of the importance of the feature, but their relative impact constitute the final set of features.

First, calculate the initial entropy of the training dataset $H(D)$:

$$H(D) = -\Sigma \left(p_i * \log_2 \left(p_i \right) \right). \tag{1}$$

where D is the training dataset with features X and class y, and p_i is the probability of each class in the dataset. For each feature $A \in X$, calculate its conditional entropy $H(D \mid A)$:

$$H(D \mid A) = \Sigma \left(p\left(A = a_i\right) * H\left(D \mid A = a_i\right) \right), \tag{2}$$

where $p(A = a_i)$ represents the probability of a certain value of feature A in the D, and $H(D \mid A = a_i)$ represents the information entropy of the dataset under the condition that the value of feature A is a_i. Then compute information gain $IG(A)$:

$$IG(A) = H(D) - H(D \mid A). \tag{3}$$

Furthermore, we adopt an ensemble learning approach to improve the accuracy of malware detection. Ensemble learning combines multiple base models to enhance predictive performance and generalization. A simple technique within this framework is the voting classifier, which classifies by aggregating the predictions of various learners. Each learner acts as a voter and the category that receives the most votes is selected as the final classification result. In this study, we employed three base classifiers: Random Forest, Extra Trees, and XGBoost, to construct a voting classifier. Random Forest utilizes randomized data sampling and feature selection, often employing the Gini coefficient or information gain, though it may overfit in noisy environments. Extra Trees trains on the entire dataset and randomly selects features for node splitting, reducing variance at the expense of increased bias. XGBoost sequentially builds trees with

Algorithm 1 Feature Selection using Information Gain

1: **Input:** Training dataset D with features X and class y
2: $H(D) \leftarrow$ compute (1)
3: **for** each feature A in X **do**
4:     $H(D \mid A) \leftarrow$ compute (2)
5:     $IG(A) \leftarrow$ compute (3):
6:     Store $IG(A)$ and feature A
7: **end for**
8: Sort features by IG in descending order
9: **Initialize:** Sum $= 0$, $selected\_features\_IG = []$
10: **for** i in range$(0, \text{len}(features))$ **do**
11:     Sum $\leftarrow$ Sum $+ IG(features[i])$
12:     $selected\_features\_IG$.append$(features[i])$
13:     **if** Sum ≥ 0.95 **then**
14:         **break**
15:     **end if**
16: **end for**
17: **Output:** Selected features $selected\_features\_IG$

regularization to prevent overfitting but requires careful hyperparameter tuning. By integrating these classifiers into a voting classifier, we leverage their collective strengths, mitigating individual limitations and enhancing robustness and reliability in classification tasks.

3 Experiments

3.1 Dataset and Experimental Configuration

In this work, we chose a public dataset CICAndMal2017 [17] to validate the effectiveness of the proposed approach. The CICAndMal2017 dataset contains multiple malware samples and normal samples, covering a wide range of malware families. These samples were obtained through simulation experiments, virtual network environments, and network capture techniques to ensure the authenticity and diversity of the data. The data used in our experiments were the raw Pcap files of Adware, Ransomware, Scareware, SMS Malware, and Benign 2017.

In this work, we focus on identifying and classifying encrypted malware traffic from Android. For malware detection, we define four binary classification scenarios: B1, B2, B3, and B4. Additionally, we conduct a coarse-grained classification of malware into four categories: adware, ransomware, smsmalware, and scareware, designated as the M1 task. We further classify malware into three categories of malware within a family, namely Adware-Youmi, Adware-Ewind, and Adware-Kemoge, designated as the M2 task. Details on data usage for these scenarios are provided in Table 3, which also correlates with the categories discussed in the Experimental Results section. The dataset used originates from a malware detection system for mobile devices, with a training-to-test ratio of 8:2.

The experiments were carried out on an Omen 30L machine equipped with an i7-11700K CPU (6 cores, 3.60 GHz) and 16 GB of memory. The proposed method and comparative algorithms were implemented using Python and Scikit-Learn version 0.24.2.

Table 3. Data usage information

Classification task	Dataset	Categories	Label
Binary classification	Binary classification-1 (B1)	Benign	0
		Adware	1
	Binary classification-2 (B2)	Benign	0
		Ransomware	1
	Binary classification-3 (B3)	Benign	0
		Scareware	1
	Binary classification-4 (B4)	Benign	0
		SMSmalware	1
Multi-classification	Multi-classification-1 (M1)	Adware	0
		Ransomware	1
		Scareware	2
		SMSmalware	3
	Multi-classification-2 (M2)	Adware-Youmi	0
		Adware-Ewind	1
		Adware-Kemoge	2

3.2 Evaluation Metrics

we employ six evaluation metrics to assess our model's performance on imbalanced datasets from various perspectives. The selected metrics are balanced accuracy, weighted precision, weighted recall, and weighted F1-Score, calculated as follows:

Balanced Accuracy is the average recall obtained for each class, crucial for evaluating classifier performance on imbalanced datasets:

$$\text{Balanced Accuracy} = \frac{1}{n}\sum_{i=1}^{n}\frac{TP_i}{TP_i + FN_i} \quad (4)$$

Weighted Precision calculates the weighted average of precision across all classes:

$$\text{Weighted Precision} = \frac{1}{n}\sum_{i=1}^{n}\frac{TP_i}{TP_i + FP_i} \quad (5)$$

Weighted Recall computes the weighted average of recall across all classes:

$$\text{Weighted Recall} = \sum_{i=1}^{n}w_i\frac{TP_i}{TP_i + FN_i} \quad (6)$$

Weighted F1-Score is the weighted average of the F1-Scores for each class, combining precision and recall:

$$\text{Weighted F1-Score} = \sum_{i=1}^{n}w_i\frac{2TP_i}{2TP_i + FN_i + FP_i} \quad (7)$$

AUC-ROC (Receiver Operating Characteristic) is the area under the ROC curve, which reflects the model's trade-off between true and false positive rates at different thresholds.

$$\text{AUC-ROC}_i = \int_0^1 TPR_i\left(FPR_i^{-1}(t)\right) dt \tag{8}$$

AUC-PR (Precision-Recall Curve) is the area under the PR curve, which reflects the trade-off between Precision and Recall under different thresholds.

$$\text{AUC-PR}_i = \int_0^1 P_i\left(R_i^{-1}(t)\right) dt \tag{9}$$

where $P_i = \frac{TP_i}{TP_i + FP_i}$, $R_i = \frac{TP_i}{TP_i + FN_i}$. The subscript i denotes the i_{th} class, TP denotes True Positive, FP denotes False Positive, FN denotes False Negative, TPR is True Positive Rate, FPR is False Positive Rate, n is the number of classes, and w is the weight of each class.

3.3 Performance Comparison of Different Classifiers

We conducted experiments on the CICAndMal2017 dataset using various classifiers based on the proposed enhanced feature set. Given the resource constraints of mobile devices, we choose traditional machine learning models, including Extra Trees, Random Forest, XGBoost, and a voting classifier, over more resource-intensive deep learning models.

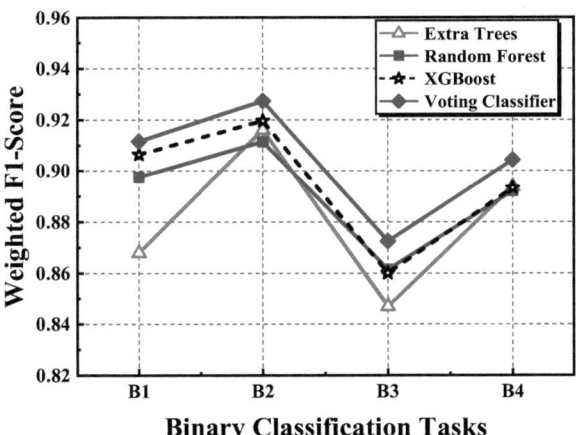

Fig. 3. Performance comparison of different classifiers in four binary classification tasks.

Figure 3 illustrates the performance comparison of various classifiers across four binary classification tasks (B1–B4), utilizing the weighted F1-Score as the evaluation metric. The results indicate that the voting classifier consistently outperforms others in all tasks. Figure 4 shows the performance of different classifiers in the multi-classification tasks M1 and M2, where the voting classifier also exhibits superior performance. Specifically, in M1, which involves distinguishing between malware families, the models achieved a weighted F1-Score of 0.87. In M2, which focuses on variants within a malware family, performance slightly decreases to a weighted F1-Score of 0.84. This analysis indicates that multi-class models generally underperform compared to binary models, primarily due to the challenges in distinguishing variants that often share similar communication patterns and malicious behaviors, complicating their differentiation. Moreover, it is observed that while XGBoost and the voting classifier perform similarly in the M2 multi-classification task, the voting classifier consistently achieves better performance across various binary tasks. This suggests that our voting classifier exhibits stronger robustness, potentially due to its ability to aggregate diverse model outputs effectively.

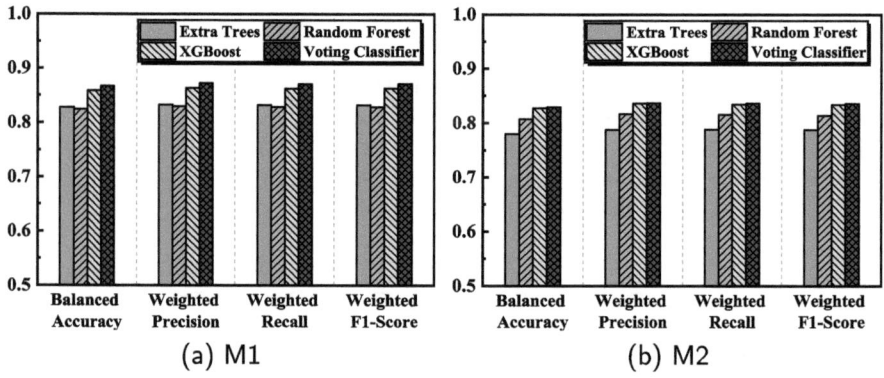

Fig. 4. Performance comparison of different classifiers in the M1 and M2 task.

3.4 Enhanced Feature Importance and Superiority

Based on a comparison of classifier performance using the enhanced feature set, the voting classifier shows superior performance in both binary and multi-classification tasks. Therefore, we use the voting classifier to conduct feature importance analysis. Feature Importance Analysis aims to examine the weights of each feature in a dataset to ascertain their relationship with the classes in the same dataset. We used IG as the metric, selecting the top nine features for detailed analysis, focusing on those related to the TLS protocol and session-based features, visually represented by red and blue, respectively.

Figure 5 illustrates the top nine feature importance rankings post-selection using IG. We observed notable differences in feature importance across these tasks. Specifically, in binary tasks B1 and B3, the top features are predominantly TLS-related. However, in binary tasks B2 and B4, session-based features like "Bytes_in" emerge as crucial, suggesting their relevance in specific contexts. These observations underline the significant role of TLS features in malware identification across several scenarios.

The experimental results reveal the significance and superiority of the TLS protocol-related and session-based features for different tasks. Consequently, selecting suitable feature sets and classifier structures can yield better classification performance for varying tasks.

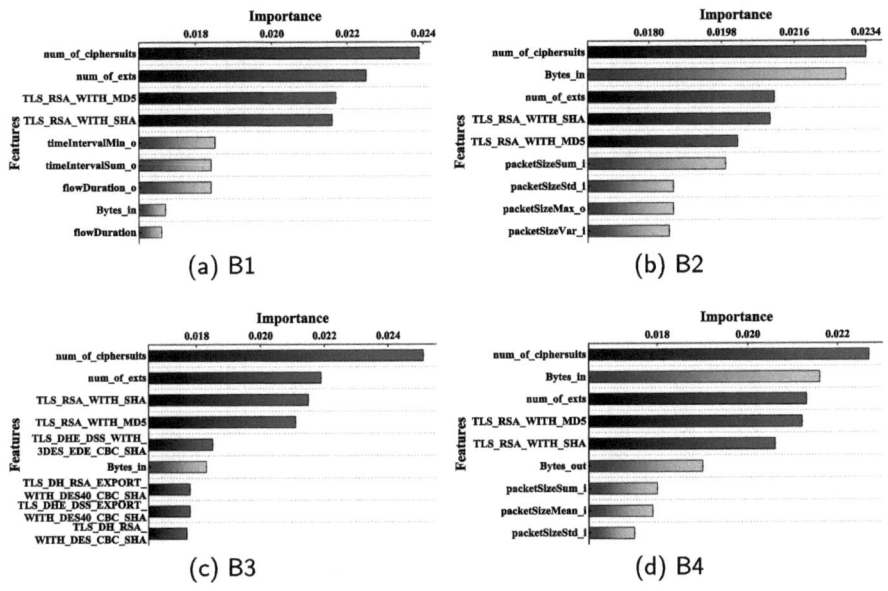

Fig. 5. Feature importance ranking in four binary tasks. (Red: TLS protocol-related features; Blue: session-based features) (Color figure online)

3.5 Performance Comparison of Different Feature Sets

In the study [18], the authors developed the CICAndMal2017 dataset and used CICFlowMeter to extract features, explicitly excluding protocol-related features in their analysis. In contrast, our study incorporated an enhanced feature set that includes TLS protocol-related features. We employed IG and a voting classifier to train and test both the enhanced and statistical feature sets extracted by CICFlowMeter.

Figure 6 shows the comparative detection performance of different feature sets across four binary classification tasks (B1–B4). The results demonstrate that our enhanced feature set significantly outperforms the feature set extracted by CICFlowmeter in all tasks. The balanced accuracy and weighted F1-Score of the enhanced set exceed 0.92 in the B2 task, compared to approximately 0.80 for the statistical set. In addition, the performance of the enhanced feature set in the B4 task reaches the highest gap of about 0.16 compared to the statistical feature set.

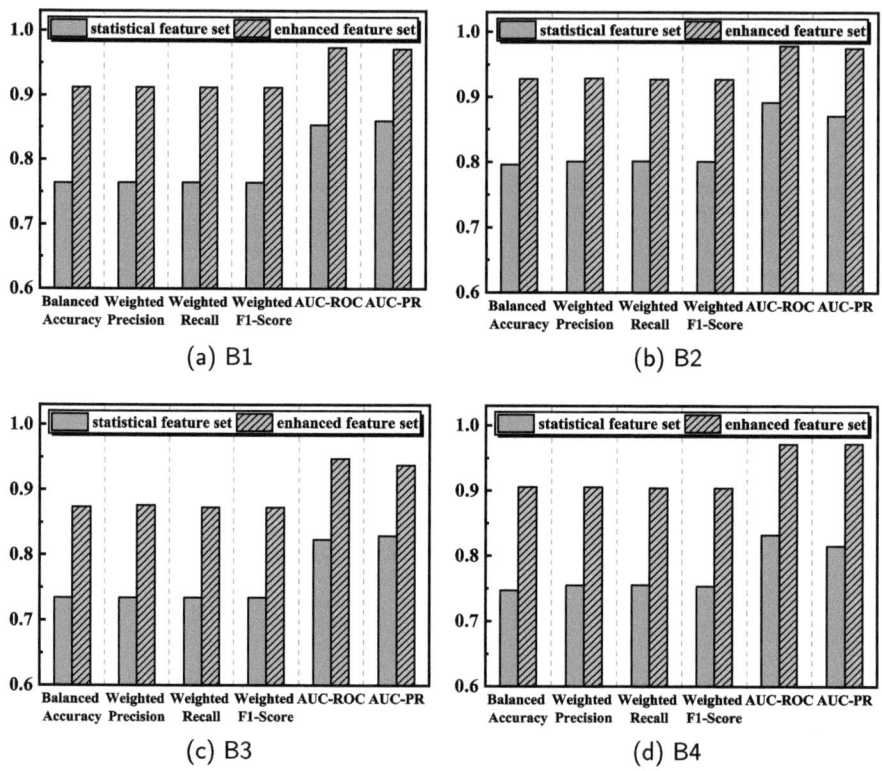

Fig. 6. Comparison of detection performance for different feature sets in four binary tasks.

Table 4 and Table 5 present the results of comparing the detection performance for different feature sets in M1 and M2 multi-classification scenarios, respectively. Experimental results show that the enhanced feature set achieves a 47.46% increase in balanced accuracy over the statistical feature set for the M1 task. In the M2 task, the enhanced feature set also shows superior performance across all evaluated metrics, with balanced accuracy achieving an approximate improvement of 22.06%.

From the experimental results, it can be concluded that our proposed enhanced feature set shows better classification results in all tasks, both in terms of overall performance in each task and detection ability in different categories. This suggests that the addition of features related to the TLS protocol helps

Table 4. Comparison of different feature sets in the M1 task

Model	Voting Classifier							
Method	statistical feature set				enhanced feature set			
Class	Precision	Recall	F1-Score	Balanced Accuracy	Precision	Recall	F1-Score	Balanced Accuracy
0	0.61	0.68	0.64	0.59	0.8	0.82	0.81	0.87
1	0.7	0.73	0.71		0.97	0.98	0.98	
2	0.55	0.55	0.55		0.9	0.83	0.87	
3	0.52	0.42	0.47		0.8	0.83	0.81	
Weighted Average	0.60	0.60	0.60		0.87	0.87	0.87	

Table 5. Comparison of different feature sets in the M2 task

Model	Voting Classifier							
Method	statistical feature set				enhanced feature set			
Class	Precision	Recall	F1-Score	Balanced Accuracy	Precision	Recall	F1-Score	Balanced Accuracy
0	0.62	0.59	0.61	0.68	0.77	0.69	0.73	0.82
1	0.74	0.81	0.77		0.98	0.99	0.98	
2	0.67	0.63	0.65		0.73	0.8	0.76	
Weighted Average	0.68	0.68	0.68		0.82	0.83	0.83	

to improve the classification performance of malware from mobile applications. Our feature extraction method considers multiple features of malicious traffic, including network protocols, traffic patterns, and packet contents, to more comprehensively capture the characteristics of mobile applications and improve the performance of the classifier. In addition, the enhanced feature set can better adapt to encrypted traffic data and classify encrypted TLS traffic more accurately. This is because, with the addition of TLS protocol-related features based on the TLS protocol, the model is better able to detect cleartext segments during the TLS handshake, thereby improving classification accuracy.

4 Conclusion

In this paper, we propose a voting classifier method based on enhanced features to identify and classify malware traffic encrypted by mobile devices. By introducing features related to TLS-based protocols, we extend the original feature set to capture malware features in mobile device traffic more comprehensively. Meanwhile, by using an ensemble learning-based voting classifier, we can effectively integrate the prediction results of multiple base classifiers, thereby improving the accuracy and robustness of the classification. Extensive experiments using the CICAndMal2017 dataset have consistently demonstrated the superiority of our proposed method across all six tasks, as evidenced by higher weighted F1-Scores. Notably, our approach has achieved a balanced accuracy improvement of up to 47.46% over the baseline method.

In future research, we will continue to optimize and improve the proposed approach, including trying more feature selection and ensemble learning strategies to further improve the performance of the classifier.

Acknowledgments. This research is supported by the National Key R&D Program of China under Grant (No. 2022YFB3104900).

References

1. IDC: Worldwide smartphone shipments forecast to recover with 4.0% growth in 2024, fueled by android growth in emerging markets (2024). https://www.idc.com/getdoc.jsp?containerId=prUS52306524
2. Taylor, P.: Market share of mobile operating systems worldwide from 2009 to 2024, by quarter (2024). https://www.statista.com/statistics/272698/global-market-share-held-by-mobile-operating-systems-since-2009/
3. Senanayake, J., Kalutarage, H., Al-Kadri, M.O.: Android mobile malware detection using machine learning: a systematic review. Electronics **10**(13), 1606 (2021)
4. Şahin, D.Ö., Kural, O.E., Akleylek, S., Kılıç, E.: A novel permission-based android malware detection system using feature selection based on linear regression. Neural Comput. Appl., 1–16 (2021)
5. Roy, A., Jas, D.S., Jaggi, G., Sharma, K.: Android malware detection based on vulnerable feature aggregation. Procedia Comput. Sci. **173**, 345–353 (2020)
6. Sihag, V., Vardhan, M., Singh, P.: A survey of android application and malware hardening. Comput. Sci. Rev. **39**, 100365 (2021)
7. Musikawan, P., Kongsorot, Y., You, I., So-In, C.: An enhanced deep learning neural network for the detection and identification of android malware. IEEE Internet Things J. (2022)
8. Wang, S., et al.: Deep and broad URL feature mining for android malware detection. Inf. Sci. **513**, 600–613 (2020)
9. Chen, R., Li, Y., Fang, W.: Android malware identification based on traffic analysis. In: Sun, X., Pan, Z., Bertino, E. (eds.) ICAIS 2019. LNCS, vol. 11632, pp. 293–303. Springer, Cham (2019). https://doi.org/10.1007/978-3-030-24274-9_26
10. Draper-Gil, G., Lashkari, A.H., Mamun, M.S.I., Ghorbani, A.A.: Characterization of encrypted and VPN traffic using time-related. In: Proceedings of the 2nd International Conference on Information Systems Security and Privacy (ICISSP), pp. 407–414 (2016)
11. Gohari, M., Hashemi, S., Abdi, L.: Android malware detection and classification based on network traffic using deep learning. In: 2021 7th International Conference on Web Research (ICWR), pp. 71–77. IEEE (2021)
12. Zscaler: Infographic: The state of encrypted attacks | 2021 threatlabz report (2021). https://www.zscaler.com/resources/infographics/infographic-state-of-encrypted-attacks-2021.pdf
13. Zscaler: The state of encrypted attacks | 2021 threatlabz report (2021). https://www.zscaler.com/resources/industry-reports/state-of-encrypted-attacks-2021.pdf
14. McGrew, D., Anderson, B., Perricone, P., Hudson, B.: Joy: a package for capturing and analyzing network flow data and intraflow data (2016). https://github.com/cisco/joy

15. Netresec: SplitCap: a tool designed to split capture files into smaller files (n.d). https://www.netresec.com/index.ashx?page=SplitCap
16. Anderson, B., Paul, S., McGrew, D.: Deciphering malware's use of TLS (without decryption). J. Comput. Virol. Hack. Techn. **14**, 195–211 (2018)
17. Lashkari, A.H., Kadir, A.F.A., Taheri, L., Ghorbani, A.A.: Toward developing a systematic approach to generate benchmark android malware datasets and classification. In: 2018 International Carnahan Conference on Security Technology (ICCST), pp. 1–7. IEEE (2018)
18. Lashkari, A.H., Kadir, A.F.A., Gonzalez, H., Mbah, K.F., Ghorbani, A.A.: Towards a network-based framework for android malware detection and characterization. In: 2017 15th Annual Conference on Privacy, Security and Trust (PST), pp. 233–23309. IEEE (2017)

An Energy Efficient and High Accuracy Detection Scheme for Dual Function Radar and Communication Systems

Pengzun Gao[1], Long Zhao[1(✉)], and Kan Zheng[2]

[1] Beijing University of Posts and Telecommunications (BUPT),
Beijing 100876, China
{gaopengzun,z-long}@bupt.edu.cn
[2] Ningbo University (NBU), Ningbo 315211, China

Abstract. In sixth generation (6G) mobile communications, Dual Function Radar and Communication (DFRC) signals are employed in Internet of Vehicles (IoV) to ensure traffic safety by simultaneously sensing and communication. This paper considers a high-accuracy target detection scheme for pedestrian with potential safety risks while minimizing the total power consumption. Therefore, an optimization problem is formulated to maximize the accuracy-to-power ratio (APR) under the communication quality of service (QoS) constraint. After detection accuracy analysis and problem transformation, a feasible solution is derived based on convex optimization theory. The detection performance of the proposed scheme under various conditions is evaluated, and the results demonstrate that the proposed scheme can achieve a tradeoff between detection accuracy and total power consumption.

Keywords: Internet of vehicles · dual function radar and communication · target detection · power allocation

1 Introduction

As urbanization accelerates and cities expand, the safety challenges associated with urban traffic are increasingly pronounced [1]. Internet of Vehicles (IoV), serving as the developmental focus of the intelligent traffic system (ITS), hold paramount significance in addressing urban traffic challenges [2,3]. In order to enhance safety, the existing IoV system must improve its capability to gather sensing information from the surrounding environment while maintaining the previous communication quality of service (QoS). As a result, certain scholars believe that sensing services will become a crucial role in IoV system in the forthcoming sixth generation (6G) mobile communications [4,5].

The coexistence and multiplexing of existing sensing and communication systems is a feasible solution; however, some potential issues of spectrum conflicts still exist [6,7]. Fortunately, the Integrated Sensing and Communication (ISAC) technology in 6G mobile communications is anticipated to ensure both sensing and communication QoS simultaneously. In current research, given the advancement of massive Multiple Input Multiple Output (mMIMO) and millimeter wave technology, Dual Function Radar and Communication (DFRC) is frequently employed as the primary technical solution for implementing ISAC functions [8]. DFRC has dual advantages over the traditional coexistence and multiplexing scheme [9,10]. Firstly, sensing and communication share the same high-frequency signal, effectively avoiding the potential spectrum conflict typically caused by using two separate signals at high frequencies. Secondly, DFRC integrates sensing and communication functions onto a unified physical platform, reducing redundancies in transmissions, equipment, and infrastructure, thereby realizing integration benefits.

Within the existing literature, the optimization objective commonly revolves the detection probability in the DFRC system [11]. This objective inherently aims to balance sensing and communication performance. Moreover, literature [12] explored the detection probability tradeoff among multiple sensing targets, ensuring the preservation of communication performance. Notably, the aforementioned articles overlook the energy efficiency of the gNB when evaluating detection performance.

In this paper, considering a target detection scenario in IoV, an indicator is introduced, i.e., the ratio of detection accuracy to the total power consumption (APR), which can reflect both detection accuracy and energy consumption. Meanwhile, an optimization problem to maximize APR while ensuring communication QoS is formulated. Through problem transformation, an energy efficient and high accuracy (EEHA) detection scheme is designed to effectively address the optimization problem. Finally, simulation results demonstrate that the proposed scheme achieves a tradeoff between detection accuracy and energy consumption compared to the baseline scheme.

The remainder of the paper is organized as follows. Section 2 describes the DFRC system model in IoV and formulates the optimization problem. In Sect. 3, a EEHA detection scheme is proposed to solve the optimization problem. Section 4 is dedicated to presenting simulation results and conducting analysis. Finally, the paper is summarized and concluded in Sect. 5.

2 System Model and Problem Formulation

2.1 Scenario Description

As depicted in Fig. 1, a millimeter wave gNB employs a uniform linear arrays (ULA), consisting of N_t transmit antennas and N_r receive antennas. The gNB transmits downlink DFRC signals to communicate with M single-antenna information users and sense a target user, i.e., potentially a pedestrian at a zebra crossing, simultaneously. To achieve temporally continuous target detection and enhance detection accuracy, we consider a total of L time slots, each lasting ΔT. Without loss of generality, given the different speeds of vehicles, it is assumed that vehicles keep moving at a constant speed throughout a time slot, while pedestrian remains stationary across multiple time slots.

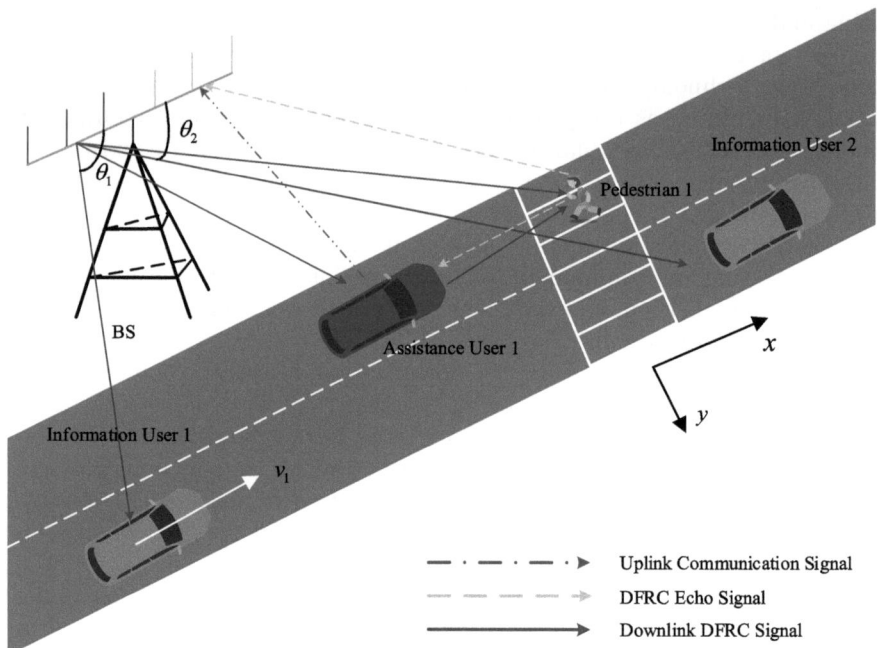

Fig. 1. Illustration of DFRC system in IoV.

2.2 Channel Model

Denote $\theta_{l,M+1}$ and $\theta_{l,m}$ as the angle of departure (AoD) of the signal from the gNB to the potential pedestrian and the mth information vehicle at time slot $l \in \mathcal{L} = [1, \cdots, L]$, respectively. Moreover, it is assumed that the estimated value of the AoD equals the true value, i.e., $\hat{\theta}_l = \theta_l$. If a detection target is present, the AoA between the gNB and the pedestrian at time slot l can also be denoted as $\theta_{l,M+1}$. Considering the antenna spacing of ULA at the gNB is half wavelength, the transmit and receive steering vectors can be expressed respectively as

$$\mathbf{a}_\chi(\theta) = N_\chi^{-1/2} \left[1, e^{j\pi \cos\theta}, \cdots, e^{j\pi(N_\chi-1)\cos\theta}\right]^{\mathrm{T}}, \qquad (1)$$

where $\chi \in \{\mathrm{t},\mathrm{r}\}$ and $\theta \in \{\theta_{l,m}, \forall m = 1, 2, \cdots, M+1\}$.

Assuming that the speed of the mth information vehicle at time slot l is $v_{l,m}$, the Doppler shift between the mth communication vehicle and the gNB is $\varpi_{l,m} = v_{l,m} f_{\mathrm{c}} \cos(\pi - \theta_{l,m})/\mathrm{c}$, where f_{c} and c denote the carrier frequency and the speed of light, respectively. Meanwhile, assuming that the distances between the gNB and the potential pedestrian and the mth information vehicle at time slot l are denoted as $d_{l,M+1}$ and $d_{l,m}$, respectively, therefore the delays of the sensing channel and the mth communication channel are $\tau_{l,M+1} = 2d_{l,M+1}/\mathrm{c}$ and $\tau_{l,m} = d_{l,m}/\mathrm{c}$.

The potential pedestrian that requires detection can be considered a stationary point target. When a pedestrian is present at the zebra crossing at time slot l, the radar echo channel between the gNB and the detection target can be characterized as

$$\mathbf{H}_{l,M+1} = \sqrt{N_\mathrm{t} N_\mathrm{r}} \beta_{l,M+1} \mathbf{a}_\mathrm{r}\left(\theta_{l,M+1}\right) \mathbf{a}_\mathrm{t}^\mathrm{H}\left(\theta_{l,M+1}\right), \tag{2}$$

where $\beta_{l,M+1} \sim \mathbb{CN}\left(0, \hat{\sigma}_\beta^2\right)$ denotes the loss factor for the round trip transmission, encompassing the impact of the radar cross section (RCS) [12]. Likewise, the communication channel between the gNB and the mth vehicle at time slot l can be denoted as

$$\mathbf{h}_{l,m} = \sqrt{N_\mathrm{t}} \alpha_{l,m} e^{j2\pi \varpi_{l,m} t} \mathbf{a}_\mathrm{t}\left(\theta_{l,m}\right), \tag{3}$$

where $\alpha_{l,m}$ signifies the large-scale fading coefficient [12]. The communication channel matrix between the gNB and all vehicles are $\mathbf{H}_l = \left[\mathbf{h}_{l,1}, \mathbf{h}_{l,2}, \cdots, \mathbf{h}_{l,M}\right]^\mathrm{H}$.

2.3 Transmit Signal

At time slot l, $(M+1)$ symbols at the gNB are transmitted concurrently to a potential pedestrian and M vehicles. These baseband symbols can be represented as $\mathbf{s}_l(t) = \left[s_{l,1}(t), \cdots, s_{l,M}(t), s_{l,M+1}(t)\right]^\mathrm{T}$, with $\mathbb{E}\left[\mathbf{s}\mathbf{s}^\mathrm{H}\right] = \mathbf{I}_{M+1}$, which means that $s_{l,M+1}(t)$ is employed to execute the sensing function by the gNB.

Consequently, let $\mathbf{p}_l = \left[p_{l,1}, \cdots, p_{l,M}, p_{l,M+1}\right]^\mathrm{T}$ denotes the power allocation vector. And the signal transmitted by the gNB can be expressed as $\mathbf{x}_l(t) = \mathbf{B}_l \mathrm{diag}^{1/2}(\mathbf{p}_l) \mathbf{s}_l(t)$, where $\mathbf{B}_l = \left[\mathbf{b}_{l,1}, \cdots, \mathbf{b}_{l,M}, \mathbf{b}_{l,M+1}\right] \triangleq \left[\mathbf{B}_{l,M}, \mathbf{b}_{l,M+1}\right]$ represents the beamforming matrix, as well as $\mathbf{b}_{l,M+1}$ and $\mathbf{B}_{l,M}$ indicate the beamforming for a potential pedestrian and communication vehicles, respectively. In this study, to simplify complexity, matched filter is utilized as the beamforming scheme in the sensing process, i.e., $\mathbf{b}_{l,M+1} = \mathbf{a}_\mathrm{t}\left(\theta_{l,M+1}\right)$. While zero forcing precoding is adopted in the communication process, i.e., $\mathbf{B}_{l,M} = \mathbf{H}_l^\mathrm{H}\left(\mathbf{H}_l \mathbf{H}_l^\mathrm{H}\right)^{-1} \mathbf{L}_{l,M}$, where $\mathbf{L}_{l,M}$ is the normalised coefficient matrix.

2.4 Received Signal

Target Echo Signal. The sensing receiver at the gNB also employs matched filter, i.e., $\mathbf{w}_{l,M+1} = \mathbf{a}_\mathrm{r}\left(\theta_{l,M+1}\right)$. Based on (2), the received sensing echo signal at the gNB at time slot l can be expressed as

$$\begin{aligned} y_{l,M+1}(t) = &\mathbf{w}_{l,M+1}^\mathrm{H} \mathbf{H}_{l,M+1} \mathbf{x}_l\left(t - \tau_{l,M+1}\right) \\ &+ \mathbf{w}_{l,M+1}^\mathrm{H} \mathbf{n}_{l,M+1}(t), \end{aligned} \tag{4}$$

where $\mathbf{n}_{l,M+1} \sim \mathbb{CN}\left(0, \sigma_\mathrm{s}^2\right)$ denotes Additive Gaussian White Noise (AWGN).

Received Communication Signal. According to (3), the communication signal received by the mth vehicle at time slot l can be represented by

$$y_{l,m}(t) = \sqrt{p_{l,m}}\mathbf{h}_{l,m}^H\mathbf{b}_{l,m}s_{l,m}(t-\tau_{l,m})$$
$$+ \sqrt{p_{l,M+1}}\mathbf{h}_{l,m}^H\mathbf{b}_{l,M+1}s_{l,M+1}(t-\tau_{l,m}) + \mathbf{n}_{l,m}(t), \quad (5)$$

where $\mathbf{n}_{l,m}(t) \sim \mathbb{CN}(0, \sigma_c^2)$ represents AWGN.

Based on (5), it is demonstrated that the communication signal received by the mth vehicle is only affected by the sensing signal. Therefore, the signal-to-interference-plus-noise ratio (SINR) can be expressed as

$$\gamma_{l,m} = \frac{p_{l,m}\left|\mathbf{h}_{l,m}^H\mathbf{b}_{l,m}\right|^2}{p_{l,M+1}\left|\mathbf{h}_{l,m}^H\mathbf{b}_{l,M+1}\right|^2 + \sigma_c^2}. \quad (6)$$

2.5 Problem Formulation

Assume that the detection probability is P_D and the probability of false alarm is P_FA for the detection task in this paper. If the probability of pedestrian presence is p, then the detection accuracy can be mathematically represented as

$$P_\text{true} = pP_\text{D} + (1-p)(1-P_\text{FA}), \quad (7)$$

where the first item represents that the pedestrian is accurately detected as present, while the other item indicates that a pedestrian is correctly sensed as absent.

Considering the power constraint of the gNB, it is necessary to give a detection scheme with high detection accuracy and low power consumption, while guaranteeing the communication QoS. Therefore, the objective of this paper is to maximize the APR, and the optimization problem can be formulated as

$$\mathcal{P}0: \max_{\mathbf{p}_l} \frac{P_\text{true}}{\sum_{m=1}^{M+1} p_{l,m}} \quad (8a)$$

$$\text{s.t.} \gamma_{l,m} \geq \gamma_{\text{th},c}, \forall m, \quad (8b)$$

$$\|\mathbf{p}_l\|_2^2 \leq P_\text{M}. \quad (8c)$$

The constraint (8b) stipulates that the SINR for the communication vehicle must exceed a defined threshold $\gamma_{\text{th},c}$ to guarantee the communication QoS. Additionally, the constraint (8c) indicates the total power constraint, capped at P_M.

3 EEHA Detection Scheme

3.1 Problem Analysis

Detection Accuracy. The target detection task entails identifying the presence or absence of a designated target within a defined area. Therefore, the primary focus of this paper is to precisely locate a potential pedestrian on a zebra crossing, we operate under the assumption that the gNB knows prior information concerning angle $\hat{\theta}_l$.

According to (1), the beam gain at time slot l can be expressed as

$$\varepsilon_{l,t} = \left| \mathbf{a}_t^H (\theta_{l,M+1}) \mathbf{a}_t (\hat{\theta}_{l,M+1}) \right|, \tag{9}$$

$$\varepsilon_{l,r} = \left| \mathbf{a}_r^H (\theta_{l,M+1}) \mathbf{a}_r (\hat{\theta}_{l,M+1}) \right|, \tag{10}$$

where $\varepsilon_{l,t}, \varepsilon_{l,r} \in [0,1]$. Then, the output of the received signal (4) after matched filtering can be represented as

$$\begin{aligned} r_{l,M+1} &= \int y_{l,M+1}(t) s_{l,M+1}^* (t - \tau_{l,M+1}) e^{-j2\pi \mu_{l,M+1} t} dt \\ &= \sqrt{p_{l,M+1}} \beta_{l,M+1} \sqrt{N_t N_r} \varepsilon_{l,t} \varepsilon_{l,r} + n_{l,M+1}. \end{aligned} \tag{11}$$

Considering that the potential pedestrian is treated as relatively stationary with respect to the gNB, the Doppler shift coefficient $\mu_{l,M+1} = 0$ holds, i.e., $e^{-j2\pi \mu_{l,M+1} t} = 1$. Therefore, the match filtering noise which can be expressed as

$$n_{l,M+1} = \int \mathbf{w}_{l,M+1}^H \mathbf{n}_{l,M+1}(t) s_{l,M+1}^*(t - \tau_{l,M+1}) dt, \tag{12}$$

and $n_{l,M+1} \sim \mathbb{CN}(0, \sigma_s^2)$.

The target detection problem discussed in this paper can be framed as a composite binary hypothesis. The null hypothesis ($\mathcal{H}_0$) posits the absence of pedestrians at the crosswalk during a red light, while the alternative hypothesis ($\mathcal{H}_1$) posits the presence of pedestrians [13]. Hence, the detection model can be defined through the following hypothesis testing problem [14]

$$r_{l,M+1} = \begin{cases} n_{l,M+1}, & \mathcal{H}_0 \\ \sqrt{p_{l,M+1}} \beta_{l,M+1} \sqrt{N_t N_r} \varepsilon_{l,t} \varepsilon_{l,r} + n_{l,M+1}. & \mathcal{H}_1 \end{cases} \tag{13}$$

Following the Neyman-Pearson criterion, the optimal detector is given by [15]

$$E = |r_{l,M+1}|^2 \underset{\mathcal{H}_0}{\overset{\mathcal{H}_1}{\gtrless}} \delta, \tag{14}$$

where δ is determined to meet the given probability of false alarm. It is apparent that the sensing statistic E follows the subsequent distribution [14]

$$E \sim \begin{cases} \frac{\sigma_s^2}{2} \chi_2^2, & \mathcal{H}_0 \\ \left(\frac{\sigma_s^2}{2} + \frac{\mu_{1,M+1}}{2} \right) \chi_2^2, & \mathcal{H}_1 \end{cases} \tag{15}$$

where χ_2^2 is the the central chi-squared distribution with two degrees of freedom and $\mu_{1,M+1} = p_{l,M+1}\hat{\sigma}_\beta^2 N_\mathrm{t} N_\mathrm{r}(\varepsilon_{l,\mathrm{t}}\varepsilon_{l,\mathrm{r}})^2$. Moreover, the expression for the probability of false alarm can be represented as

$$P_\mathrm{FA} = \Pr\left(\chi_2^2 > \frac{2\delta}{\sigma_\mathrm{s}^2}\right). \tag{16}$$

Thus, the threshold can be further derived as

$$\delta = \frac{\sigma_\mathrm{s}^2}{2} F_{\chi_2^2}^{-1}\left(1 - P_\mathrm{FA}\right), \tag{17}$$

where $F_{\chi_2^2}(\cdot)$ represents the cumulative distribution function (CDF), while $F_{\chi_2^2}^{-1}(\cdot)$ represents the inverse operation of the chi-square random variable. Similarly, the detection probability can be written as

$$\begin{aligned}P_\mathrm{D} &= \Pr\left(E > \delta \,|\, \mathcal{H}_1\right) = 1 - F_{\chi_2^2}\left(\frac{2\delta/\sigma_\mathrm{s}^2}{1 + \rho_1 p_{l,M+1}}\right) \\ &= e^{\frac{-\delta}{\sigma_\mathrm{s}^2\left(1+\rho_1 p_{l,M+1}\right)}},\end{aligned} \tag{18}$$

where

$$\rho_1 = \frac{\hat{\sigma}_\beta^2 N_\mathrm{t} N_\mathrm{r}(\varepsilon_{l,\mathrm{t}}\varepsilon_{l,\mathrm{r}})^2}{\sigma_\mathrm{s}^2}. \tag{19}$$

Problem Transformation. When the probability of false alarm P_FA is certain, the threshold value δ is determined according to (17). If the probability of the presence of a pedestrian p is also certain at this time, based on (7) and (18), it is established that enhancing detection accuracy is feasible by power allocation. Therefore, the optimization problem $\mathcal{P}0$ can be transformed into

$$\mathcal{P}1 : \min_{\mathbf{p}_l} \frac{1}{P_\mathrm{D}} \sum_{m=1}^{M+1} p_{l,m} \tag{20a}$$

$$\text{s.t. } (8b) \text{ and } (8c). \tag{20b}$$

Meanwhile, based on (6), (8b) can be rewritten as

$$\gamma_{\mathrm{th,c}} k_{l,m}^2 p_{l,M+1} - k_{l,m}^1 p_{l,m} + \gamma_{\mathrm{th,c}} \sigma_\mathrm{c}^2 \leqslant 0, \forall k, \tag{21}$$

where

$$k_{l,m}^1 \triangleq \left|\mathbf{h}_{l,m}^H \mathbf{b}_{l,m}\right|^2, \tag{22}$$

$$k_{l,m}^2 \triangleq \left|\mathbf{h}_{l,m}^H \mathbf{b}_{l,M+1}\right|^2. \tag{23}$$

Substituting (18) into (20a), we have

$$\mathcal{P}2: \min_{\mathbf{p}_l} e^{\frac{A}{1+\rho_1 p_{l,M+1}}} \sum_{m=1}^{M+1} p_{l,m}, \tag{24a}$$

$$\text{s.t. (21) and (8c)}, \tag{24b}$$

where $A \triangleq \delta/\sigma_s^2$.

3.2 Problem Solution

For the sake of simplicity, omit l on the problem solution part of the expression and let $Q_1 \triangleq \gamma_{\text{th,c}} \sum_{i=1}^{M} (k_i^2/k_i^1)$ and $Q_2 \triangleq \gamma_{\text{th,c}} \sigma_c^2 \sum_{i=1}^{M} (1/k_i^1)$. The solution to $\mathcal{P}2$ is proposed as follows, which is also the solution to $\mathcal{P}0$.

Proposition 1. *The solution to $\mathcal{P}2$ can be found in the following two cases, while no solution exists in the remaining case.*

- **Case I:** When P_M satisfies

$$P_M \geq \frac{(A - 2 - 2Q_1) + \sqrt{(A - 4Q_1 - 4)A}}{2\rho_1} + Q_2$$

$$\triangleq B_1, \tag{25}$$

the optimal solution that guarantees high detection accuracy can be expressed as

$$p_{M+1} = \frac{(A - 2 - 2Q_1) - \sqrt{(A - 4Q_1 - 4)A}}{2\rho_1 (1 + Q_1)}, \tag{26}$$

$$p_m = \frac{\gamma_{\text{th,c}} k_m^2}{k_m^1} p_{M+1} + \frac{\gamma_{\text{th,c}} \sigma_c^2}{k_m^1}, \forall m. \tag{27}$$

- **Case II:** When P_M satisfies

$$B_2 \triangleq (1 + Q_1) \frac{A - 2 - \sqrt{A(A-4)}}{2\rho_1} + Q_2 < P_M$$

$$< (1 + Q_1) \frac{A - 2 + \sqrt{A(A-4)}}{2\rho_1} + Q_2 \triangleq B_3, \tag{28}$$

the optimal solution can be represented as

$$p_{M+1} = \frac{P_M - Q_2}{1 + Q_1}, \tag{29}$$

$$p_m = \frac{\gamma_{\text{th,c}} k_m^2}{k_m^1} p_{M+1} + \frac{\gamma_{\text{th,c}} \sigma_c^2}{k_m^1}, \forall m. \tag{30}$$

- **Case III:** When $P_M \in [0, B_2] \cup [B_3, B_1)$, the optimal solution cannot be obtained.

Proof. The Lagrange function of $\mathcal{P}2$ is given by

$$L(\mathbf{p}, \vartheta, \mathbf{\Lambda}) = e^{\frac{A}{1+\rho_1 p_{M+1}}} \sum_{m=1}^{M+1} p_m + \vartheta \left(\sum_{m=1}^{M+1} p_m - P_M \right)$$

$$+ \sum_{m=1}^{M} \lambda_m \left(\gamma_{\text{th,c}} k_m^2 p_{M+1} - k_m^1 p_m + \gamma_{\text{th,c}} \sigma_c^2 \right), \quad (31)$$

where $\mathbf{\Lambda} = [\lambda_1, \lambda_2, \cdots, \lambda_M]^{\text{T}}$. Therefore, based on the Karush Kuhn Tucker (KKT) condition, (31) can be transformed into

$$\frac{\partial L}{\partial p_m} = e^{\frac{A}{1+\rho_1 p_{M+1}}} - \lambda_m k_m^1 + \vartheta = 0, \forall m \quad (32a)$$

$$\frac{\partial L}{\partial p_{M+1}} = e^{\frac{A}{1+\rho_1 p_{M+1}}} - \frac{A \rho_1 p_{M+1}}{(1 + \rho_1 p_{M+1})^2} e^{\frac{A}{1+\rho_1 p_{M+1}}}$$

$$+ \gamma_{\text{th,c}} \sum_{m=1}^{M} \lambda_m k_m^2 + \vartheta = 0, \quad (32b)$$

$$\lambda_m \left(\gamma_{\text{th,c}} k_m^2 p_{M+1} - k_m^1 p_m + \gamma_{\text{th,c}} \sigma_c^2 \right) = 0, \forall m, \quad (32c)$$

$$\vartheta \left(\sum_{m=1}^{M+1} p_m - P_M \right) = 0, \quad (32d)$$

- **Case I ($\vartheta = 0$)**: Based on (32a), we have

$$\lambda_m = \frac{1}{k_m^1} e^{\frac{A}{1+\rho_1 p_{M+1}}} > 0, \forall m. \quad (33)$$

Therefore, according to (32c), the following equation holds

$$\gamma_{\text{th,c}} k_m^2 p_{M+1} - k_m^1 p_m + \gamma_{\text{th,c}} \sigma_c^2 = 0, \forall m. \quad (34)$$

Then, by transforming (34), the power allocation scheme for communication user can be expressed as

$$p_m = \frac{\gamma_{\text{th,c}} k_m^2}{k_m^1} p_{M+1} + \frac{\gamma_{\text{th,c}} \sigma_c^2}{k_m^1}, \forall m. \quad (35)$$

Substituting (33) into (32b), we have

$$-A \rho_1 p_{M+1} + (1 + Q_1)(1 + \rho_1 p_{M+1})^2 = 0. \quad (36)$$

When a suitable probability of false alarm is given, $A \geq 4(Q_1 - 1)$ holds if the number of antennas in the simulation experiment is greater than 4 (which is easily satisfied in 6G mobile communication systems), i.e., $\Delta = \rho_1^2 (A - 4Q_1 - 4) A \geqslant 0$ holds. Additionally, there are two solutions to (36): the smaller solution consumes less total power, while the other provides higher target detection accuracy. To enhance traffic safety, a heightened level of detection accuracy is essential. Therefore, the optimal power allocation scheme for sensing can be expressed as

$$p_{M+1} = \frac{(A - 2 - 2Q_1) + \sqrt{(A - 4Q_1 - 4)A}}{2\rho_1(1 + Q_1)}. \tag{37}$$

Substituting (35) and (37) into (32d), the boundary of the maximum power of gNB can be expressed as

$$\sum_{m=1}^{M+1} p_m = \frac{(A - 2 - 2Q_1) + \sqrt{(A - 4Q_1 - 4)A}}{2\rho_1(1 + Q_1)} + Q_2$$
$$= B_1 \leq P_M. \tag{38}$$

- **Case II** ($\vartheta > 0$): According to (32a), the following inequality holds, i.e.,

$$\lambda_m = \frac{1}{k_m^1} e^{\frac{A}{1+\rho_1 p_{M+1}}} + \frac{1}{k_m^1}\vartheta > 0, \forall m. \tag{39}$$

Similar to the derivation process of (35), the optimal communication power allocation scheme can also be expressed as

$$p_m = \frac{\gamma_{\text{th},c} k_m^2}{k_m^1} p_{M+1} + \frac{\gamma_{\text{th},c}\sigma_c^2}{k_m^1}, \forall m. \tag{40}$$

Based on (32d), we have

$$\sum_{m=1}^{M} p_m + p_{M+1} = P_M. \tag{41}$$

Substituting (40) into (41), the sensing power allocation scheme can be expressed as

$$p_{M+1} = \frac{P_M - Q_2}{1 + Q_1}. \tag{42}$$

In order to obtain the boundary of the maximum power of gNB, substituting (42) into (32b) to ensure that (32b) has a solution, we have

$$B_2 = (1 + Q_1)\frac{A - 2 - \sqrt{A(A-4)}}{2\rho_1} + Q_2 < P_M$$
$$< (1 + Q_1)\frac{A - 2 + \sqrt{A(A-4)}}{2\rho_1} + Q_2 = B_3. \tag{43}$$

The boundaries of $\mathcal{P}2$ with solutions have been discussed, and the remaining cases ($P_M \in [0, B_2] \cup [B_3, B_1)$) are the no-solution intervals of $\mathcal{P}2$. Thus, *Proposition 1* was proved.

4 Simulation Results and Discussions

4.1 Simulation Configuration

In the simulation, seven communication vehicles and one potential pedestrian are taken into account, as well as the distance between the center of the road and the gNB is $H = 5$ m. Within the entire area, the road has a length of $L_x = 300$ m, the gNB located at the midpoint with coordinates $x = 0$, and the zebra crossing situated at $x \in [19, 21]$. The system bandwidth and carrier frequency of the signal are $B = 100$ MHz and $f_c = 100$ GHz, respectively. The power spectral density for both sensing and communication noise is -162 dBm/Hz [12]. The probability of the presence of a pedestrian and the false alarm are assumed to be 0.005 and 10^{-4}, respectively.

4.2 Simulation Results and Analysis

A baseline scheme is taken for comparison, where the aforementioned detection method in [12] is adopted for one detection target.

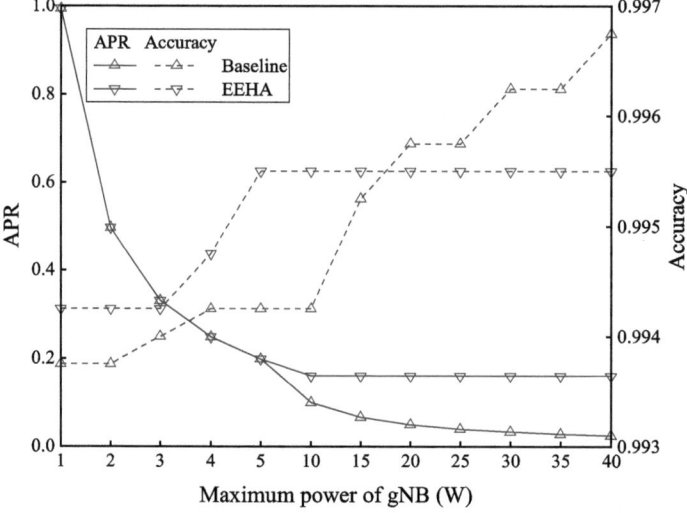

Fig. 2. APR and detection accuracy versus maximum power of gNB ($N_r = 256$).

As depicted in Fig. 2, an increase in the maximum transmit power of gNB results in a declining trend in APR for both schemes. Notably, the APR of EEHA scheme stabilizes after its initial decrease, whereas the APR of the baseline continues to decrease persistently. Simultaneously, both schemes demonstrate an overall upward trend in detection accuracy. Specifically, the detection accuracy of EEHA scheme tends to stabilize following the initial increase, while the detection accuracy of the baseline experiences a gradual rise. It is important to note that the baseline scheme necessitates the continuous consumption of the entire gNB transmit power, whereas the EEHA scheme utilizes the full power only at low power levels (**Case II** in (28)) and a fraction of it at higher power levels (**Case I** in (25)). Upon (7) and (18) and considering the definition of APR, it becomes evident that with an escalation in transmit power at the gNB, the detection accuracy of the baseline scheme progressively approaches 1, and the APR gradually converges to 0. Conversely, the EEHA scheme tends to exhibit smooth convergence. In contrast to the baseline scheme, the proposed EEHA scheme takes into account the tradeoff between detection accuracy and energy efficiency, which could achieve a maximized APR while maintaining an acceptable level of detection accuracy.

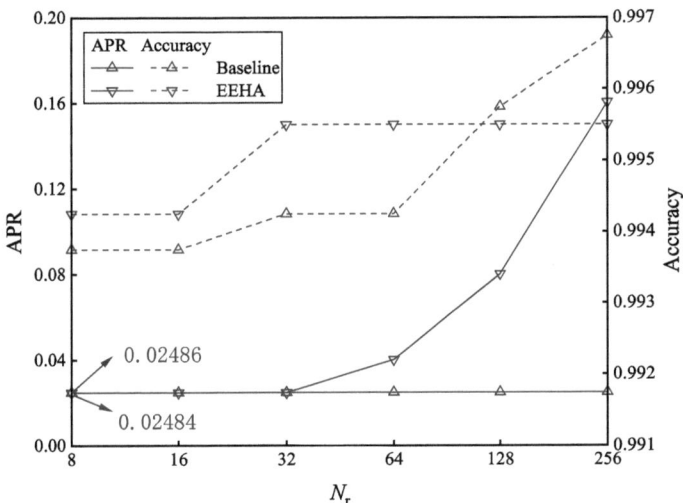

Fig. 3. APR and detection accuracy versus number of gNB receive antennas ($P_M = 40$ W).

Figure 3 illustrates the APR and detection accuracy of two schemes in relation to the number of receive antennas in gNB. As N_r increases, the detection accuracy of the proposed EEHA scheme experiences a gradual ascent. The APR of the baseline scheme also shows an increase, while it consistently remains smaller than that of the EEHA scheme. Concurrently, the detection accuracy of the EEHA scheme initially rises and then stabilizes, in contrast to the continuous increase in detection accuracy of the baseline scheme. Based on (19), as N_r grows, the proposed EEHA scheme gradually transitions from **Case II** to **Case I**, leading to a gradual reduction in the power required for sensing and communication. According to (7) and (18), it is observed that the detection accuracy of the EEHA scheme increases slightly but with a small magnitude (the magnitude is related to the value of p). Thus overall, the APR of the EEHA scheme shows an upward trend with the increase of N_r. Similarly, as N_r increases in the baseline scheme, the immunity of the received signals to interference increases, resulting in sensing signals that contain a higher proportion of sensing information. Consequently, the detection accuracy experiences a notable increase. However, the APR displays only a marginal upward trend. This phenomenon can be attributed to the baseline scheme consuming the full transmit power of gNB, which is numerically much larger than the detection accuracy. In summary, when confronted with limited hardware conditions (small N_r), the EEHA scheme has the capability to attain a relatively high APR while simultaneously maintaining a specific level of detection accuracy.

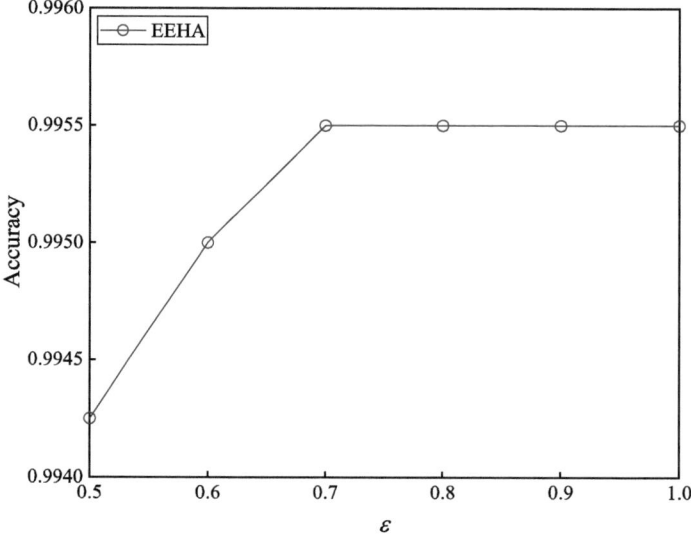

Fig. 4. Detection accuracy versus non-ideal estimation ($P_M = 40$ W and $N_r = 256$).

Figure 4 plots the correlation between detection accuracy and beam gain. With the consequent weakening of the non-ideal degree (indicated by an increase in ε), the detection accuracy initially stabilizes before ascending to a peak. The proposed EEHA scheme maintains acceptable detection accuracy even under non-ideal conditions.

5 Conclusions

In a DFRC system, a detection scheme, aiming to balance detection accuracy and energy consumption, is proposed in this paper. After problem analysis, an EEHA detection scheme is proposed, and the optimal solution is obtained by means of convex optimization theory. The simulation results demonstrate that the proposed EEHA scheme could achieve high APR compared to the baseline scheme, while concurrently maintaining commendable detection accuracy.

Acknowledgment. This work was supported in part by the China Natural Science Funding under Grant 61931005

References

1. Cheng, X., Duan, D., Gao, S., Yang, L.: Integrated sensing and communications (ISAC) for vehicular communication networks (VCN). IEEE Internet Things J. **9**(23), 23 441–23 451 (2022)
2. Dokhanchi, S.H., Shankar, M.R.B., Alaee-Kerahroodi, M., Ottersten, B.: Adaptive waveform design for automotive joint radar-communication systems. IEEE Trans. Veh. Technol. **70**(5), 4273–4290 (2021)
3. Zheng, K., Mei, J., Yang, H., Hou, L., Ma, S.: Digital retina for IoV towards 6G: architecture, opportunities, and challenges. IEEE Netw. **38**(2), 62–69 (2024)
4. Lei, L., Kuang, Y., Shen, X.S., Yang, K., Qiao, J., Zhong, Z.: Optimal reliability in energy harvesting industrial wireless sensor networks. IEEE Trans. Wireless Commun. **15**(8), 5399–5413 (2016)
5. Zhang, J.A., et al.: Enabling joint communication and radar sensing in mobile networks–a survey. IEEE Commun. Surv. Tutor. **24**(1), 306–345 (2022)
6. Yang, T., Lv, C.: A secure sensor fusion framework for connected and automated vehicles under sensor attacks. IEEE Internet Things J. **9**(22), 22 357–22 365 (2022)
7. Zhang, H., Zong, B., Xie, J.: Power and bandwidth allocation for multi-target tracking in collocated MIMO radar. IEEE Trans. Veh. Technol. **69**(9), 9795–9806 (2020)
8. Liu, A., et al.: A survey on fundamental limits of integrated sensing and communication. IEEE Commun. Surv. Tutor. **24**(2), 994–1034 (2022)
9. Chiriyath, A.R., Paul, B., Bliss, D.W.: Radar-communications convergence: coexistence, cooperation, and co-design. IEEE Trans. Cogn. Commun. Netw. **3**(1), 1–12 (2017)
10. Liu, F., Masouros, C., Petropulu, A.P., Griffiths, H., Hanzo, L.: Joint radar and communication design: applications, state-of-the-art, and the road ahead. IEEE Trans. Commun. **68**(6), 3834–3862 (2020)
11. Liu, F., et al.: Integrated sensing and communications: toward dual-functional wireless networks for 6G and beyond. IEEE J. Sel. Areas Commun. **40**(6), 1728–1767 (2022)
12. Dong, F., Liu, F., Cui, Y., Wang, W., Han, K., Wang, Z.: Sensing as a service in 6G perceptive networks: a unified framework for ISAC resource allocation. IEEE Trans. Wireless Commun. **22**(5), 3522–3536 (2023)
13. Richards, M.A.: Fundamentals of Radar Signal Processing. McGraw-Hill Education (2022)
14. Fishler, E., Haimovich, A., Blum, R., Cimini, L., Chizhik, D., Valenzuela, R.: Spatial diversity in radars–models and detection performance. IEEE Trans. Signal Process. **54**(3), 823–838 (2006)
15. Kay, S.M.: Fundamentals of Statistical Signal Processing: Detection Theory. Prentice-Hall, Inc., Englewood Cliffs (1993)

Task Scheduling and Blockchain

A Network Intrusion Detection Method Based on Multi-scale Spatiotemporal Feature Extraction

Yushu Zhang[1], Xuanrui Xiong[1], Yuan Zhang[2(✉)], Tianyu Li[1], Canpu Liu[3(✉)], and Xiaolin Fan[1]

[1] School of Communications, Information Engineering, Chongqing University of Posts Telecommunications, Chongqing 400065, China
[2] School of Computer and Internet of Things, Chongqing Institute of Engineering, Chongqing 400056, China
zhangyuan@cqie.edu.cn
[3] College of Electronic Science and Technology, National University of Defense Technology, Changsha 410073, China
liucanpu24@nudt.edu.cn

Abstract. To address the problems of feature redundancy and insufficient utilization of hierarchical features in the classification process of convolutional neural network models in deep learning, this paper proposes a novel deep learning model termed as Gated Convolution and Feature Pyramid Network (GCFPN). This model incorporates a gating mechanism in the conventional convolutional layers to filter redundant features and extract useful temporal features, and then utilizes a feature pyramid structure to integrate features from different hierarchical levels, thereby obtaining more comprehensive feature information for input into the classification module. Furthermore, the model is trained using the Focal Loss function to enhance its attention towards minority class and hard-to-classify samples during training process. The experimental results show that the proposed GCFPN model outperforms the comparison algorithms in various detection indicators, improving the weighted average of Precision, Recall, and F1 scores of all samples in the test set by 3.27%, 3.42%, and 6.13%, respectively.

Keywords: convolutional neural network · Gated Convolution · Feature Pyramid Network · Focal Loss function

1 Introduction

With the development of the Internet, the complexity and size of cyber intrusion data have changed significantly. Traditional machine learning classifiers usually need to extract features manually and have limited capability in handling complex information data. Therefore, deep learning classification models are widely used in network intrusion detection.

This work was supported by the Natural Science Foundation of China under Grant No. 62171449 , by the Science and Technology Research Program of Chongqing Municipal Education Commission under Grant KJQN202301902.

Deep learning models usually build their feature extraction components through convolutional or fully connected layers. However, due to the large number of parameters involved in building fully connected layers, they are not suitable for handling high-dimensional network traffic data. In contrast, convolutional neural networks (CNNs) are more suitable for extracting features from network traffic data. Convolutional kernels are locally connected to and shared across the feature map with fewer parameters, making them more suitable for this type of data.

Due to the presence of certain similarities among feature maps extracted by different convolutional kernels in each convolutional layer, information redundancy can occur. This accumulation of redundant information throughout the layers increases the computational load on the model and can result in a loss in its final detection performance. As a result, some researchers have started incorporating gate units into convolutional neural networks to control the flow of information and filter the extracted features. For example, in reference [1], gate convolutions were applied to filter the final feature maps extracted by the model, which were then passed to the decision-making module for classification. Reference [2] went a step further by replacing all the convolutional layers in the entire model with gate convolutions. Although this led to an increase in the number of parameters and computational requirements, various classification metrics improved. Therefore, this paper introduces gate mechanisms into the convolutional layers of the proposed GCFPN model to filter the extracted features.

As convolutional layers progress from shallow to deep, the size of the output feature maps gradually decreases, and the concentration of features increases.[3] Each layer's feature maps contain varying levels of information richness and semantic complexity, making them all valuable for the model's output. For example, in reference [4], the proposed SPC-CNN model leveraged group convolutions to extract macro features and point convolutions to capture fine-grained details. The model computed feature map weights using global average pooling and fused these two feature components, resulting in classification performance that surpassed traditional CNN and RNN models. In the field of image processing, Feature Pyramid Networks (FPN) have demonstrated the effectiveness of fusing multiple features from different network layers to create comprehensive representations, making them particularly useful for tasks like object detection and image segmentation. Therefore, this paper introduces gate mechanisms into the traditional GCFPN network to filter the extracted features. At the output stage, a feature pyramid is employed for feature fusion. This involves channel convolutions and upsampling to combine feature maps containing information from different hierarchical levels. The result is a comprehensive feature map that facilitates subsequent classification and decision-making tasks.

Furthermore, while cross-entropy loss is commonly used during training for models dealing with multi-class classification tasks, this paper opts for the Focal Loss as the loss function. This choice is driven by the imbalanced distribution of samples among different classes in datasets related to network intrusion detection. Focal Loss enhances the model's focus on minority classes and hard-to-classify samples, ultimately resulting in significantly improved classification performance compared to other neural network models. The main contributions of this paper are as follows:

1) A network intrusion detection model based on multi-scale spatiotemporal feature extraction is proposed for network intrusion detection, effectively improving the accuracy of intrusion detection;
2) In the convolutional feature extraction module of the model, a gating mechanism is introduced to filter redundant and similar feature information to ensure that only the most representative features are used for subsequent classification decisions. Additionally, the utilization of a feature pyramid structure fuses multi-scale features from different levels, resulting in a more comprehensive feature representation for more accurate classification decisions;
3) Focal Loss is adopted as the loss function during the model training process, replacing the traditional cross-entropy loss to enhance the focus on minority classes and hard-to-categorize samples. Experimental results show that the proposed GCFPN model outperforms the comparison algorithms in various detection metrics;

The rest of the paper is arranged as follows. Section 2 reviews the methods for object detection. Section 3 outlines our research approach. In Sect. 4, the experimental results and evaluation results are described. Finally, Sect. 5 draws the conclusion.

2 Related Work

Research on network intrusion detection technology has gone through several stages: signature detection, anomaly detection, machine learning, and deep learning [5–7]. Signature detection identifies potential attack behaviors by comparing known attack patterns and features. The characteristic of this technology is that it can only recognize known attack patterns and cannot effectively detect new intrusion behaviors. Anomaly detection establishes a baseline based on patterns of normal behavior and considers deviations from this baseline as anomalies. The characteristic of this technology is that it detects all types of attacks as anomalies but cannot identify the specific intrusion behavior of the current anomaly. Machine learning and deep learning techniques build intrusion detection models by designing complex algorithms and training the models with large amounts of network data, achieving automatic recognition of network intrusions after training. This method requires a large amount of data and complex algorithms but can identify unknown attack behaviors.

Currently, classical machine learning classifiers such as Decision Tree (DT), Random Forest (RF), Naive Bayes (NB), Logistic Regression (LR), etc., are widely used in multi-classification tasks for network intrusion detection. BHATI et al. [8] used the Extreme Gradient Boosting (XGBoost) algorithm to couple multiple DT classifiers for serial training, obtaining a strong classifier from weak classifiers and improving the accuracy of intrusion detection. Abbas et al. [9] utilized the VotingClassifier to train DT, NB, and LR classifiers in parallel, and the method significantly improved the classification accuracy in both binary and multi-classification scenarios of network intrusion detection. Zhang et al. [10] achieved better intrusion detection results by using a stacked ensemble learning method to use DT and RF classifiers as a hierarchical ensemble learning model.

Machine learning classifiers have low model complexity, and they quickly output results during training and testing, but they rely on feature engineering. Feature engineering is the process of selecting the best combination of attribute features from raw data to train a machine learning model. In addition, machine learning models are limited in their ability to handle complex information data, and integrated training of multiple machine learning models is often required to build stronger classifier models. On the other hand, constructing basic network layers in deep learning models, such as convolutional and fully connected layers, allows for feature extraction and data dimension reduction by controlling the dimensions of output tensors, thus providing natural feature engineering capabilities. Moreover, deep learning models are highly adaptable, easy to transfer and convert [11]. For example, using pre-trained neural network models can save model training time and is applicable to different application scenarios within the same research field. Therefore, current researchers are focusing on designing deep learning models and applying them to network intrusion detection.

Deep learning models have powerful learning capabilities and are suitable for processing network traffic data. Among them, Deep Belief Networks [12, 13], Convolutional Neural Networks [14, 15], Long and Short Term Memory Networks [16], and Autoencoder Networks (AEs) [17] have been widely used in the field of intrusion detection.

The current design approach for deep learning-based network intrusion detection models focuses on improving the methods of feature extraction from network traffic data and the methods of merging features extracted from different network layers to make the obtained feature information more comprehensive and facilitate subsequent classification tasks. For example, Hu et al. [4] proposes an SPC-CNN network model for intrusion detection. This structure applies grouped convolution and point convolution to the feature maps after initial convolution to extract macro features and detail features separately. Finally, the two parts of features are weighted and fused to obtain comprehensive features, improving the accuracy of intrusion detection. Li et al. [18] proposes a detection model based on the fusion of multiple CNNs. This model groups features based on the correlation between features of network traffic data and uses multiple CNN models to extract features separately. It then superimposes local features to obtain global features for classification decision-making. This method is simple and accurate. Mulyanto et al. [19] uses Focal Loss (FL) as the loss function during CNN training. FL enhances the model's attention to minority class samples by amplifying the training error of minority class samples. At the same time, it dynamically adjusts the loss weight based on the model's accuracy in classifying samples, accelerating the convergence of the model.

Deep learning is efficient in feature extraction and data modeling. Therefore, using deep learning technology to build detection models for analyzing and classifying complex, high-dimensional data such as network traffic is a hot research topic in the current field of network intrusion detection and has significant research prospects.

3 Network Intrusion Detection Model Based on Gated Convolution and Feature Pyramid

3.1 The Overall Network Architecture of the Model

This paper introduces a deep learning model based on gated convolutions and a feature pyramid for the purpose of accomplishing intrusion detection classification tasks. The model incorporates gating mechanisms to enhance traditional convolutional approaches and combines them with a feature pyramid network to amalgamate various feature maps from the model's deep layers. This results in a more comprehensive and information-rich feature set for making classification decisions. The complete network structure of the GCFPN model is illustrated in Fig. 1.

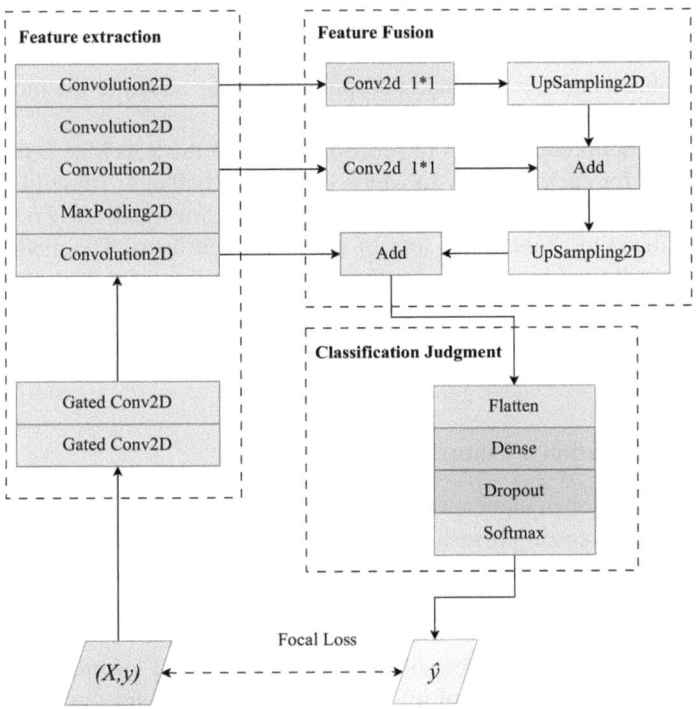

Fig. 1. Network structure of the GCFPN model.

As can be seen from Fig. 1, the feature extraction part of the model consists of five convolutional layers, with the first two layers utilizing gated convolutional technology, and the last three layers using conventional convolution. Gated convolution operates by multiplying the output of a standard convolution with a gating signal generated by a Sigmoid activation function, effectively filtering and controlling the flow of information. However, due to the increased number of parameters and computational load, gated convolution layers lead to a larger and more complex model, thus their use is limited within the model. Since the features extracted by the initial convolutional layers of the model are less focused and redundant, employing a gating mechanism for feature filtering is appropriate. In contrast, the features extracted by the deeper convolutional layers are more concentrated; adding gating mechanisms here would complicate the model unnecessarily. Therefore, these features are typically merged using a feature pyramid structure to enhance the model's performance in classification decisions.

In the feature fusion of the output of the three regular convolutional layers at the end of the network with the feature pyramid structure, the channel convolution used for the output of each convolutional layer first reduces the number of channels to the same as that of the output of the previous layer of the network, and then the size of the feature maps is expanded to the same size as that of the previous layer using up-sampling. After the two layers of feature maps have the same size and the same number of channels, they are summed up to get the comprehensive feature maps that contain different levels of semantic information. Finally, the obtained multi-layer composite feature maps are compressed into one-dimensional vectors using the Flatten operation and fed into the fully connected neural network for dimensionality reduction. To prevent overfitting problems during training, a dropout layer was added to the model with the parameter set to 0.5.

The final model produces a set of probabilities from the Soft Max layer. These are the probabilities for each category to which the sample belongs. These likelihoods are compared with the genuine labels of the sample categories, and the Focal Loss loss function is utilised to evaluate the loss of error between them. The model's network parameters are adjusted by minimizing the loss value using the Adam optimizer. This process enhances the model's output for the next round of training to fit better with the sample's true category. Following the completion of model training, the test set data is assessed for discrimination.

3.2 Gated Convolutional Feature Extraction

In the feature extraction of input network intrusion data by convolutional neural network, the extracted feature tensors are reshaped into two-dimensional matrices for visualization in the form of grayscale images. The multiple feature grayscale images extracted by different convolutional kernels in each layer are illustrated in Fig. 2. As indicated by the green boxes in Fig. 2, there is a discernible similarity among rows of grayscale images, where they exhibit varying degrees of brightness at identical locations. These similar features represent a certain level of informational redundancy for the subsequent layer of the neural network. Consequently, this study employs gated convolution within the deep learning model to enhance selective feature extraction.

The gated convolution refers to the forgetting gate in the long and short-term memory network, and a gating unit immediately follows the feature map output from each layer of convolution. The gating unit consists of a regular convolution connected to a Sigmoid function with an output value between 0 and 1, which serves as a weight parameter for the feature maps, retaining the parts of the features with weights close to 1 and filtering the parts with weights close to 0.

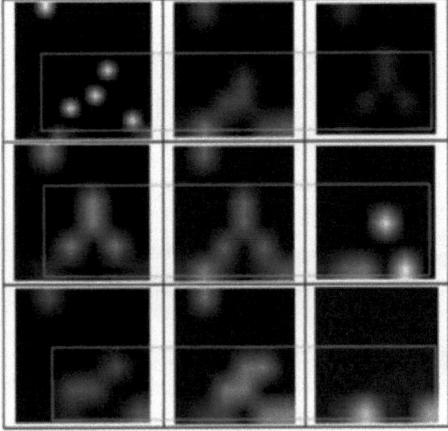

Fig. 2. The feature maps extracted by different convolution kernels in each convolutional layer.

The expression for the gated convolution is as follows:

$$\begin{cases} Feature_X = X^*W_1 + b_1 \\ Gating_X = \delta(X^*W_2 + b_2) \\ Output_X = Feature_X \otimes Gating_X \end{cases} \quad (1)$$

X represents the input data of every convolutisonal layer. W denotes the weight of the convolutional kernel, while b stands for the bias parameter. Additionally, δ signifies the Sigmoid activation function. In comparison to the ReLU activation function, which uses only 0 or 1 to weigh the feature map, the gating unit outputs weights varying from 0 to 1. This helps in identifying the components of the extracted features that require attention or can be disregarded. Compared to the Tanh activation function, the gating mechanism has a linear channel, ensuring a stable gradient drop during the training process. This results in less sharp back propagation reduction and faster model convergence when using the gating unit as the activation function.

As illustrated by Fig. 3, gating unit parameters are trained, differentiating it from traditional activation functions such as ReLU and Tanh. By using the gating unit as the feature map's activation function, the output weight value can be learnt during training, allowing for dynamic adjustment of weight values to better fit subsequent classification judgments. In this study, the proposed GCFPN model employs gated convolution for initial feature extraction and filtering in the first two network layers.

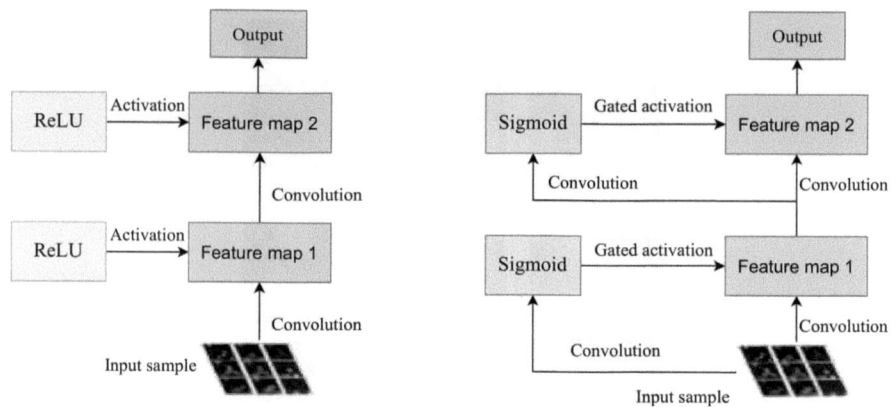

Fig. 3. Differences in model construction between traditional convolution (left) and gated convolution (right).

3.3 Feature Pyramid Fusion Hierarchy Features

As the size of the feature map produced by each convolutional layer and the level of semantic information contained varies, the shallow convolutional layer generates feature maps with greater size and more detailed information, while the deeper convolutional layer generates feature maps with smaller size and more concentrated feature information. Therefore, this paper utilises the feature pyramid structure to enhance the model's network structure. The feature information from various network layers consolidates to form a more comprehensive and integrated feature map, enabling the model to make more effective classification decisions. Typically, conventional CNN models only rely on the feature map output from the last convolutional layer as the comprehensive features for subsequent classification decisions. The feature pyramid, however, combines the individual feature maps with varying levels of semantic knowledge in the model's deeper layers to create a more all-encompassing feature map. Figure 4 illustrates the feature pyramid's structure.

The feature map obtained is combined with the feature map of its preceding layer to create a feature map that has more comprehensive information. This process is then replicated multiple times, following the model's layers, until the feature map with the most extensive feature information is constructed. In this paper, we implement a feature pyramid structure in the final three regular convolutional layers of our proposed model. This enables us to extract a more comprehensive feature map, which is then passed to the classification module for intrusion detection.

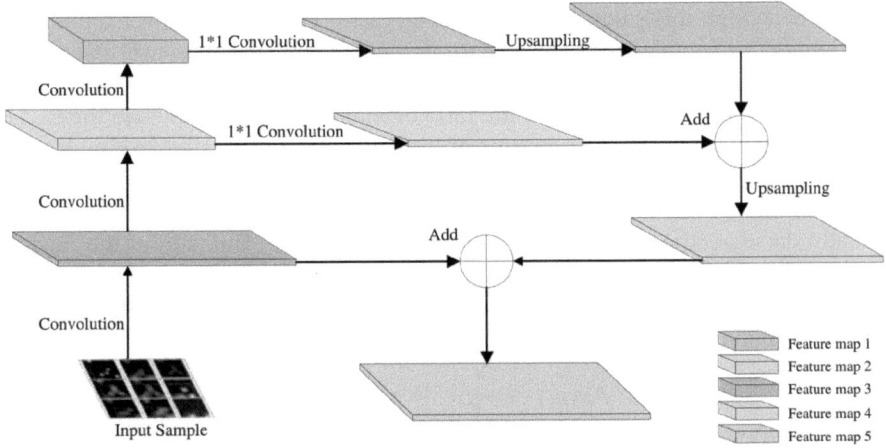

Fig. 4. Schematic diagram of the feature pyramid structure.

3.4 Focus Loss Function

Network intrusion detection is a multi-classification problem, and the loss function of the model usually uses Cross Entropy Loss (CE), which is formulated as follows:

$$CE(p, y) = \begin{cases} -log(p) & \text{if } y = 1 \\ -log(1-p) & \text{otherwise} \end{cases} \quad (2)$$

y denotes the category label of the sample; p denotes the probability that the test sample is predicted to be a positive example. If p_t is defined as:

$$p_t = \begin{cases} p & \text{if } y = 1 \\ 1-p & \text{otherwise} \end{cases} \quad (3)$$

Then the cross-entropy loss can be expressed as follows:

$$CE(p_t) = -log(p_t) \quad (4)$$

Since the samples in the network intrusion dataset are not evenly balanced across all classes, there is a high proportion of majority class samples in each batch during the model's training. As a result, this leads to a higher weight placed on the majority class samples in the overall loss function. When training the model to reduce loss through back propagation, the reduction in loss for majority class samples will be greater, ultimately creating a bias towards the majority class in the detection performance of the trained model. Furthermore, the network intrusion dataset is dominated by normal traffic samples, which the model can easily classify accurately. Consequently, the model's training process may exhibit a bias towards majority-class samples with low complexity, namely normal traffic. To counteract this imbalance, it is necessary to enhance the model's loss function.

Focal Loss introduces weight factors into the cross-entropy loss to adjust the loss of samples belonging to different categories and to regulate the model's focus on the classification accuracy of each category of samples during the training process. For network intrusion detection, this study uses a weighting factor based on the inverse proportion of the number of samples in each category in the dataset. This approach scales up the loss for categories with fewer samples, thus mitigating classification loss. Furthermore, it is imperative to not only enhance the ratio of minority class samples in the loss but also consistently diminish the proportion of straightforwardly classifiable samples in the loss. As the model's accuracy in identifying easy-to-classify samples improves swiftly during continuous training, the Focal Loss function introduces a modulation factor to gradually decrease the classification loss of such samples. This allows the model to concentrate on optimising the loss of difficult-to-classify samples, resulting in a logical progression towards improving its performance. The complete expression of the introduced modulation factor is provided below:

$$FL(p_t) = -\alpha_t(1-p_t)^\gamma \log(p_t) \tag{5}$$

where, p_t denotes the probability that the sample is classified correctly; α_t denotes the weight of this class of samples in the calculation of the loss function; $(1-p_t)^\gamma$ is the modulation factor, and γ is the focusing parameter. From Eq. 5, it can be seen that setting the value of α_t can adjust the focus of the model on the class of samples in the training process. And under different values of the focusing parameter γ, with the growth of the horizontal coordinate p_t, the decay process of the vertical coordinate loss function value is shown in Fig. 5.

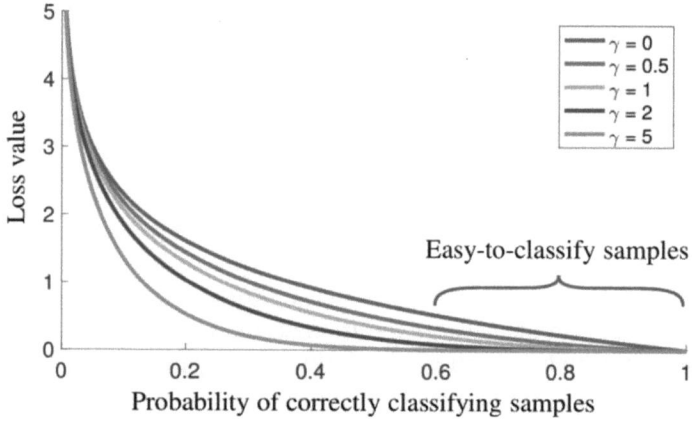

Fig. 5. The impact of the modulation factor of Focal Loss on the loss value.

From Fig. 5, we can see the principle that the modulation factor can adjust the loss weights of easy and difficult to classify samples: when the value of p_t will tend to 1, the sample is correctly classified (at this time, the sample belongs to the easy to classify samples), and the modulation factor will tend to 0, so that the value of the loss function also tends to 0; when the value of p_t tends to 0, the sample is classified incorrectly (at this time, the sample belongs to the difficult to classify samples), and the modulation factor will tend to 1, so that the value of the the value of the loss function to be maintained. Since the focusing parameter γ is in the exponential position in the formula, adjusting the value of γ can accelerate the loss decay rate of the easy-to-classify samples, however, the value of γ should not be taken too large, or else it will affect the effect of the convergence of the model loss curve. And when the value of γ is taken as 0, the Focal Loss is degraded into the cross-entropy loss again. In this paper, Focal Loss is used for GCFPN model training, where the value of the α_t array is set to the inverse of the percentage of the number of samples in each category, and the value of γ is set to 2.

4 Experiments

4.1 Experimental Datasets

The dataset used for the experiments is NSL-KDD, which is improved from the benchmark dataset KDD-CUP99 commonly used in the field of network intrusion detection by removing duplicated samples and taking the number of samples from each group according to the detection difficulty level group inversely proportional to the proportion of that level in the dataset, so that the samples obtained are more reasonable in terms of the difficulty of detection, and thus the detection performances of the different classifiers can be evaluated more effectively. Detection performance of different classifiers. There are five categories of samples in NSL-KDD: the normal category Normal and four attack categories: Dos, Probe, R2L, and U2R, and the introduction of the attack categories is shown in Table 1.

Table 1. Introduction to attack categories in NSL-KDD

Type of attack	Full name of attack	Description of the attack
Dos	Denial-of-service	denial of service
Probe	surveillance and Probing	port monitoring or scanning
R2L	Remote to Local	unauthorised access from remote hosts
U2R	User to Root	unauthorised superuser privileged access

The NSL-KDD dataset contains features in 41 dimensions. The number of the samples of each category in the training set and test set in NSL-KDD are shown in Table 2. Where a feature named num_outbound_cmds is the same in all the sample data, then this feature cannot distinguish the categories of different samples, so it is a useless feature and can be eliminated.

Table 2. Quantity for each category in the training and testing sets of NSL-KDD

Typology	Number of training sets	Number of test sets
Normal	67343	9710
Dos	45927	7457
Probe	11656	2421

(*continued*)

Table 2. (*continued*)

Typology	Number of training sets	Number of test sets
R2L	995	2754
U2R	52	200
Total	125973	22544

From Table 2, it can be seen that the number of samples for both attack types, R2L and U2L, is much less than that of Normal and Dos, both in the training set and in the test set, so R2L and U2R are classified as the minority class, and Normal and Dos are classified as the majority class.

4.2 Data Preprocessing

The dataset contains three categorical features, which need to be encoded numerically because they are difficult to input directly into the model for computation. We use tag encoding to convert character features into numeric values. For example, the three attribute values of protocol_type, TCP, UDP, and ICMP, are encoded as 0, 1, and 2, respectively, so that they can be differentiated according to their magnitude, which makes it easier to input them into the model for computation.

The characteristic of data standardization is that when the attribute values are near the mean, the gradient of the attribute values distributed near 0 is larger after the transformation, which is conducive to increasing the variance of the attribute values near the mean and making the values near the mean more diverse. The gradient of the attribute value distribution near the left and right extremes after the transformation is small, so that the standardization can effectively constrain the range of the transformed extreme deviation, and achieve the effect of unifying the attribute value scale of each dimensional feature. In this paper, the Z-value standardization method was chosen with the formula: $x' = \frac{x-u}{\sigma}$; where x' is the transformed output value; x is the value of each attribute in the original data; u is the mean value of each dimension attribute value of the original data; σ is the variance.

Intrusion detection systems (IDS) aim to effectively classify and identify different types of attack traffic, thus constituting a multi-class classification task. In such a setting, each category of samples is treated as the positive class while all other categories are considered negative, leading to the categorization of classification outcomes into four types: True Positives (TP), True Negatives (TN), False Positives (FP), and False Negatives (FN). TP denotes the count of samples correctly predicted as positive within the positive class, TN reflects the count of samples correctly predicted as negative within the negative class, FP represents the count of negative class samples incorrectly predicted as positive, and FN indicates the count of positive class samples incorrectly predicted as negative. These categories together form the confusion matrix of classification outcomes, as shown in Table 3.

Table 3. Classification result confusion matrix

The real situation	Projected results	
	normal practice	counter-example
normal practice	TP	FN
counter-example	FP	TN

For the categorical performance of each class of samples in the dataset, the following evaluation metrics are used in this paper:

$$\begin{cases} Presion = \frac{TP}{TP+FP} \\ Recall = \frac{TP}{TP+FN} \\ F1\text{-}score = \frac{2*Precision*Recall}{Precision+Recall} \end{cases} \quad (6)$$

In the formula, Precision represents the accuracy rate, Recall represents the completeness rate, and F1-score is the average of the two, which is a comprehensive evaluation index. Evaluating Precision, Recall and F1-score for all samples in the test set as a whole is to find out the average value of the classification indexes for each type of samples in the test set. There are two methods for calculating the average: the macro method and the weighted method. The macro method calculates the arithmetic mean of the metrics in all categories, assigning equal weight (1/N) to each category, where N is the total number of categories. This method ensures that each category contributes equally to the overall mean, regardless of the prevalence of the category in the dataset. In contrast, the weighting method adjusts the contribution of each category based on its proportion in the overall dataset. As a result, categories with larger sample sizes have a proportionately larger impact on the overall metric calculation. This method provides an average value that reflects the distribution of categories in the dataset, resulting in a more realistic assessment of model performance in unbalanced data. The calculation formula is as follows:

$$\begin{cases} WeightedP = \sum_{i=1}^{n} \frac{Support_i}{Total} * Precision_i \\ WeightedR = \sum_{i=1}^{n} \frac{Support_i}{Total} * Recall_i \\ WeightedF1 = \sum_{i=1}^{n} \frac{Support_i}{Total} * F1-score_i \end{cases} \quad (7)$$

where i denotes the sample of category i; n denotes the total number of sample categories with n categories; $Support_i$ denotes the number of samples of category i in the test set; Total denotes the sum of the number of samples of all categories in the test set. This calculation avoids the effect of the imbalance of the number of samples in the test set on the overall classification result, but the result of the operation may make the F1-score not between Precision and Recall.

4.3 GCFPN Model Parameterization

The parameter settings for each network layer of the GCFPN model are shown in Table 4.

Table 4. Network layer parameter setting of GCFPN

Layer	Type	Size	Active Function
L1	Gated Conv2d_1	32@5*5	-
L1_1	Conv2D	32@5*5	-
L1_2	Conv2D	32@5*5	Sigmoid
L1_3	Multiply	-	-
L2	Gated Conv1d_2	64@5*5	-
L3_1	Conv2D	128@3*3	ReLU
L3_2	Maxpooling	2	-
L4_1	Conv1D	256@3*3	ReLU
L4_2	Maxpooling	2	-
L5	Conv1D	512@3*3	ReLU
L6	FPN_1	-	-
L6_1	Conv2D	128@1*1	ReLU
L6_2	Upsampling	2	-
L6_3	Add	-	-
L7	FPN_2	-	-
L8	Flatten	-	-
L9	Dense	512	ReLU
L10	Dropout	0.5	-
L11	Dense	5	Softmax

In the table, L2 and L1 have the same layer structure, both are gated convolutional layers, L3 and L4 are both convolutional + pooling layers, and L7 and L6 have the same layer structure, both are FPN layers. The parameters for model training are set as follows: epoch = 200, Loss = Focal Loss, the optimiser is Adam, and the learning rate is initialised to 0.01.

4.4 Experimental Results and Discussions

This study utilized the KDDTrain + dataset to train the proposed GCFPN model. To ascertain the impact of the GCFPN model components on performance detection, ablation experiments were conducted, with the results post-training presented in Table 5.

Table 5. Results of ablation contrast experiment of each module of GCFPN model

Model			Weighted average		
Gated Conv	FPN	Focal Loss	Precision	Recall	F1
✗	✗	✗	81.36	76.94	73.26
✔	✗	✗	83.41	79.33	77.94
✗	✔	✗	83.56	78.84	76.49
✗	✗	✔	83.22	78.69	76.59
✔	✔	✔	84.63	80.45	79.47

From Tables 5, it is evident that the traditional CNN models, after incorporating gated convolution, feature pyramid structures, and Focal Loss, each show improvements in the overall F1 score. Among these, gated convolution has the most significant impact, increasing the F1 score by 4.68%.

To assess the extent of the GCFPN model's enhancement compared to the conventional CNN, this study conducts experiments using the traditional CNN model. The model is structured with an identical number of layers and parameter settings as the GCFPN, and the cross-entropy loss function is utilised. The experimental results are shown in Figs 6, 7 and 8.

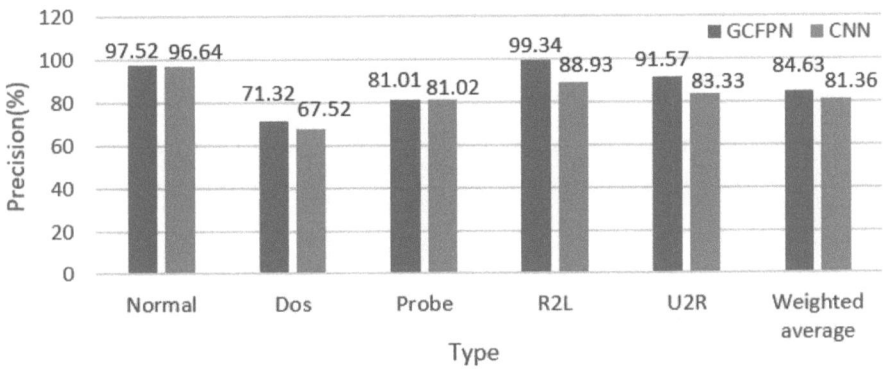

Fig. 6. Comparison of Precision (%) between GCFPN and CNN models on the test set KDDTest+

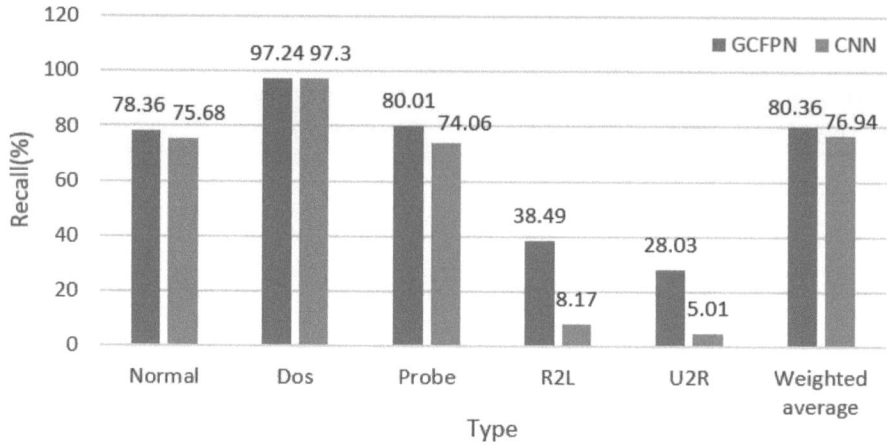

Fig. 7. Comparison of Recall (%) between GCFPN and CNN models on the test set KDDTest+

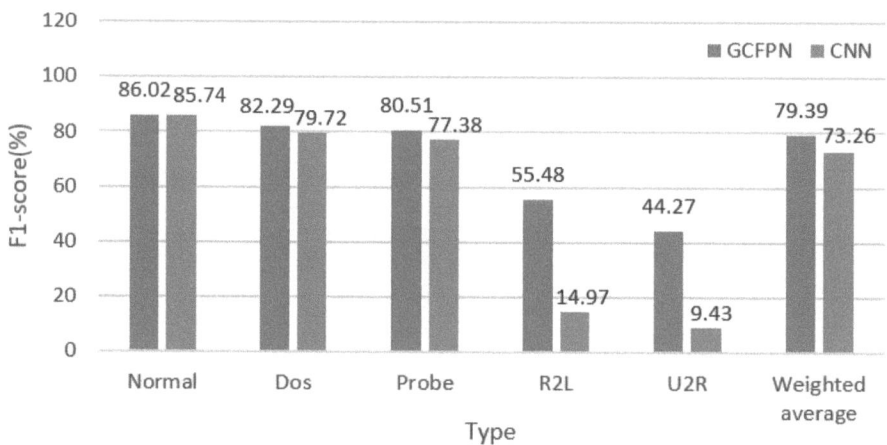

Fig. 8. Comparison of F1-score (%) between GCFPN and CNN models on the test set KDDTest+

The results of the comparison experiments by precision show that GCFPN demonstrates higher precision than CNN in almost all categories, especially notable in Dos, R2L, and U2R attack types. The most significant difference appears in R2L where GCFPN's precision significantly outperforms CNN. In terms of recall, GCFPN also exhibits superior performance for R2L and U2R attacks, boosting recall from very low percentages (8.17% and 5.01% respectively) for CNN to much higher values (38.49% and 28.03%). This suggests GCFPN's enhanced ability to identify minority class samples which are usually harder to detect. The F1-score, which balances both precision and recall, further highlights GCFPN's strengths across the board, with significant improvements in R2L and U2R categories. This metric demonstrates GCFPN's effectiveness in maintaining a balance between precision and recall, particularly in minority classes where performance enhancements are most needed.

In addition, the classification accuracy, recall and F1 score of the model are 84.63%, 80.36% and 79.39%, respectively, which are quite good. Compared with traditional CNN, the GCFPN model's comprehensive classification metrics improved by 3.27%, 3.42% and 6.13%, respectively.

5 Conclusion

Aiming at the problems of redundancy of features extracted from network data by convolutional neural network model and insufficient feature utilization in the classification process, this paper proposes a network intrusion detection model based on gated convolution and feature pyramid. The method adds a gating mechanism to the low level of the conventional convolutional neural network model to filter and screen the features and remove redundant information and retain useful temporal features. Then the feature pyramid structure is used for feature fusion at the higher level of the model, which makes use of the features at different levels to obtain more comprehensive and integrated feature information. Finally, after the classification results are output from the Softmax layer of the classification module, the Focal Loss is used as the loss function during training to improve the model's focus on the classification effect of a few types of samples during training. This paper conducts experiments on the NSL-KDD dataset. The ablation experiment of GCFPN proves the effect of each module in the proposed model, among which the gated convolution module has the most obvious improvement effect on the model. Compared with the same type of deep convolutional neural network algorithm, the proposed GCFPN model improves the weighted mean values of Precision, Recall, and F1-score of the overall samples in the test set by 3.27%, 3.42%, and 6.13%, respectively.

References

1. Zhang, X., et al.: RANet: network intrusion detection with group-gating convolutional neural network. J. Netw. Comput. Appl. **198**, 103266 (2022)
2. Wang, Y., Wang, J., Jin, H.: Network intrusion detection method based on improved CNN in internet of things environment. Mob. Inf. Syst. **2022**(1), 3850582 (2022)
3. Ning, Z., Yang, Y., Wang, X., Song, Q., Guo, L., Jamalipour, A.: Multi-agent deep reinforcement learning based UAV trajectory optimization for differentiated services. IEEE Trans. Mob. Comput. **23**(5), 5818–5834 (2024)
4. Hu, Z., Wang, L., Qi, L., Li, Y., Yang, W.: A novel wireless network intrusion detection method based on adaptive synthetic sampling and an improved convolutional neural network. IEEE Access **8**, 195741–195751 (2020)
5. Telo, J.: Intrusion detection with supervised machine learning using smote for imbalanced datasets. J. Artif. Intell. Mach. Learn. Manage. **5**(1), 12–24 (2021)
6. Ning, Z., et al.: Joint user association, interference cancellation and power control for Multi-IRS assisted UAV communications. IEEE Trans. Wirel. Commun., 1 (2024). https://doi.org/10.1109/TWC.2024.3401152

7. Ahmad, Z., Khan, A.S., Shiang, C.W., et al.: Network intrusion detection system: a systematic study of machine learning and deep learning approaches. Trans. on Emerg. Telecommun. Technol. **32**(1), e4150 (2021)
8. Bhati, B.S., Chugh, G., Al-Turjman, F., Bhati, N.S.: An improved ensemble based intrusion detection technique using XGBoost. Trans. Emerg. Telecommun. Technol. **32**(6), e4076 (2021)
9. Abbas, A., Khan, M.A., Latif, S., Ajaz, M., Shah, A.A., Ahmad, J.: A new ensemble-based intrusion detection system for internet of things. Arabian J. Sci. Eng., 1–15 (2022)
10. Zhang, H., Li, J.L., Liu, X.M., Dong, C.: Multi-dimensional feature fusion and stacking ensemble mechanism for network intrusion detection. Futur. Gener. Comput. Syst. **122**, 130–143 (2021)
11. Wang, X., Li, J., Ning, Z., Song, Q., Guo, L., Jamalipour, A.: Wireless powered metaverse: joint task scheduling and trajectory design for multi-devices and Multi-UAVs. IEEE J. Sel. Areas Commun. **42**(3), 552–569 (2024). https://doi.org/10.1109/JSAC.2023.3345433
12. Jia, H., Liu, J., Zhang, M., He, X., Sun, W.: Network intrusion detection based on IE-DBN model. Comput. Commun. **178**, 131–140 (2021)
13. Ning, Z., et al.: Mobile edge computing and machine learning in the internet of unmanned aerial vehicles: a survey. ACM Comput. Surv. **56**(1), 1–31 (2023)
14. Kim, J., Kim, J., Kim, H., Shim, M., Choi, E.: CNN-based network intrusion detection against denial-of-service attacks. Electronics **9**(6), 916–937 (2020)
15. Wang, X., et al.: Integration of sensing, communication, and computing for metaverse: a survey. ACM Comput. Surv. **56**(10), 1–38 (2024)
16. Xu, C., Shen, J., Du, X., et al.: An intrusion detection system using a deep neural network with gated recurrent units. IEEE Access **6**, 48697–48707 (2018)
17. Andresini, G., Appice, A., Malerba, D.: Autoencoder-based deep metric learning for network intrusion detection. Inf. Sci. **569**, 706–727 (2021)
18. Li, Y., et al.: Robust detection for network intrusion of industrial IoT based on multi-CNN fusion. Measurement **154**, 107450 (2020)
19. Mulyanto, M., Faisal, M., Prakosa, S.W., Leu, J.S.: Effectiveness of focal loss for minority classification in network intrusion detection systems. Symmetry **13**(1), 4 (2021)

Investigating the Correlation Between Choice of Spreading Factor and Duty Cycle Calculations on Energy Consumption Profiles for LoRa: Insights from Optimized Image and Audio Data Transmission in Beehive Monitoring

Ephrance Eunice Namugenyi[1(✉)], Julianne Sansa Otim[2], Marco Zennaro[3], Stephen Wolthusen[4], Mary Nsabagwa[2], and David Tugume[2]

[1] College of Computing and Informatics Sciences, Makerere University, Kampala, Uganda
[2] Internet of Things Research and Applications Lab, Makerere University, Kampala, Uganda
{sansa,mnsabagwa}@cit.ac.ug
[3] Marconi Laboratory, ICTP, Trieste, Italy
mzennaro@ictp.it
[4] NTNU, Trondheim, Norway
stephen.wolthusen@ntnu.no

Abstract. This study optimizes energy efficiency in the LoRa communication module for beehive monitoring, focusing on image and audio data transfer. It investigates the effects of duty cycle calculations and spreading factor (SF) choice on power consumption and data transmission reliability. An experimental setup involved running optimized audio and image models on an Arduino Nano 33 BLE board. These models captured probabilities of different hive states—being robbed, missing queen, or active hive. The category with the highest probability indicated the current state of the hive. Optimized data results were transferred via the LoRa Grove E5 and displayed upon reception. Power and duty cycle measurements were taken on the LoRa module for spreading factors 7, 8, and 12 at set delay intervals during data transfer to the Mile sight gateway and back. Statistical analysis techniques evaluated the gathered data, revealing a high correlation between SFs, calculated duty cycles, and energy consumption profiles. These findings demonstrate the importance of optimizing duty cycles and SFs to minimize power consumption and ensure effective data transfer, thereby enhancing system reliability and reducing the environmental impact of smart bee monitoring. This promotes sustainable beekeeping practices. Moreover, the implications of this work extend beyond beekeeping, offering valuable insights into energy-efficient Internet of Things applications in environmental and agricultural monitoring.

Keywords: LoRa · Duty Cycle · Spreading Factor · Power Consumption · Beehive Monitoring · Energy Efficiency

1 Introduction

Beehive monitoring is indispensable in modern beekeeping practices, serving as a cornerstone for beekeepers to ensure hive health, productivity, and ecological balance [1]. By monitoring parameters like hive temperature, humidity, and activity levels, beekeepers can proactively address challenges such as disease outbreaks, pest infestations, and environmental stressors, thereby fostering the well-being of bee colonies and contributing to broader ecosystem health [2].

Recent advancements in wireless communication have revolutionized beehive monitoring, with Long-Range (LoRa) [3] modules emerging as a favored technology due to their capability for long-range, low-power communication in remote and challenging environments [4]. LoRa modules in combination with the requisite sensors empower beekeepers to remotely monitor hive conditions, receive real-time alerts, and collect valuable data without necessitating direct physical presence at the hive-site [5].

The main characteristics of Low Power Wireless Area Networks (LPWAN) technologies, such as Sigfox, LoRaWAN, NB-IoT, and LTE Cat-M1, are outlined in Table 1 below. These technologies provide extended battery life, low bandwidth (tens of kbps), and large data transmission ranges (up to many tens of kilometers). Since LPWANs may be deployed more affordably than cellular networks, new entrants into the telecommunications industry can compete with more established Mobile Network Operators (MNOs). The choice of LoRa technology in this paper is because of its energy-saving and long-range coverage capabilities [3, 6, 7]. Several MNOs like Orange, SKTelecom, Bouygues Telecom, Swisscom, SoftBank, and the like, have started building on LoRa and LoRaWAN infrastructure in response to this trend to supplement their current cellular network deployments [6].

Table 1. Important LPWAN technology parameters and features (LoRaWAN, Sig-fox, NB-IoT, and LTE Cat-M1.) [7].

	LoRaWAN	Sigfox	NB-IoT	LTE Cat-M1
Coverage (MCL)	157 dB	162 dB	164 dB	155 dB
Technology	Proprietary	Proprietary	Open LTE	Open LTE
Spectrum	Unlicensed	Unlicensed	Licensed (LTE/any)	Licensed (LTE/any)
Duty cycle limit	Yes	Yes	No	No
Output power restrictions	Yes (14 dBm = 25 mW)	Yes (14 dBm = 25 mW)	No (23 dBm = 200 mW)	No (23 dBm = 200 mW)
Downlink data rate	0.3–50 kbps	<1 kbps	0.5–27.2 kbps	<300 kbps
Uplink data rate	0.3–50 kbps	<1 kbps	0.3–32.25 kbps	<375 kbps
Battery life/Current consumption	8+ years < 2 uA	10+ years < 2 uA	10+ years < 3 uA	10+ years < 8 uA
Module cost	<$ 10	<$ 10	$ 10 (2019); $ 3 (2020)	<$ 25 (2019)
Security	Medium (AES-128)	Low (AES-128)	Very high (LTE Security)	Very high (LTE Security)

This research in essence aims to maximize energy efficiency specifically beehive monitoring using the LoRa Grove E5 module. By strategically managing spreading factors and duty cycles, our goal is to minimize power consumption while maintaining reliable data transmission capabilities. Through this maximization, we seek to address the dual challenge of preserving battery life for prolonged monitoring periods and reducing the environmental footprint of monitoring operations in beekeeping which can further be investigated for future work.

1.1 Hypothesis

In LoRa-based monitoring systems, a combined optimization of spreading factor selection and duty cycle control [6, 7] informed by the analysis of optimized audio and image data transmission experiments can significantly reduce power consumption in the active state which in turn minimizes energy being utilized in comparison with the minimum (lower bound) theoretical value of 7dB $= 5.0119$ mW (from the equation $PdBm = 10 * \log(PmW)$) for the LoRa Grove E5 module. This optimization in energy efficiency will consider the trade-off between:

- *Spreading Factor:* Higher spreading factors (SF) may lead to increased power consumption during active transmission, potentially resulting in less energy saved during beehive data transfer. (quantified based on experiment data: difference in average active power between lowest and highest SF).
- *Duty Cycle:* Reducing the duty cycle, or the percentage of time in active mode, directly contributes to lower average power consumption resulting in higher energy savings during data transfer. Quantitative: calculate the reduction in average power consumption based on sleep and active power levels and desired duty cycle reduction).
- *Data Type Optimization:* Optimizing the data type, such as beehive audio or image data, further enhances energy efficiency and overall energy savings.

To achieve this optimization:

- Use optimized efficient image and audio models during data transfer across the LoRa network
- Utilize measured values of average power consumption (active and sleep), sleep time, active time, and cycle time across different spreading factors (SF 7, 8, and 12).
- Define a desired duty cycle reduction based on application requirements, focusing on maximizing energy efficiency during data transfer for bee-keeping monitoring practices.
- Calculate the expected reduction in average energy consumption observed when transferring images and audio data from bee hives based on the targeted duty cycle reduction, spreading factor, and sleep/active power levels.

1.2 Expected Outcome

We expect the analysis to support the efficacy of duty cycle and spreading factor selection techniques in maximizing energy efficiency and performance in LoRa-based beehive monitoring systems by testing and verifying this premise [4, 6, 7]. This hypothesis forms the basis of our study, directing future research and analysis to bolster the argument for energy-efficient monitoring techniques in beekeeping.

1.3 Research and Technical Contributions

This paper makes the following significant contributions to the field of beehive monitoring using the LoRa module:

- Through a detailed analysis, the study provides a thorough understanding of power consumption and duty cycles in beehive monitoring, covering a comparison of both optimized image and audio data collection.
- It offers crucial insights for maximizing energy efficiency while using LoRa Technology in farming and environmental monitoring practices like beekeeping.
- By identifying trends in power consumption across spreading factors, the study highlights the importance of tailored strategies to balance energy efficiency effectively. The findings have practical implications for implementing monitoring systems, emphasizing the need to minimize power consumption while maintaining effectiveness for longer battery life experiences.
- Serving as a foundation for future developments, the research guides the advancement of energy-efficient monitoring technologies that guarantee long-term battery life and lessen environmental effects for sustainable beekeeping benefiting both beekeepers and ecosystem health.

2 Literature and Related Research

2.1 Duty Cycle Regulation in Uganda for Short-Range Devices (SRDs) and Long-Range Devices

Uganda regulates the duty cycle for both Short-Range Devices (SRDs) and Long-Range Devices (potentially including LoRa) [23] under the guidelines set by the Uganda Communications Commission (UCC) [24]. The specific duty cycle limits for short-range devices/ultra-wideband devices depend on the sub-band used:

- 863.7–868.7 MHz $\leq$ 1% duty cycle OR require Detect and Avoid (DAA) mitigation technique.
- 868.7–869.2 MHz $\leq$ 0.1% duty cycle OR require DAA.
- 869.4–869.65 MHz $\leq$ 10% duty cycle OR require DAA. (This is relevant for LoRa applications)
- 869.7–870 MHz operating below 5 mW, no requirement.

There aren't currently specific regulations documented for Long-Range Devices like LoRa that operate outside the ISM bands mentioned above. Long-range communication typically requires a license from UCC. Devices need to comply with the Uganda Communications Act (2013) and any relevant regulations issued by UCC. This might involve limitations on transmit power, spectrum usage, and potential duty cycle restrictions depending on the allocated frequency band. As mentioned before, a 10% duty cycle would only be legal for SRDs operating in the specific 869.4–869.65 MHz sub-band and fulfilling all other requirements (type approval, DAA if needed, etc.). For long-range devices, using a 10% duty cycle might be possible depending on the allocated frequency band and the specific license obtained from UCC. However, confirmation and potential limitations would need to be obtained directly from UCC.

2.2 Impact of Spreading Factor on Duty Cycle

Since duty cycle is a key parameter regulated for SRDs, choosing a Spreading Factor will ultimately affect the achievable duty cycle for a given data rate. Lower Spreading Factors (SF7, SF8) offer faster transmission but consume more power and increase duty cycle. Higher Spreading Factors (SF10, SF12) offer slower transmission but use less power and lead to lower duty cycle [23, 24].

2.3 Compliance of Spreading Factor with Duty Cycle Limits

For SRDs [23] operating in the 863–870 MHz band, users must ensure their chosen Spreading Factor configuration, along with other factors like data rate and packet size, stays within the allowed duty cycle limits for the specific sub-band they're using (1% or 10% depending on the sub-band).

For Long-Range Devices like LoRa, regulations might focus on licensing and spectrum usage rather than Spreading Factor specifically. However, similar to SRDs, the chosen Spreading Factor will indirectly impact the achievable data rate and power consumption, which might need to be considered for overall system design and compliance with any limitations imposed by the license obtained from UCC [24].

2.4 Applications and Related Research

Bee monitoring technologies have undergone significant advancements in recent years, driven by the growing recognition of bees' critical role in pollination and ecosystem health [1, 2]. According to Jiang et. al, traditional monitoring methods, such as manual hive inspections and stationary sensor networks, are labor-intensive, time-consuming, and often limited in scalability and real-time data accessibility [8]. In contrast, emerging wireless communication technologies [7] offer promising solutions to address these challenges, with LoRa technology standing out as a prominent enabler of remote and energy-efficient beehive monitoring.

LoRa technology, based on the LoRaWAN protocol, enables long-range communication with low power consumption, making it well-suited for monitoring applications in remote and resource-constrained environments [9, 10] By leveraging LoRa modules, beekeepers can collect real-time data on hive conditions, including temperature, humidity, sound, and activity levels, without the need for frequent onsite visits [2]. This capability not only enhances operational efficiency but also allows for timely intervention in response to emerging hive issues, thereby improving colony health and productivity.

Previous studies have highlighted the energy-efficient nature of LoRa technology and its potential for reducing power consumption in IoT applications by optimizing spreading factors and duty cycles, LoRa-based monitoring systems can achieve prolonged battery life, minimizing the need for frequent battery replacements and reducing environmental impact [4, 11–13]. Moreover, the scalability and flexibility of LoRa networks enable seamless integration with existing infrastructure, facilitating the deployment of large-scale monitoring networks across diverse geographical regions.

The accomplishment of ongoing research initiatives advances our knowledge and defines the state-of-the-art for LoRaWAN installations in both lab and real-world contexts. Coverage distance measurements are the most strongly weighted criterion in all the previous research. Remarkably, a wide range of assessment techniques were presented, such as: distance traveled [10, 13–15], data communication success rate [16], payload sizes [11], different spreading factors or impairments [3, 9], and rural versus urban scenarios [17]. The time needed for data transmissions for different spreading factor (SF) configurations is given in [18]. Moreover, [12] shows the network throughput for different message sizes as a function of SF.

While research on energy-efficient communication protocols [7] in IoT applications is abundant, studies specifically focusing on beehive monitoring are relatively limited. Therefore, there is a need for further investigation into the efficacy of LoRa technology in optimizing energy efficiency in farming and environmental monitoring practices like beekeeping. By building upon existing literature and empirical evidence, this study aims to contribute valuable insights into the potential benefits and challenges of deploying LoRa-based monitoring systems in beekeeping operations.

3 Methodology

3.1 Experimental Network Setup

The Arduino Nano 33 BLE board and Seeedstudio LoRa Grove E5 [8] module (model LSN50V2-S3B) were used in the beehive monitoring project. The board will be powered via its 3.3 V and GND input pins with this modification. The LoRa Grove E5 module [19] is based on the Semtech SX1276 chipset, which is well-known for its long-range communication capabilities. It runs on the 868 MHz frequency band. Notably, the LoRa Grove E5 is appropriate for long-distance communication because of its remarkable transmission range of up to −10 km in open spaces. With a high sensitivity range of −116.5 dBm to −136 dBm and a maximum output power of 20.8 dBm, the module guarantees dependable communication even in challenging environments. The module also has an embedded GPS module (NEO-6M) for exact location tracking, which allows the beehives to be positioned accurately. It is compatible with LoRaWAN. Because it supports both LoRaWAN Class A and Class C protocols [7], communication methods can be customized.

Moreover, an OLED display facilitates real-time data visualization and user interaction, enhancing the monitoring experience. The Arduino Nano 33 BLE board [20], based on the nRF52840 microcontroller, provides the necessary processing power and interfaces for integrating the LoRa module into the monitoring system. With features such as digital input/output pins, PWM pins, UART, SPI, I2C, analog input pins, and native USB support, the Arduino Nano 33 BLE board serves as a versatile platform for deploying IoT applications with LoRa connectivity. Additionally, the low operating voltage of 3.3 V, compact dimensions (45 mm length, 18 mm width), and lightweight design (5g with headers) of the Arduino Nano 33 BLE board make it well-suited for compact and portable monitoring solutions. The nano 33 can be powered by USB. An output pin can have a maximum current of 10 mA. It is advised to use the lowest power modes and **decrease CPU activity to minimize self-heating. Furthermore, the board could be powered without using the DC**-DC regulator by cutting the connection between the 3.3V pads (see Fig. 1. Below).

Data Collection and Preprocessing:

Set Up-Hardware

The Arduino Nano 33 BLE Sense Rev2: combines a tiny form factor, different environment sensors and the possibility to run AI using TinyML and TensorFlow™ Lite.

ArduCam OV7675: The camera module with the matrix OV7675 0,3 MPx with a resolution of 640x 480 px and a speed of up to 60 frames per second. The device has the lens of 1/9", it communicates through a parallel interface.

LoRa Module-Grove - Wio-E5: Grove Wio-E5 embedded with Wio-E5 STM32WLE5JC, powered by ARM Cortex M4 ultra-low-power MCU core and Wio SX126x, is a wireless radio module supporting LoRa® and LoRaWAN® protocol on the EU868 & US915 frequency.

Fig. 1. Set Up- LoRa Module with Arduino Board

- Collected audio and image data from beehives under various conditions.
- Preprocessed the data to remove noise and enhance relevant features.

Model Training and Data Optimization:

- Trained Tiny ML models using Edge Impulse platform for audio and image classification.
- Optimized the audio and image models for accuracy and efficiency (Fig. 2 and Table 2).

Table 2. Dataset categories

Bee Hive Type	Image Data Set	Audio Data Set
Healthy	Healthy	Active
Hive being robbed	hbr	no_bee
Missing queen	mis_q	no_qbee

Arduino Nano 33 BLE Integration:

- Integrated the trained Tiny ML models into Arduino Nano 33 BLE devices.
- Developed C++ code to collect data from microphone and camera sensors, process it using the models, and prepare it for transmission (Fig. 3).

LoRa Beehive Monitoring Network Setup:

- Set up a LoRa network using the LoRa Grove E5 module and the Milesight UG67 outdoor Gateway [19, 21].
- Transmission of processed data over the LoRa network.

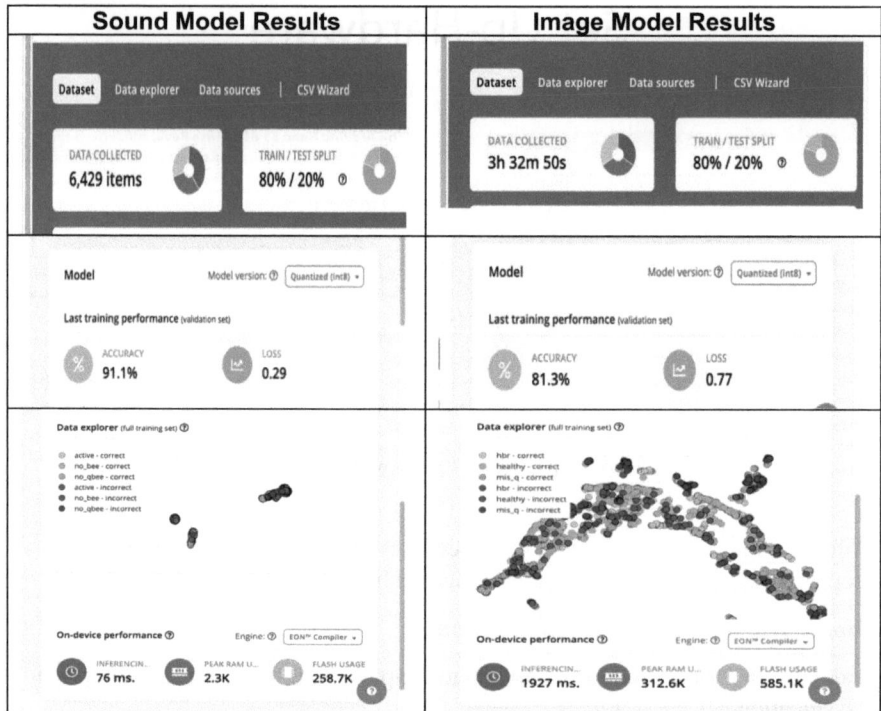

Fig. 2. Beehive Audio and Image File Model Validation and Training Results in Edge Impulse

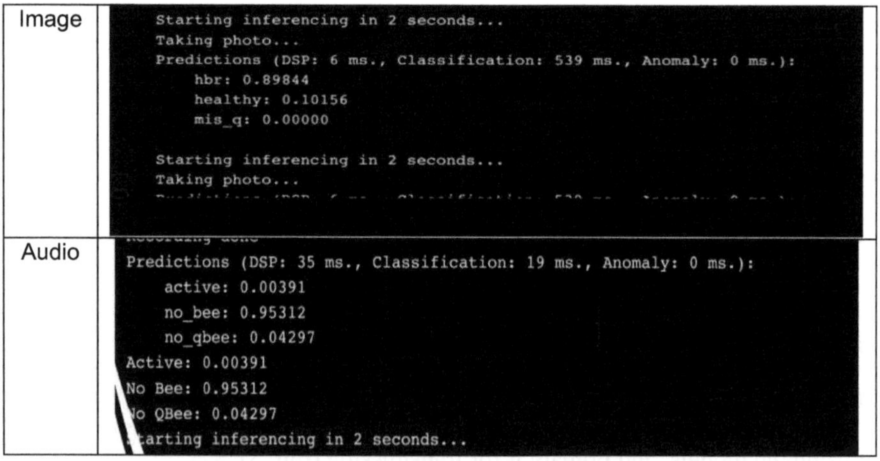

Fig. 3. Running Audio and Image Models in Arduino

3.2 Data Transmission

For transmitting image and audio data, the LoRa module was configured to adhere to specific parameters optimized for energy efficiency and data integrity. The packet size for data transmission was carefully chosen to balance payload size with transmission efficiency, ensuring minimal overhead while maximizing data throughput. The transmission frequency of 868MHz was selected to comply with regulatory requirements and leverage the propagation characteristics of the ISM band. Modulation schemes supported by the LoRaWAN protocol, such as Chirp Spread Spectrum (CSS), were utilized [7, 12, 13, 18] to achieve robust communication in noisy environments and over long distances. The LoRa modules were programmed to transmit data at regular intervals, synchronized with the monitoring schedule, to capture real-time insights into hive conditions. Additionally, error detection and correction mechanisms were implemented to mitigate data loss and ensure the integrity of transmitted information. The Milesight UG67 outdoor gateway [21] is used in our experiment. UG67 is a powerful 8-channel outdoor LoRaWAN®-gateway. With its high-performance quad-core CPU and SX1302 LoRa chip, UG67 can connect to more than 2000 nodes. With its IP67 waterproof housing and up to 15 km of line of sight, the UG67 is perfect for smart metering, smart agriculture, and a host of other outdoor applications. In addition to supporting various back-haul backups over Ethernet, Wi-Fi, and cellular, UG67 also includes built-in network servers and Milesight IoT Cloud for simple deployment, as well as integrated mainstream network servers (such TTI, ChirpStack, etc.). We used the MQTT broker destination server in this case as its preferred for IoT applications (Fig. 4).

Overall, the experimental setup aimed to harness the capabilities of the LoRa modules [11, 12] effectively while maintaining energy-efficient operation and reliable data transmission for beehive monitoring applications.

3.3 Power Measurement

The experimental setup utilized the OTII device [22] for precise power measurement during the transmission of data by the LoRa module. The OTII device offers a versatile output voltage range from 0.5 V to 5 V with a resolution of 1mV, ensuring compatibility and accurate voltage control. It supports a continuous output current of 2.5 A, with a peak current capability of 5 A, providing ample power delivery for stable operation. Additionally, the device allows for sink currents ranging from 0 to 2.5 A, enabling flexible current flow control and measurement with a resolution of 39 µA. With exceptional accuracy in current measurement ($\pm 0.1\% + 50$ nA) and voltage measurement ($\pm 0.1\% + 1.5$ mV), the OTII device ensures reliable monitoring of power consumption dynamics. Its sample rate of up to 4 ksps and analog bandwidth of 400 Hz facilitate rapid data acquisition and precise measurement of power signals within the specified frequency range. Overall, the OTII device's comprehensive specifications make it an indispensable tool for assessing the power consumption characteristics of electronic devices like the LoRa module in experimental studies and analysis (Fig. 5).

Other details of the methodology are covered in the table below (Table 3).

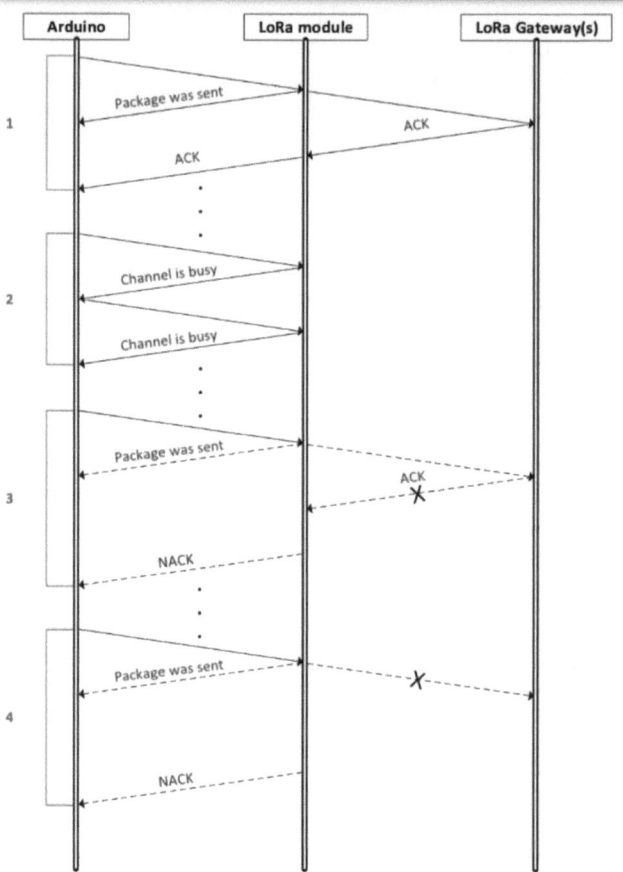

Fig. 4. A simplified representation of the message exchange that occurs while sending data.

Fig. 5. OTII Device

Table 3. Other details of the methodology

Section	Description	Details (Based on Available Information)
Data Collection	Process of gathering data	- Gathered image and audio data from beehive monitoring experiments conducted using the LoRa module - Parameters collected: Spreading factor, voltage, current consumption (sleep & active modes), energy consumption, time in sleep mode, cycle time
Data Analysis	Techniques used to analyze data	- Programming language: Python - Libraries: Pandas, Matplotlib, Seaborn - Techniques: Descriptive statistics, visualizations (line graphs), grouping by spreading factor
Power Consumption Measurements and Analysis		- Calculated average power consumption (sleep & active) for each spreading factor - Analyzed variations and trends in power consumption - Estimated total energy consumption for transfer of image and audio data across a LoRa Network for bee monitoring
Duty Cycle Analysis		- Defined duty cycle (percentage of active time) - Calculated duty cycle for each spreading factor and analyzed variations - Explored relationship between spreading factor and duty cycle for power management
Comparison & Interpretation		- Compared power consumption and duty cycle trends between spreading factors for both audio and image data - Interpreted results for energy efficiency of LoRa-based beehive monitoring - Discussed implications for optimizing energy usage and sustainable beekeeping practices
Validation & Discussion		- Validation against existing literature on power-efficient communication protocols and IoT applications - Discussion of limitations and future research for improving energy efficiency
Conclusion	Key findings and contributions	- Summarized key findings on optimizing energy efficiency with LoRa for beehive monitoring - Highlighted significance for sustainable beekeeping practices - Concluded with future research directions and practical applications

4 Results and Discussions

Calculations and Graphical observations were done in Python in google colab to provide insights into how various parameters described below were affected by the duration of sleep mode, shedding light on the behavior of the LoRa system module under different spreading factors. Further analysis was done to help in understanding the implications of these trends for optimizing energy consumption and duty cycle monitoring performance for both bee audio and image inferencing applications.

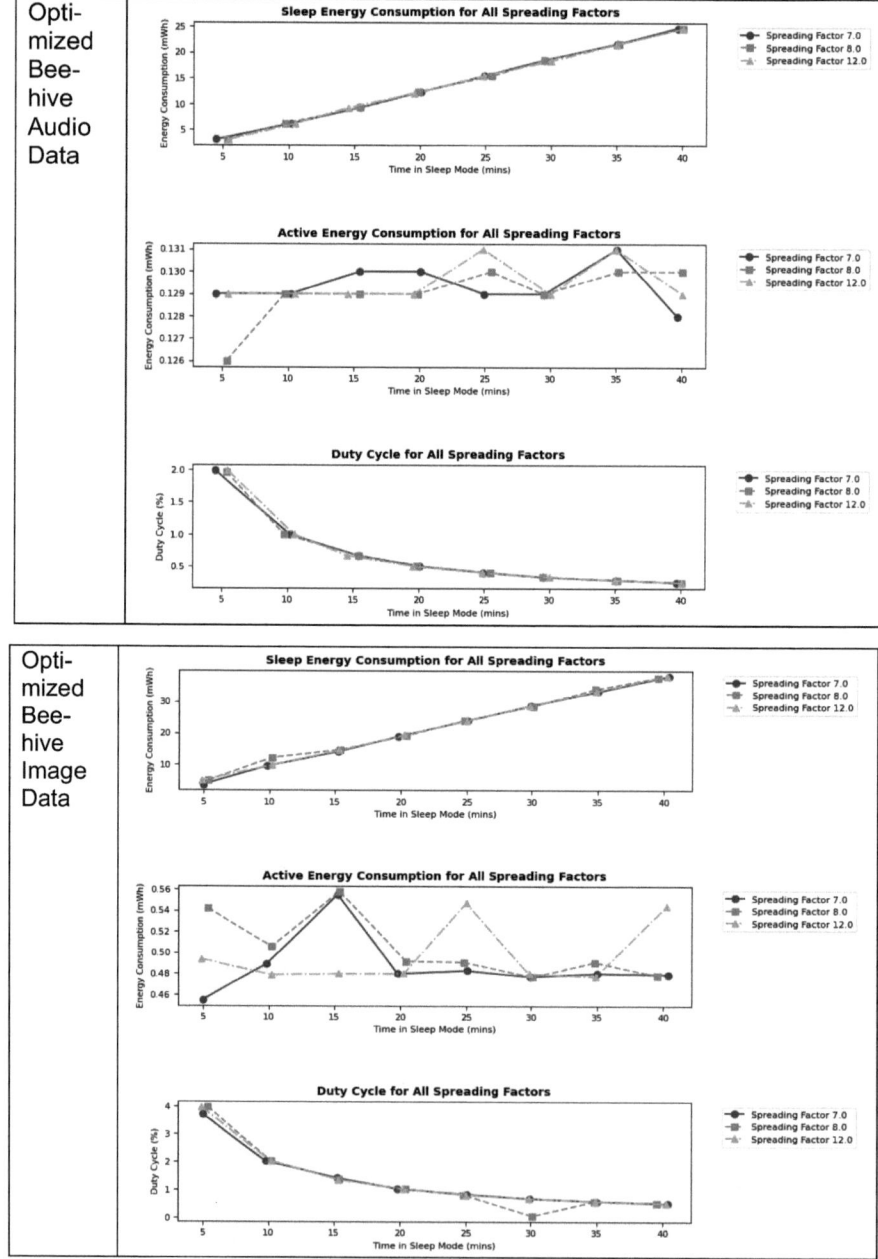

Fig. 6. Analysis of Energy Consumption and Duty Cycle Trends for Image and Audio data based on SFs.

Investigating the Correlation Between Choice of Spreading Factor 253

4.1 Formulae and Definition of Terms

$$Duty\ Cycle\ (\%) = (Time\ Active/Cycle\ Time) * 100 \quad (1)$$

$$Energy\ Consumption\ (mWh) = (Average\ Current\ Active * Time\ Active)/3600 \quad (2)$$

$$Power\ Consumption\ (mW) = Average\ Current\ Active\ (mA) * Voltage\ (V) \quad (3)$$

$$Time\ to\ Transmit\ a\ Symbol = (Symbol\ Length * 1000)/(Bandwidth * Spreading\ Factor) \quad (4)$$

4.2 Analysis of Energy Consumption (Both Active and Sleep States) and Duty Cycle Trends Based on SFs 7, 8 and 12

From the provided data statistics, we can observe the following trends in energy consumption and duty cycle across spreading factors (Fig. 6).

Energy Consumption Trends for Audio Data

Sleep Energy Consumption: The average sleep energy consumption ranges from approximately 12.51 mWh to 12.60 mWh across spreading factors 7, 8, and 12. The standard deviation of 7.93 mWh indicates relatively low variability in sleep energy consumption among different spreading factors.

Active Energy Consumption: The average active energy consumption is very low, ranging from approximately 0.126 mWh to 0.131 mWh across spreading factors 7, 8, and 12. The standard deviation of 0.001 mWh is also very low, suggesting consistent active energy consumption among spreading factors.

Total Energy Consumption: The total energy consumption is the sum of sleep and active energy consumption. It appears to be consistent across spreading factors, with no significant variation observed.

Duty Cycle Trends for Audio Data

Duty Cycle Variation: The duty cycle (%) represents the percentage of time the device is in active mode compared to the total cycle time. It ranges from approximately 0.12% to 0.13% across spreading factors 7, 8, and 12. The standard deviation is minimal, but the cycle time data is needed for exact calculation.

Impact of Spreading Factor: There is no clear trend in duty cycle variation based on spreading factors 7, 8, and 12. The duty cycle values are relatively consistent, suggesting that spreading factors may not significantly influence the duty cycle in this context.

Overall, the energy consumption for audio data remains consistent across spreading factors, with sleep energy consumption dominating and active energy consumption being relatively low. Duty cycle values also show consistency, indicating stable operational patterns regardless of the spreading factor.

Energy Consumption Trends for Image Data

Sleep Energy Consumption: The average sleep energy consumption ranges from approximately 19.36 mWh to 19.83 mWh across spreading factors 7, 8, and 12. The standard deviation of 12.12 mWh indicates moderate variability in sleep energy consumption among different spreading factors.

Active Energy Consumption: The average active energy consumption is relatively higher compared to the audio data, ranging from approximately 0.455 mWh to 0.564 mWh across spreading factors 7, 8, and 12. The standard deviation of 0.0337 mWh suggests some variability in active energy consumption among spreading factors.

Total Energy Consumption: The total energy consumption is the sum of sleep and active energy consumption. It shows a moderate variation across spreading factors, with spreading factor 8 having the highest total energy consumption.

Duty Cycle Trends for Image Data

Duty Cycle Variation: The duty cycle (%) ranges from approximately 0.07% to 0.09% across spreading factors 7, 8, and 12. The standard deviation of 0.0276 indicates some variability in duty cycle values among different spreading factors.

Impact of Spreading Factor: Similar to the audio data, there is no clear trend in duty cycle variation based on spreading factors 7, 8, and 12. The duty cycle values are relatively consistent, suggesting that spreading factors may not significantly influence the duty cycle in this context.

Overall, the energy consumption for image data is higher compared to audio data, with moderate variability observed among spreading factors. Duty cycle values remain relatively consistent across spreading factors, indicating stable operational patterns. However, further analysis and optimization may be required to minimize energy consumption and improve efficiency.

4.3 Performance Comparison Analysis of the Performance of the Lora Module Based on Energy Consumption and Duty Cycle Monitoring for Both Audio and Image Beehive Data

This analysis compares the performance of a LoRa module based on power consumption and duty cycle monitoring for transmitting audio and image beehive data across three spreading factors (SF): 7, 8, and 12.

Energy Consumption

Audio Data:

- Sleep energy consumption remains low and relatively consistent across spreading factors, with minimal variation (standard deviation of 7.93 mWh).
- Active energy consumption is very low and shows minimal variation across spreading factors (standard deviation of 0.001 mWh).
- Total energy consumption also remains consistent, with sleep energy dominating overall consumption.

Image Data:

- Sleep energy consumption is higher compared to audio data and exhibits moderate variability across spreading factors (standard deviation of 12.12 mWh). This could be due to factors like image size or processing requirements during transmission.

- Active energy consumption is significantly higher compared to audio data (around 3–4 times higher) due to the larger data size of images requiring more transmission time. This value exhibits some variability across spreading factors (standard deviation of 0.0337 mWh).
- Total energy consumption shows moderate variation across spreading factors, with SF 8 having the highest consumption likely due to its slightly higher active energy usage.

Duty Cycle:
Both audio and image data exhibit relatively consistent duty cycle values across spreading factors. This suggests that spreading factors may not significantly influence the percentage of time the device is active in this context. However, the duty cycle values are very low (around 0.13% for audio and 0.09% for image data), indicating short active periods compared to sleep time.

Key Observations:

- LoRa module performance for audio data transmission demonstrates consistent energy consumption with minimal variation across spreading factors, making it suitable for applications prioritizing low power usage.
- Image data transmission has a higher overall energy consumption due to larger data size but still exhibits moderate variability across spreading factors. Optimizing image size or compression techniques might be beneficial.
- Duty cycle is low and relatively consistent across spreading factors for both data types, suggesting efficient operation with minimal active time compared to sleep time.

4.4 Insights into LoRa Module Performance Measurements for Audio and Image Transmission Across Spreading Factors 7, 8 and 12

This table provides insights of the average performance measurements taken into LoRa module performance for audio and image transmission across three spreading factors (SF): 7, 8, and 12 (Table 4).

Table 4. Average Performance Measurements for SFs 7, 8 & 12 for both Audio and Image Data

Data Type	Spreading Factor	Bandwidth Usage (bits)	Power Consumption (mW)	Energy Consumption (mWh)	Time to Transmit a Symbol (ms)
Audio	7	438163.672	0.021271	25.864	0.292
Audio	8	437611.032	0.021206	25.738	0.585
Audio	12	438321.824	0.021281	25.855	9.345
Image	7	892702.08	0.038993	95.970	0.143
Image	8	893073.92	0.04114	101.994	0.287
Image	12	891440.792	0.04079	100.915	4.595

Here's a breakdown of the key observations, incorporating specific value differences and calculations of standard deviation for energy consumption:

Spreading Factor and Transmission Efficiency: A higher SF leads to wider signal spread (increasing potential range) but significantly increases the time to transmit a symbol (slower data rate). This trade-off is evident in both audio and image data. For example, while SF 7 takes 0.29 ms to transmit a symbol for audio data, SF 12 takes 9.34 ms (over 32 times longer).

Bandwidth Usage: Both audio and image data show relatively consistent bandwidth usage across spreading factors. Audio data exhibits minimal variation, with values around 438,000 bits for all SFs. Image data also shows consistency, with values around 892,000 bits for all SFs. This suggests a fixed bit rate for the audio and potentially similar image sizes or bit depths for the image data.

Power Consumption and Energy Consumption: Both audio and image data exhibit minimal variation in power consumption across spreading factors, with values in the range of milliwatts (mW). Audio data: Power consumption for audio data varies slightly, from 0.021 mW (SF 7) to 0.021 mW (SF 12). Image data:

Power consumption for image data is consistently higher compared to audio, ranging from 0.039 mW (SF 7) to 0.041 mW (SF 12). This is likely due to the larger data size of images requiring more transmission time.

Energy consumption follows a similar trend to power consumption, with close values across spreading factors for both audio and image data. However, due to high bandwidth usage for image data, energy consumption might be slightly higher. We calculated the standard deviation for each data type using the formula for population standard deviation:

$$\sigma = \sqrt{\left(\Sigma(x_i - \mu)^2 / N\right)} \qquad (6)$$

where:

σ = standard deviation.

x_i = individual energy consumption value for each spreading factor.

μ = average energy consumption for all spreading factors (mean).

N = total number of spreading factors (3 in this case).

Audio data has a standard deviation of approximately 0.010 mWh.

Image data has a standard deviation of around 3.02 mWh.

These values are relatively small compared to the mean energy consumption, suggesting minimal variation across spreading factors.

Time to Transmit a Symbol (ms): As observed in the table, the Time to Transmit a Symbol increases significantly with a higher spreading factor:

SF 7: This has the fastest transmission time (around 0.14 ms for image and 0.29 ms for audio).

SF 8: Transmission time doubles compared to SF 7 (around 0.29 ms for image and 0.58 ms for audio).

SF 12: Transmission time increases significantly compared to lower SFs (around 4.59 ms for image and 9.34 ms for audio).

This highlights the trade-off between range and data rate. Higher spreading factors offer potentially longer range but require considerably longer transmission times.

Key Differences Between Audio and Image Data

- Image data transmission has a consistently higher power consumption compared to audio data (approximately double the value). This is likely due to the larger data size of images requiring more transmission time.
- Despite the higher power consumption, image data still shows minimal variation in power consumption across spreading factors.
- The standard deviation of energy consumption is considerably higher for image data (around 3.02 mWh) compared to audio data (around 0.010 mWh). This suggests slightly more variation in energy consumption for image data transmission.

4.5 Energy Efficiency Calculations

To calculate the energy saved for both audio and image data given the energy efficiency values, we can use the theoretical minimum power value used by the LoRa Grove E5 Module in active mode is 7 dB, equivalent to 5.0119 mW. The energy utilized for our practical case by the module in active mode is already given in the percentage above, so we can derive the energy saved by subtracting these percentages from 100%.

Audio Data Energy Efficiency:

	Spreading Factor	Total Energy per cycle (mWh)	Energy Efficiency (%)
0	7	12.439833	1.021631
1	8	18.653666	0.692869
2	12	24.917384	0.526301

Image Data Energy Efficiency:

	Spreading Factor	Total Energy per cycle (mWh)	Energy Efficiency (%)
0	7	28.694351	1.550465
1	8	19.320758	2.480802
2	12	292.151373	0.178066

Audio data energy in mW

	Energy Active (mWh)	Energy Active (mW)
0	0.127089	0.021153
1	0.129245	0.021292
2	0.131140	0.021432

Image data energy in mW

	Energy Active (mWh)	Energy Active (mW)
0	0.444896	0.038549
1	0.479310	0.038688
2	0.520222	0.041889

Audio Data Energy Saved:

	Spreading Factor	Energy Saved (mW)	Energy Saved (%)
0	7	4.990747	99.577938
1	8	4.990607	99.575161
2	12	4.990468	99.572384

Image Data Energy Saved:

	Spreading Factor	Energy Saved (mW)	Energy Saved (%)
0	7	4.973351	99.230847
1	8	4.973212	99.228071
2	12	4.970011	99.164206

4.6 Results Analysis

Results indicate significant energy savings achievable by optimizing duty cycles, optimizing data transfer, and observing spreading factors while using the LoRa Grove E5 Module. For instance, the spreading factor of 8 achieves the highest power consumption saving of 4.973212 mW (over 99.23%) for image data with slower data rates, compared to a theoretical minimum value of 5.0119 mW. For audio data, a spreading factor of 7 achieves the highest power saving of 4.990747mW. But since the energy-saving capabilities are minimal across the three spreading factors we can use SF 12 to achieve a longer range at faster data rates. These findings emphasize the importance of efficient LoRa communication module configuration to minimize energy consumption during data transmission in bee hive monitoring.

4.7 Overall Observations

- LoRa offers a trade-off between range and data rate through spreading factor selection. Optimizing this trade-off depends on application requirements. For scenarios prioritizing fast data transmission and lower power consumption lower spreading factors (like SF 7) might be preferable due to faster transmission times and slightly lower power consumption. When long-range communication is essential, even at the cost of slower data rates (e.g., sending periodic sensor data from beehives), higher spreading factors (like SF 12) become more suitable despite potentially slightly higher energy consumption.
- Both audio and image data transmission demonstrate minimal variation in power consumption across spreading factors, suggesting other factors like module overhead might play a significant role in overall power usage.
- The standard deviation of energy consumption provides insights into the variability of energy usage across spreading factors. Image data exhibits a higher standard deviation compared to audio data, suggesting slightly more variation in energy consumption for image transmission.

4.8 Performance Evaluation

- Efficiency: The LoRa module demonstrates efficient power management, maintaining low energy consumption during both active transmission and sleep modes. This efficiency is essential for prolonging battery life and ensuring reliable long-term operation in remote beehive monitoring applications.
- Trade-offs: There exists a trade-off between spreading factor, communication range, and power consumption. While higher spreading factors may offer increased range and better signal penetration, they can also result in longer duty cycles and higher power consumption. Balancing these factors is crucial to meet the specific requirements of the monitoring application while optimizing power usage.

The analysis above highlights the effectiveness of the LoRa module in maintaining efficient power consumption and duty cycle management for beehive monitoring applications. By carefully optimizing spreading factors and duty cycles, it is possible to achieve prolonged battery life and reliable performance in remote and resource-constrained environments.

5 Research Considerations and Recommendations

5.1 Research Considerations

- The hypothesis discussed in the paper focuses on optimizing energy efficiency. Real-world factors like environmental conditions and interference might impact actual performance.
- The optimal spreading factor and duty cycle settings will depend on specific application requirements, balancing power consumption and latency.

5.2 Recommendations

- For audio data transmission, higher spreading factors (like SF 12) might be preferable due to their minimal impact on power consumption and faster transmission times (assuming sufficient range is achieved).
- For image data transmission, a trade-off analysis is necessary. Lower spreading factors offer faster transmission but potentially lower range. Higher spreading factors might be suitable if longer range is critical, but techniques to minimize image size or optimize transmission can help reduce energy consumption.
- The battery life of an end device is highly dependent on the spreading factor used and duty cycles. Higher spreading factors and duty cycles result in longer active times for the radio transceivers and shorter battery life of beehive nodes. However, this needs to be balanced with communication range requirements

6 Conclusion

In this work, we used LoRa modules to monitor beehives and carried out a thorough examination of power consumption and duty cycles, paying particular attention to the collection of both image and audio bee-hive data. Our research provides important new information about how to optimize energy efficiency for long-term, successful beehive monitoring procedures.

By carefully analyzing power consumption in the active and sleep modes across a range of spreading parameters, we were able to identify some noteworthy tendencies that highlight the importance of energy optimization. The findings show that the spreading factor selection has a substantial impact on duty cycles and power consumption, emphasizing the need for customized approaches to strike a compromise between range and energy economy.

Moreover, our research clarifies the trade-offs involved in choosing the appropriate spreading factor, highlighting the necessity of finding a careful balance between power usage and data transmission range. Without sacrificing data quality or transmission reliability, beekeepers can attain maximum energy efficiency by carefully modifying spreading parameters according to particular monitoring requirements.

The practical use of beehive monitoring systems, where increasing energy efficiency is critical for extended operation and less environmental effect, is affected by our findings. Stakeholders may design well-informed strategies to reduce power usage while preserving efficient monitoring capabilities by implementing the lessons learned from our study, which will eventually support the sustainability of beekeeping practices and the health of the ecosystem.

Essentially, our work lays the groundwork for the development of energy-efficient beehive monitoring systems and provides insightful advice to interested parties looking to leverage LoRa modules for sustainable and data-driven beekeeping methods.

Acknowledgments. The authors gratefully acknowledge the support of the Marconi Lab in ICTP Trieste Italy and the IoTRA Lab in Makerere University Uganda for the information provided and the design of the figures in this document.

Author Contributions. All authors contributed equally to this work. All authors have read and agreed to the published version of the manuscript.

Funding. This research was supported by funding from NORAD through the NORHED2 program under grant agreement QZA-21/0159 as part of the AdEMNEA project.

Conflict of Interest. The authors declare no conflicts of interest.

References

1. Zaman, A., Dorin, A.: A framework for better sensor-based beehive health monitoring (2022). https://doi.org/10.1101/2022.11.15.516676
2. Van Espen, M., Williams, J.H., Alves, F., Hung, Y., de Graaf, D.C., Verbeke, W.: Beekeeping in Europe facing climate change: a mixed methods study on perceived impacts and the need to adapt according to stakeholders and beekeepers. Sci. Total. Environ. **888**, 164255 (2023). https://doi.org/10.1016/j.scitotenv.2023.164255
3. Wendt, T., Volk, F., Mackensen, E.: A benchmark survey of long range (LoRaTM) spread-spectrum-communication at 2.45 GHz for safety applications. In: Proceedings of the 2015 IEEE 16th Annual Wireless and Microwave Technology Conference (WAMICON), pp. 1–4. IEEE (2015)
4. Aarif, L., Tabaa, M., Hachimi, H.: Performance evaluation of LoRa communications in harsh industrial environments. J. Sens. Actuator Netw. **12**(6), 80 (2023). https://doi.org/10.3390/jsan12060080
5. Cota, D., Martins, J., Mamede, H., Branco, F.: BHiveSense: an integrated information system architecture for sustainable remote monitoring and management of apiaries based on IoT and microservices. J. Open Innov. Technol. Mark. Complexity **9**(3), 100110 (2023). ISSN 2199-8531. https://doi.org/10.1016/j.joitmc.2023.100110. https://www.sciencedirect.com/science/article/pii/S2199853123002123
6. Pötsch, A., Haslhofer, F.: Practical limitations for deployment of LoRa gateways. In: Proceedings of the 2017 IEEE International Workshop on Measurement and Networking (M&N), pp. 1–6. IEEE (2017)
7. Poluektov, D., et al.: On the performance of LoRaWAN in smart city: end-device design and communication coverage (2019). https://doi.org/10.1007/978-3-030-36614-8_2
8. Jiang, J.-A., et al.: A WSN-based automatic monitoring system for the foraging behavior of honeybees and environmental factors of beehives. Comput. Electron. Agric. **123**, 304–318 (2016). https://doi.org/10.1016/j.compag.2016.03.003

9. Wixted, A.J., Kinnaird, P., Larijani, H., Tait, A., Ahmadinia, A., Strachan, N.: Evaluation of LoRa and LoRaWAN for wireless sensor networks. In: Proceedings of the 2016 IEEE Sensors, pp. 1–3. IEEE (2016)
10. Xiong, X., Zheng, K., Xu, R., Xiang, W., Chatzimisios, P.: Low power wide area machine-to-machine networks: key techniques and prototype. IEEE Commun. Mag. **53**(9), 64–71 (2015)
11. Aref, M., Sikora, A.: Free space range measurements with Semtech LoRaTM technology. In: Proceedings of the 2014 2nd International Symposium on Wireless Systems within the Conferences on Intelligent Data Acquisition and Advanced Computing Systems, pp. 19–23. IEEE (2014)
12. Augustin, A., Yi, J., Clausen, T., Townsley, W.: A study of LoRa: long range & low power networks for the Internet of Things. Sensors **16**(9), 1466 (2016)
13. Petri´c, T., Goessens, M., Nuaymi, L., Toutain, L., Pelov, A.: Measurements, performance and analysis of LoRa FABIAN, a real-world implementation of LPWAN. In: Proceedings of the 2016 IEEE 27th Annual International Symposium on Personal, Indoor, and Mobile Radio Communications (PIMRC), pp. 1–7. IEEE (2016)
14. Cenedese, A., Zanella, A., Vangelista, L., Zorzi, M.: Padova smart city: an Urban Internet of Things experimentation. In: Proceeding of IEEE International Symposium on a World of Wireless, Mobile and Multimedia Networks 2014, pp. 1–6. IEEE (2014)
15. Centenaro, M., Vangelista, L., Zanella, A., Zorzi, M.: Long-range communications in unlicensed bands: the rising stars in the IoT and smart city scenarios. IEEE Wirel. Commun. **23**(5), 60–67 (2016)
16. Petajajarvi, J., Mikhaylov, K., Roivainen, A., Hanninen, T., Pettissalo, M.: On the coverage of LPWANs: range evaluation and channel attenuation model for LoRa technology. In: Proceedings of the 2015 14th International Conference on ITS Telecommunications (ITST), pp. 55–59. IEEE (2015)
17. Radcliffe, P.J., Chavez, K.G., Beckett, P., Spangaro, J., Jakob, C.: Usability of LoRaWAN technology in a central business district. In: Proceedings of the 2017 IEEE 85th Vehicular Technology Conference (VTC Spring), pp. 1–5. IEEE (2017)
18. Vatcharatiansakul, N., Tuwanut, P., Pornavalai, C.: Experimental performance evaluation of LoRaWAN: a case study in Bangkok. In: Proceedings of the 2017 14th International Joint Conference on Computer Science and Software Engineering (JCSSE), pp. 1–4. IEEE (2017)
19. https://wiki.seeedstudio.com/Grove_LoRa_E5_New_Version/
20. https://store.arduino.cc/products/arduino-nano-33-ble
21. https://resource.milesight-iot.com/milesight/document/ug67-datasheet-en.pdf
22. https://connectedthings.store/gb/lorawan-development/qoitech-otii-power-optimising-tool.html
23. https://www.ucc.co.ug/wp-content/uploads/2023/10/Technical-Requirements-for-operation-of-868.docx.pdf
24. https://www.ucc.co.ug/

GPT Promotes Intelligent Autonomy in Communication Networks

Yifan Yang[1], Zheng Yang[2], Jie Zeng[2(✉)], Yuran Dan[2], Zhenming Bai[2], and Chen Xu[2]

[1] School of Information and Electronics, Beijing Institute of Technology, Beijing 100081, China
3220230923@bit.edu.cn
[2] School of Cyberspace Science, Beijing Institute of Technology, Beijing 100081, China
{3120231286,zengjie,1120222004,1120221445,1120220671}@bit.edu.cn

Abstract. With the continuous progress of mobile communication technology and the continuous growth of network demand, the network structure is becoming increasingly complex. However, traditional network management is difficult to meet the needs of future development. In the future, intelligent autonomous networks could perform flexibly and efficiently with the help of AI-driven automated analysis and multidimensional data perception. Still, at the same time, this also requires a more intelligent approach to network management. The large language models (LLMs) represented by generative pre-trained transformer (GPT) will play an important role in promoting intelligent autonomy of communication networks. Therefore, this paper studies the specific methods of GPT promoting intelligent autonomy of communication networks, and analyzes how GPT enables intelligent autonomy in communication networks from different perspectives. Specifically, it includes GPT-assisted base station site selection, antenna design optimization and virtualized intelligent slicing, as well as network operations and maintenance from anomaly detection to automatic recovery, and network traffic optimization, coverage optimization and signaling tracing. Finally, we also propose some challenges, such as the inconsistent quality of training data sets, insufficient computing resources, and high risks to network privacy and security. We also propose some corresponding solutions and predict future development trends.

Keywords: Autonomous Networks · GPT · Large Language Models · Network Intelligence

1 Introduction

1.1 Research Background

In the development of artificial intelligence (AI), "large language models" have gradually attracted attention, the most famous of which is the GPT series released by OpenAI. GPT has been applied in plentiful fields, becoming a dominant key technology and

---

This work was supported by the National Key Research and Development Program of China under Grant 2024YFE0200300, the National Natural Science Foundation of China (No. 92367201 and No. 62371039), and BIT Research and Innovation Promoting Project (Grant No. 2024YCXY027).

playing a vital role in commercial and social development. Nowadays, applying AI in communications sheds light on breakthroughs in the deployment and operation of communication infrastructures.

The current network management model mainly relies on manual intervention and has many limitations. Manual management is not only inefficient but also prone to problems such as delayed responses and inaccurate decision-making when faced with complex network environments and changing business needs. AI-empowered autonomous networks, however, can make network management more efficient, flexible and precise through automation and intelligent means. The network automation capabilities brought about by AI in mobile networks are a vital fourth dimension [1] in addition to the three dimensions of the fifth Generation (5G) mobile communication system, as shown in Fig. 1.

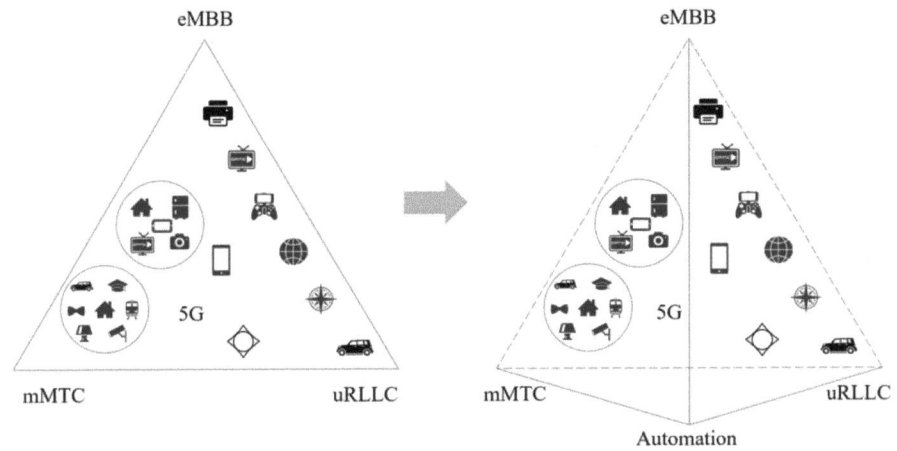

Fig.1. Network automation becomes the fourth dimension of 5G.

Autonomous networks, which can be further empowered by AI, could empower next-generation communications with self-configuration [2], self-optimization, self-healing, as well as self-evolution. "AI + communication" has been proposed as one typical scenario in the sixth generation (6G) mobile communication system [3]. In the future, intelligent networks will have a comprehensive understanding of network operating conditions through multi-dimensional data perception, including business data, network status data, and so on. With these data, intelligent analysis can be performed, and flexible and efficient network strategies can be provided.

1.2 Main Contribution

Currently, many operators and vendors are studying network autonomy with the help of AI [4]. Therefore, based on the latest research progress of GPT applied to intelligent communication networks, this paper discusses the specific processes of GPT enhancing the intelligent autonomy of communication networks, as shown in Fig. 2.

The main contributions of this paper are given below:

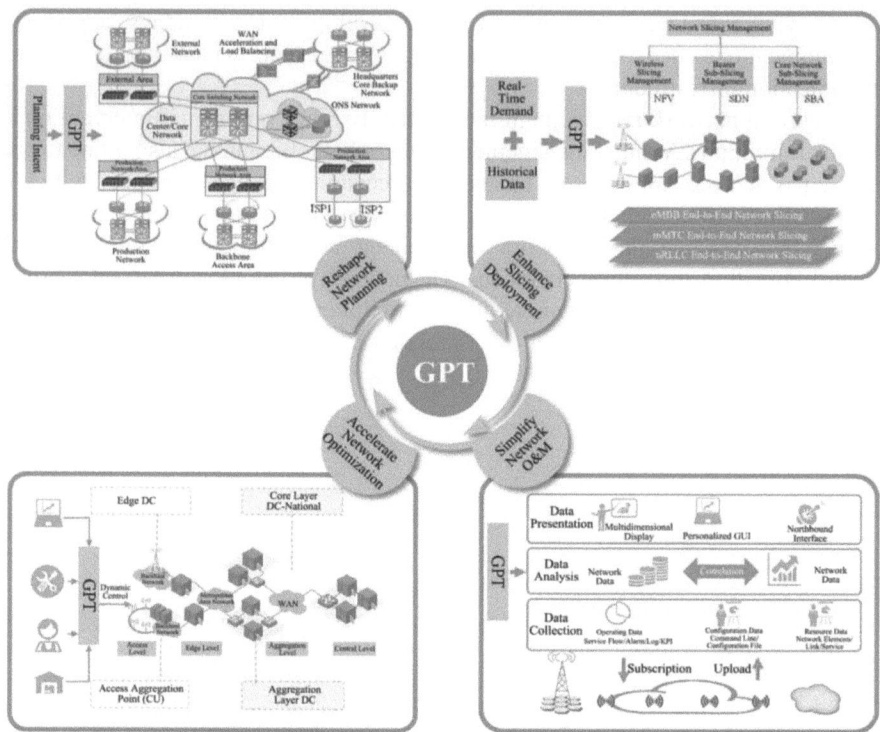

Fig. 2. Intelligent network autonomy with GPT.

- The concept of intelligent autonomous networks is introduced, and the method of GPT promoting intelligent autonomy of communication networks is studied. On this basis, the details of how to empower the communication network are given.
- Considering network planning, slice deployment and so on, the specific applications of GPT to promote the intelligent and autonomous development of communication networks are discussed, and some new applications and architectures are studied to improve network performance.
- The application of GPT in existing intelligent communication networks is summarized, and challenges that GPT will face in future network intelligence, as well as corresponding solutions and plans, are introduced.

The remainder of this paper is organized as follows. Section II introduces the GPT-based base station location selection and antenna design optimization methods, and proposes the specific process of using GPT as an intent engine to implement network planning. Following Section III will introduce network slicing techniques and present a specific approach to enhance network slicing deployment by optimizing VNF mapping with GPT. In Section IV, we analyze the simplification of GPT to network operation and maintenance (O&M), including the complete process from anomaly detection, fault diagnosis, and event alert to an intelligent decision. Then, in Section V, how to use GPT for the optimization of network traffic and coverage is studied, and the corresponding process framework is given. In Section VI, the challenges to be faced are presented. The conclusions and future work can be found in Section VII.

2 GPT Reshapes Network Planning

Today, the Internet has an unprecedented and growing impact on our business and our lives. At the same time, the construction of mobile communication networks is developing rapidly, the number of sites is increasing quickly, and the number of end users is exploding. In this case, operators are faced with many problems and challenges, such as accurate location, continuous coverage, interference control, and so on. In addition, the emergence of new techniques and different business characteristics require that network architectures can quickly adapt to these changes. Consequently, when designing and deploying networks, it is particularly important to carry out reasonable network planning, and the addition of GPT can quickly realize this process.

2.1 Base Station Location Selection

Since the number of wireless devices grows quickly, operators need to deploy more network infrastructure. Traditionally, the selection of new base station sites could be carried out by coverage simulation tools. In this case, each site can be evaluated by Key Performance Indicators (KPIs). However, when there are a large number of available base station options, traditional planning methods become expensive and it is difficult to consider all the factors. Artificial intelligence-driven planning solutions can help operators reduce the costs of network planning by recommending optimal locations for new cellular base stations.

The AI-based selection scheme determines the location of candidate sites based on a site screening algorithm model, and generates corresponding 360° satellite and 3D environment photos by combining satellite and building 3D maps. At the same time, the pole tower height, AAU coverage height, and azimuth angle are determined based on the location and corresponding coverage area of the candidate site, as well as the height of the existing candidate site, and a site selection report is generated for each candidate site [5].

Recently, an AI-based site selection method is proposed [6]. The location selection process of the base station based on AI is shown in Fig. 3.

Then, GPT can be utilized to plan network site selections. By collecting spatio-temporal feature data, the changing law of wireless resource utilization, and monitoring and evaluating the KPIs of the covered cells. GPT comprehensively analyzes aspects such as network coverage and user distribution, and performs homogeneous clustering based on cell attributes. Relationships between cell properties can be captured by supervised regression models. Based on the regression model, a simulation algorithm is constructed to estimate the site traffic load. Finally, these base stations can be further specifically ranked, and the top-ranked base stations can be included in the candidate base station list. The experimental results show that as the number of clusters increases, the error decreases and the accuracy of the corresponding model increases. This proves that clustering and building separate regression models for base stations of a similar nature can indeed improve the accuracy.

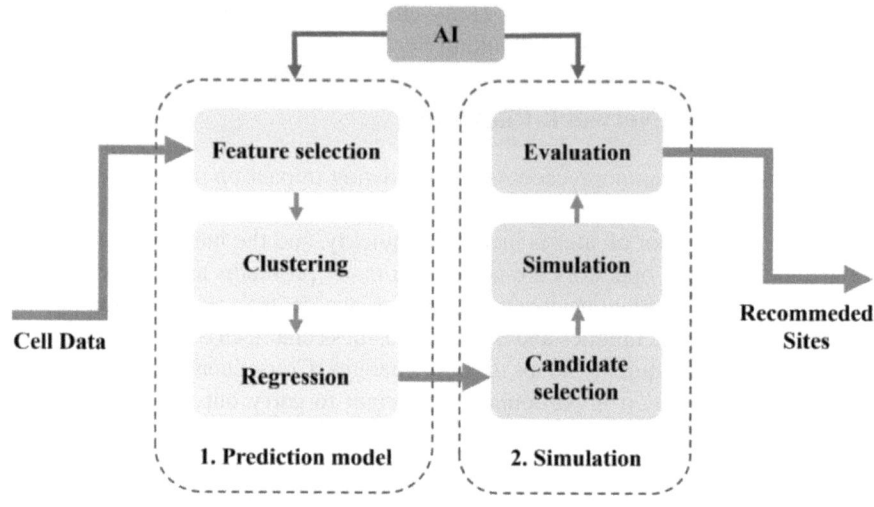

Fig. 3. AI-based location selection method.

2.2 Antenna Design Optimization

In the stage of planning the base stations, it is important to design antennas. When designing a mobile communication network, many factors need to be considered before the design of the base station antenna, and the base station antenna should be reasonably selected according to the actual situation of network coverage requirements, call distribution, anti-jamming requirements and network service quality. First of all, the selection of antenna type is an important step in the design of base station antenna. However, in the actual antenna optimization and design process, many antenna parameters are usually involved, the antenna geometry is becoming more and more complex, and the performance requirements of antennas are often contradictory, which brings a lot of challenges to the antenna selection and design.

Integrating GPT into the design of antenna simulations could supplant electromagnetic simulation software's function in modifying antenna settings based on simulated scenarios and employing particle swarm intelligent optimization algorithms [7] for rapid antenna simulation and optimization planning. In contrast to EM simulation software, this method has the potential to enhance computational effectiveness. The results are shown in Fig. 4, which shows that the human model designed by the engineer is regular with a limited number of parameters. In contrast, the model designed by artificial intelligence is irregular, with more parameters, a higher degree of freedom and a more natural shape [8].

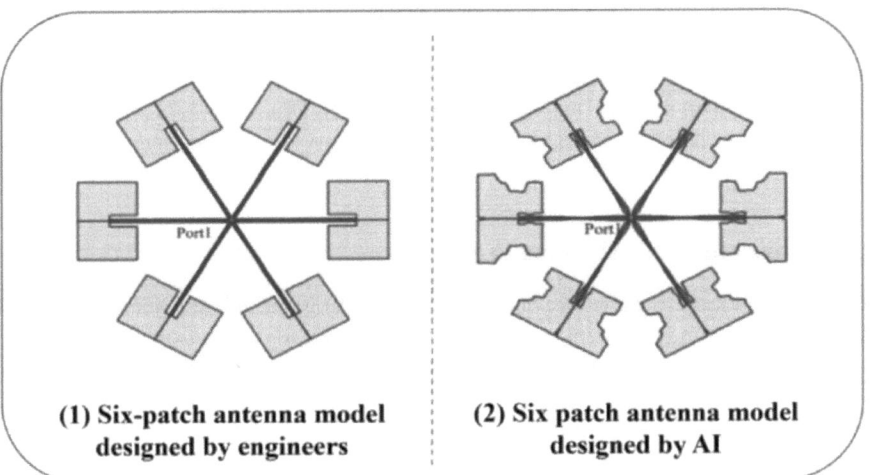

Fig. 4. A comparison between a human engineer and an AI-designed six patch antenna model.

3 GPT Enhances Slicing Deployment

With the advent of diverse new services in the 5G and cloud era, different industries, businesses, and users have put a variety of service quality requirements on the network. Therefore, 5G networks should have massive access, deterministic delay, high reliability, and other capabilities. It is necessary to build flexible and dynamic networks to meet the diversified business needs of users and vertical industries. Faced with the above needs, network slicing technology has emerged.

During the deployment of network slicing, the division of various service scenarios imposes distinct resource requirements on the base physical network, along with variations in the structure of the deployment. Conventional algorithms pose challenges in addressing the issue of deploying multi-scenario slicing. Utilizing technologies related to GPT enables the implementation of network slicing from start to finish, simultaneously lowering the cost of deployment and enhancing security.

3.1 Auxiliary Network Slicing Management

The technique of network slicing facilitates the development of tailored virtual networks within a common physical framework. However, existing orchestration and management approaches still have limitations and are unable to meet the more complex demands for new services in a multi-managed host environment. 6G network architectures will open up new revenue streams and allow organizations with different needs to share network and spectrum resources. At the same time, based on the evolving Open Radio Access Network (ORAN) paradigm, 6G networks can offer unparalleled openness, customization, automation, and software [9].

A novel network slicing architecture driven by LLM and multi-agent systems such as GPT is proposed in reference [10]. At the same time, multi-agent systems like GPT also facilitate collaboration across different management domains.

Ramraj Dangi et al. also propose an efficient artificial intelligence-based network slicing framework, and make the construction of intelligent 6G networks easier [11]. Artificial intelligence can enhance the stability of 5G networks [12]. The architecture should have built-in security mechanisms to deal with attacks and threats [13], thereby supporting faster data transmission rates, better quality of service, and higher network efficiency.

3.2 Optimize the VNF Mapping Process

The implementation of network slicing entails situating Virtualized Network Functions (VNFs) and choosing pertinent connections. In contrast to conventional heuristic methods, GPT has the capability to evaluate the status of the network environment and smartly modify network parameters based on various criteria. Collaboration with the agent enables the execution of certain tasks, reorganization of network resource usage, and complete assertion of state information.

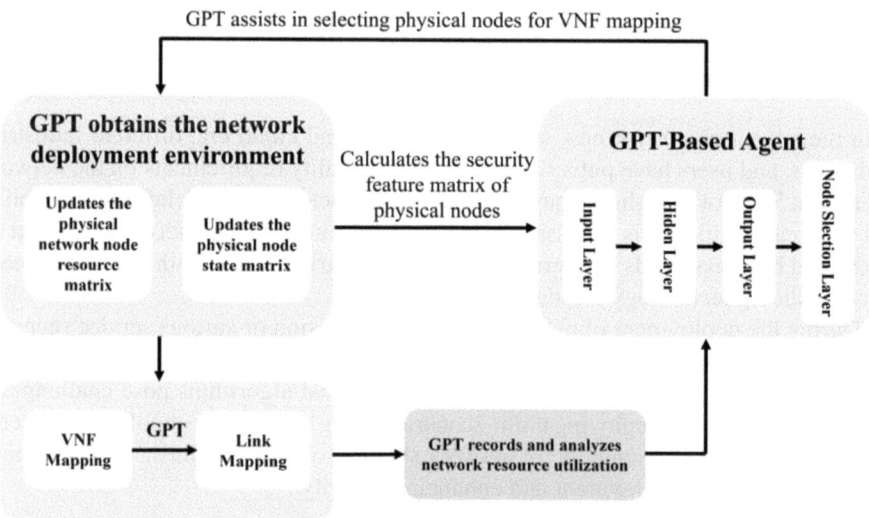

Fig. 5. GPT optimizes VNF mapping.

As demonstrated in Fig. 5, the GPT aids in acquiring the network deployment setting and preserving the physical node data as a matrix of security features. The agent is characterized as a policy network dependent on the GPT for calculating the likelihood of mapping physical nodes. The GPT assists in determining the probability of mapping physical nodes, subsequently generating the security feature matrix, selecting the most likely physical node, and implementing VNF mapping. Following this, GPT identifies the optimal link mapping strategy tailored to varying service needs, employs network resource usage as a reward mechanism, offers agent feedback, and aligns to refresh the status data. Adopting this method can greatly enhance the precision in deploying network slicing.

4 GPT Streamlines Network Operation and Maintenance

Typical applications of network intelligent O&M include identifying anomalies, diagnosing faults, issuing event warnings, and enhancing performance. In standard network operations and management, employees must collect network status information through manual verification and analysis, a process deemed inefficient. The implementation of GPT-linked technologies enables immediate, effective monitoring of network states, alongside automated analysis and processing, significantly enhancing network stability and dependability. Figure 6 displays the streamlined structure of network operation and Maintenance, supported by GPT.

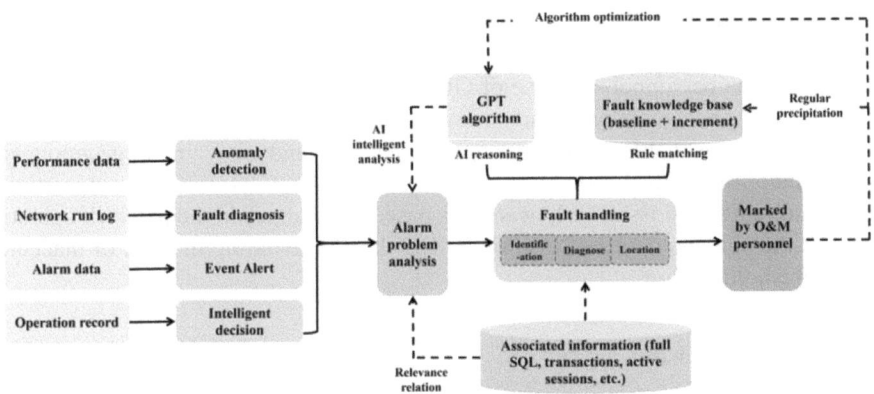

Fig. 6. GPT streamlines network operation and maintenance.

4.1 Anomaly Detection

GPT intelligent anomaly detection relies on the perception ability of network state, and can continuously and automatically collect all kinds of state data in the network, and carry out intelligent analysis of these data. Once any abnormal state in the network is detected, it is immediately identified and the detection results are reported [14]. First, according to different network status awareness tasks, different status detectors can be generated, and corresponding awareness tasks can be started according to the requirements, such as performance, alarm, log, configuration and other tasks, and then the indicators are subscribed and sent to the data acquisition platform. Then, the correlation analyzer will be started to quickly analyze and detect anomalies using GPT-related technology. This method is highly practical and effective in practical applications, especially in complex network environments, and can significantly improve the efficiency of fault detection and processing.

4.2 Fault Diagnosis

GPT can find out the strong correlation between different factors, and use these relationships to infer which factors are fundamental factors, to help users quickly diagnose the problem, improve the fault location speed and repair efficiency, and then prevent similar abnormal problems in the next time. GPT can analyze the collected network data through the inference engine based on a knowledge graph so as to quickly locate the root cause of the fault. The knowledge graph is a semantic network containing entities and inter-entity relationships, which can be used for reasoning and representation of knowledge. For some unknown faults, GPT can also learn fault inference, helping operation and maintenance personnel to deeply explore the root causes of unknown faults.

4.3 Event Alert

In terms of early warning, the traditional early warning management generally uses fixed thresholds and requires manual setting by operation and maintenance personnel, which not only requires a huge workload but also depends on the experience of operation and maintenance personnel. The use of GPT-related technologies can greatly improve the intelligence and accuracy of early warning management. First, GPT can automatically determine reasonable threshold ranges by learning and analyzing large amounts of historical data, rather than relying on manual experience. GPT can also automatically identify anomalies and issue early warnings based on changes in the network operating status and the characteristics of historical data, thereby avoiding the risk of inaccurate manual threshold setting.

4.4 Intelligent Decision

In the process of intelligent decision-making, GPT can analyze historical data and real-time performance indicators, and use its powerful generation capabilities to automatically perform fault diagnosis and repair processes. This includes running automated scripts to restart services, reconfigure network settings, or return to a previous stable version. Initially, the network collector sends real-time network data to the GPT, which includes the CPU, memory, congestion specifics, and records of network activities. Upon receiving this data, GPT conducts a rapid statistical analysis to ascertain the present state of the network's condition. Consequently, GPT was amalgamated with various network business scenarios to forecast network conditions and make appropriate operational and maintenance choices.

5 GPT Accelerates Network Optimization

GPT has revolutionized network optimization through its powerful data processing and analysis capabilities. GPT can quickly analyze massive amounts of network data, accurately identify performance bottlenecks, and generate optimization strategies to significantly improve network efficiency and stability. Network engineers can use GPT to improve network performance, optimize network architecture, and resolve network failures. Operators can also use the huge amount of data in the communication network to train the communication GPT to achieve intelligent network analysis, real-time prediction, code generation and vulnerability scanning, thereby improving the level of network security.

5.1 Network Traffic Optimization

All data on the Internet is transmitted via network traffic, so accurately modeling network traffic can help improve the quality of network services and protect data privacy. In recent years, the Internet industry has continued to develop,, the number of users connected to the Internet has continued to expand, and mobile Internet access traffic has also grown rapidly. According to data from the communications industry statistical bulletin, mobile Internet access traffic reached 301.5 billion GB in 2023, an increase of 15.2% over the previous year. In addition, by the end of 2023, there will be 1.517 billion mobile Internet users, a net increase of 63.16 million users throughout the year [15], reflecting the increasingly important position of the mobile Internet in daily life and users' growing demand for digital services.

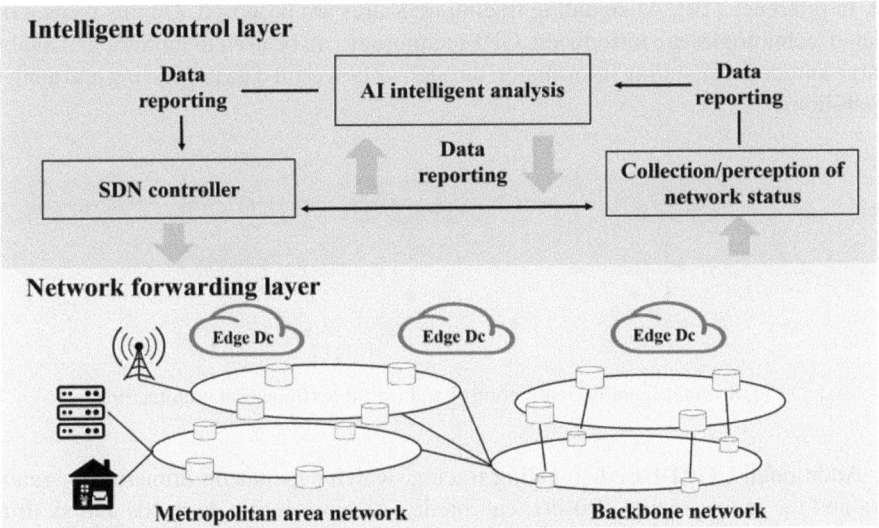

Fig. 7. Intelligent network control and traffic optimization architecture.

Network traffic pre-trained models utilize extensive raw data to understand network traffic's key features and produce unique outcomes for input traffic, disregarding particular downstream activities. Proficient models used in pre-training can greatly enhance the efficiency and productivity of subsequent tasks like classifying applications, identifying attacks, and creating traffic [16]. For example, reference [17] proposes a network intelligent control and traffic optimization method based on software-defined network (SDN) and AI, as shown in Fig. 7.

5.2 Radio Access Network Coverage Optimization

According to statistics, there are more than 8000 wireless parameters of various equipment manufacturers in the LTE network, so it is difficult to use manual experience to configure them. Certain scholars suggest that employing AI for a thorough examination of communication networks could lead to precise configuration of network parameters [18], paving the way for the introduction of GPT-related technologies. In wireless network coverage optimization, GPT can also optimize resource utilization efficiency, improve network capacity and coverage according to real-time environment and network conditions, thus reducing the complexity of coverage optimization and improving optimization efficiency and accuracy.

5.3 Network Signaling Tracking

Signaling messages play a crucial role in mobile communication networks. They not only carry user data, but also control the transmission of information, including call establishment, maintenance, removal and management of various services. Signaling data mainly has the characteristics of large volume, unfixed data and obvious fluctuation [1]. In reference [19], AI signaling tracing measures are proposed. On this basis, GPT-related technologies are introduced. GPT technology can be used to monitor and analyze a large amount of signaling information through its powerful data processing and analysis capabilities.

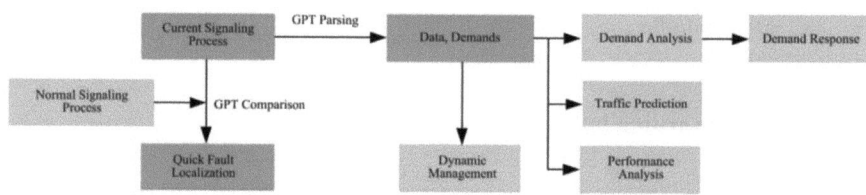

Fig. 8. Intelligent network control and traffic optimization architecture.

Additionally, GPT-based signaling tracing, which depends on immediate signaling data and the requirements of users, can predict network traffic demands and skillfully handle, allocate, and schedule resources to adapt to changes over time, regionally, and tailored to individual users. The diagram in Fig. 8 illustrates how GPT-based network signaling is traced.

6 Challenges

Nonetheless, the practical application of the GPT model in communication typically results in a noticeable discrepancy between the actual application needs of the scenario. Numerous obstacles remain in the GPT process to enhance the smart independence of communication networks. So, we also need to carefully consider the following:

6.1 Training Data Set Quality

The quality of the content produced is directly influenced by the training data set, with the network's data set quality being uncertain, and the precision of GPT in comprehending intricate or unconventional instructions is subpar. Furthermore, continuous training of the model using just one data set could lead to overfitting, thereby greatly diminishing its ability to generalize. Owing to its specialized characteristics, data originating from untrustworthy sources might include technical inaccuracies, obsolete information, or deceptive material. Within the realm of communications, extensive models educated using imprecise data can produce material filled with factual inaccuracies, logical inaccuracies, or prejudiced views, resulting in technical misapprehensions and erroneous choices. Consequently, training an extensive model with restricted data for various communication-related tasks requires a thorough evaluation of elements like the nature of communication data, the intricacy of the model, and the computational expense. The large model that is suitable for the task needs to be selected, and the model may need to be 'pruned' and 'compressed' appropriately [20].

6.2 Computing Power and Resources

In order to realize intelligent autonomous networks, huge computing power is needed, which consumes a lot of resources. However, the current computing power and hardware resources are obviously insufficient, which makes the deployment of large models very difficult, and its operation efficiency cannot be guaranteed.

During their deployment, extensive models necessitate substantial memory for parameter storage and demand significant computational energy and power usage for intricate computing operations [21]. Nonetheless, mobile gadgets like smartphones suffer from restricted hardware and battery life, with their lightweight implementation encountering numerous obstacles, primarily in memory limitations, inadequate computing capacity, and elevated power usage.

6.3 Network Security and Privacy

GPT continues to face security challenges, with attackers potentially employing diverse methods to manipulate, taint, or pilfer extensive model training or input data. Moreover, the current extensive model data probably holds substantial user data, leading to the revelation of privacy details.

Consequently, nations and areas typically place significant emphasis on investigating and tackling AI's security concerns, along with a thorough examination of its associated risks and challenges. Nonetheless, the dissemination of pertinent policies lags behind the advancement of major model technology. The absence of prompt legal restrictions could enable certain offenders to take advantage of legal gaps and engage in actions like employing extensive models to pilfer data and privacy, thereby jeopardizing social security [22]. Consequently, there should be a focus on the synchronized advancement of major model research and development, along with related regulatory backing. Countries and regions around the world also need to strengthen the interoperability of governance frameworks and deepen joint cooperation in order to find an artificial intelligence governance mechanism suitable for the entire international community.

7 Conclusions and Future Work

Briefly, the significance of GPT in enhancing the smart independence of communication networks is paramount, with its initial applications being in network planning, slicing implementation, network functioning, and network enhancement. In this paper, we describe these contents in detail. In network planning, GPT can not only provide codes and scripts of professional planning tools in network planning, but also identify and analyze various forms of user input, so as to help professional planners analyze user intentions more accurately and efficiently, and provide corresponding planning schemes, greatly improving work efficiency. During the implementation of slicing, GPT aids in managing network slicing, choosing the optimal algorithm for link mapping based on varied service needs, and enhancing the VNF procedure. Within the realm of network O&M, GPT is crucial in various standard O&M applications, including identifying anomalies, diagnosing faults, alerting to events, and making smart decisions, thereby enhancing the network's stability and dependability. Finally, in network optimization, GPT can significantly improve the efficiency and stability of the network and provide a better user experience.

In the future, we believe that GPT will also achieve more applications in automated network management, network security defense and other aspects. GPT can be used to analyze descriptions of cybersecurity incidents to help understand the patterns and motivations of attacks. GPT can simulate the behavior of attackers and generate simulated attacks to test network security defense capabilities. GPT can also assist in the development of more accurate intrusion detection systems, improving defenses by continuously learning and adapting to new threat patterns.

References

1. GSMA: AI in Network Intelligent Autonomous Network Case Report (2019)
2. Gelenbe, E., Domanska, J., Fröhlich, P., Nowak, M.P., Nowak, S.: Self-aware networks that optimize security, QoS, and energy. Phil. Trans. Roy. Soc. London **A247**, 529–551 (1955)
3. Series, M.: Framework and overall objectives of the future development of IMT-2000 and systems beyond IMT-2000. Rec. ITU-R, M, 1645 (2003)
4. Future Mobile Communications Forum. GPT and Communication (2024)
5. Liu, Y., Gong, K., Zhou, C.: Research on 5G base station site selection platform based on AI technology. Commun. Power Supply Technol. (2021). https://doi.org/10.19399/j.cnki.tpt.2021.11.023
6. Shakya, S., Roushdy, A., Khargharia, H.S., Musa, A., Omar, A.: AI based 5G RAN planning. In: Proceedings of the 2021 International Symposium on Networks, Computers and Communications (ISNCC), pp. 1–6, October 2021
7. Vijayakumar, D., Nema, R.K.: Superiority of PSO relay coordination algorithm over non-linear programming: a comparison, review and verification. In: Proceedings of the 2008 Joint International Conference on Power System Technology and IEEE Power India Conference, pp. 1–6, October 2008. https://doi.org/10.1109/ICPST.2008.4745385
8. J. Liu et al., "Microwave Integrated Circuits Design with Relational Induction Neural Network." arXiv, Jan. 03, 2019. https://doi.org/10.48550/arXiv.1901.02069
9. Dangi, R., Choudhary, G., Dragoni, N., et al.: 6G Mobile networks: key technologies, directions, and advances. Telecom. MDPI **4**(4), 836–876 (2023)

10. A. Dandoush, V. Kumarskandpriya, M. Uddin, and U. Khalil, "Large Language Models meet Network Slicing Management and Orchestration." arXiv, Mar. 20, 2024. https://doi.org/10.48550/arXiv.2403.13721
11. Dangi, R., Jadhav, A., Choudhary, G., et al.: ML-Based 5G network slicing security: a comprehensive survey. Future Internet **14**, 116 (2022)
12. Abubakar, A.I., Omeke, K.G., Ozturk, M., et al.: The role of artificial intelligence driven 5G networks in COVID-19 outbreak: Opportunities, challenges, and future outlook. Front. Commun. Netw. **1**, 575065 (2020)
13. Choudhary, G., Sharma, V.: A survey on the security and the evolution of osmotic and catalytic computing for 5G networks. In: Jayakody, D., Srinivasan, K., Sharma, V. (eds) 5G Enabled Secure Wireless Networks, 69–102. Springer, Cham (2019). https://doi.org/10.1007/978-3-030-03508-2_3
14. ZTE: White Paper on 5G Network Intelligence (2018)
15. Ministry of Industry and Information Technology. 2023 Communications Industry Statistical Bulletin (2023)
16. Meng, X., Lin, C., Wang, Y., Zhang, Y.: NetGPT: generative pretrained transformer for network traffic. arXiv, 17 May 2023. http://arxiv.org/abs/2304.09513. Accessed 27 Jun 2024
17. Guo, A., Yuan, C.: Network intelligent control and traffic optimization based on SDN and artificial intelligence. Electronics **10**(6), 700 (2021)
18. Song, L., Hu, X., Zhang, G., Spachos, P., Plataniotis, K.N., Wu, H.: Networking systems of AI: on the convergence of computing and communications. IEEE Internet Things J. **9**(20), 20352–20381 (2022). https://doi.org/10.1109/JIOT.2022.3172270
19. Hu, Z., Dong, Y., Wang, K., Chang, K.-W., Sun, Y.: GPT-GNN: generative pre-training of graph neural networks. In: Proceedings of the 26th ACM SIGKDD International Conference on Knowledge Discovery and Data Mining, KDD 2020, pp. 1857–1867. Association for Computing Machinery, New York, August 2020. https://doi.org/10.1145/3394486.3403237
20. Lei, J., Gao, X., Song, J., et al.: A survey of deep network model compression. J. Softw. **29**(2), 251–266 (2017)
21. Mutlu, O., Ghose, S., Gómez-Luna, J., et al.: Processing data where it makes sense: enabling in-memory computation. Microprocess. Microsyst. **67**, 28–41 (2019)
22. Qiu, X., Sun, T., Xu, Y., et al.: Pre-trained models for natural language processing: a survey. Sci. China Technol. Sci. **63**(10), 1872–1897 (2020)

Multipath Transaction Scheduling for Payment Channel Networks

Xiaojie Wang[1], Zhonghui Zhao[1], Yu Wu[2(✉)], Hailin Zhu[1], Ling Yi[1], Li Zhou[3(✉)], and Zhaolong Ning[1]

[1] School of Communications and Information Engineering, Chongqing University of Posts and Telecommunications, Chongqing 400065, China
[2] School of Cyber Security and Information Law, Chongqing University of Posts and Telecommunications, Chongqing 400065, China
wuy@cqupt.edu.cn
[3] College of Electronic Science and Technology, National University of Defense Technology, Changsha 410073, China
zhouli2035@nudt.edu.cn

Abstract. In order to solve the problem of large-value transactions that are prone to failure in payment channel networks, we propose an innovative scheme named Multipath Forwarding based on Transaction Splitting (MFTS), considering insufficient channel balance. First, we propose a path-window based transaction segmentation mechanism to divide transactions that do not satisfy the transaction conditions into different small-value transactions. Then, we design a deep reinforcement learning-driven channel probing algorithm to find the best transaction routes to optimize the transaction throughput. Meanwhile, to ensure transaction security, homomorphic encryption is used to encrypt the segmented microtransactions. Finally, we verify MFTS in the Watts-Strogatz small-world model by simulating payments in conjunction with the Kaggle credit card and Ripple dataset, and the results demonstrate the effectiveness of the designed scheme in improving the transaction success rate and the network throughput.

Keywords: Payment channel networks · Deep reinforcement learning · Transaction segmentation

1 Introduction

Blockchain technology, as a distributed ledger with decentralisation, trust, anonymity and tamper-proof features [1–3], enables secure, privacy-preserving

---

This work was supported by the Natural Science Foundation of China under Grant 62171449, Grant 62272075, and Grant 62403092; by the National Natural Science Foundation of Chongqing under Grant CSTB2024NSCQ-JQX0013 and Grant 2024NSCQ-MSX1192; by the Science and Technology Research Program for Chongqing Municipal Education Commission under Grant KJZDM202200601 and Grant KJZDK202300608.

transactions between two untrustworthy nodes without a third party. However, since blockchain technology is widely used in fields such as healthcare [4] and IoT [5], its inherent scalability problems have gradually emerged. For example, Bitcoin and Ether networks require consensus validation from nodes across the network for each transaction, which limits the system's transaction processing capacity. In fact, their transaction processing rates are of about 7 and 15 transactions per second, respectively [6]. Because each transaction must undergo full consensus before it can be confirmed, this process can last from minutes to hours [7]. To overcome this challenge, Payment Channel Networks (PCNs) have emerged as an off-chain scaling solution. PCNs significantly increase transaction speeds and reduce costs by creating payment channels outside of the blockchain, allowing for fast, low-cost transactions among nodes without the need to record them on-chain each time [8].

The current studies on PCNs can be mainly divided into two categories based on their objectives: The first considers the transaction privacy [9,10], and the second focuses on the transaction success rate. For the second category, it can be further divided into single-path transactions [11–14] and multi-path transactions [15–18] according to transaction types. However, existing studies treat the two objectives as separate ones, which can not maximize the transaction rate under the condition of protecting privacy.

To handle the above challenge, we propose Multipath Forwarding based on Transaction Splitting (MFTS) to maximize transaction throughput while protecting transaction privacy. The main contributions are as follows:

- The system model takes into account the characteristics of PCNs that may lead to privacy leakage and possible blockage of the channel during the transaction process, and proposes a throughput maximization problem. To solve it, we decompose the problem into two subproblems, for transaction segmentation and microtransaction routing, respectively.
- In order to solve the transaction segmentation problem, a dynamic transaction segmentation algorithm is developed, which can analyze the network state and transaction demand dynamically, to avoid transaction congestion, and decompose original transactions into atomic microtransactions to enhance the network's processing ability for a large number of transactions.
- In order to solve the microtransaction routing problem, an improved Deep Reinforcement Learning (DRL)-based path selection scheme is designed, enabling intelligent selection of the shortest and non-intersecting path to meet transaction requirements, while leveraging homomorphic encryption to ensure transaction privacy.
- Based on Watts-Strogatz small-world model, the performance of MFTS is verified through simulating payments with the Kaggle credit card and Ripple dataset, and comparative results show that it can effectively improve the transaction success rate and the network throughput.

2 Related Work

To ensure transaction privacy and security, authors in [9] use the smart contract based on the watch tower to monitor the offline transactions of PCNs to prevent collusion, but do not consider the issue of transaction balance. While authors in [10] propose a cryptographic primitive-anonymous multi-hop branching easy to ensure path privacy, and propose anonymous multi-hop payment based on bilinear pairing to achieve a balance between transaction privacy and communication cost, but do not consider the problem of transaction congestion. In order to improve the transaction success rate, authors in [11] propose a DRL-based privacy-aware high-throughput multi-path routing algorithm. Authors in [12] propose a PCN balancing algorithm based on DRL, decomposing the original problem and utilizing DRL for long-term optimization. Authors in [13] design an enhanced Dijkstra routing algorithm to select the lowest-cost path while improving transaction success rates, ensuring transaction balance. However, these studies do not address privacy concerns. To enhance transaction privacy, authors in [14] devise an online balance-aware fee-setting algorithm, dynamically adjusting transaction fees to influence path selection and protecting privacy through channel balance updates. However, when large-value transactions occur, simply by finding the best transaction channel may result in low transaction success rates, because insufficient channel balances may cause the transaction path to face congestion.

In order to solve the problem of transaction blocking caused by insufficient balance, researchers consider distributed transaction to improve the success rate. Authors in [15] design distributed PCN routing by considering transaction duration and channel availability, prioritizing short routes for transaction immediacy. Authors in [16] introduce a distributed and robust transaction routing algorithm by constructing two transaction paths for individual transactions. While authors in [17] improve transaction efficiency and success rates through hash-driven transaction splitting and multipath routing strategies, it neglects transaction balance. In contrast, authors in [18] propose a priority-based PCNs using a multi-agent deep Q-learning algorithm for priority allocation, yet this method is specific to the Lightning Network and lacks portability.

Although previous research has made some progress in improving transaction success rates and transaction privacy, none of the considerations are comprehensive. For example, the smart contract mentioned in [9] does not consider the problem of transaction blocking, although it can monitor offline transactions to prevent collusion. Authors in [11,13] propose a DRL-based multipath routing algorithm and an enhanced Dijkstra routing algorithm, but they do not adequately address the transaction congestion problem, and privacy is not considered comprehensively. Authors in [15,16], while considering distributed transactions to improve the success rate, neglect transaction balancing and privacy protection. In this paper, we provide a comprehensive and innovative solution to address transaction privacy protection, transaction congestion, and transaction success rate improvement in PCNs, considering not only the efficiency but also the privacy of transactions.

3 System Model

The PCN can be viewed as a direct graph $G = (\mathcal{V}, \mathcal{E})$, where $\mathcal{V} = \{1, ..., \nu, ...V\}$ is the set of all nodes, and V denotes the number of all nodes. Variable $\mathcal{E}$ is the set of all channels, and $\mathcal{E} = \{e_{i,j}\}, i, j \in \mathcal{V}$. Each node has at least one channel to connect to other nodes, and channels in the PCN can be unidirectional or bidirectional. Each node can either initiate a transaction as a starting point or accept a transaction as an end point, and even it can forward the transaction as a relay node. We focus on multipath scheduling of PCN transactions. Transaction $\mathbb{T}_x$ is characterised by start point u, end point v, timestamp τ_x^s (when the transaction is generated), transaction amount d_x, and deadline τ_x^d, i.e., $\mathbb{T}_x = \{u, v, \tau_x^s, d_x, \tau_x^d\}, x \in \mathcal{N}, \mathcal{N} = \{1, \ldots, x, \ldots, N\}$. Let n be the maximum number of hops of a valid transaction path, and $\mathcal{P}_x \subseteq \mathcal{P}$ denotes the set of paths that satisfy the constraints between u and v, where $\mathcal{P}$ denotes the set of all paths from the start point to the end point with no more than n nodes. A path can be defined by $p_k = \{e_1, e_2 \ldots, e_{h_k+1}\}$, where both e_1 and $e_{i,j}$ can represent a channel of path p_k, and h_k denotes the number of hops of path p_k. The set of microtransaction paths is P_k, $p_k \in P_k$ and $P_k \subseteq P_x$.

3.1 Transaction Segmentation Model

The transaction segmentation mechanism splits a large-value transaction into multiple microtransactions which can be forwarded through different paths, thus relieving the pressure on one path while preventing channel balance skews.

A path window size $w_{i,j}$ is set for channel $e_{i,j}$ where transaction $\mathbb{T}_x$ may complete a transaction, and defined as the maximum transaction amount not confirmed on the path (from the sender to the receiver). The window size can limit the speed of transaction sending by the sender to avoid network congestion.

How to partition transaction $\mathbb{T}_x$ is determined by the transaction cost of each possible paths. For example, in Fig. 1, transaction $\mathbb{T}_x$ cannot reach end point D regardless of the path taken; consequently, it is subdivided into three microtransactions $\mathbb{T}_1$, $\mathbb{T}_2$ and $\mathbb{T}_3$ to facilitate its completion. One needs to send a microtransaction with transaction amount d_1 through path p_1 with unconfirmed transaction amount d_1' and window size d_w. The microtransaction can pass through path p_1 only if $d_1 + d_1' < d_w$. Let the number of microtransactions split by $\mathbb{T}_x$ be n, then

$$n = \frac{d_x}{s_x}, \qquad (1)$$

where d_x is the transaction amount forwarded to the end point; s_x is the microtransaction size. When transaction segmentation occurs for transaction $\mathbb{T}_x$, transaction cost d_k on path p_k is

$$d_k = s_x + h_k \sigma, \qquad (2)$$

where σ is the forwarding cost at an intermediate node, and h_k is the number of hops of path p_k. The transaction cost to be prepared at the beginning of the transaction is

$$f_x = \sum_{k=1}^{n} d_k, \tag{3}$$

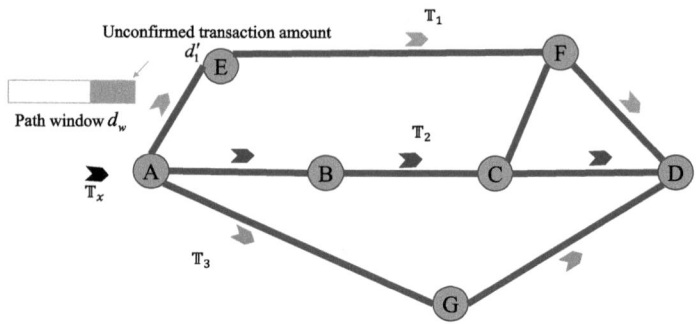

Fig. 1. The illustrative paths and path windows.

Each channel has a certain channel balance $\beta_{i,j} \in (0,1)$, which is the distribution of balances of nodes at both ends of the channel. When $\beta_{i,j} = 0.5$, the channel is perfectly balanced, because both nodes of the channel own half of the total channel amount. When $\beta_{i,j} = 0$, the current node has a balance of 0 in channel $e_{i,j}$. Depleting the funds in that channel means that no further transactions can be forwarded in the direction of i to j. As a result, to maintain long-term transaction forwarding, it is necessary to achieve the balance in the payment channel.

3.2 Transaction Privacy

To enhance transaction privacy, homomorphic encryption can be utilised to prevent any biased processing or selective forwarding by intermediate nodes due to the fact that it is a microtransaction. Let $\mathbb{T}_x$ be partitioned into n microtransactions $(\mathbb{T}_1, \mathbb{T}_2, \ldots, \mathbb{T}_n)$ with transaction amount $(d_1, d_2, \ldots, d_k, \ldots, d_n)$ respectively. When the random number of $\mathbb{T}_x$ is x_R and the hash value is y_R, its hash lock is y, and the ciphertext of random number x is c as shown in Eq. (4) and Eq. (5).

$$y = \mathcal{Y}(x_R + x) = y_R + \mathcal{Y}(x), \tag{4}$$

$$c = \varphi_{pk}(x_R + x), \tag{5}$$

where $\mathcal{Y}$ denotes the homomorphic hash function, and φ_{pk} denotes the additive homomorphic public key cryptographic function.

For a microtransaction from transaction $\mathbb{T}_x$, we can generate the corresponding uniformly distributed random number $(x_1, x_2, \ldots, x_n)$, and compute the corresponding hash lock $(y_1, y_2, \ldots, y_n)$ according to Eq. (6), where the corresponding ciphertext $(c_1, c_2, \ldots, c_n)$ is given by Eq. (7).

$$y_k = y + y(x_k) = y_R + \mathcal{Y}(x) + \mathcal{Y}(x_k) = \mathcal{Y}(x_R + x + x_k). \tag{6}$$

$$c_k = c + \varphi_{pk}(x_k) = \varphi_{pk}(x_R + x) + \varphi_{pk}(x_k) = \varphi_{pk}(x_R + x + x_k). \tag{7}$$

The receiver decrypts c_k with its own private key to obtain y_k, and computes $\mathcal{Y}(x_k)$. The random number of microtransactions can be derived and the transaction success rate can be judged based on whether the random satisfies a uniform distribution.

Finally, when the equilibrium state of the payment channel is considered in finding the optimal path, it may give rise to privacy leakage. We define the privacy leakage as the number of channels $\Pr(p_{i,j})$ involved in the exploration process, which has to be strictly controlled below predefined threshold ρ, i.e., $\sum_{p_{i,j} \in \mathcal{P}_x} \Pr(p_{i,j}) \leq \rho$ (the maximum number of exploration channels that can be tolerated in a PCN).

3.3 Problem Formulation

In order to maximise the transaction throughput of the PCN while ensuring the transaction privacy, the overall optimisation objective is as follows:

$$P1: \max_{s_x, \Pr(p_{i,j})} \sum_{x=1}^{N} \sum_{k=1}^{n} d_k(e), \tag{8}$$

$$\text{s.t. } C1: 0 \leq s_x \leq d_x,$$

$$C2: \sum_{p_{i,j} \in \mathcal{P}_x} \left[\Pr(p_{i,j}) - \rho \right] \leq 0,$$

$$C3: \tau_x^s + (h_p)_{\mathcal{P}_x}^{\max} \overline{\tau} \leq \tau_x^d,$$

$$C4: \frac{d_x}{s_x} \leq |\mathcal{P}_x|,$$

$$C5: \sum_{k=1}^{n} d_k < \beta_{i,j} * C_{i,j}.$$

where constraint $C1$ is the size constraint of each microtransaction; $C2$ indicates that the total number of channels involved in the exploration process should below the threshold for privacy protection; $C3$ indicates that the actual transaction delay of each transaction is to be within its deadline; $C4$ expresses the number of microtransactions of a transaction should be no more than the number of potential paths; and $C5$ indicates the transaction amount constraint of microtransactions.

4 MFTS Algorithm

Given the NP-hard nature of Problem $P1$, we decompose it into two subproblems: dynamic transaction segmentation and microtransaction routing, which are detailed in Sects. 4.1 and 4.2 respectively. Specifically, dynamic transaction segmentation is implemented based on the state of PCNs in the case of potential routing paths. Then, the routing scheme for microtransactions is optimised subject to transaction partition.

4.1 Dynamic Transaction Segmentation

Under the premise of determining the transaction routing path set, the transaction segmentation scale is optimised according to the routing scheme and the current network state, to maximise the network throughput, as shown in Problem $P2$.

$$P2: \max_{s_x} \sum_{x=1}^{N} \sum_{k=1}^{n} d_k(e), \tag{9}$$

$$\text{s.t. } C1: 0 \leq s_x \leq d_x,$$

$$C2: \tau_x^s + (h_p)_{\mathcal{P}_x}^{\max} \bar{\tau} \leq \tau_x^d,$$

$$C3: \frac{d_x}{s_x} \leq |\mathcal{P}_x|,$$

$$C4: \sum_{x=1}^{n} d_x < \beta_{i,j} * C_{i,j},$$

where $C1$ and $C4$ is derived from $C1$ and $C5$ in $P1$; $C2$ and $C3$ is the of $C3$ and $C4$ in $P1$.

For adapting to the uncertainty of transaction amount and the dynamics of PCN, a dynamic transaction segmentation algorithm based on the network state is set up. It dynamically adjusts the size and number of microtransactions based on the path window to improve transaction efficiency and throughput.

Path window size $w_{i,j}$, reflects node funding in the current channel. Since there are micro-transactions and large transactions, dynamic transaction splitting is crucial. The size of microtransactions for $\mathbb{T}_x$ is

$$s_x = \mathbb{E}[w] \times \gamma, \tag{10}$$

where $\gamma = \frac{1}{1+c^{-(z-\delta)}}$, $z = \frac{\tau_x^d}{\bar{\tau}}$. Variable $\mathbb{E}[w]$ denotes the average window size of all paths between sender u and receiver v, and parameter $\gamma \in (0,1)$. Variable $\bar{\tau}$ denotes the average time taken to complete a transaction over all paths, including the entire time from when the transaction is sent to completed. Variables c and δ are two constants that control the size of the segmentation.

The window size also shows the upper limit of the amount of microtransactions that can be sent on a given path. This is achieved by combining the funds of path, the size of transaction, and the urgency of transaction, which can be expressed by

$$w_{i,j} = \frac{C_{i,j} \times \beta_{i,j}}{d_k + \sum_{p_k} h_k \varepsilon} f(\Delta t) g(N_k), \tag{11}$$

where $f(\Delta t)$ is a deadline difference function to account for urgent transactions. The more urgent the transaction, the larger the path window should be. Variable $g(N_k)$ is the congestion level function of the transaction on path p_k, and $g(N_k) \in (0,1)$. Symbol $C_{i,j}$ is the capacity of the payment channel, and $\beta_{i,j}$ is the payment channel balance. Expression $d_k + \sum_{p_k} h_k \varepsilon$ is the cost of the microtransaction that needs to be forwarded by the current path. The path congestion level function is

$$g(N_k) = \exp\left(-\frac{N_k}{\lambda}\right), \qquad (12)$$

where λ is a positive parameter controlling the sensitivity to the impact of congestion. When N_k is small, the path is less congested and $g(N_k)$ is close to 1, and the opposite is true when N increases.

4.2 Intelligent Microtransaction Routing

With the size of microtransactions, the corresponding paths need to be determined for them. To obtain the corresponding routing paths, the following subproblems need to be solved:

$$P3: \max_{\Pr(p_{i,j})} \sum_{x=1}^{N} \sum_{k=1}^{n} d_k(e), \qquad (13)$$

$$\text{s.t. } C1: \sum_{p_{i,j} \in \mathcal{P}_x} [\Pr(p_{i,j}) - \rho] \leq 0,$$

$$C2: \frac{d_x}{s_x} \leq |\mathcal{P}_x|,$$

$$C3: \tau_x^s + (h_p)_{\mathcal{P}_x}^{\max} \overline{\tau} \leq \tau_x^d,$$

$$C4: \sum_{k=1}^{n} d_k < \beta_{i,j} \cdot C_{i,j},$$

where $C1$ and $C3$ is derived from $C2$ in $P1$; $C2$ is the relaxation of $C4$ in $P1$; $C4$ is derived from $C5$ in $P1$.

To solve Problem $P3$, a multipath routing mechanism based on node disjointness is proposed to distribute transactions and balance the network load with fault tolerance. When a transaction is forwarded, the node locks its transaction amount and forwarding cost and reduces the corresponding channel balance on that side of the channel. To satisfy the above characteristics, the selection of candidate routing paths follows the following principles: (1) To ensure feasibility, all routing configurations should not exceed the maximum tolerable number of probing channels among nodes; (2) One channel should only be included in one path; and (3) Priority is given to the shortest path.

Based on the above principles, an improved DRL-based routing algorithm is designed for microtransactions. According to the payment demand, the time period can be divided into multiple time slots, and one time slot is the path decision process for one transaction. For each microtransaction, the DRL agent observes network state s_m and then make a path selection decision, and then obtain reward r_m. The reward r_m incentivizes the DRL agent to select paths that reduce transaction delay and maximize throughput. On the other hand, the cost value c_m penalizes the agent for violating key constraints, such as exceeding the privacy limit by using too many probing channels or selecting paths that lead to excessive delays. The agent continuously adjusts its path selection strategy based on these rewards and costs, aiming to find the optimal balance between transaction success rate, privacy protection, and load distribution. After the PCN performs the path decision, it moves to the next state and then starts a new cycle until a suitable path is selected for all the microtransactions of transaction $\mathbb{T}_x$. As shown in Fig. 2, the path selection algorithm is structured using an actor-critic framework. The actor network is responsible for making path selection decisions based on the observed network state, while the critic network evaluates these decisions by computing the reward and cost values. This iterative process allows the agent to improve its decisions over time, continuously refining its path selection strategy based on feedback from the critic.

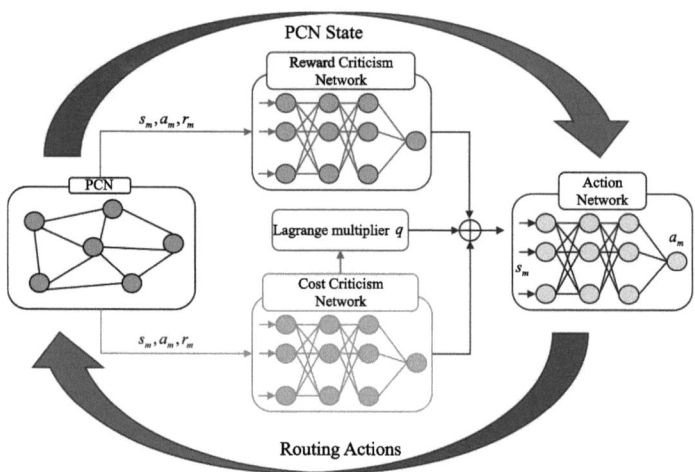

Fig. 2. The structure of DRL-based routing algorithm.

By adaptive Lagrange multiplier based proximal strategy optimisation, we can transform the optimisation objective and constraint $C1$ in Problem $P3$ into:

$$\max_{\pi_\theta} \min_{k \geq 0} \mathcal{L}(\pi_\theta, k) = f(\pi_\theta) - qg(\pi_\theta), \tag{14}$$

where $f(\pi_\theta) = \mathbb{E}_{\pi_\theta}\left[\sum_{m=1}^{n} \gamma^{m-1} r(s_m, a_m)\right]$, $g(\pi_\theta) = \mathbb{E}_{\pi_\theta}\left[\sum_{m=1}^{n} \gamma^{m-1} c(s_m, a_m)\right] - d$, and $\gamma \in (0, 1]$ is a discount factor measuring the future state; π_θ is a parameterised policy; θ is a parameter of the deep neural network; $\mathbb{E}_{\pi_\theta}$ denotes that the state-action distribution follows the policy; d is a hyper-parameter of the privacy constraint. When $d \leq 0$, the path policy is prevented from violating the constraint; when $d > 0$, the policy is allowed to violate the constraint.

In order to achieve adaptive control, Lagrange multiplier q is used as a learning parameter. In this case, Eq. (14) can be solved alternatively by gradient ascent on θ and gradient descent on q, i.e., by implementing gradient updating based on

$$J(\theta) = \mathbb{E}[(p_m(\theta)(A_m - q(C_m - d)))], \qquad (15)$$

where $p_m(\theta)$ denotes the probability ratio between the action strategy for collecting experience and the update strategy, represented by

$$p_m(\theta) = \frac{\pi_\theta(a_m \mid s_m)}{\pi_{old}(a_m \mid s_m)}, \qquad (16)$$

where $\pi_\theta(a_m \mid s_m)$ denotes the probability of following policy π_θ to adopt action a_m under state s_m and $\pi_{old}(a_m \mid s_m)$ is similar.

A_m is the long-term reward function and can be computed by

$$A_m = \sum_{j=0}^{n} \gamma^j \left[r_m + \gamma V_\omega^r(s_{m+1}) - V_\omega^r(s_m) \right], \qquad (17)$$

where $V_\omega^r(\bullet)$ denotes the long term reward after mapping the state to the action network.

C_m is the long-term cost function and can be computed by

$$C_m = \sum_{j=0}^{n} \gamma^j \left[c_m + \gamma V_\delta^c(s_{m+1}) - V_\delta^c(s_m) \right], \qquad (18)$$

where $V_\delta^c(\bullet)$ is denotes the long term cost after mapping the state to the action network.

Since the PCN is a distributed system and each user independently implements transactions via paths, a completely independent approach for path decision making is used to develop a distributed training framework. All nodes share an adaptive Lagrange multiplier, a reward-criticism network, a cost-criticism network and a PCN. Training and interaction are completely independent and each user leverages its own collected experience (s_m, a_m, r_m, s_{m+1}) to update the learning model, and then join the global environment to implement path decisions for microtransactions.

5 Simulation

5.1 Experiment Settings

We implement the proposed MFTS based on the Watts-Strogatz small-world model [19] by Python 3.8 in the PyCharm2021 software. The Watts-Strogatz model is created by introducing a certain degree of random reconnection of edges on top of a regular lattice graph. The resulting networks are characterised by short path lengths and high clustering coefficients, both of which are consistent with the characteristics of networks in many real systems, and so the model has been widely used to describe real-world connections. In the model, the values of the average channel capacity are 4000, and the transmission delay of transactions is set to 20 ms. The learning rates of the policy network, the two critic networks, and the Lagrange multiplier are set to 3×10^{-4}, 1×10^{-3}, and 5×10^{-2} respectively. The discount factor is $\gamma = 0.99$, and $\rho = 10$ and $d = 0$ are set for privacy constraints.

To evaluate the performance of different algorithms, we construct a SimPy-based discrete event simulator for payment channels [9]. The simulator allows to parameterise the initial channel balance, the distribution of transaction generation on both sides of the channel (frequency, number and maximum buffer time), the total number of transactions to be simulated and the scheduling strategy followed by each node. Each node is set to send an average of 30 transactions per second and the transaction sending process arrives as a Poisson process. The number of network nodes is set to 512. The payment channel $\mathcal{E}$ is set to 3212. The payment channel capacity C is set to 4000. The transaction forwarding cost σ is set to 4. The threshold for the number of transaction path hops h_k is set to 5. The channel detection threshold η is set to 10. The number of transactions N is set to 1×10^9. The transaction amount d_x is set to 0-400. The credit card dataset for training the neural network is downloaded from Kaggle and Ripple. The Kaggle credit card dataset contains transaction records of real users, providing a typical sample of large-scale transaction behaviour, while the Ripple dataset simulates a decentralised payment network, allowing this experiment to test the performance of the algorithms in different transaction scenarios.

In order to evaluate the effectiveness of this experiment, MFTS is compared with the classical Spider algorithm [11], Waterfilling algorithm [17] and the shortest path algorithm.

5.2 Simulation Analysis

Transaction Success Rate Analysis (Fig. 3): As transaction amounts increase, MFTS, Spider, Waterfilling, and Shortest Path algorithms exhibit a decrease in transaction success rates. However, MFTS consistently outperforms others, showcasing the highest transaction success rate. This simulation results effectively underscore the effectiveness of dynamic transaction segmentation and multipath forwarding in MFTS.

Transaction Delay Analysis (Fig. 4): As transaction amounts increase, it can be demonstrated that the Shortest Path has the lowest transaction latency, attributed to the fact that the shortest path is selected for transactions. It can be observed that MFTS ranks second in terms of latency, with a difference that is almost negligible. From Figs. 3 and 4, we can discover that although MFTS sacrifices some latency, it achieves a significant improvement in transaction success rate.

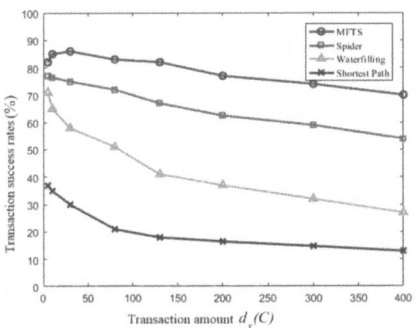
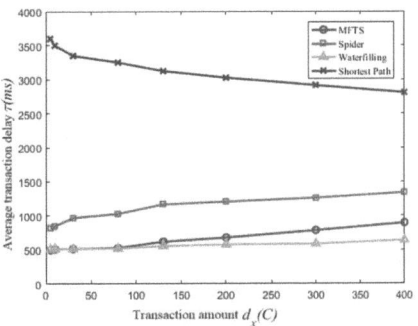

Fig. 3. Transaction success rate for different transaction amounts.

Fig. 4. Average transaction delay for different transaction amounts.

Impact Analysis (Fig. 5): It is evident that the value of threshold ρ increases, the normalized transaction throughput of all four algorithms also increases. Notably, threshold ρ enables the discovery of suitable paths for forwarding microtransactions, consequently reducing transaction forwarding failure rates. Furthermore, it can be observed that algorithms like MFTS and Spider, which split transactions for forwarding, have lower requirements for channel balancing, resulting in a relatively lower growth rate of transaction throughput compared to Waterfilling and Shortest Path algorithms.

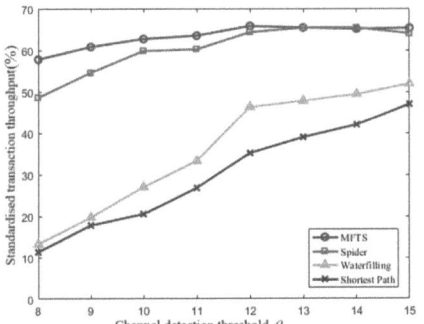
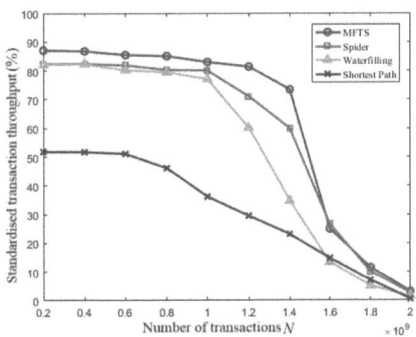

Fig. 5. Normalized transaction throughput with different threshold ρ.

Fig. 6. Transaction throughput with different number of transactions.

Impact of the total number of Transactions Analysis (Fig. 6): It shows that, except for the Shortest Path algorithm, the number of transactions below 1×10^9 does not significantly affect the normalized transaction throughput. However, when the number of transactions exceeds 1.4×10^9, the normalized transaction throughput gradually decreases. Because congestion in certain payment channels caused by the excessive number of transactions, leading to the depletion of channel balances and subsequent transaction failures. Among them, the shortest path algorithm is more prone to congestion because it tends to choose the shortest path.

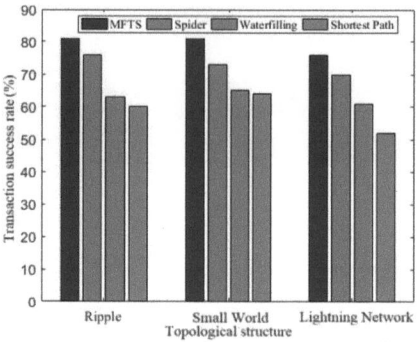

Fig. 7. Normalised transaction throughput in different topologies.

Comparison of Normalized Throughput in Different Topologies (Fig. 7): In the Watts-Strogatz small world topology, the gap in standardized transaction throughput between MSTS and other algorithms is notably wide. This discrepancy arises from the utilization of non-duplicated payment channel by MSTS. Specifically, in the Watts-Strogatz small world topology, unlike the Lightning Network and Ripple, the payment channel balance is not guaranteed to be relatively balanced, making it more susceptible to channel skew. When significant skew exists in the payment channel balance, MFTS utilizes non-duplicated paths to better utilize the capacity of the payment channels.

6 Conclusion

This paper proposes an MFTS scheme to improve the success rate of transactions in PCNs while protecting the privacy of transactions. First, we dynamically segment the transactions based on the state of the PCN to avoid channel blockage. Subsequently, the routing of microtransactions is optimized by DRL with a determined segmentation size, while the hashes of segmented microtransactions are encrypted using homomorphic encryption-based techniques. Finally, by utilizing a simulation of PCNs based on the Watts-Strogatz small-world model and conducting payment simulations based on the Kaggle credit card dataset and the Ripple dataset, experimental results demonstrate the success of the proposed scheme in terms of transaction success rate and standardized network throughput. In the future, the MFTS scheme can be integrated with distributed ledger technology and smart contracts to further enhance the system's scalability and automation. Additionally, more privacy protection mechanisms and dynamic resource allocation strategies are expected to further improve the applicability of the algorithm.

References

1. Ning, Z., Sun, S., Wang, X., Guo, L., Wang, G., Gao, X., Kwok, R.Y.: Intelligent resource allocation in mobile blockchain for privacy and security transactions: a deep reinforcement learning based approach. Sci. China Inf. Sci. **64**(6), 162303 (2021)
2. Ning, Z., Sun, S., Wang, X., Guo, L., Guo, S., Hu, X., Hu, B., Kwok, R.Y.K.: Blockchain-enabled intelligent transportation systems: A distributed crowdsensing framework. IEEE Trans. Mob. Comput. **21**(12), 4201–4217 (2022)
3. Wang, X., Ning, Z., Guo, L., Guo, S., Gao, X., Wang, G.: Mean-field learning for edge computing in mobile blockchain networks. IEEE Trans. Mob. Comput. **22**(10), 5978–5994 (2023)
4. Liu, Y., Wang, X., Zheng, G., Wan, X., Ning, Z.: An AOI-aware data transmission algorithm in blockchain-based intelligent healthcare systems. IEEE Trans. Consum. Electron. **70**(1), 1180–1190 (2024)
5. Ning, Z., Chen, H., Wang, X., Wang, S., Guo, L.: Blockchain-enabled electrical fault inspection and secure transmission in 5G smart grids. IEEE J. Sel. Top. Signal Process. **16**(1), 82–96 (2022)
6. Buterin, V., et al.: A next-generation smart contract and decentralized application platform. white paper **3**(37), 2–1 (2014)
7. Wang, X., Zhu, H., Ning, Z., Guo, L., Zhang, Y.: Blockchain intelligence for Internet of vehicles: challenges and solutions. IEEE Commun. Surv. Tutorials **25**(4), 2325–2355 (2023)
8. Wang, X., Gu, H., Li, Z., Zhou, F., Yu, R., Yang, D.: Why riding the lightning? equilibrium analysis for payment hub pricing. In: ICC, pp. 5409–5414 (2022)
9. Du, M., Yang, P., Tian, W., Han, Z.: Anti-collusion multiparty smart contracts for distributed watchtowers in payment channel networks. IEEE J. Sel. Areas Commun. **40**(12), 3600–3614 (2022)
10. Zhang, Y., Jia, X., Pan, B., Shao, J., Fang, L., Lu, R., Wei, G.: Anonymous multi-hop payment for payment channel networks. IEEE Trans. Dependable Secure Comput. **21**(1), 476–485 (2024)
11. Qiu, X., Chen, W., Tang, B., Liang, J., Dai, H.N., Zheng, Z.: A distributed and privacy-aware high-throughput transaction scheduling approach for scaling blockchain. IEEE Trans. Dependable Secure Comput. **20**(5), 4372–4386 (2023)
12. Chen, W., Qiu, X., Cai, Z., Tang, B., Du, L., Zheng, Z.: Graph neural network-enhanced reinforcement learning for payment channel rebalancing. IEEE Trans. Mob. Comput. **23**(6), 7066–7083 (2024)
13. Chen, Y., Ran, Y., Zhou, J., Zhang, J., Gong, X.: MPCN-RP: a routing protocol for blockchain-based multi-charge payment channel networks. IEEE Trans. Netw. Serv. Manage. **19**(2), 1229–1242 (2022)
14. Wang, X., Yu, R., Yang, D., Xue, G., Gu, H., Li, Z., Zhou, F.: Fence: Fee-based online balance-aware routing in payment channel networks. IEEE/ACM Trans. Networking **32**(2), 1661–1676 (2024)
15. Yu, R., Xue, G., Kilari, V.T., Yang, D., Tang, J.: Coinexpress: a fast payment routing mechanism in blockchain-based payment channel networks. In: ICCCN, pp. 1–9 (2018)
16. Zhang, Y., Yang, D.: RobustPay+: robust payment routing with approximation guarantee in blockchain-based payment channel networks. IEEE/ACM Trans. Networking **29**(4), 1676–1686 (2021)

17. Zhang, Y., Gai, K., Xiao, J., Zhu, L., Choo, K.K.R.: Blockchain-empowered efficient data sharing in Internet of things settings. IEEE J. Sel. Areas Commun. **40**(12), 3422–3436 (2022)
18. Luo, X., Li, P.: Learning-based off-chain transaction scheduling in prioritized payment channel networks. IEEE J. Sel. Areas Commun. **40**(12), 3589–3599 (2022)
19. Watts, D.J., Strogatz, S.H.: Collective dynamics of 'small-world' networks. Nature **393**(6684), 440–442 (1998)

An Energy Payment Transaction Scheduling Solution for Electric Vehicles Based on Off-Chain Computing

Ziyi Liu[1], Yu Wu[2(✉)], Qi Guo[1], Qianwen Liu[1], Yuzhen Zhang[1], Xinfeng Deng[3], Qiuping Li[4(✉)], and Xuanrui Xiong[1]

[1] School of Communications and Information Engineering, Chongqing University of Posts and Telecommunications, Chongqing 400065, China
[2] School of Cyber Security and Information Law, Chongqing University of Posts and Telecommunications, Chongqing 400065, China
wuy@cqupt.edu.cn
[3] College of Electronic Science and Technology, National University of Defense Technology, Changsha 410073, China
[4] National Computer Network Emergency Response Technical Team/Coordination Center of China (CNCERT/CC), Beijing 100029, China
qiupingli_bj@163.com

Abstract. To solve the problem of inefficient energy allocation in traditional charging methods for electric vehicles, and considering the high concurrency of transactions in transaction-intensive scenarios, we propose an energy payment transaction scheduling solution for electric vehicles (EVs) based on off-chain computing. The solution utilizes blockchain to guarantee the security of inter-vehicle (V2V) energy payment and improves the transaction efficiency through an off-chain payment channel. We first construct a joint optimization problem aiming at selecting the optimal payment routing and setting the priority of payment forwarding. To solve this problem, we propose a multi-route multi-hop transaction scheduling algorithm (MRMH), which mainly contains two parts: a heuristic routing channel selection algorithm based on ant colony optimization for determining the optimal transaction paths, and a reinforcement learning-based (RL) relay forwarding algorithm for optimizing the relay selection during the transaction process. Finally, we verify the effectiveness of MRMH in the reliability and throughput of transactions by simulation experiments. The experiment results also show that MRMH can satisfy the demand for EVs charging in transaction-intensive scenarios while ensuring the security and efficiency of the transactions.

Keywords: EV Charging · Transaction Security and Efficiency · Joint Optimization · Reinforcement Learning Algorithms

---

This work was supported by the Natural Science Foundation of China under Grant No. 62171449.

1 Introduction

The number of electric vehicles (EVs) worldwide has grown exponentially over the past decade, leading to a dramatic increase in charging demand that is difficult to meet. If EV users are unable to find suitable charging stations promptly, travel plans will be seriously affected. Although energy transactions and scheduling can be carried out over the network when EVs are connected [1], the complex transportation network topology makes it very difficult to guarantee transaction security [2]. Blockchain technology can effectively secure energy transactions in the Internet of Vehicles by its traceability, confidentiality, and transparency [3,4]. However, it still faces the challenge of scalability [5]. Specifically, blockchain has poor throughput and high settlement latency compared to existing payment systems, which are not able to meet EV energy trading needs [6].

Off-chain computing technology becomes a promising way to solve the scalability problem of blockchain [7]. Both parties of the transaction put forward the transaction demand to the blockchain when establishing the off-chain transaction channel and report to it after the completion of the transaction, and a large number of transaction calculations exist off-chain without the need to be carried out on the blockchain. This approach can not only guarantee the security of EV energy transactions but also improve resource utilization and reduce transaction processing delay [8]. However, the off-chain payment channel faces the challenge of congestion in the transaction channel [9–11], thus bringing the problem of a low transaction success rate. The transaction nodes are in a complex topology of the off-chain transaction network, and there are multiple transaction paths between each transaction, so the path decision and task scheduling of the transaction become the key to improving the transaction throughput.

Therefore, this paper proposes an innovative off-chain computing-based transaction scheduling solution for EV energy payment. It ensures the security of V2V energy payment through blockchain technology and optimizes transaction efficiency through an off-chain payment channel network. The main work is designing a multi-route multi-hop transaction scheduling algorithm (MRMH), which aims to improve the success rate of the transaction and reduce the initial cost of the transaction by selecting the optimal transaction path. MRMH integrally considers the forwarding amount of the transaction node and the transaction tolerance of the transaction routing node, which contains two parts: a heuristic routing channel selection algorithm based on ant colony optimization for determining the optimal transaction paths, and a reinforcement learning-based (RL) relay forwarding algorithm for optimizing the relay selection during the transaction process. The main contributions of this paper are as follows:

- We design a heuristic routing channel selection algorithm based on ant colony optimization to solve the routing problem of off-chain payments. It intelligently selects the most suitable routing channel for each transaction and optimizes the process of selecting transaction paths.
- We design a relay forwarding algorithm based on reinforcement learning to determine the transaction order of off-chain payments. It dynamically deter-

mines the forwarding priority of each relay node, thus improving the efficiency and reliability of transactions.
- We compare and analyze the proposed MRMH with traditional methods through simulation experiments. The results show that MRMH improves the transaction success rate, effectively alleviates the congestion problem of the transaction channel, and enhances the transaction throughput of the whole network.

The rest of the paper is organized as follows. We introduce related work in Sect. 2. In Sect. 3, we present the system model and formulate the optimization problem. The proposed MRMH algorithm is provided in Sect. 4. In Sect. 5, we provide simulation results and verify the effectiveness of MRMH. Finally, the paper is summarized in Sect. 6.

2 Related Work

The transaction implementation of blockchain as well as its off-chain network is an intricate research field, and this section will mainly analyze the current research status of transaction research based on off-chain computing from two aspects, which mainly contain the transaction path decision of off-chain network and the transaction order selection of off-chain network.

To increase the success rate of transactions and reduce transaction costs, researchers optimize the transaction path decision. The authors of the literature [12] classify transactions as atomic and use packet-switching architecture and multipath transport protocols to achieve high throughput routing in Payment Channel Networks(PCNs). The authors of literature [13] propose a homomorphic encryption-based transaction splitting model to ensure the fairness and security of the split microtransactions. They also propose an intelligent multipath routing scheme based on a multipoint relay mechanism to obtain the current routing topology and balanced view of the entire PCN, selecting the appropriate path to complete the transaction forwarding. The authors of literature [14] design an optimal distributed algorithm called CheaPay. This algorithm minimizes transaction costs, optimizes the transaction success rate, and achieves the minimization of the total transaction cost of the payment request through three concise steps: initialization, iterative update, and determining the routes, all while satisfying timeliness and feasibility constraints. The authors of literature [15] design a transaction payment protocol that includes three parts: payment determination, routing determination, and payment execution. In the routing confirmation part, optimal multipath routing is designed using genetic algorithms to avoid causing transactions to be blocked on the same path by controlling the transaction path.

To solve the channel congestion problem caused by excessive traffic, researchers consider using optimized transaction orders to improve the success rate. The authors of literature [16] propose a hybrid protocol for the Bitcoin network based on zero-knowledge proof to resist DoS attacks and conspiracy attacks. This protocol cleverly utilizes hash-time-lock transactions to reconstruct the order of transactions to mitigate DoS attacks and also performs congestion control on PCN transactions to improve the success rate of transactions. The authors of literature [17] consider the case where the starting point and the endpoint are connected by a channel and propose the strategy of setting a buffer at each node. This strategy aims to prevent unnecessary blocking of transactions in the channel, make decisions about the transaction order, and maximize the throughput of transactions.

Although the aforementioned path decision optimization schemes and transaction ordering optimization schemes each make some progress in improving transaction success rates, they all have certain limitations in real trading environments. For example, the Spider routing scheme in [12] only addresses two specific transaction demand patterns and lacks universality. The optimal distributed algorithm CheaPay proposed by the authors in [14] minimizes transaction fees, and the multi-path routing algorithm based on genetic algorithms proposed by the authors in [15] also does not fully address transaction congestion issues. The authors of [16,17] improve transaction success rates by considering transaction ordering optimization, but this incurs certain transaction locking costs and results in more communication overhead. Therefore, we aim to provide a comprehensive and innovative solution to address the electric vehicle energy transaction scheduling problem in transaction-intensive scenarios, taking into account both channel congestion and optimizing transaction costs.

3 System Model and Problem Formulation

This section focuses on constructing a transaction scheduling network model based on off-chain computing, covering the network structure, relay node roles, transaction order optimization, as well as quantitative analysis of throughput and initial funding, aiming at optimizing transaction efficiency and guaranteeing transaction security. Furthermore, we formulate the optimization problem in Subsect. 3.5.

3.1 Network Model

We model the system as a graph $G(\mathcal{H}, \mathcal{E})$, where $\mathcal{H}$ is the set $\mathcal{H} = \{1, ..., h, ..., H\}$ of all nodes in the off-chain payment network and H denotes the number of all nodes in the network. $\mathcal{E}$ is the set of off-chain payment network channels, $\mathcal{E} = \{e_{i,j}\}, i, j \in \mathcal{H}$, and each node has at least one channel connected to the other nodes. We set the transaction channels are all unidirectional. In addition, each node can act as a transaction initiator or receiver and as a relay node to get the corresponding payment reward by forwarding transactions from other payment channels. Suppose there are A users initiating energy payment transaction requests at the same time in period T. Each transaction a, where $a \in \mathcal{A} = \{1, ..., A\}$, needs to send a request $\mathcal{Q}_a$ to the blockchain to establish a transaction channel, where the request to establish a transaction channel contains: the transaction start node u, the transaction end node v, the transaction timestamp τ_a, the amount of money e_a of the transaction and the deadline τ_a^d of the transaction, i.e., $\mathcal{Q}_a = \{u, v, \tau_a, e_a, \tau_a^d\}$. Unlike the traditional known origin-to-destination routing paths, in this paper, we assume that the routing path of transaction a is p_a, and the sequence of nodes of this path is $r_a = \{u, ..., i, ..., j ..., v\}$, taking into account the unknown nature of the vehicle topology. When a relay node performs forwarding, the relay node needs to charge a certain amount of forwarding fee f_i^a. Since different transactions have different latency tolerances, the forwarding fee provided for each transaction is also different. Similar to the approach in [18], the relay forwarding fee for transactions at relay nodes is:

$$f_i^a = f_i + \Delta f_i^a \tag{1}$$

where f_i is the fixed node relaying cost of the node in the off-chain payment channel network, and Δf_i^a is the proportional relaying cost of transaction a at relay node i. We set the proportional relay fee to be $0 \leq \Delta f_i^a \leq 0.7\% \cdot e_a$. In this case, the transaction needs to pay the relaying cost at each relay node, and different relaying costs affect the order of relaying, which in turn affects the success rate of the transaction.

To prevent malicious intermediate node users from locking the transaction funds for their use, this paper utilizes Hash Time Lock Contracts (HTLC) to generate a delay tolerance for each relay node, if a random value R is not received within the delay tolerance time, then the funds of this transaction will be returned to the previous relay node. We set a delay tolerance for each payment path, and let h_a be the number of intermediate nodes per transaction, the total forwarding delay tolerance needs to be satisfied:

$$\tau_a^d - \tau_a \geq \lambda \cdot h_a \tag{2}$$

3.2 Relay Node Transaction Order

The order of task forwarding affects the success rate of transaction tasks. As shown in Fig. 1, each edge $e_{i,j}$ has its channel constraints, and $\Delta c_{i,j}$ denotes the cost that node i to node j can maximize can be transferred. For a transaction a, the fixed starting capital $b_{u,v}$ of its transaction initiating node and the forwarding order of the intermediate nodes involved in the whole transaction channel determine whether this transaction can be completed or not, i.e., the fixed starting capital of the transaction initiating node needs to be greater than or equal to the amount of the transaction plus the forwarding cost of each relay node.

We set a forwarding priority d_i^a, $d_i^a = w$ for each relay node, where d_i^a is the forwarding priority of relay node i in the routing path p_a for transaction event a, and w is the value of the priority, where $w \in \mathcal{W} = \{1, ..., w, ..., W\}$, W is the number of maximal events that can be forwarded by this relay node i. The smaller the numerical representation of the transaction priority we set, the higher the transaction priority of that transaction at the current relay node. Thus, a relay forwarding total F_a exists on the transaction path for each transaction a, then:

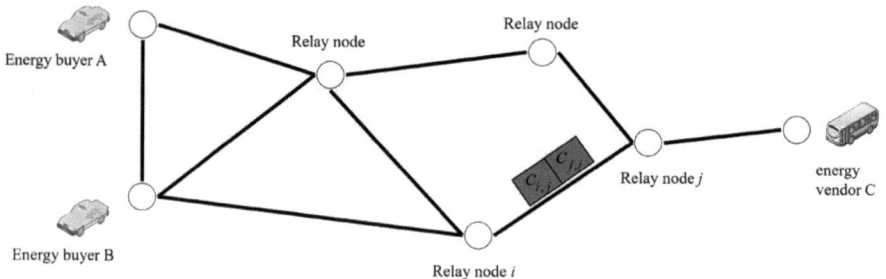

Fig. 1. Schematic diagram of the transaction and payment network.

$$F_a = \sum_{i \in p_a} f_i^a = \sum_{i \in p_a} \mathcal{X}_i^a f_i^a \qquad (3)$$

where f_i^a is the forwarding cost of transaction a at relay node i, $\mathcal{X}_i^a$ is a binary variable that evaluates to 1 if a forwarding priority is assigned at the relay node and can be forwarded to the next node, and 0 otherwise. Differences in forwarding priority greatly affect transaction throughput and starting capital. A transaction with a higher priority value may result in the transaction not being able to be completed within the transaction time limit, resulting in a failed transaction.

3.3 Transaction Throughput Model

The throughput of the entire payment network is mainly related to the success rate of each transaction. We define a variable ϕ as the success rate of transactions per unit of time on the whole network, which can be expressed as:

$$\phi = \frac{V}{A} = \frac{\sum_{a=1}^{A} \prod_{i \in p_a} \psi_i^a}{A} \qquad (4)$$

where A is the total number of transaction tasks in time T, and V is the number of transactions completed in time T. Since the success rate of each transaction is not only related to the amount initially locked by the transaction initiating node, but also to the success rate of forwarding by each relay node in the selected routing path. The binary variable ψ_i^a is used to indicate whether the relay node i in the transaction a is forwarded successfully or not, it has a value of 1 if the transaction a is forwarded successfully at the relay node and 0 otherwise.

3.4 Transaction Amount Model

We categorize the nodes in the transaction path into start node, relay node, and end node. The locking amount of the start node is the sum of the actual transaction amount and the forwarding cost of all the relay nodes passing through the selected path. The lock amount of the relay node is the sum of the actual transaction amount and the forwarding cost of the relay nodes after that path. The lock amount of the end node is the actual amount of this transaction.

Nodes on a payment channel network rarely play only one role. A node may be the end node for a particular transaction and at the same time may be a relay node for other transactions. In addition, a relay node may need to forward amounts for multiple transactions, thus requiring a systematic determination of the initial funds locked in by each node. Based on the above requirements, the starting funds locked at each node e_a including the initial and end nodes can be expressed as:

$$e_a = c_a + \sum_{i \in p_a} f_i^a \tag{5}$$

where c_a is the amount of actual transaction, and f_i^a is the amount of the transaction event a forwarded at relay node i. Thus we conclude that the amount initially locked by the transaction is related to the actual amount of the transaction and the forwarded amount. Due to the channel capacity limitation, we utilize Eq.(6) to indicate that the spend passing through relay node i cannot exceed the channel capacity limit, where C_i is the forwarding capacity of node i.

$$\sum_{a \in \mathcal{A}} (c_a + f_a^i) \leq C_i \tag{6}$$

3.5 Problem Formulation

To ensure the security and efficiency of energy payment transactions in transaction-intensive scenarios, this paper introduces federated blockchain technology to ensure the reliability of transactions and employs off-chain payment channels to optimize transaction processing speed and reduce latency. On this basis, this paper jointly optimizes the transaction forwarding order and the choice of transaction routing to ensure that the transaction throughput of the network is maximized and the starting capital of the transaction is minimized. Thus, the problem can be formulated as:

$$\max_{\mathcal{X}_i^a, f_i^a} \sum_{a \in \mathcal{A}} \phi_a$$

$$\min_{\mathcal{X}_i^a, f_i^a} \sum_{a \in \mathcal{A}} e_a$$

s.t.:

C1: $0 \leq f_i^a \leq 0.7\% \cdot e_a, \forall i \in \mathcal{H}, \forall a \in \mathcal{A}$ (7)

C2: $\tau_a^d - \tau_a \geq \lambda \cdot h_a, \forall a \in \mathcal{A}$

C3: $\sum_{a \in \mathcal{A}} (c_a + \mathcal{X}_i^a \psi_i^a f_i^a) \leq C_i, \forall i \in \mathcal{H}, \forall a \in \mathcal{A}$

C4: $\mathcal{X}_i^a \in \{0, 1\}, \forall i \in \mathcal{H}, \forall a \in \mathcal{A}$

C5: $\psi_i^a \in \{0, 1\}, \forall i \in \mathcal{H}, \forall a \in \mathcal{A}$

where constraint C1 is the range of forwarding cost of the relay node; C2 is the forwarding time limit of the relay node's forwarding task; C3 is the channel capacity limit of the relay node; C4 is a binary variable indicating whether the transaction task is assigned a forwarding priority at the node or not; and C5 is a binary variable indicating whether the transaction task is forwarded successfully at the node or not.

In response to the aforementioned issue, this paper employs a sequential optimization approach to tackle these two core optimization problems step by step. Specifically, after determining the transaction routing path, the forwarding priority at the relay node is set based on the relay forwarding costs provided by each transaction.

4 Problem Solution

We propose MRMH, an off-chain computing-based scheduling solution for EV energy payment transactions, to solve the problem presented in Subsect. 3.5. MRMH consists of two algorithms: the heuristic routing channel selection algorithm based on ant colony optimization algorithm is used for determining the routing channel for each transaction, and the relay scheduling based on the RL algorithm is used to determine the forwarding priority of each relay node.

4.1 Routing Channel Selection

The routing channel selection algorithm is heuristic and based on ant colony optimization algorithm The main idea is based on a stable network topology and utilizes a periodic update mechanism to simulate the path-finding behavior of ants to intelligently determine efficient transaction routes.

We assume that the network topology is stable and does not change until the end of each transaction. It is assumed that each user in the network is aware of the existing payment channels and updates them periodically through some gossip protocol. We use a meta-heuristic approach strategy based on an improved ant colony to select the optimal routing transaction channel for each transaction.

For the payment request $\mathcal{Q}_a = \{u, v, \tau_a, c_a, \tau_a^d\}$, the sending node u will send a forwarding ant T. T is randomly sent to the receiving node v based on the forwarding node information in the routing table of each node, and the overall pathway information is collected. When T reaches the receiving node v, it forwards backward and forwards the formed pathway information back to the sending node. The routing information is represented as:

$$T(a) = \{(\mu_1, \eta_1, C_1), (\mu_2, \eta_2, C_2), ..., (\mu_N, \eta_N, C_N)\} \tag{8}$$

where $T(a)$ denotes the feasible routing channel from the transmitting node u to the receiving node v for this transaction event, where (μ, C) denotes the information of the nodes in the routing channel. C denotes the channel capacity of a node on the path, μ denotes the number of relay nodes on the routing channel, and η denotes the proportion of forwarding cost of the relay nodes. In the initialization phase of the algorithm, the main task of the algorithm is the acquisition of the relevant state. State acquisition involves obtaining the current state of the nodes in the network in real-time or at regular intervals to update the topology in the network and initialize the routing table.

We define the probability of forwarding to the next hop in the routing table based on three different scenarios. In the first scenario, the starting node u and the terminating node v are neighboring nodes, and $C_{u,v}^{T_a}$ satisfies the constraints of Eq.(7), then a high priority is assigned to this pathway. In the second scenario, the start node u and the end node v are neighboring points, but $C_{u,v}^{T_a}$ do not satisfy the constraints of Eq.(7), then the path is discarded; In the third scenario, the start node u and the termination node v is not adjacent nodes, then the priority of the next hop selection is determined based on whether $C_{u,v}^{T_a}$ satisfies the constraints of Eq.(7), if not, then the path is discarded, and if it does, the priority of the next hop selection is determined based on the next-hop channel capacity and the forwarding amount.

For the above description of the finite set selection area, we propose a forwarding node selection prioritization formula, i.e.:

$$W_{i,j}^{T_a} = \begin{cases} 1, & \text{if } i = u, j = v, \text{ and } c_a(1+\eta_j^{T_a}) \leq C_{i,j}^{T_a} \\ \frac{(\eta_j^{T_a})^\beta}{((C_{i,j}^{T_a})^\alpha N_i)^2}, & \text{if } i \neq u, j \neq v, \text{ and } c_a(1+\eta_j^{T_a}) \leq C_{i,j}^{T_a} \\ 0, & \text{if } c_a(1+\eta_j^{T_a}) \geq C_{i,j}^{T_a} \end{cases} \quad (9)$$

where i and j are the nodes in the pathway p_n, N_i is the number of next hops that can be selected by node i, and α and β are the impact factors of the channel capacity constraints and the forwarding cost, respectively. Calculating the selection priority from the current node to the next hop node allows prioritizing all the routing paths fulfilled from the start node to the termination node so that the optimal routing path can be obtained by prioritization. After a transaction event selects a certain routing path, if other transaction events select routing paths containing the same relay node, the forwarding capacity of the same relay node will change, i.e.:

$$C_i = C_i - e_a \quad (10)$$

When a new transaction event is re-routed for routing path selection, the optimal routing path is selected by forwarding path selection based on the updated channel forwarding capacity.

4.2 Relay Forwarding Scheduling

The relay forwarding scheduling strategy is based on reinforcement learning, aiming to maximize the transaction success rate and minimize the initial amount of the transaction. The main idea is transforming the transaction prioritization problem into a Markov decision process and optimizing the transaction success rate and initial cost in the payment channel network using a multi-intelligent deep Q-network.

Once the optimal transaction routing path is determined for each transaction, the order in which transaction events are forwarded to the relevant relay nodes needs to be determined. Next, we transform the optimization problems of joint channel capacity, initial amount per transaction, and transaction deadline per transaction into Markov decision processes, and then design a relay forwarding strategy based on the RL algorithm to achieve the maximization of the success rate of the network transactions and the minimization of the initial amount of the transactions. Due to privacy and security concerns, the relay cost of each transaction needs to be determined before performing the transaction, and the relay node's historical mid-cost in the routing path of each transaction is unknown to the other nodes, so the relay-forwarding scheduling problem can be thought of as a decentralized, partially observable Markov decision-making process, which is denoted as $\mathcal{M} = (\mathbb{S}_i, \mathbb{A}_i, \mathbb{P}_i, \mathcal{R}_i, \mathcal{O}, \gamma)$. Since each transaction involves multiple relay nodes to carry out, and node-to-node forwarding decisions have an impact on the success rate as well as the initial amount of each transaction, we use each relay node as a learning agent, which maintains the interaction of each transaction with the network environment of the dynamic payment channel by sequentially assigning a forwarding priority assignment policy in discrete time.

Each learning agent engages in interactions with the environment, which are characterized by a state space $\mathcal{S} \triangleq \{\mathbb{S}_i, i \in I\}$ and an action space $\mathcal{A} = \{\mathbb{A}_i, i \in I\}$. Relay node i transitions from the current state to the next state based on the probability $\mathcal{P} \triangleq \{\mathbb{P}_i, i \in I\}$. In addition, $\gamma \in (0,1)$ is the discount factor. Each agent i can make a partial observation $o_i = \mathcal{O}(s, i)$ of the payment channel network based on an observation of their current state a_i, where $\mathcal{O}(s, i)$ is an observation function $\mathcal{S} \times \{1 \cdots, N\} \to \mathcal{O}$. When a relay node uses a specified forwarding policy for task forwarding, each agent can measure the reward $r: \mathcal{S} \times \mathcal{A} \to \mathcal{R}$ by the total forwarding cost and transaction success rate. At the same time, each agent learns a policy $\pi_i(\mathbb{A}_i | o_i)$, based on its experience, and the policies of all the agents form an overall policy $\boldsymbol{\pi} = \langle \pi(\mathbb{A}_1 | o_1), \ldots, \pi(\mathbb{A}_i | o_i), \ldots, \pi(\mathbb{A}_I | o_I) \rangle$. The goal of each agent is to find an optimal strategy $\boldsymbol{\pi}^*$ to maximize its expected cumulative discount reward:

$$\boldsymbol{\pi}^*(o_i^0) \in \arg\max_{a_t \in \mathcal{A}} \left[\sum_{t=0}^{\infty} \gamma^t r_i(o_i^t, \mathbb{A}_t) \right] \quad (11)$$

From Eq. (11), the objective function of this paper is to maximize the transaction success rate and minimize the initial amount of the transaction. Since the initial amount of the transaction is fixed, the optimization objective can be viewed as maximizing the transaction success rate and minimizing the amount of relay forwarding for each transaction. And in the setting of rewards, our method uses a separate reward for each subject. To better balance the impact of these two metrics, we use standardized rates and fee values with a weighting factor α to show user preferences. Thus, an agent's independent reward at each time step can be expressed as:

$$r_i(t) = \alpha |\phi_a| - (1 - \alpha) |f_{i,a}^t| \quad (12)$$

The equilibrium varies with the value of α. If the value increases, the learning method finds the minimized forwarding fee to ensure that the realized transaction success rate meets the requirements. Conversely, it tends to find the maximum achievable transaction success rate for a given forwarding fee.

To ensure the success rate of the transaction, we propose a prioritized relay forwarding scheduling policy based on multi-agent DQN. To train the network, each agent chooses an action based on a policy $\pi_i(\mathbb{A}_i | o_i)$, which results in a reward $r(o_t, \mathbb{A}_t)$. The expected total discount reward $Q_i(o, \mathbb{A})$ is defined as a function of the values of the state-action pairs of an agent i with a given strategy π, which can be expressed as:

$$Q_i(o, \mathbb{A}) = \mathbb{E}[\sum_{t=1}^{\infty} \gamma^t r_i(o_t, \mathbb{A}_t) | o_1 = 0, \mathbb{A}_1 = \mathbb{A}, \pi \quad (13)$$

The goal of the agent is to find a strategy that maximizes the cumulative value of $Q_i(o, \mathbb{A})$ from the start state. Other agents can adjust their strategies to maximize their profits, and each agent's strategy has an impact on the environment. The optimal strategy for a multi-intelligent body environment is to ensure that the total reward is maximized under adversarial equilibrium. Thus, combining Eq. (11) and Eq. (13), the expected cumulative discount reward for agent i can be described as follows:

$$V_i(\pi^*) = [Q_i(o_i^t, \mathbb{A}_i^t) | \mathbb{A}_i^t \in \mathbb{A}_i, \pi^*(o_i^0) \in \arg\max_{a_t \in \mathcal{A}} \left[\sum_{t=0}^{\infty} \gamma^t r_i(o_i^t, \mathbb{A}_t) \right]] \quad (14)$$

Deep Q-learning supports Q-value approximation by applying a deep Q-network, where each agent i maintains its action-value function $Q_i(o_i, \mathbb{A}_i, \theta_i)$ using a local DQN parameter θ_i. The DQN stores each agent's transformation record $\langle o_i^t, \mathbb{A}_i^t, r_i^t, o_i'^t \rangle$ to an experience replay $\mathcal{M}_i$. By sampling B round transitions from $\mathcal{M}_i$, the learning agent learns the action-value function to minimize the error function. The loss function is as follows:

$$\mathcal{L}_i(\theta_i) = \sum_{m=1}^{B} [((r_p + \gamma \max_{\mathbb{A}'_i} Q_i(o'_i, \mathbb{A}'_i, \hat{\theta}_i)) - Q_i(o_i, \mathbb{A}_i, \theta_i))^2] \quad (15)$$

Therefore, the higher the forwarding priority of the event at i, the faster it will be forwarded to the next node in its routing path. If a transaction event forwarded later finds that there are not enough events to forward the current amount if it comes to its forwarding, the task will be returned to the previous relay node, which will then select a suitable routing path for the transaction again according to the solution step of the routing algorithm. The robustness of relay node forwarding is ensured by the above forwarding strategy.

5 Performance Evaluation

In this section, we compare the proposed MRMH algorithm with the shortest path algorithm (Dijkstra), the CheaPay algorithm [15], and the MILPA-PCN algorithm [16]. The experimental results show that MRMH is advantageous in reducing the amount of locking of the starting node, increasing the network throughput, and improving the transaction success rate. Additionally, MRMH demonstrates a competitive algorithmic runtime compared to the other algorithms.

5.1 Experiment Settings

To evaluate the performance between different algorithms, we use Python SimPy to build a simulator for the discrete payment channel transaction task. It parameterizes for the initial channel balance, the generation of transactions on both sides of the channel such as frequency, quantity, etc., and the full set of transactions to be simulated. Considering the randomness of the emergence of transaction tasks, we assume that the users who generate transaction demands obey a Poisson distribution. To make the simulated transactions in this paper cover both small and medium-sized transactions, we set the transaction amounts from 1 to 102 ETC [15]. In addition, during the simulation, the number of trading network nodes H is set to 1000 and the channel capacity C is set to 102-103 ETC.

To evaluate the effectiveness of this experiment, MRMH is compared with the classical Dijkstra algorithm, the ChePaay algorithm [15], and the MILPA-PCN algorithm [16].

5.2 Simulation Analysis

This subsection analyzes the algorithmic performance of the MRMH algorithm and three other algorithms for different network sizes and transaction volumes, including the transaction success rate, the initial lock amount, and the algorithmic runtime.

1) Transaction Success Rate Analysis

This part compares transaction success rates for different networks and the number of transactions. Figure 2 analyzes the transaction success rates of the four algorithms with different node sizes. With the number of nodes increasing, the transaction success rates of all four algorithms remain stable without significant changes. Among them, the MRMH algorithm has the highest transaction success rate, which is 10% higher than the best-performing MILPA-PCN algorithm, demonstrating its advantage in transaction-intensive scenarios. These simulation results effectively prove the effectiveness of routing channel selection and relay forwarding scheduling in MRMH.

Figure 3 analyzes the transaction success rates of the four algorithms under varying transaction amounts. The success rates of all four algorithms decrease as the transaction amounts increase. The MRMH algorithm achieves the highest transaction success rate, outperforming MILPA-PCN, CheaPay, and Dijkstra by 7%, 7.6%, and 22.5% respectively. Due to channel capacity limitations, an increase in the number of transactions in the network leads to fewer available pathways, resulting in transaction stacking and a lower success rate for transaction events. The MRMH algorithm schedules in two stages: first, it selects the routing path; second, it optimizes relay costs and transaction deadlines to generate the best scheduling decision, enhancing the transaction success rate.

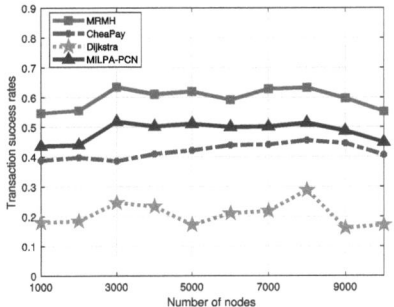

Fig. 2. Transaction success rates for different network sizes

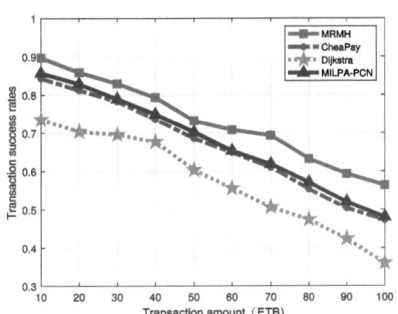

Fig. 3. Transaction success rates for different transaction amounts

2) Initial Lock Amount Analysis

Figure 4 analyzes the initial locked transaction volume of the four strategies for different network sizes with a fixed transaction volume of 102 ETC. As the number of nodes increases, the initial locked transaction volume of all four algorithms increases. Among them, the MRMH algorithm has the lowest initial locked transaction volume, which is 2.4%, 5.7%, and 12.4% lower than MILPA-PCN, CheaPay, and Dijkstra, respectively. The MRMH algorithm selects the routing path by considering the channel capacity and the number of relay nodes during relay node transaction forwarding. It also decides the forwarding order of the transactions by considering the transaction deadline and forwarding cost, thus reducing the initial node locking to ensure each transaction's success rate.

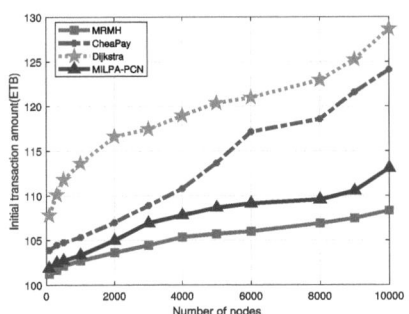

Fig. 4. Initial lock-in amount for transactions with different network sizes

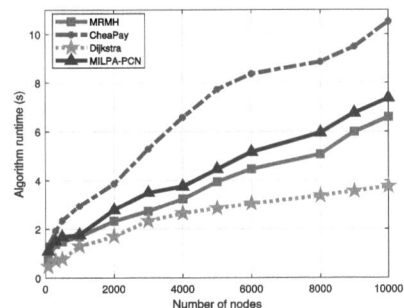

Fig. 5. Algorithm runtime for different network sizes

3) Algorithmic Runtime Analysis

Figure 5 analyzes the algorithmic running time of the four algorithmic strategies for different node sizes. As the number of nodes increases, the algorithmic running time of all four algorithms gradually increases, with the MRMH algorithm being second only to the Dijkstra algorithm. This is because the Dijkstra algorithm only considers finding the shortest routing path for a transaction event and does not take into account transaction failures due to channel capacity limitations. Although the MRMH algorithm has a large path-finding delay compared to the Dijkstra algorithm, the MRMH algorithm takes into account the channel capacity limitations when selecting the routing path and has a lower delay than the other two algorithms.

6 Conclusion

In this paper, we introduced an off-chain computing-based transaction scheduling solution to enhance the efficiency of energy payment transactions for electric vehicles (EVs). We developed an MRMH algorithm that incorporates two key components: a heuristic routing channel selection algorithm utilizing ant colony optimization to identify the most efficient transaction routes, and an RL-based relay forwarding algorithm to refine the selection of relay nodes, ensuring transaction security and efficiency. Through extensive simulation experiments, we demonstrated that our MRMH algorithm significantly improves transaction throughput and success rates in EV charging scenarios.

References

1. Wu, Y., Zhang, C., Zhu, L.: Privacy-preserving and traceable blockchain-based charging payment scheme for electric vehicles. IEEE Internet Things J. **10**(24), 21254–21265 (2023). https://doi.org/10.1109/JIOT.2023.3283415
2. Wang, Y., et al.: A fast and secured vehicle-to-vehicle energy trading based on blockchain consensus in the internet of electric vehicles. IEEE Trans. Veh. Technol. **72**(6), 7827–7843 (2023). https://doi.org/10.1109/TVT.2023.3239990
3. Wang, X., Zhu, H., Ning, Z., Guo, L., Zhang, Y.: Blockchain intelligence for internet of vehicles: challenges and solutions. IEEE Commun. Surv. Tutorials **25**(4), 2325–2355 (2023). https://doi.org/10.1109/COMST.2023.3305312
4. Ning, Z., et al.: Intelligent resource allocation in mobile blockchain for privacy and security transactions: a deep reinforcement learning based approach. Sci. China Inf. Sci. **64**(6), 162303 (2021)
5. Wang, X., Ning, Z., Guo, L., Guo, S., Gao, X., Wang, G.: Mean-field learning for edge computing in mobile blockchain networks. IEEE Trans. Mob. Comput. **22**(10), 5978–5994 (2023). https://doi.org/10.1109/TMC.2022.3186699
6. Zhang, J., Ye, Y., Wu, W., Luo, X.: Boros: secure and efficient off-blockchain transactions via payment channel hub. IEEE Trans. Dependable Secure Comput. **20**(1), 407–421 (2023). https://doi.org/10.1109/TDSC.2021.3135076
7. Wang, X., et al.: Future communications and energy management in the internet of vehicles: Toward intelligent energy-harvesting. IEEE Wirel. Commun. **26**(6), 87–93 (2019). https://doi.org/10.1109/MWC.001.1900009

8. Ning, Z., Huang, J., Wang, X., Rodrigues, J.J.P.C., Guo, L.: Mobile edge computing-enabled internet of vehicles: Toward energy-efficient scheduling. IEEE Network **33**(5), 198–205 (2019). https://doi.org/10.1109/MNET.2019.1800309
9. Ning, Z., Dong, P., Wang, X., Guo, L., Rodrigues, J.J.P.C., Kong, X., Huang, J., Kwok, R.Y.K.: Deep reinforcement learning for intelligent internet of vehicles: an energy-efficient computational offloading scheme. IEEE Trans. Cognitive Commun. Networking **5**(4), 1060–1072 (2019). https://doi.org/10.1109/TCCN.2019.2930521
10. Liu, Y., Wang, X., Zheng, G., Wan, X., Ning, Z.: An aoi-aware data transmission algorithm in blockchain-based intelligent healthcare systems. IEEE Trans. Consum. Electron. **70**(1), 1180–1190 (2024). https://doi.org/10.1109/TCE.2024.3365198
11. Ning, Z., Chen, H., Wang, X., Wang, S., Guo, L.: Blockchain-enabled electrical fault inspection and secure transmission in 5g smart grids. IEEE J. Sel. Top. Signal Process. **16**(1), 82–96 (2022). https://doi.org/10.1109/JSTSP.2021.3120872
12. Sivaraman, V., et al.: High throughput cryptocurrency routing in payment channel networks. In: Proceedings of the 17th Usenix Conference on Networked Systems Design and Implementation, pp. 777–796. NSDI'20. USENIX Association, USA (2020)
13. Zhang, Y., Gai, K., Xiao, J., Zhu, L., Choo, K.K.R.: Blockchain-empowered efficient data sharing in internet of things settings. IEEE J. Sel. Areas Commun. **40**(12), 3422–3436 (2022). https://doi.org/10.1109/JSAC.2022.3213353
14. Zhang, Y., Yang, D., Xue, G.: Cheapay: an optimal algorithm for fee minimization in blockchain-based payment channel networks. In: ICC 2019 - 2019 IEEE International Conference on Communications (ICC), pp. 1–6 (2019). https://doi.org/10.1109/ICC.2019.8761804
15. Bi, H., Chen, Y., Zhu, X.: A multipath routing for payment channel networks for internet of things microtransactions. IEEE Internet Things J. **9**(20), 19670–19681 (2022). https://doi.org/10.1109/JIOT.2022.3167098
16. Xie, H., Fei, S., Yan, Z., Xiao, Y.: Sofitmix: a secure offchain-supported bitcoin-compatible mixing protocol. IEEE Trans. Dependable Secure Comput. **20**(5), 4311–4324 (2023). https://doi.org/10.1109/TDSC.2022.3213824
17. Papadis, N., Tassiulas, L.: Payment channel networks: Single-hop scheduling for throughput maximization. In: IEEE INFOCOM 2022 - IEEE Conference on Computer Communications, pp. 900–909 (2022). https://doi.org/10.1109/INFOCOM48880.2022.9796862
18. Zhang, J., Xiao, S., Wu, W., Zhou, J.: A payment channel network fee allocation strategy integrating auction theory. In: 2023 IEEE International Conference on Metaverse Computing, Networking and Applications (MetaCom), pp. 648–652 (2023). https://doi.org/10.1109/MetaCom57706.2023.00114

Local Descriptors Aided Few-Shot Learning for Wireless Spectrum Status Recognition

Zixin Wang[1], Bianzheng Wang[2], Xin Wang[1], Yue Li[1], and Bin Shen[1(✉)]

[1] School of Communications and Information Engineering, Chongqing University of Posts and Telecommunications, Chongqing 400065, China
shenbin@cqupt.edu.cn
[2] College of Electronics and Information Engineering, Sichuan University, Chengdu 610065, China

Abstract. Recognizing Primary User (PU) activities in cognitive radio networks is indispensable for dynamic spectrum utilization. Due to stringently limited spectrum observing time, the problems of data deficiency and category imbalance hamper traditional spectrum sensing methods from agilely discerning the PU activities with high accuracy. In this paper, we define multiple PU transmitters' joint operating modes as the PU activity scenes and propose a local descriptors-aided adaptive prototype rectification network, named LDAPRNet, to pinpoint the scene type. Specifically, to cope with the data deficiency problem at first, we use a Convolutional Neural Network (CNN) to extract Local Descriptors (LDs) from the few spectrum samples available. Then, we construct a classifier that utilizes the extracted LDs to identify the scenes, where the imbalanced categories are given equal attention by introducing the prototypical network. Experimental results show that the LDAPRNet achieves significant accuracy and generalization ability improvements compared to traditional methods, and therefore, it can serve as an easy-to-implement candidate solution for few-sample-based spectrum sensing.

Keywords: primary user activity · scene recognition · prototypical network · local descriptor

1 Introduction

With the capability of spectrum sensing, Cognitive Radio (CR) technology allows terminal devices to utilize the licensed spectrum opportunistically, therefore improving the overall spectrum efficiency [1, 2]. In the early years, many spectrum sensing methods for ascertaining the PU transmitter's on/off status have been proposed, where binary decisions are made periodically through statistical signal processing.

Traditional spectrum status recognition methods [3, 4] are mainly based on the statistical characteristics of received signals, such as mean, variance, power spectral density, etc. If a wide frequency bandwidth is under consideration, the receivers perform Discrete Fourier Transform (DFT) or Fast Fourier Transform (FFT) on received signal samples to obtain the spectrum observations in frequency domain and analyze the amplitude, frequency distribution and characteristics [5,6]. With an aim to gain more accurate spectrum status decisions in rapidly varying spectrum environment, more advantageous statistical methods and models are necessary to overcome the difficulties and in-adaptability that traditional methods often encounter in practice. Moreover, traditional methods are often implemented by a single or multiple receivers over a relatively small area and accordingly the spectrum decisions are drawn on the proximity of the receivers, thus resulting in a limited geographical area that dynamic spectrum management can cover. In recent years, Machine Learning (ML) has provided new promising solutions for spectrum sensing [2,7].

In Cognitive Radio Networks (CRN), the joint operating modes of multiple PU transmitters can be viewed as PU activities since they exhibit the PU transmitters' whereabouts and the spectrum holes that can be exploited by the Secondary Users (SU) across the geographical area of the CRN. In this sense, recognition of the PU activity scenes is crucial for avoiding interference with the PU receivers and ensuring fairness in spectrum sharing. However, achieving accurate and nimble recognition of the PU activities is still challenging due to data deficiency and category imbalance in practically collecting spectrum observations.

When used for signal classification, conventional ML methods usually perform with high accuracy, but it is generally restrained under the condition of sufficient data, fixed data types, or stable data characteristics. Deep Learning (DL) methods have demonstrated proficient generalization capabilities and better performance in spectrum sensing [8,9] by demanding a large amount of labeled data for training to capture the subtle differences and characteristics between different categorical data. In case the data is insufficient, it is likely to encounter the problem of overfitting. Moreover, the number of collected samples of different categories may vary in a wide range, resulting in a data imbalance problem. Therefore, the model after training is usually biased towards the categories with a large number of samples and performs poorly for those with insufficient samples.

Bearing in mind that data deficiency and imbalance are two nuisances for spectrum status recognition, we notice that Few-Shot Learning (FSL) inherently serves to solve the problem of insufficient samples and provides models with strong generalization ability from new tasks under limited supervisory experience [10–12]. Particularly as one typical FSL approach, prototypical networks can represent each data category by calculating the category prototypes [13,14]. Even if there is a data imbalance problem between different categories, it will not have much impact on the model obtained [15]. However, when operating on insufficient data, prototypical networks cannot effectively seize the true distribution of the categorical data, resulting in a drawback of deviations in the obtained categorical prototypes [16].

In this paper, we propose a novel PU activity scene recognition method based on a local descriptor-aided adaptive prototype network called LDAPRNet. To combat the data deficiency effect at first, we extract the Local Descriptors (LDs) from the limited number of spectrum data via the intermediate layers of a CNN, which are capable of supplying a wider receptive field to understand the overall data contents. The extracted LDs intensively and implicitly reflect the spatial distribution of the multiple neighboring Primary User Transmitters' (PUT) radio signal strength in the CRN. A prototypical network-based classifier is subsequently constructed to identify the scenes using the extracted LDs, where the effects of imbalanced categorical data are alleviated through prototype calculation. In other words, the calculated prototypes help allocate equal attention to different categorical data instead of focusing on the categories with relatively more data, thus reducing the classification bias towards the category with relatively more data.

In model training, we adopt the meta-learning strategy to enhance the scene classifier's generalization ability with a limited number of data samples. Experimental results show that, compared to the existing baseline methods, the proposed LDAPRNet performs significantly better in PU activity scene recognition when there are merely a few data samples available under uneven data distributions among different scene categories.

2 System Model

We consider that there are N PUTs and M Sensing Devices (SD) in the CRN. The operating status of the n-th PUT is denoted as u_n, where $u_n = 1$ indicates the n-th PUT is in the active mode, and $u_n = 0$ indicates inactive. A vector $\mathbf{u} = [u_1, u_2, \cdots, u_N]^T$ is used to represent the joint operating mode of all the N PUTs. We define the joint mode of the N PUTs as their activity scene in this paper. Therefore, there are a total of 2^N possible scenes, among which we need to identify the actual one within each sensing interval. The geographical area of the CRN is divided into $M = O \times P$ grids equally, and we assume that there is at most one SD in each grid. The signal received by the (o, p)-th SD in the CRN is a superposition of the N PUTs' signals as

$$y_m[i] = \sum_{n=1}^{N} \sqrt{P_n} u_n h_{n,m} x_n[i] + n_\sigma[i] \quad (1)$$

where $y_m[i]$ represents the signal received at the i-th time instant by the m-th SD with $m = (o-1)P + p$, P_n is the transmit power of the n-th PUT, $x_n[i]$ is the transmit symbol of the n-th PUT with $E[|x_n[i]|^2] = 1$, $n_\sigma[i]$ is the additive Gaussian white noise with zero mean and variance σ^2, and $h_{n,m}$ denotes the channel coefficient from the n-th PUT to the m-th SD, which can be specifically expressed as:

$$h_{n,m} = \sqrt{\text{PL}(\|\mathbf{S}_m - \mathbf{R}_n\|)} \cdot \mu_{n,m} \cdot \eta_{n,m} \quad (2)$$

where $\mathbf{R}_n = [R_{n,x}, R_{n,y}]^T$ is the position of the n-th PUT, $\mathbf{S}_m = [S_{m,x}, S_{m,y}]^T$ is the position of the m-th SD, $\mathrm{PL}(\|\mathbf{S}_m - \mathbf{R}_n\|) = (d_{n,m}/d_0)^{-\lambda}$ denotes the propagation pathloss under the reference distance d_0 when the distance between the n-th PUT and the m-th SD is $d_{n,m}$, λ is the pathloss index, $\mu_{n,m}$ represents the shadowing factor, and $\eta_{n,m}$ stands for the multipath fading factor.

According to Eq. (1), the received signal energy measured by the m-th SD at the l-th sensing interval is expressed as:

$$Y_m^{(l)} = \frac{1}{2w\tau} \sum_{i=1}^{2w\tau} \left| y_m^{(l)}[i] \right|^2, \quad l = 1, 2, \cdots, L \tag{3}$$

where w is the received signal bandwidth and τ is the spectrum sensing time duration. It is worth noting that the total number of available spectrum samples L is assumed to be small due to the agile sensing requirements in practice.

3 Local Descriptors Aided Prototypical Networks

3.1 Data Preparation

According to Eq. (3), the energy samples collected by the M SD during the l-th observing period can be obtained and aggregated in matrix form as

$$\mathbf{Y}_l = \begin{bmatrix} Y_{11}^{(l)} & Y_{12}^{(l)} & \cdots & Y_{1P}^{(l)} \\ Y_{21}^{(l)} & Y_{22}^{(l)} & \cdots & Y_{2P}^{(l)} \\ \vdots & \vdots & \ddots & \vdots \\ Y_{O1}^{(l)} & Y_{O2}^{(l)} & \cdots & Y_{OP}^{(l)} \end{bmatrix} \tag{4}$$

where $Y_{op}^{(l)}$ represents the spectrum energy observed by the m-th SD at the (o, p) grid.

Considering that the insufficient data and imbalanced distribution of samples are not appropriate for utilizing DL models, we propose an LD-aided prototypical network named LDAPRNet to fulfill the PU activity scene classification task. Since the LDs are inherently utilized for image feature processing, we transform each spectrum energy matrix into an image as the input data to the LDAPR-Net. Specifically, we first normalize the data matrix $\mathbf{Y}_l$ in Eq. (4) and set the pixel range of the spectrum image as $[0, 255]$. Then we map each entry in the normalized $\mathbf{Y}_l$ to the corresponding image position to obtain $\mathbf{Y}_l^{\mathrm{IMG}}$, which is an image representation of the PU activity scene. Figure 1 shows the spectrum status maps for different statuses.

3.2 Model Architecture

The overall architecture of the proposed LDAPRNet is shown in Fig. 2. The LDAPRNet consists of three main components, namely an LD-extractor, which is used to extract LDs from the input samples; a prototype calculator, which is used to calculate the prototype of each category; and a similarity measurement module, which is used to evaluate the similarity between query samples and each category prototype for classification. The LDAPRNet performs end-to-end data feature extraction and classification by first extracting LDs from the input data and subsequently mapping them into categorical prototypes.

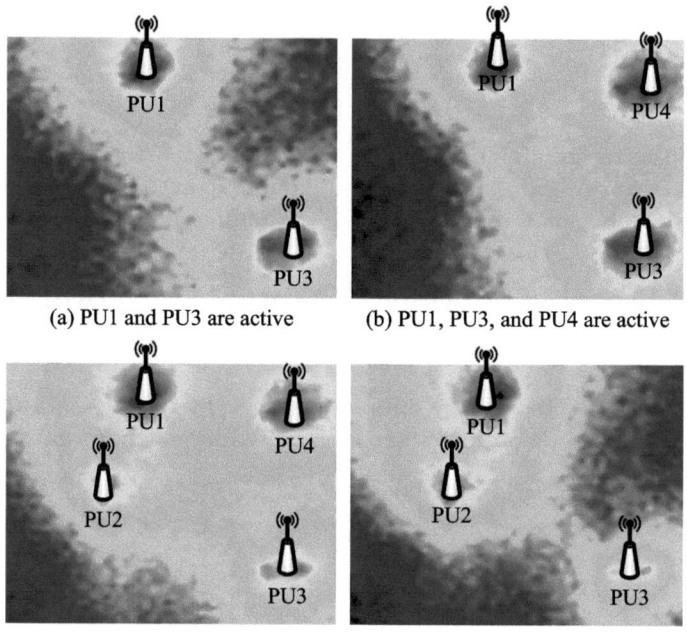

Fig. 1. Spectrum status maps.

3.3 Local Descriptors Extractor

The advantage of bringing in LDs is that they can inherently capture the local structure and texture information of images and, therefore, are robust enough to handle complicated scenes or, equivalently, the data categories. In PU activity scene recognition, the extracted LDs endow the model with more attention to the local details of the spectrum images, thereby improving the recognition accuracy and generalization ability. In this paper, we use three CNN blocks to perform convolution operations and feature extraction to obtain LDs of the PU scene images.

Each CNN layer consists of four parts: the Convolution Layer (Conv), Batch Normalization layer (BNLayer), ReLU layer, and Maximum Pooling (MaxPool) layer. By entering the spectrum images into the CNN, a three-dimensional

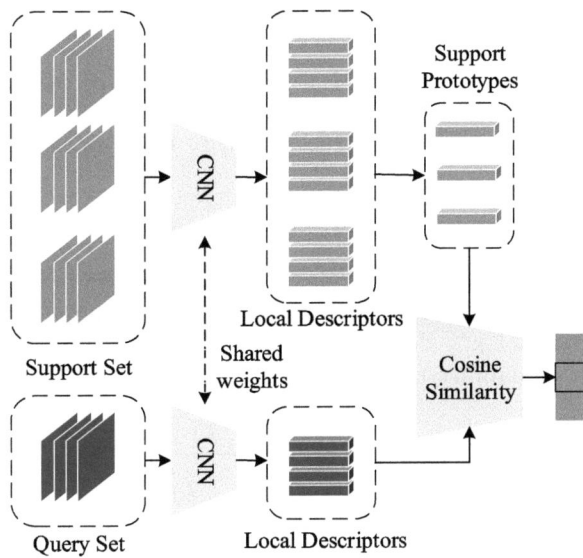

Fig. 2. Architecture of the proposed LDAPRNet.

sample tensor set can be obtained. The role of CNN can be represented as $\phi_\theta(\cdot) \in \mathbb{R}^{h \times w \times d}$, where θ refers to the set of learnable parameters, and h, w, and d denote the three dimensions of the sample tensor, respectively. After feeding the image $\mathbf{Y}_l^{\text{IMG}}$, we can obtain the tensor $\phi_\theta\left(\mathbf{Y}_l^{\text{IMG}}\right)$ with $h \times w \times d$ dimension, which can be regarded as a local descriptor of $\eta = h \times w$ dimension:

$$\phi_\theta\left(\mathbf{Y}_l^{\text{IMG}}\right) = [\mathbf{x}_1, \mathbf{x}_2, \cdots, \mathbf{x}_\eta] \in \mathbb{R}^{d \times \eta} \tag{5}$$

where $\mathbf{x}_\eta$ represents the η-th local descriptor of the image $\mathbf{Y}_l^{\text{IMG}}$. Figure 3 depicts the dimensionality change of a spectrum image through an LD-extractor consisting of a 3-layer CNN.

3.4 Prototype Calculator

A prototype serves as a central point for representing a category by capturing common characteristics. To enhance accuracy and generalization, the prototype module selects relevant LDs, improving prototype calculation. To mitigate deviations from background-related LDs, the module identifies the nearest K LDs in categories for each support set. Calculating the mean value of the obtained K LDs, we obtain the category prototype as

$$\mathbf{c}_\ell = \frac{1}{K} \sum_{k=1}^{K} \mathbf{x}_k \tag{6}$$

where $\mathbf{c}_\ell$ represents the categorical prototype of category ℓ.

3.5 Similarity Measure

The input for the similarity measure is the prototypes of each category of the support set and the K LDs of the query set samples. We determine the category of query set samples by calculating the similarity between the two:

$$s_{i,j} = \sum_{k=1}^{K} cos(\mathbf{x}^*_{i,k}, c_j) \tag{7}$$

where $s_{i,j}$ represents the similarity score between the i-th query set sample and the j-th category, and $\mathbf{x}^*_{i,k}$ denotes the k-th local descriptor of the i-th query set sample. The probability that the i-th query set sample belongs to the j-th category is

$$P_{i,j} = \frac{\exp(s_{i,j}/T)}{\sum\limits_{j=1}^{2N} \exp(s_{i,j}/T)} \tag{8}$$

where T denotes a temperature hyperparameter.

The LDAPRNet model is designed to classify the PU activity scenes by transforming spectrum energy matrices into images and utilizing LDs for enhanced feature extraction. This approach enhances classification accuracy and generalization by focusing on local details within the spectrum images, making it robust for handling complex scenes and imbalanced data distributions.

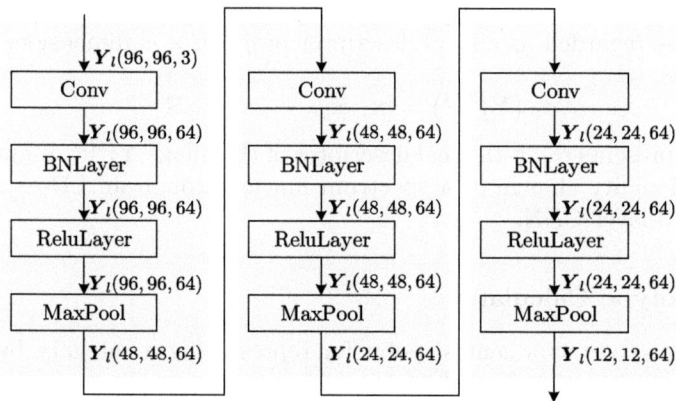

Fig. 3. The CNN-Block structure and image dimension change of the LD extractor.

4 Experiment

4.1 Datasets and Simulation Setup

We evaluate the performance of LDAPRNet over the dataset obtained under the system model described in Sect. 2. Detailed parameter settings are shown in Table 1. In this paper, an geographical area of 5 km × 5 km is divided into 50 × 50 grids, and we assume that there is only one SD in each grid. The input image size of the proposed model is 96 × 96. In experiments, the total number of data images obtained is totally $L = 320$. Each category of the PU activity scene has an unevenly distributed number of samples, and the dataset contains 32 categories where each category has an unknown number of samples.

In this paper, various A-way B-shot types of FSL classifications are performed, where $A \in \{5, 10\}$ and $B \in \{1, 5, 10\}$. For each episodic task, we randomly select A categories from the total 32 ($N = 5$) categories and B samples from each category to form the support set. To make the results general, we use the Adam algorithm for training all models for 40 epochs with 100 randomly constructed episode tasks per epoch. As mentioned before, each CNN block in Fig. 2 consists of one 3 × 3 convolutional kernel, one BNLayer, one ReLULayer, and one 2 × 2 MaxPool, with 64 channels.

4.2 Baselines

We compare the proposed model in this paper with six baseline models: (1) Decision Tree (DT) [2]; (2) K-Nearest Neighbor (KNN) [2]; (3) CNN [3]; (4) Support Vector Machine (SVM); (4) Model-Agnostic Meta-Learning (MAML) [5]; (5) MatchingNet [6]; (6) PrototypeNet [7].

Table 1. Simulation parameter settings.

Parameters	Value
Number of PUTs N	5
Number of SUEs M	2500
LFB bandwidth w	5 MHz
Data collection time τ	$100\mu s$
Path-loss exponent α	4
Shadow fading factor μ	3 dB
Multipath fading factor η	5 dB
Noise power spectral density	−174 dBm/Hz

Table 2. Accuracy of the baseline models, the typical FSL models, and the proposed LDAPRNet on two kinds of FSL tasks.

Methods	5-way 1-shot	5-way 5-shot
DT	0.4300	0.5000
KNN	0.3281	0.4062
CNN	0.6250	0.6563
SVM	0.7629	0.8967
MAML	0.9580	0.9603
MatchingNet	0.9677	0.9733
PrototypeNet	0.9211	0.9307
our model	**0.9899**	**0.9955**

4.3 Experiment Results and Discussions

Table 2 demonstrates the test results when the SNR is 15 dB, where the models investigated are grouped into conventional ML models, the FSL models, and the LDAPRNet model. It can be seen that CNN performs better than KNN and DT, but it is difficult to adapt to situations with fewer samples. The SVM model is more suitable for few-shot conditions than others in the first group since it only has to search the support vector. However, compared with the FSL models in the second group, there is still a performance gap due to data imbalance-led overfitting. Among the three FSL models, metric-based MatchingNet and PrototypeNet show better performance than the optimization-based MAML, indicating that the loss function-based metric learning model is more suitable for PU activity scene recognition than the gradient-based weight parameter-updating method. Compared with MatchingNet and PrototypeNet, the proposed LDAPRNet in this paper exhibits the best performance and is easier to generalize to new PU activity scenes.

Figure 4 shows the sample mapping in the embedded space, where subfigs (a) and (b) represent the sample mapping in the embedding space without using the LDs Extractor, while subfig (c) and (d) illustrate the sample mapping with extracted LDs. As shown, without LDs, the samples that can be used are highly limited, whereas with the LDs extractor, the samples are remarkably augmented. With these augmented samples to support each categorical data, the deviation resulting from data imbalance is significantly eliminated. The increase of the B value can indeed improve the classification accuracy to a certain extent. However, when the B value tends to be saturated, further increasing the B value may only introduce redundant samples and increase the complexity of training, but the improvement of classification accuracy is not obvious.

Figure 5 shows the test results under different A and B values in the A-way B-shot task. This paper evaluates the classification accuracy of the model in 3 to 8 categories. It was found that as the number of categories increases, the accuracy rate will decrease. This is because when the value of A increases, more similar

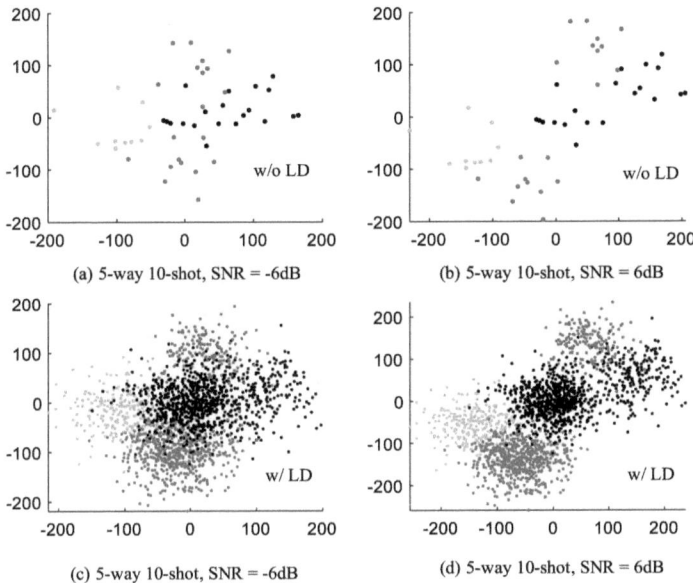

Fig. 4. The impact of LDs on sample augmentation.

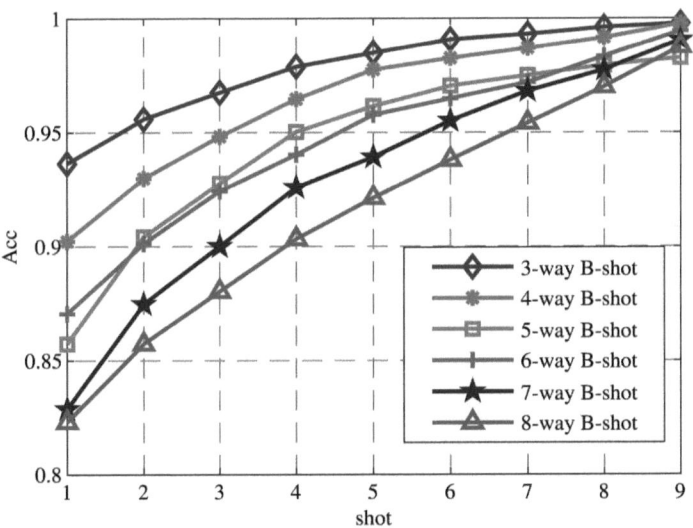

Fig. 5. Accuracy of the proposed method on different values of A and B.

categories may appear, which increases the difficulty of the classification task. In this case, even with more support set samples (larger B value), the classifier may still face confusion between classes. However, when the B value tends to be saturated, further increasing the B value may only introduce redundant samples

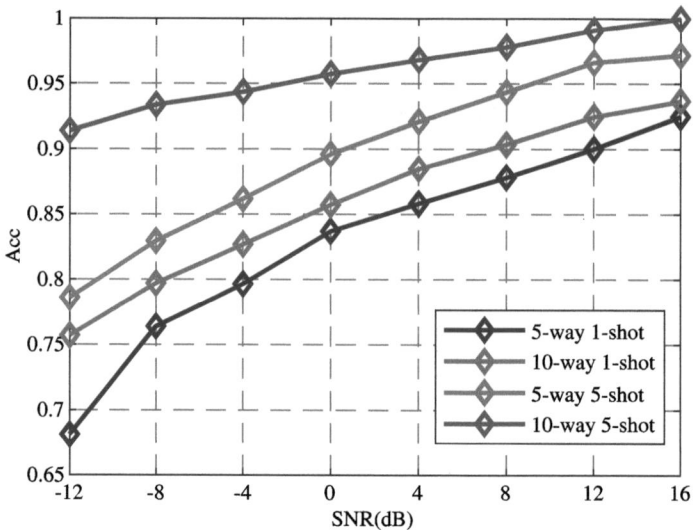

Fig. 6. Accuracy of the proposed method on different values of SNR.

and increase the complexity of training, but the improvement of classification accuracy is not obvious.

Considering that the SNR will affect the clarity of the spectrum status maps, Fig. 6 shows the test results of several A-way B-shot tasks under different SNR conditions. As expected, the accuracy increases significantly as the SNR increases. This is because the spectrum status maps will be clearer when the SNR is higher. Also, at high SNRs, the noise will have less influence on the energy distribution and shape of the signal in the spectrum status maps.

5 Conclusion

This paper proposes LDs-aided prototypical networks to deal with the data deficiency and categorical imbalance problems in PU activity scene recognition. Compared with the baseline models, the proposed LDAPRNet uses LDs to capture fine-grained features in the spectrum energy images, enhancing the model's perception of target differences and effectively dealing with few samples. It proves the LDAPRNet has important application potential in licensed spectrum status recognition.

Acknowledgments. This work was supported by the Chongqing University of Posts and Telecommunications Ph.D. Postgraduate Talent Cultivation Project under Grant BYJS202315.

References

1. Lee, J., Tejedor, E., Ranta-aho, K., et al.: Spectrum for 5G: Global status, challenges, and enabling technologies. IEEE Commun. Mag. **56**(3), 12–18 (2018)
2. Zhang, Y., Hu, G., Cai, Y.: Proactive spectrum monitoring for suspicious wireless powered communications in dynamic spectrum sharing networks. China Commun. **18**(12), 119–138 (2021)
3. Niu, L., Li, F.: Cooperative spectrum sensing for Internet of Things using modeling of power-spectral-density estimation errors. IEEE Internet Things J. **9**(10), 7802–7814 (2021)
4. Sun, C., Lu, P., Cao, K.: Phase-rotated spectral correlation detection for spectrum sensing at low SNR regimes. IEEE Signal Process. Lett. **26**(7), 991–995 (2019)
5. Yizhou, H., Gaofeng, C., Pengxu, L.I., et al.: Timing advanced estimation algorithm of low complexity based on DFT spectrum analysis for satellite system. China Commun. **12**(4), 140–150 (2015)
6. Sun, B., Zheng, Z., Zhou, Y., et al.: Research on fast acquisition algorithm of spread spectrum signal based on PMF-FFT. In: 7th International Conference on Communication, Image and Signal Processing (CCISP), pp. 291–296. IEEE, Chengdu, China (2022)
7. Wang, Y., Wang, X., Shen, B., et al.: Clustering optimization and hog feature extraction based primary user activity scene recognition scheme. In: 2022 IEEE 95th Vehicular Technology Conference: (VTC2022-Spring), pp. 1–5. IEEE, Helsinki, Finland (2022)
8. Zhang, Y., Shen, B., Wang, J., et al.: CNN based wideband spectrum occupancy status identification for cognitive radios. In: 2020 International Conference on Wireless Communications and Signal Processing (WCSP), pp. 569–574. IEEE, Nanjing, China (2020)
9. Zhen, P., Zhang, B., Chen, Z., et al.: Spectrum sensing method based on wavelet transform and residual network. IEEE Wirel. Commun. Lett. **11**(12), 2517–2521 (2022)
10. Song, Y., Wang, T., Cai, P., et al.: A comprehensive survey of few-shot learning: evolution, applications, challenges, and opportunities. ACM Comput. Surv. **55**(13s), 1–40 (2023)
11. Puri, R., Zakhor, A., Puri, R.:Few shot learning for point cloud data using model agnostic meta learning. In: 2020 IEEE International Conference on Image Processing (ICIP), pp. 1906–1910. IEEE, Location (2020)
12. Cai, Q., Pan, Y., Yao, T., et al.: Memory matching networks for one-shot image recognition. In: 2018 IEEE/CVF Conference on Computer Vision and Pattern Recognition, pp. 1–2. IEEE, Salt Lake City, UT, USA (2018)
13. Sun, J., Takeuchi, S., Yamasaki, I.: Prototypical inception network with cross branch attention for time series classification. In: 2021 International Joint Conference on Neural Networks (IJCNN), pp. 1–7. IEEE, Shenzhen, China (2021)
14. Lin, J., Shen, J., He, X.: Gaussian prototype rectification for few-shot image recognition. In: 2021 International Joint Conference on Neural Networks (IJCNN), pp. 1–8. IEEE, Shenzhen, China (2021)
15. Liu, D., Bai, L., Yu, T., et al.: Learning a good representation for metric-based few-shot classification. In: 2023 15th International Conference on Computer Research and Development (ICCRD), pp. 187–192. IEEE, Hangzhou, China (2023)
16. Li, W., Wang, L., Xu, J., et al.: Revisiting local descriptor based image-to-class measure for few-shot learning. In: 2019 IEEE/CVF Conference on Computer Vision and Pattern Recognition (CVPR), pp. 7260–7268. IEEE, Long Beach (2019)

A Variational Bayesian Based Adaptive Kalman Filter Time-Scale Algorithm for Atomic Clock Ensemble

Buyun Ma[1], Zhengkang Wang[2], Yiyi Yao[1], Jiahui Cheng[1], Xinyu Miao[1], and Yaojun Qiao[1(✉)]

[1] State Key Laboratory of Information Photonics and Optical Communications, Beijing University of Posts and Telecommunications, Beijing, China
qiao@bupt.edu.cn
[2] Beijing Key Laboratory of Space-Ground Interconnection and Convergence, Beijing University of Posts and Telecommunications, Beijing, China

Abstract. To obtain a time scale with better stability and robustness, integrating atomic clock ensemble is a common approach. As a celebrated optimal estimator, the Kalman filter (KF) can be employed to construct time-scale algorithms for atomic clock ensemble to generate a time scale. The original KF time-scale algorithm typically sets a priori measurement noise covariance matrix which kept constant throughout the operation process. However, practical measuring equipment would introduce non-stationary noise, causing the mismatch of noise covariance matrices and corrupting the stability of the generated time scale. To address this problem, a variational Bayesian adaptive Kalman filter (VB-AKF) time-scale algorithm is proposed for estimating the variance matrix of non-stationary noise in real time and improving the stability of time scale. As shown through the simulation that the proposed VB-AKF time-scale algorithm can quickly track the measurement noise variance and conquer the corruption due to the mismatch of noise covariance matrices. Under the same noise circumstance, the stability of time scale can be improved from 5.42×10^{-12}@1s to 1.46×10^{-12}@1s and from 4.87×10^{-12}@1s to 2.82×10^{-12}@1s by VB-AKF in set scenarios of clock ensemble respectively, achieving the equivalent stability as KF with priori true noise covariance matrix. Compared with the KF, the VB-AKF time-scale algorithm is better at handling the impact of non-stationary measurement noise on the stability of time scale.

Keywords: Kalman filter · Time-scale algorithm · Variational Bayesian method · Atomic clock ensemble

1 Introduction

The atomic clock, as the core of time-frequency system, can generate ultra-high stability time scale, which widely used in various research fields, e.g., positioning, navigation, and timing [1]. Due to possible abnormalities to any physical device which would corrupt the stability of time scale, most international time-reference laboratories currently employ multiple high-performance atomic clocks as the basis to constitute an atomic clock ensemble for timekeeping. By integrating the clock ensemble, several time-scale algorithms which produce a virtual clock have emerged to improve the robustness and performance of time scale [2].

Approaches using Kalman filter (KF) as time scale seem to establish a promising method for which provides the optimal estimation of time deviation in the sense of least squares, thus abandoning the framework of weighted average in traditional time-scale algorithms [3]. Therefore, several attempts at generating time scale with KF were made in recent decades [4–7]. Reference [4] reported the JY1 time scale with hydrogen-maser based on KF, which reduced the likelihood of being influenced by an abnormal clock by detecting a clock error automatically. Y. Yan et al. proposed a structured KF which associated with the transformation matrix to generate a time scale with better accuracy [5]. Considering ensembling different clock types which exhibiting well for distinct time scales can benefit from the virtue of single clocks, Marion Gödel et al. discussed the rationality for modeling three-state clock based on Markov processes and proposed the KF method for a mixed clock ensemble [6]. H. Song et al. proposed a robust KF time-scale algorithm which introduces the inflation factor and optimal adaptive factor into conventional KF progress, maintaining the stability of time scale when measuring outliers and phase jumps occur [7]. In practice, the measurement noise superimposed on clock difference would change over time, which make obtaining the noise characteristics accurately being difficult, and is often only a crude and invariant prior-approximation as substitute, degrading the performance of the algorithm. This gives rise to the need to estimate measurement noise characteristics in real time based on actual conditions to operate KF time-scale algorithm reliably. Fortunately, variational Bayesian (VB) approach with low computational cost has been employed for signal processing widely, which can approximate the joint posterior distribution of the state and the noise variance on each time step separately [8,9]. However, the VB approach for noise variance estimation in time-scale algorithm has not been fully studied.

In this paper, we propose a variational Bayesian adaptive Kalman filter (VB-AKF) time-scale algorithm, which aims to solve the problem of the stability degradation of the original KF employed for time scale generation when dealing with non-stationary measurement noise. The proposed VB-AKF time-scale algorithm can resist the deterioration of noise characteristic mismatch on time scale performance by estimating the covariance of measurement noise between independent clocks and adjust the corresponding elements of the covariance matrix in real time. The simulation shows that, although non-stationary noise exists, the VB-AKF can still accurately estimate the variance and improve the stability of time scale from $5.42 \times 10^{-12}@1s$ to $1.46 \times 10^{-12}@1s$ and from $4.87 \times 10^{-12}@1s$ to $2.82 \times 10^{-12}@1s$ in set scenarios of clock ensemble respectively. Further more, the time scale generated by VB-AKF can obtain the same stability as KF with priori true noise covariance matrix.

The paper is organized as follows: Sect. 2 discusses the clock ensemble model and VB-AKF time-scale algorithm in detail. Section 3 provides comparison of the results obtained by employing VB-AKF and original KF respectively for generating the time scale.

2 Principle

2.1 The General Clock Ensemble

Accurate modeling of the state and measurement equation of the atomic clock ensemble is necessary, as it forms the foundation of Kalman filtering. The former equation describes the transition of the dynamical system's predicted state at next epoch, and the latter conveys the observation relationship within the clock ensemble.

The Sate-Space Model. Considering an ensemble of N independent clocks, the state vector of which has a size of $3N \times 1$ and can be expressed as

$$X(k) = [x_1(k), f_1(k), d_1(k), \cdots, x_N(k), f_N(k), d_N(k)]^T, \quad (1)$$

where $x_i(k)$ represents the time deviation between ith clock reading and ideal clock reading at kth epoch, while $f_i(k)$ is frequency deviation and $d_i(k)$ represents frequency drift which mainly originates from component aging of atomic clock. According to the quadratic polynomial for the time deviation, the sate-space model of single clock can be written as below

$$X_i(k) = \Phi X_i(k-1) + W_i(k), i = 1, \cdots, N, \quad (2)$$

where Φ is the transition matrix which related to sampling time τ_0 and has diagonal blocks as follows

$$\Phi = \begin{bmatrix} 1 & \tau_0 & \frac{\tau_0^2}{2} \\ 0 & 1 & \tau_0 \\ 0 & 0 & 1 \end{bmatrix}. \quad (3)$$

Furthermore, $W_i(k) = [\xi_i(k), \eta_i(k), \zeta_i(k)]^T$ respectively represents the phase white noise, frequency white noise, and frequency random walk noise of ith clock at kth epoch, and has covariance matrix [10]

$$\mathbf{Q}_i = \begin{bmatrix} q_{1i}\tau_0 + q_{2i}\frac{\tau_0^3}{3} + q_{3i}\frac{\tau_0^5}{20} & q_{2i}\frac{\tau_0^2}{2} + q_{3i}\frac{\tau_0^4}{8} & q_{3i}\frac{\tau_0^3}{6} \\ q_{2i}\frac{\tau_0^2}{2} + q_{3i}\frac{\tau_0^4}{8} & q_{2i}\tau_0 + q_{3i}\frac{\tau_0^3}{3} & q_{3i}\frac{\tau_0^2}{2} \\ q_{3i}\frac{\tau_0^3}{6} & q_{3i}\frac{\tau_0^2}{2} & q_{3i}\tau_0 \end{bmatrix}, \quad (4)$$

where parameter q_{1i}, q_{2i}, and q_{3i} reflect the three noise components of each clock.

The Measurement Model. Due to the fact that the only observable quantity of clock ensemble is the difference of clock readings $h(t)$ of two clocks, which called clock difference and defined as

$$x_{ij}(k) = h_i(k) - h_j(k) = x_i(k) - x_j(k), i,j = 1,...,N, \quad (5)$$

where $i \neq j$. Thus, an overall matrix-vector equation for the measurement model of clock ensemble can be given by

$$Z(k) = HX(k) + V(k), \quad (6)$$

where H represents the $(N-1) \times 3N$ measurement matrix and $Z(k) = [z_{1,N}(k), z_{2,N}(k), \cdots, z_{N-1,N}(k)]^T$ is measurement clock difference vector. The measurement noise $V(k) = [v_{1,N}(k), v_{2,N}(k), \cdots, v_{N-1,N}(k)]^T$ is a vector of statistically independent Gaussian variables with zero mean and has diagonal covariance matrix comprising of these noise variances by $R = diag(\sigma_{1,N}^2, \sigma_{1,N}^2, \cdots, \sigma_{N-1,N}^2)$.

2.2 VB-AKF Time-Scale Algorithm

The proposed VB-AKF time-scale algorithm which estimates state vector $X(k)$ and adjusts the covariance of measurement noise dynamically using only the new observation $Z(k)$ and the previous estimation $\widehat{X}(k-1)$ in every epoch k consists 3 steps: *prediction*, *VB estimation* and *update*, and the block diagram is depicted in Fig. 1.

Prediction. The estimated state $\widehat{X}$ and its covariance matrix $P_{\widehat{X}}$ at k-1 are projected one step forward to obtain the a priori estimates at k as

$$\widehat{X}^-(k) = \Phi \widehat{X}^+(k-1), \quad (7)$$

$$P_{\widehat{X}}^-(k) = \Phi P_{\widehat{X}}^+(k-1)\Phi^T + Q(k), \quad (8)$$

where the superscript "+" indicates a posteriori value and "−" is priori value.

VB Estimation. Based on the principle of heuristic dynamics for the variances, the parameters $\alpha_{k-1,i}$ and $\beta_{k-1,i}$ which employed for calculating covariance matrix R_k in kth epoch can be obtained by the following, for $i = 1,\ldots,N-1$:

$$\alpha_{k,i}^- = \rho \alpha_{k-1,i}, \quad (9)$$

$$\beta_{k,i}^- = \rho \beta_{k-1,i}, \quad (10)$$

where ρ is variance decreasing factor. Then, the parameters of VB estimation are set as $\widehat{X}_{VB}^{(0)}(k) = \widehat{X}^-(k)$, $P_{\widehat{X},VB}^{(0)}(k) = P_{\widehat{X}}^-(k)$, $\alpha_{k,i}^{(0)} = 1/2 + \alpha_{k,i}^-$, $\alpha_{k,i}^{(0)} = 1/2 + \alpha_{k,i}^-$

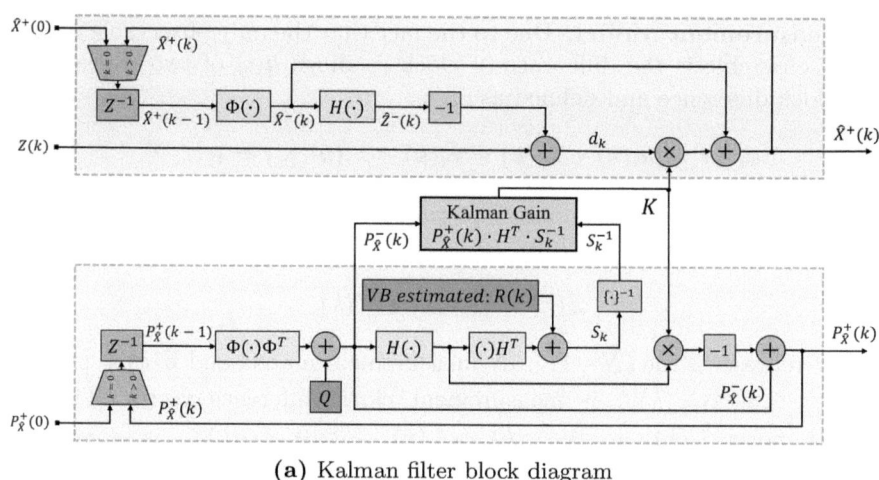

(a) Kalman filter block diagram

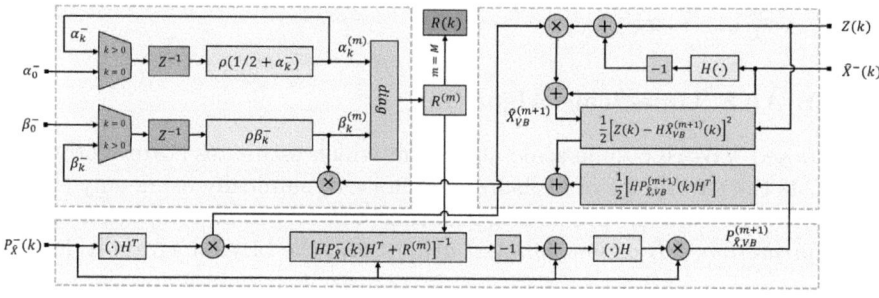

(b) VB estimation block diagram

Fig. 1. VB-AKF time-scale algorithm flowchart. $R(k)$ represents the measurement noise matrix estimated by the VB section, and $\{\cdot\}^T$ denotes transpose and Z^{-1} is the unit delay.

and $\beta_{k,i}^{(0)} = \beta_{k,i}^-$. The process for estimating noise covariance matrix R_k includes the following steps with M iterations:

$$R_k^{(m)} = diag\left(\beta_{k,1}^{(m)}/\alpha_{k,1}^{(m)}, \cdots, \beta_{k,N-1}^{(m)}/\alpha_{k,N-1}^{(m)}\right), \tag{11}$$

$$S_k^{(m)} = H P_{\widehat{X}}^-(k) H^T + R_k^{(m)}, \tag{12}$$

$$d(k) = Z(k) - H\widehat{X}^-(k), \tag{13}$$

$$\widehat{X}_{VB}^{(m+1)}(k) = \widehat{X}^-(k) + P_{\widehat{X}}^-(k) H^T \left[S_k^{(m)}\right]^{-1} \times d(k), \tag{14}$$

$$P_{\widehat{X},VB}^{(m+1)}(k) = P_{\widehat{X}}^-(k) H^T \left[S_k^{(m)}\right]^{-1} H P_{\widehat{X}}^-(k), \tag{15}$$

$$\beta_{k,i}^{(m+1)} = \beta_{k,i}^{-} + \frac{1}{2}\left[Z(k) - H\hat{X}_{VB}^{(m+1)}(k)\right]_{i}^{2} + \frac{1}{2}\left[HP_{\hat{X},VB}^{(m+1)}(k)H^{T}\right]_{ii}. \quad (16)$$

The iteration tends to converge expeditiously that 5 rounds of iterative operations are already sufficient in practice. Finally, the output $R_k^{(M)}$ is the estimated covariance matrix of measurement noise in kth epoch and would be rewritten as $R(k)$ in the update step.

Update. Based on the previous discussion, the Kalman gain matrix can be calculated as

$$K = P_{\hat{X}}^{-}(k)H^{T}\left[HP_{\hat{X}}^{-}(k)H^{T} + R(k)\right]^{-1}. \quad (17)$$

Thus, the state estimate update is given by

$$\hat{X}^{+}(k) = \hat{X}^{-}(k) + K\left[Z(k) - H\hat{X}^{-}(k)\right], \quad (18)$$

whose covariance is

$$P_{\hat{X}}^{+}(k) = [I - KH]P_{\hat{X}}^{-}(k), \quad (19)$$

where I represents the $3N \times 3N$ identity matrix.

3 Results

In order to analyze the performance of the proposed VB-AKF time-scale algorithm, data of time deviation for the clock ensemble which consists of 3 cesium clocks and 3 hydrogen-maser clocks (one of which set as the reference clock) was simulated [11]. In addition, we add another simulation scenario which consists

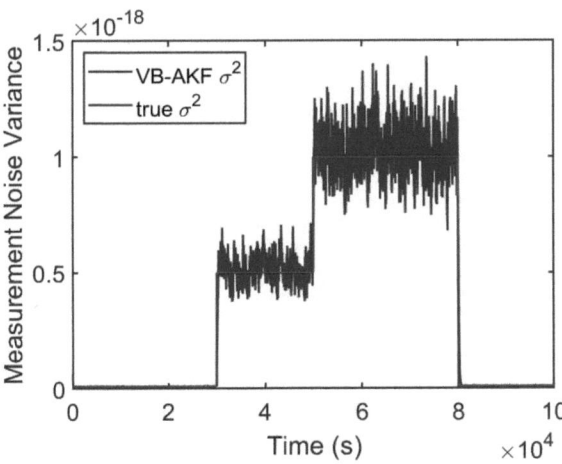

Fig. 2. Result of tracking the noise variance by VB-AKF.

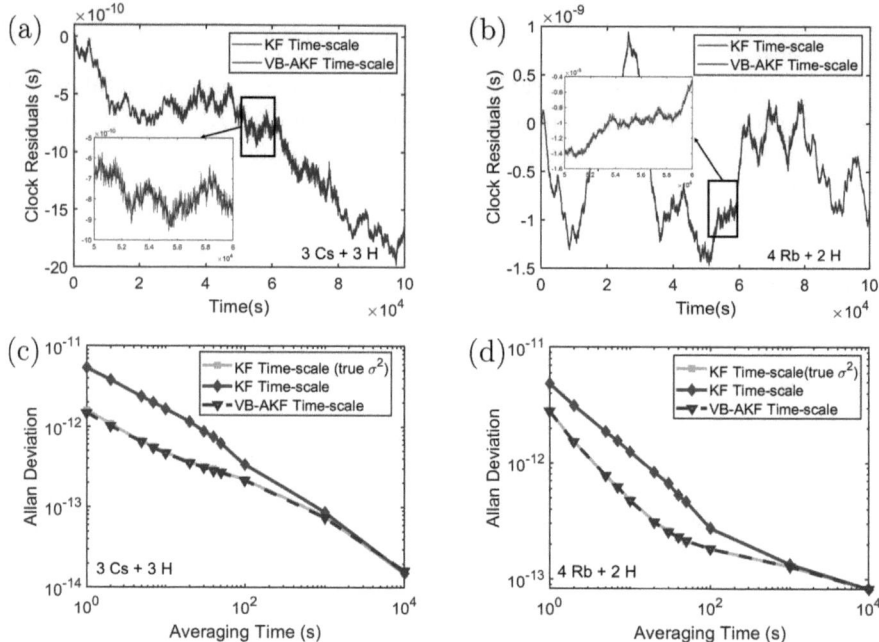

Fig. 3. The clock deviations and the stability comparison of time scale generated by KF and VB-AKF time-scale algorithms. (a) and (c) is the scenario of clock ensemble consists of 3 cesium clocks and 3 hydrogen-maser clocks, while (b) and (d) is the scenario with 4 rubidium clocks and 2 hydrogen-maser clocks.

of 4 rubidium clocks and 2 hydrogen-maser clocks to further verify the robustness and applicability of the algorithm. The measurement clock difference vector which generated by (6) is corrupted by a non-stationary white phase Gaussian noise. In the simulation, the measurement noise with variance which changing within the range of $1 \times 10^{-20} s^2$ to $1 \times 10^{-18} s^2$ dynamically as shown in Fig. 2 is added into the clock difference between the first clock and the reference.

The conventional KF and the VB-AKF time-scale algorithm are used respectively to generate a time scale which can be calculated as

$$TA(k) = \sum_{i=1}^{N} w_i E_i(k), \qquad (20)$$

where $E_i(k) = x_i(k) - \hat{x}_i(k)$ is the vector of residuals for the ith clock, and w_i represents the normalized weight of single clock in the ensemble and typically defined to be inversely proportional to the Allan variance σ_i^2 of the time deviation to optimize the stability of $TA(k)$ when the clocks are statistically independent, i.e. $w_i \propto (1/\sigma_i^2)$.

As shown in Fig. 2, the initial value of measurement noise variance which represented as true σ^2 is set to $1 \times 10^{-20} s^2$. At time $t = 3 \times 10^4 s$ and $t = 5 \times 10^4 s$, the variance rises to $5 \times 10^{-19} s^2$ and $1 \times 10^{-18} s^2$ respectively, and drops to $1 \times 10^{-20} s^2$ at time $t = 8 \times 10^4 s$. However, despite the existence of fluctuations, the VB method can quickly estimate the change in measurement noise variance whether increasing or decreasing. Thus, the implementation of estimation endows VB-AKF with the ability to dynamically adjust the measurement noise matrix R to adapt to changes in noise.

The advantage of VB-AKF for establishment of time scale can be seen in the following discussion of results. The clock residuals of time scale generated by conventional KF and VB-AKF and their frequency stability which evaluated with Allan variance are demonstrated in Fig. 3. It can be observed in Fig. 3a and Fig. 3b that the conventional KF fails to cope with the change of measurement noise within a time interval of $3 \times 10^4 s$ to $8 \times 10^4 s$ and has experienced significant fluctuations on clock residuals, while the VB-AKF overcomes the impact of increased noise variance of non-stationary measurement noise and improving the accuracy of the atomic clock state estimation. Furthermore, the Allan variance of time scale based on the two algorithms is depicted in Fig. 3c and Fig. 3d, and the result of conventional KF using the measurement variance consistent with truth are plotted in comparison. It can be seen that the VB-AKF without priori true variance can improve the stability of time scale from 5.42×10^{-12}@1s to 1.46×10^{-12}@1s in the former scenario, and from 4.87×10^{-12}@1s to 2.82×10^{-12}@1s in the latter scenario. What's more, VB-AKF can just obtain the equivalent stability as the KF with true variance because the VB method successfully estimates and tracks the variance changes in measurement noise, and the time scale based on KF with invariant prior-variance has worse stability for which mismatching the variance of non-stationary measurement noise.

In addition, as the averaging time increases, it can be seen that the impact on stability due to noise variance mismatch becomes smaller. This phenomenon originates from the characteristic that measurement noise is phase white noise, which mainly corrupts the short-term stability of the time scale and has little impact on the long-term stability.

4 Conclusion

In order to address the situation where the measurement noise variance mismatch caused by non-stationary noise which leading to a corruption in the stability of the time scale established by KF, we propose the VB-AKF time-scale algorithm which can estimate the variance of measurement noise and adjust the noise matrix dynamically to adapt to the non-stationary noise. Simulation results demonstrate that, even at an ensemble of clocks with unknown non-stationary measurement noise, the VB-AKF time-scale algorithm could still precisely estimate the states of atomic clocks and improve the stability of time scale from 5.42×10^{-12}@1s to 1.46×10^{-12}@1s and from 4.87×10^{-12}@1s to 2.82×10^{-12}@1s in different scenarios of clock ensemble respectively. In particular, the time scale generated by VB-AKF can achieve the same stability as KF with priori true noise covariance matrix. Above all, the proposed VB-AKF can overcome the impact of non-stationary measurement noise and provide a more reliable scheme for the establishment of time scale.

Acknowledgment. This work was supported in part by the National Natural Science Foundation of China under Grant 62271080, and in part by the Fund of State Key Laboratory of Information Photonics and Optical Communications(lPOC2022ZT06).

References

1. Liang, Y., Xu, J., Wu, M., Li, F.: Analysis of the long-term characteristics of bds on-orbit satellite atomic clock: since bds-3 was officially commissioned. Remote Sens. **14**(18), 4535 (2022)
2. Panfilo, G., Arias, F.: The coordinated universal time (utc). Metrologia **56**(4), 042001 (2019)
3. Galleani, L., Tavella, P.: Time and the kalman filter. IEEE Control Syst. Mag. **30**(2), 44–65 (2010)
4. Yao, J., Parker, T.E., Levine, J.: Jy1 time scale: a new kalman-filter time scale designed at nist. Meas. Sci. Technol. **28**(11), 115004 (2017)
5. Yan, Y., Kawaguchi, T., Yano, Y., Hanado, Y., Ishizaki, T.: Structured kalman filter for time scale generation in atomic clock ensembles. IEEE Control Syst. Lett. (2023)
6. Gödel, M., Schmidt, T.D., Furthner, J.: Kalman filter approaches for a mixed clock ensemble. In: 2017 Joint Conference of the European Frequency and Time Forum and IEEE International Frequency Control Symposium (EFTF/IFCS), pp. 666–672. IEEE (2017)
7. Song, H., Dong, S., Qu, L., Wang, X., Guo, D.: A robust kalman filter time scale algorithm with data anomaly. J. Instrum. **16**(06), P06032 (2021)
8. Zhang, L., Sidoti, D., Bienkowski, A., Pattipati, K.R., Bar-Shalom, Y., Kleinman, D.L.: On the identification of noise covariances and adaptive kalman filtering: a new look at a 50 year-old problem. IEEE Access **8**, 59362–59388 (2020)
9. Sarkka, S., Nummenmaa, A.: Recursive noise adaptive kalman filtering by variational bayesian approximations. IEEE Trans. Autom. Control **54**(3), 596–600 (2009)
10. Zucca, C., Tavella, P.: The clock model and its relationship with the allan and related variances. IEEE Trans. Ultrason. Ferroelectr. Freq. Control **52**(2), 289–296 (2005)
11. Diez, J., D'Angelo, P., Fernández, A.: Clock errors simulation and characterisation. In: Proceedings of the 19th International Technical Meeting of the Satellite Division of the Institute of Navigation (ION GNSS 2006), pp. 815–821 (2006)

Cost-Optimized Dynamic Offloading and Resource Scheduling Algorithm for Low Earth Orbit Satellite Networks

Jinhong Li, Kangan Gui, Chengchao Liang[✉], and Rong Chai

School of Communications and Information Engineering, Chongqing University of Posts and Telecommunications, Chongqing, China
liangcc@cqupt.edu.cn.com, chairong@cqupt.edu.cn

Abstract. This paper addresses the joint task offloading and resource scheduling problem in Low Earth Orbit (LEO) satellite edge computing networks. The proposed network comprises a number of source low earth orbit (SLEO) satellites attempting to transmit their data flows to the designated ground stations (GSs). To address the long-term cost minimization problem in refeq:pro, a Dijkstra-based strategy is proposed for the transmission scheduling problem, while a deep learning method using DQN is adopted for dynamic task scheduling. Simulation results show significant improvements in average system cost, queue length, energy consumption, and task completion rate compared to baseline strategies.

Keywords: LEO Satellite Networks · task offloading · resource scheduling · DQN

1 Introduction

In the rapidly advancing realm of the Internet of Things (IoT), the emphasis on achieving global connectivity and intelligence has never been greater, leading to an exponential rise in data volume and the number of edge devices. Mobile Edge Computing (MEC) stands out as a pivotal technological advancement to meet these needs by decentralizing computing resources and facilitating processing at the network peripheries. By offloading tasks to these localized devices, MEC reduces latency, enhances bandwidth availability, improves the user experience, and eases the strain on core network infrastructures [6,10].

Terrestrial networks mainly depend on base stations to provide real-time services. However, their deployment is geographically constrained and not viable in remote or disaster-affected regions. Terrestrial networks are inherently vulnerable to natural disasters such as earthquakes and tsunamis, which can cause severe communication breakdowns, leading to substantial socio-economic impacts. Satellite communication networks, with their global coverage and flexible deployment capabilities, complement terrestrial systems. In high-density areas, they help to reduce network congestion, while in remote regions lacking conventional network coverage, satellites offer essential communication links

[5]. Traditionally, satellite systems acted as relay nodes, sending data to the cloud for processing. However, this model is increasingly inadequate for modern, latency-sensitive applications requiring instant data processing. Integrating satellite communication with edge computing creates a future-ready communication framework. By deploying computing and storage resources directly on satellites, their inherent low-latency and high-reliability attributes are leveraged, significantly reducing dependence on central cloud systems. This integration meets current demands for localized processing power and storage, supporting new application scenarios that require robust resource availability [14,21].

Diving into low Earth orbit (LEO) satellite networks, integrating MEC signifies a crucial advancement in broadening service capabilities. Unlike traditional relay methods, placing MEC servers directly on LEO satellites leverages their unique chain routes for more efficient data transmission. This approach upgrades the infrastructure necessary to manage the increasing demands for quicker and more reliable data processing services. While the advantages are clear, challenges like signal delays, bandwidth restrictions, and energy limitations remain. Ongoing innovations in battery technology and resource management are vital to address these issues, making the development of satellite-integrated MEC networks a key element in the future of global IoT connectivity and network performance.

Task offloading in Low Earth Orbit (LEO) satellite networks has gained significant attention due to the necessity for energy-efficient and delay-optimized algorithms. Reference [27] introduces a cloud-edge cooperative computing strategy with a focus on service quality constraints, while [20] presents a hybrid architecture aimed at lowering energy consumption for ground users by employing game theory. Simultaneously, references [11,25,26] target the reduction of task execution delays, with [11] showcasing a space-ground integrated network using deep reinforcement learning for optimal offloading decisions. The cooperative computing approaches described in [26] further underscore the importance of reducing task response delays via satellite-ground collaboration.

Beyond these innovations, references [3,16,23,24] explore both energy efficiency and delay optimization. Reference [23] examines the influence of satellite-ground communication delays on overall performance, using a heuristic search algorithm to balance computational loads. Similarly, [3,16] propose task offloading strategies in small satellite systems, stressing the importance of optimizing energy use and minimizing execution delays through effective algorithms.

Resource scheduling algorithms are also pivotal in enhancing the performance of LEO satellite networks. References [1,18,19] address transmission delays, with [1] combining ground stations and high-altitude platforms to enhance data offloading efficiency. Likewise, [2] suggests a matching algorithm to maximize data transmission rates by integrating LEO satellites with ground networks, whereas [8] employs deep Q-learning to optimize resource utilization in hybrid networks. Recent studies on joint task offloading and resource scheduling feature deep reinforcement learning strategies. References [7,9,12,15] illustrate approaches that adapt to dynamic network conditions to enhance energy efficiency and reduce delays. Notably, [4] proposes a comprehensive strategy that significantly lowers system costs.

Although these advancements have been made, research on satellite collaboration is still sparse. Numerous studies concentrate largely on optimizing individual satellite resources, thereby neglecting the potential advantages of satellite cooperation. This paper seeks to address this gap by examining task offloading and resource scheduling methods that capitalize on the distinctive features of satellite networks.

2 System Model and Problem Formulation

2.1 LEO Satellite Network Model

The devised Low Earth Orbit (LEO) satellite system is constituted of N observation satellites, K relay satellites, M IoT devices, and a ground station. Observation satellites OS_n gather terrestrial data and transmit it to relay satellites RS_k, which then relay the data to the ground station's cache. IoT devices ID_m create computational tasks and dispatch them either to the relay satellites or directly to the ground station for processing. Each relay satellite is endowed with a computational capacity of ϕ_k and interacts with several IoT devices using Orthogonal Frequency Division Multiple Access (OFDMA) technology, with a sub-channel bandwidth of B.

In this dynamic LEO satellite scenario, the system time T is divided into continuous time slots of length τ. Each LEO satellite is connected through four inter-satellite links. Links between adjacent satellites in the same orbit are stable, while links between satellites in different adjacent orbits use steerable beam technology to maintain stable connections. Consequently, the inter-satellite network topology is assumed to be stable.

To characterize the connection states of inter-satellite communication links, let $x^o_{n,k} \in \{0,1\}$ indicate the physical link between observation satellite OS_n and relay satellite RS_k: if $x^o_{n,k} = 1$, a physical link exists; if $x^o_{n,k} = 0$, it does not. Similarly, let $x^r_{k,k'} \in \{0,1\}$ represent the link indicator between relay satellites RS_k and $RS_{k'}$ with the same interpretation.

The satellite-to-ground network topology is dynamic, changing every time slot but remaining static within each slot. The connection state between IoT device ID_m and relay satellite RS_k in time slot t is denoted by $x^i_{m,k,t} \in \{0,1\}$: if $x^i_{m,k,t} = 1$, a physical link exists; if $x^i_{m,k,t} = 0$, it does not. Finally, $x^g_{k,t} \in \{0,1\}$ indicates the link existence between relay satellite RS_k and the ground station in time slot t: if $x^g_{k,t} = 1$, there is a physical link; if $x^g_{k,t} = 0$, there is not.

Assume that the computational tasks of IoT devices randomly arrive in each time slot, following a Poisson distribution. Let $\theta_{m,t}$ denote the computational task arriving at IoT device ID_m in time slot t. The task $\theta_{m,t}$ is modeled as $\theta_{m,t} = (D_{m,t}, F_{m,t})$, where $D_{m,t}$ represents the task size and $F_{m,t}$ denotes the number of central processing unit (CPU) cycles required per bit of data. The task size can be expressed as $D_{m,t} = \lambda_m \tau$ where λ_m is the average task arrival rate for terminal ID_m.

Assuming IoT devices do not perform computations, they must transmit tasks to relay satellites for execution. Relay satellites can adopt either satellite computation mode or ground station computation mode. In the satellite offloading mode, relay satellites compute the tasks upon receipt from IoT devices. Conversely, in the ground station offloading mode, relay satellites forward tasks to the ground station for execution in subsequent time slots.

Let $z_{m,t,k,t'} \in \{0,1\}$ be the task transmission variable for $\theta_{m,t}$. If $z_{m,t,k,t'} = 1$, it indicates that task $\theta_{m,t}$ is transmitted to relay satellite RS_k in time slot t'; otherwise, $z_{m,t,k,t'} = 0$. Additionally, let $\lambda^g_{m,t,k,t'} \in \{0,1\}$ denote the ground station offloading mode selection variable for task $\theta_{m,t}$. If $\lambda^g_{m,t,k,t'} = 1$, it indicates that relay satellite RS_k selects the ground station computation mode for task $\theta_{m,t}$ in time slot t'; otherwise, $\lambda^g_{m,t,k,t'} = 0$.

Observation satellites continuously collect data transmission services, denoted as D^o_n for satellite OS_n. After collecting data, each satellite transmits it to the ground station via relay satellites in subsequent time slots. Let $y^o_{n,k,t} \in \{0,1\}$ be the transmission selection variable for relay satellites. If $y^o_{n,k,t} = 1$, it indicates that OS_n transmits data to relay satellite RS_k in time slot t; otherwise, $y^o_{n,k,t} = 0$.

For transmission between relay satellites, let $y^r_{n,k,k',t} \in \{0,1\}$. If $y^r_{n,k,k',t} = 1$, RS_k transmits data D^o_n to $RS_{k'}$ in time slot t; otherwise, $y^r_{n,k,k',t} = 0$. Finally, let $y^g_{n,k,t} \in \{0,1\}$ indicate whether RS_k transmits data to the ground station in time slot t (1) or not (0).

Let $R^i_{m,k,t}$ denote the link rate between IoT device ID_m and relay satellite RS_k in time slot t. Let $R^o_{n,k}$ denote the link rate between observation satellite OS_n and relay satellite RS_k. Due to the space limitation, the modeling of channels and related achievable data rate can be found in [13,17].

2.2 Optimization Problem Modeling

Given that IoT devices generate computational tasks randomly and transmit them to relay satellites in subsequent time slots, a computation task cache queue should be established for the devices. Similarly, relay satellites must model a queue to represent their caching capabilities, as they may receive and forward data, offload computational tasks, and execute onboard tasks during each time slot.

Let $Q^i_{m,t}$ denote the length of the computational task queue at IoT device ID_m in time slot t. The queue update formula for $Q^i_{m,t}$ can be expressed as:

$$Q^i_{m,t+1} = \min\left(Q^i_{m,t} - \sum_{k=1}^{K}\sum_{t'=1}^{t} z_{m,t,k,t'} D_{m,t'} + D_{m,t}, Q^{i,\max}_m\right) \quad (1)$$

where $Q^{i,\max}_m$ is the maximum cache queue length of IoT device ID_m.

Let $Q_{k,t}$ represent the queue length of relay satellite RS_k at time t. The queue update formula at relay satellite RS_k is expressed as:

$$Q_{k,t+1} = \min \left\{ Q_k^{\max}, Q_{k,t} + \sum_{n=1}^{N} y_{n,k,t}^o D_n^o - \sum_{k'=1, k' \neq k}^{K} y_{n,k',t}^r D_n^o \right.$$
$$- \sum_{n=1}^{N} y_{n,k,t}^g D_n^o + \sum_{m=1}^{M} \sum_{t'=1}^{t-1} y_{m,t',k,t} \lambda_{m,t',t}^g D_{m,t',t}^g \quad (2)$$
$$\left. - \sum_{m=1}^{M} \sum_{t'=1}^{t-1} y_{m,t',k,t} \min \left(\frac{\varphi_{k,t}^T}{D_{m,t',t}^r F_{m,t'}}, D_{m,t',t}^r \right) \right\}$$

where $Q_k^{\max}$ is the maximum queue length of relay satellite RS_k. The task calculation identifier $y_{m,t',k,t} \in \{0,1\}$ indicates whether relay satellite RS_k executes task $\theta_{m,t'}$ at time t. If $y_{m,t',k,t} = 1$, the task is being executed; otherwise, it is not. The computing power of RS_k is represented by φ_k, and $D_{m,t',k,t}$ denotes the task volume of $\theta_{m,t'}$ that needs computation by RS_k at time t. The update formula for the task volume is given by:

$$D_{m,t',k,t+1} = D_{m,t',k,t} - \min \left(\frac{\varphi_{k,t}^T}{V_{m,t',t}^r F_{m,t'}}, D_{m,t',k,t}^r \right) \quad (3)$$

The initial task volume $D_{m,t',k,t}$ at relay satellite RS_k is defined as:

$$D_{m,t',k,t} = \begin{cases} 0, & t < t' \\ \theta_{m,t'}, & t = t' \\ \theta_{m,t'} - \sum_{\tau=t'}^{t-1} y_{m,t',k,\tau} \frac{\varphi_{k,\tau}^T}{V_{m,t',\tau}^r F_{m,t'}}, & t' < t \end{cases} \quad (4)$$

Let E_t^c represent the energy consumption for task execution at time t, which includes the energy required to transmit tasks from IoT devices to relay satellites, the energy for relay satellites to compute tasks, and the energy to transmit tasks from relay satellites to ground stations. Ground station energy consumption is neglected due to its sufficient power supply. E_t^c is expressed as:

$$E_t^c = \sum_{m=1}^{M} \sum_{k=1}^{K} E_{m,t,k}^t + \sum_{m=1}^{M} \sum_{k=1}^{K} E_{m,t,k}^c + \sum_{m=1}^{M} \sum_{k=1}^{K} E_{m,t,k}^g \quad (5)$$

where $E_{m,t,k}^t = z_{m,t,k} \frac{D_{m,t}^o P_{m,t}^i}{R_{m,t,k}^i}$ is the energy to transmit task $\theta_{m,t}$ from IoT device ID_m to relay satellite RS_k at time t; $E_{m,t,k}^c = y_{m,t,k} \epsilon_k \left(\frac{D_{m,t}^o}{\varphi_k} \right)^2$ is the energy for relay satellite RS_k to compute task $\theta_{m,t}$; $E_{m,t,k}^g = \lambda_{m,t,k} \frac{D_{m,t}^o P_{m,t}^g}{R_{m,t,k}^g}$ is the energy to transmit $\theta_{m,t}$ from relay satellite RS_k to ground stations.

Let E_t^o represent the energy consumption for data transmission at time t, including energy to transmit data from observation satellites to relay satellites, energy for transmission between relay satellites, and energy to transmit data from relay satellites to ground stations. E_t^o is given by:

$$E_t^o = \sum_{n=1}^{N}\sum_{k=1}^{K} E_{n,k,t}^o + \sum_{k=1}^{K}\sum_{k'\neq k} E_{n,k,k',t}^r + \sum_{n=1}^{N}\sum_{k=1}^{K} E_{n,k,t}^g \qquad (6)$$

where $E_{n,k,t}^o = y_{n,k,t}^o \frac{D_n^o P_n}{R_{n,k}^o}$ is the energy for observation satellite OS_n to transmit data D_n^o to relay satellite RS_k; $E_{n,k,k',t}^r = y_{n,k,k',t}^r \frac{D_n^o P^r}{R_{k,k'}^r}$ is the energy for relay satellite RS_k to transmit D_n^o to relay satellite $RS_{k'}$; $E_{n,k,t}^g = y_{n,k,t}^g \frac{D_n^o P^{rg}}{R_{k,g}^g}$ is the energy for relay satellite RS_k to transmit D_n^o to ground stations.

Considering the queue of data transmission tasks and computation tasks in the system as well as the energy consumption for execution, the system cost function U is modeled as:

$$U = \sum_{t=1}^{T} U_t \qquad (4\text{-}22)$$

where $U_t = \mu_1 E_t + \mu_2 Q_t$ is the cost function at time t. In this equation, $E_t = E_t^c + E_t^o$ represents the total energy consumption for computation and data transmission tasks; $Q_t = \sum_{m=1}^{M} Q_{m,t}^o + \sum_{k=1}^{K} Q_{k,t}$ denotes the total queue length at time t; and μ_1 and μ_2 are the weight factors for energy and queue length, respectively.

2.3 Optimization Constraints

The optimization problem must satisfy several constraints regarding transmission links and flow conservation.

At any time t, each IoT device can connect to only one relay satellite, and each observation satellite can also connect to only one relay satellite. Relay satellites can forward data from one observation satellite to another or to the ground station, but only one at a time.

Data transmission can occur only when links between the respective devices and satellites exist. Relay satellites start computing tasks only after all tasks are received and can process only one task per time slot.

Flow conservation constraints must be satisfied for both observation and relay satellites. For observation satellite OS_n:

$$\sum_{k=1}^{K}\sum_{t=1}^{T} y_{n,k,t}^o = 1, \quad \forall n \qquad (7)$$

For relay satellite RS_k processing data D_n^o:

$$\sum_{t=1}^{T} y_{n,k,t}^o + \sum_{k'\neq k}\sum_{t=1}^{T} y_{n,k,k',t}^r = \sum_{k'\neq k}\sum_{t=1}^{T} y_{n,k',k,t}^r + \sum_{t=1}^{T} y_{n,k,t}^g, \quad \forall n,k \qquad (8)$$

2.4 Optimization Model

Considering constraints such as link availability and computation limitations, the optimization model for the joint dynamic task offloading and resource allocation problem based on the long-term cost function minimization under the constraints is:

$$\min_{\{y^o_{n,k,t}, y^r_{n,k,k',t}, y^g_{n,k,t}, z^i_{m,t',k,t}, \lambda^g_{m,t',k,t}, y_{m,t',k,t}\}} \lim_{T \to \infty} \frac{1}{T} \mathbb{E}\left[\sum_{t=1}^{T} U_t\right] \quad (9)$$

3 Proposed Optimization Algorithms

To tackle the issue of minimizing long-term costs as described in 9, we have devised dynamic strategies for task offloading and computation scheduling, specifically for observation satellite data tasks, IoT device computations, and maintaining the stability of the inter-satellite network topology. The optimization challenge is segmented into data task transmission scheduling and the offloading of computation tasks. For transmission scheduling, a strategy based on Dijkstra's algorithm is introduced, while a deep Q-network (DQN) based deep learning approach is utilized for dynamic task offloading and scheduling.

3.1 Data Task Transmission Scheduling Problem Modeling and Solving

The data task transmission scheduling problem is modeled as a directed shortest path problem with weighted edges, assuming the inter-satellite network topology remains unchanged during scheduling. The Dijkstra algorithm is employed to find the shortest path from each observation satellite to the ground station, resulting in an optimized transmission strategy to address relay satellite capacity issues.

Without considering conflicts in relay satellite scheduling, the strategy determines data transmission paths between observation satellites and ground stations. Link weights, based on energy consumption, are calculated for modeling the problem.

Let $W^o_{n,k} = \frac{D^o_n P_n}{R^o_{n,k}}$ when $x^o_{n,k} = 1$ and $W^o_{n,k} = +\infty$ when $x^o_{n,k} = 0$. Let $W^r_{n,k,k'} = \frac{D^o_n P^r_k}{R^r_{k,k'}}$ when $x^r_{k,k'} = 1$ and $W^r_{n,k,k'} = +\infty$ when $x^r_{k,k'} = 0$. Let $W^g_{n,k,t} = \frac{D^o_n P^g_k}{R^g_{k,g}}$ when $x^g_{k,g} = 1$ and $W^g_{n,k,t} = +\infty$ when $x^g_{k,g} = 0$. The total energy consumption from observation satellite OS_n to the ground station is represented by W_n. The shortest path problem is modeled as:

$$\min W_n = \sum_{\substack{k=1, \\ t=1}}^{K,T} y^o_{n,k,t} W^o_{n,k} + \sum_{\substack{k=1, k'=1, \\ k' \neq k, t=1}}^{K,K,T} y^r_{n,k,k',t} W^r_{n,k,k'} + \sum_{\substack{k=1, \\ t=1}}^{K,T} y^g_{n,k,t} W^g_{n,k,t} \quad (10a)$$

s.t. *constraints in Section* 2.3 \hfill (10b)

To describe the inter-satellite link state at different times, the ground station is virtualized into T nodes, denoted as GS_t for $1 \leq t \leq T$. The link weights between each virtual ground station and relay satellites are determined based on the inter-satellite link state. Using the Dijkstra algorithm to solve the shortest path problem, super nodes are introduced, with link weights of virtual ground station nodes set to zero. The graph $G_n = (V, E, W_n)$ includes observation satellites OS_n, relay satellites, and virtual ground stations, with E representing satellite-ground links.

By applying Dijkstra's algorithm in the augmented graph G_n, the shortest path from OS_n to GS_t is identified. Let $\pi_n^t = \{y_{n,k,t}^o, y_{n,k,k',t}^r, y_{n,k,t}^g, 1 \leq t \leq T\}$ represent the data set D_n^o from OS_n to GS_t. Due to multiple hops and the dynamic nature of the links, the original transmission strategy may become infeasible. Thus, all strategies need to be checked for conflicts. If the maximum conflict time $\tau_{n,k}^t = \arg\max\{y_{n,k,t}\}$ exceeds t, the strategy is invalidated; otherwise, it is retained. The strategy with the minimum weight is chosen as the local transmission scheduling strategy set π_n^t.

When designing independent transmission strategies for observation satellites, conflicts arise if two tasks are transmitted simultaneously from the same origin to the same destination. This section proposes a priority-based transmission adjustment algorithm. For conflicting data tasks D_n^o and D_n', the algorithm is as follows:

Assuming that the task with higher cumulative transmission energy has higher priority, let $E_{n,t-1}^o$ represent the cumulative transmission energy of D_n^o before time t':

$$E_{n,t-1}^o = \sum_{k=1}^{K}\sum_{k'=1}^{K}\sum_{t=1}^{t'-1} E_{n,k,k',t}^o + \sum_{k=1}^{K}\sum_{t=1}^{t'-1} E_{n,k,t}^o + \sum_{k=1}^{K}\sum_{t=1}^{t'-1} E_{n,k,t}^g \quad (11)$$

If $E_{n,t-1}^o > E_{n,t-1}'$, then D_n^o has higher priority.

The higher-priority task D_n^o executes the strategy in $\pi_{n,t}^o$. The optimal transmission scheduling strategy set is $\pi_{n,t}^o$. For the lower-priority task D_n', return to OS_n and redesign the transmission strategy as described in above section. To prevent further conflicts, attention should be paid to the arrangement containing the strategy $\pi_{n,k,k',t}^r$, ultimately yielding the optimal strategy set $\pi_{n,t}^o$.

3.2 Dynamic Task Offloading and Computation Scheduling Problem Modeling and Solving

Given the determined data task transmission scheduling strategy and the relay satellite's buffer status at each time slot, this section employs the DQN algorithm for task offloading and computation scheduling, considering the limited buffer, dynamic satellite-ground links, and the random arrival of IoT computation tasks.

Let $\tilde{U}_t = \mu_1 E_t + \mu_2 Q_t$ represent the cost function for the relay satellite at time t. The optimization model for the dynamic task offloading and computation scheduling problem is expressed as:

$$\min_{z^i_{m,t',k,t},\lambda^g_{m,t',k,t},y_{m,t',k,t}} \lim_{T\to\infty} \frac{1}{T}\mathbb{E}\left[\sum_{t=1}^{T}\tilde{U}_t\right] \tag{12a}$$

$$s.t.\ constraints\ in\ Section\ 2.3 \tag{12b}$$

Solving problem (12) yields the relay satellite's computation mode selection strategy $z^i_{m,t',k,t}$, ground station offloading mode selection strategy $\lambda^g_{m,t',k,t}$, and computation scheduling strategy $y_{m,t',k,t}$.

Considering that problem (12) is a long-term optimization problem with random variables, it is modeled as a Markov decision process represented by a tuple (S, A, r). Here, $S = \{s_t\} = \{Q_t, Q^t_i, L^r_t, x_t\}$ denotes the system states, where $Q_t = \{Q_{1,t}, Q_{2,t}, \ldots, Q_{K,t}\}$ represents the buffer queue status of relay satellites; $Q^t_i = \{Q_{i,1,t}, Q_{i,2,t}, \ldots, Q_{i,M,t}\}$ represents the buffer status of IoT devices; $L^r_t = \{L^r_{m,k,t}\}$ indicates the rain attenuation coefficient between IoT devices and relay satellites; and $x_t = \{x_{m,k,t}\}$ shows the logical link existence status. The action set is $A = \{a_t\} = \{z^i_{m,t',k,t}, \lambda^g_{m,t',k,t}, y_{m,t',k,t}, 1 \le m \le M, 1 \le t' < t, 1 \le k \le K\}$, with r as the immediate reward function.

When IoT devices are in state s_t and execute action a_t, the immediate reward r_t is defined as:

$$r_t = -\left(\sum_{k=1}^{K} Q_{k,t} + \sum_{m=1}^{M} Q_{i,m,t} + E_t\right) \tag{13}$$

DQN introduces deep neural networks as function approximators, efficiently handling high-dimensional state spaces and improving learning efficiency. Unlike traditional Q-learning, which requires discrete action spaces, DQN estimates Q-values for each action using deep networks, enabling it to address continuous action spaces [22]. An experience replay mechanism stores agent experiences, allowing for random sampling during training to eliminate correlations between consecutive data, enhancing efficiency and stability. Thus, DQN effectively maximizes interactions between agents and random environments.

During DQN training, convolutional and recurrent neural networks approximate the state-action value function (Q-function). The DQN comprises a prediction network for generating replay data and a target network for calculating Q-values. Experience replay randomly samples data to accelerate convergence and employs smoothing techniques.

When IoT devices execute actions in state s_t, the action value function Q updates as follows:

$$Q_{t+1}(s,a) = Q(s,a) + \alpha\left[r(a,s_t) + \gamma \max_{a'} Q(s',a') - Q(s,a)\right] \tag{14}$$

Here, α is the learning rate and γ the discount factor. To manage computational complexity and avoid Q-value divergence, DQN uses a prediction network $Q(s,a;\theta)$ and a target network $Q(s,a;\theta')$. Parameters θ are updated by minimizing the loss function:

$$\theta \leftarrow \theta + \nu \nabla_\theta F_t\left(Q(s,a|\theta)\right) \tag{15}$$

Table 1. Parameter Settings for DQN Network and Simulation

Parameter	Value
Learning Rate α	0.001
Discount Factor γ	0.95
Experience Replay Buffer Capacity $D^{\max}$	10000
Sample Size D^{batch}	64
Exploration Value ϵ	[0.1, 1]
Link Bandwidth B	20 MHz
Rain Attenuation $L^{\text{rain}}_{m,k,t}$	[10, 20] dB
Boltzmann Constant k_s	1.380649×10^{-23} J/K
Thermal Noise Temperature T_s	300 K
Signal-to-Noise Ratio E_b/N_0	17 dB
Relay Satellite Transmission Power P^r	40 W
Relay Satellite Transmission Antenna Gain G^{rg}_t	27 dBi
Relay Satellite Reception Antenna Gain G^{rg}_r	24 dBi
Observation Satellite Transmission Power P_n	40 W
IoT Device Transmission Power P^i_m	0.1 W

where ν is the step size, and $F_t(Q(s,a|\theta))$ is the Q-value loss function:

$$F_t(Q(s,a|\theta)) = \mathbb{E}_{(s_t,a_t,r_t,s_{t+1}) \sim U(D)}\left[(y_t - Q(s,a;\theta))^2\right] \tag{16}$$

In this context, $(s_t, a_t, r_t, s_{t+1}) \sim U(D)$ are samples from the experience replay buffer D, and y_t is:

$$y_t = r_t + \gamma \max_{a'} Q'(s', a'; \theta') \tag{17}$$

The computation task offloading and scheduling algorithm using DQN involves initializing the prediction and target networks, state, action, and experience replay buffer parameters. Using an ϵ-greedy policy in state s_t, the optimal action a_t is selected, transitioning to state s_{t+1}. The experience sample (s_t, a_t, r_t, s_{t+1}) is stored in the replay buffer, with capacity $D^{\max}$. A batch of size D^{batch} is randomly drawn for input to the prediction network to obtain predicted Q-values. Target Q-values are calculated via Eq. (14), and the difference between predicted and target values updates the prediction network parameters per Eq. (15). The target network parameters are updated periodically. This process repeats until convergence.

4 Simulation Results and Analysis

This section uses STK simulation software to establish a low Earth orbit satellite network with 24 medium-orbit satellites, 10 observation satellites, and one ground station. The DQN network is simulated in Python using Pytorch within the Gym reinforcement learning environment, comprising 4000 training steps over 30 h, with results averaged from 600 experiments (Table 1).

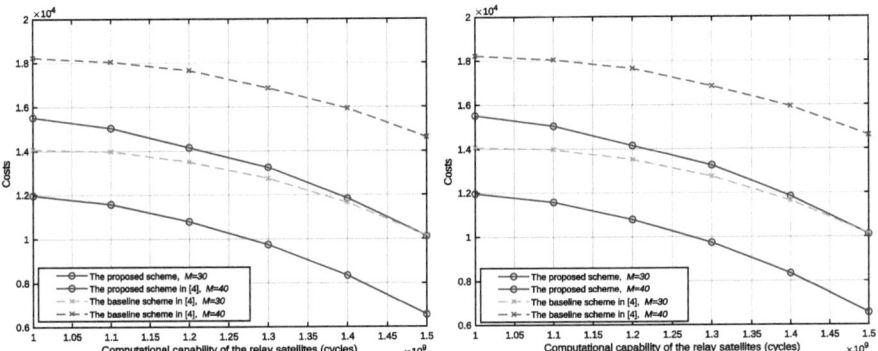

(a) System cost versus maximum queue length of relay satellites

(b) System cost versus computing capability of relay satellites

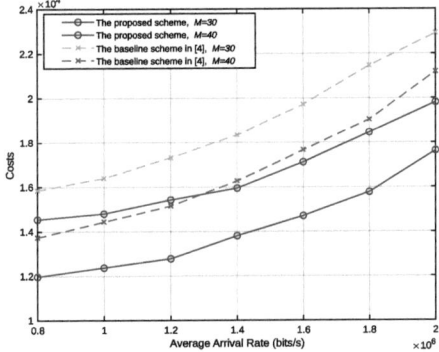

(c) System cost versus average arrival rate of the tasks

Fig. 1. Performance of the proposed schemes.

Figure 1a illustrates that increasing the relay satellite's maximum queue length reduces system costs, as it enhances data handling and task scheduling. The proposed method consistently yields lower costs than the literature method [4], though at 1000 cycles, the reduction rate slows.

Figure 1b highlights that greater computation capability of the relay satellite reduces costs unevenly, especially with more IoT devices. Improved capability shortens task completion times and stabilizes the task queue, with the proposed method outperforming the literature method [4] in cost efficiency.

Figure 1c demonstrates that as the average task completion rate increases, system costs decrease. The proposed method shows a slower cost increase compared to the literature method [4], affirming its effectiveness.

5 Conclusion

This paper addresses the joint dynamic task offloading and resource scheduling problem in Low Earth Orbit (LEO) satellite edge computing networks. The proposed model integrates data service transmission and computational task offloading, framed as a long-term cost minimization problem with constraints. Key contributions include a priority-based policy adjustment algorithm for transmission scheduling conflicts and a DQN-based algorithm for dynamic task offloading and computation scheduling, forming a joint scheduling strategy that optimizes overall system performance. Simulation results show significant improvements in average system cost, queue length, energy consumption, and task completion rate compared to baseline strategies. Future work will expand the framework to more complex scenarios and explore integrating machine learning with traditional optimization methods to enhance performance further.

References

1. Alsharoa, A., Alouini, M.S.: Improvement of the global connectivity using integrated satellite-airborne-terrestrial networks with resource optimization. IEEE Trans. Wireless Commun. **19**(8), 5088–5100 (2020)
2. B. Di, H. Zhang, L.S.: Ultra-dense leo: integrating terrestrial-satellite networks into 5g and beyond for data offloading. IEEE Trans. Wirel. Commun. **18**(1), 47–62 (2018)
3. Pang, B., Gu, S., Zhang, Q., Zhang, N., Xiang, W.: Ccos: a coded computation offloading strategy for satellite-terrestrial integrated networks. In: 2021 International Wireless Communications and Mobile Computing (IWCMC), pp. 242–247. Harbin City, China, June 2021
4. Wang, B., Feng, T., Huang, D.: A joint computation offloading and resource allocation strategy for leo satellite edge computing system. In: 2020 IEEE 20th International Conference on Communication Technology (ICCT), pp. 649–655. Nanning, China, October 2020
5. Bai, L., Zhu, L., Zhang, X., Zhang, W., Yu, Q.: Multi-satellite relay transmission in 5g: concepts, techniques, and challenges. IEEE Network Mag. **32**(5), 38–44 (2018)
6. Bin Li, Z.F., Zhou, C.: Physical-layer security in space information networks: a survey. IEEE Internet Things J. **7**(1), 33–52 (2019)
7. Ding, C., Wang, J.B., Zhang, H., Lin, M., Gy, L.: Joint optimization of transmission and computation resources for satellite and high altitude platform assisted edge computing. IEEE Trans. Wirel. Commun. **21**(2), 1362–1377 (2021)
8. C. Qiu, H. Yao, F.R.Y.: Deep q-learning aided networking, caching, and computing resources allocation in software-defined satellite-terrestrial networks. IEEE Trans. Vehicular Technol. **68**(6), 5871–5883 (2019)
9. Cheng, N., Lyu, F., Quan, W., Zhou, C., He, H., Shi, W., Shen, X.: Space/aerial-assisted computing offloading for iot applications: A learning-based approach. IEEE J. Sel. Areas Commun. **37**(5), 1117–1129 (2019)
10. De Cola, T., Bisio, I.: Qos optimisation of embb services in converged 5g-satellite networks. IEEE Trans. Vehicular Technol. **69**(10), 12098–12110 (2020)
11. Xu, F., Yang, F., Zhao, C., Wu, S.: Deep reinforcement learning based joint edge resource management in maritime network. China Commun. **17**(5), 211–222 (2020)

12. Cui, G., Long, Y., Xu, L., Wang, W.: Joint offloading and resource allocation for satellite assisted vehicle-to-vehicle communication. IEEE Syst. J. **15**(3), 3958–3969 (2020)
13. Golkar, A., i Cruz, I.L.: The federated satellite systems paradigm: concept and business case evaluation. Acta Astronautica **111**, 230–248 (2015)
14. Liu, J., Shi, Y., Fadlullah, Z.M., Kato, N.: Space-air-ground integrated network: a survey. IEEE Commun. Surv. Tutorials **20**(4), 2714–2741 (2018)
15. Wei, K., Tang, Q., Guo, J., Zeng, M., Fei, Z., Cui, Q.: Resource scheduling and offloading strategy based on leo satellite edge computing. In: 2021 IEEE 94th Vehicular Technology Conference (VTC2021-Fall). pp. 1–6. Norman, OK, USA, September 2021
16. Zhang, L., Zhang, H., Guo, C., Xu, H., Song, L., Han, Z.: Satellite-aerial integrated computing in disasters: user association and offloading decision. In: ICC 2020-2020 IEEE International Conference on Communications (ICC), pp. 554–559. Dublin, Ireland, June 2020
17. Li, J., Chai, R., Liu, C., Liang, C., Chen, Q., Yu, F.R.: Energy-aware joint route selection and resource allocation in heterogeneous satellite networks. IEEE Trans. Vehicul. Technol, Early Access (2024)
18. Zhang, M., Zhou, W.: Energy-efficient collaborative data downloading by using inter-satellite offloading. In: 2019 IEEE Global Communications Conference (GLOBECOM), pp. 1–6. Waikoloa, HI, USA, December 2019
19. Yarr, N., Ceriotti, M.: Optimization of intersatellite routing for real-time data download. IEEE Trans. Aerospace Electron. Syst. **54**(5), 2356–2369 (2018)
20. Tang, Q., Fei, Z., Li, B., Han, Z., Zhang, Y.: Computation offloading in leo satellite networks with hybrid cloud and edge computing. IEEE Internet Things J. **8**(11), 9164–9176 (2021)
21. Xie, R., Tang, Q., Wang, Q., Liu, X.: Satellite-terrestrial integrated edge computing networks: architecture, challenges, and open issues. IEEE Network **34**(3), 224–231 (2020)
22. Chen, T., Liu, J., Tang, Q., Huang, T., Liu, Y.: Deep reinforcement learning based data offloading in multi-layer ka/q band leo satellite-terrestrial networks. In: 2021 IEEE 21st International Conference on Communication Technology (ICCT), pp. 1417–1422. Tianjin, China, October 2021
23. Wang, Y., Yang, J., Guo, X.: A game-theoretic approach to computation offloading in satellite edge computing. IEEE Access **8**, 12510–12520 (2019)
24. Wang, Y., Zhang, J., Zhang, Y.: A computation offloading strategy in satellite terrestrial networks with double edge computing. In: 2018 IEEE International Conference on Communication Systems (ICCS), pp. 450–455. Chengdu, China, December 2018
25. Chen, Y., Ai, B., Niu, Y., Zhang, H., Han, Z.: Energy-constrained computation offloading in space-air-ground integrated networks using distributionally robust optimization. IEEE Trans. Vehicular Technol. **70**(11), 12113–12125 (2021)
26. Zhen Zhang, W.Z., Tseng, F.H.: Satellite mobile edge computing: improving qos of high-speed satellite-terrestrial networks using edge computing techniques. IEEE Network **33**(1), 70–76 (2019)
27. Tang, Z., Zhou, H., Ma, T., Yu, K., Shen, X.S.: Leveraging leo assisted cloud-edge collaboration for energy efficient computation offloading. In: 2021 IEEE Global Communications Conference (GLOBECOM), pp. 1–6. Madrid, Spain, December 2021

Author Index

B
Bai, Zhenming II-262
Bao, Zhicheng II-62

C
Chai, Rong II-327
Chen, Hongju II-47
Chen, Qianbin I-169
Chen, Shuhui II-177
Chen, Tao II-3, II-62
Chen, Ying II-163
Chen, Yishuo I-218
Chen, Zheyi II-33, II-47
Cheng, Jiahui II-318
Cheng, Qi II-136
Chu, Zheng I-108, I-120

D
Dai, Qinglong II-78
Dan, Yuran II-262
Deng, Xinfeng I-259, II-291

F
Fan, Mingrui II-190
Fan, Ruixin I-134
Fan, Xiaolin I-203, I-233, I-259, II-223
Feng, Jihan I-46
Feng, Xuehao I-46
Feng, Zhiyong I-134

G
Gao, Jiaqi II-190
Gao, Pengzun II-206
Gao, Xiang I-29
Gui, Kangan II-327
Guo, Qi II-291

H
He, Hongjun I-56
He, Mengting I-259

He, Yaru II-190
Hu, Aiqun II-163
Hu, Dan I-203, I-233, I-259
Huang, Chongwen I-108
Huang, Haihong I-203, I-233
Huang, Sai I-134
Huang, Xiaoge I-169, II-18
Huang, Zhiqin II-33

I
Inekwe, John N. I-184

J
Jiang, Tao I-56
Jiang, Zhaorui I-68
Jin, Shuang I-56
Jokthan, Grace E. I-184

L
Li, Boxian I-248
Li, Jiaxue I-108
Li, Jinhong II-327
Li, Liyan I-134
Li, Qiuping II-291
Li, Ran II-78
Li, Simin II-93
Li, Tianyu I-203, I-233, I-259, II-223
Li, Wenjing II-18
Li, Xingkuan I-3
Li, Xue I-29
Li, Ying I-29
Li, Yue II-306
Li, Zhen I-29
Li, Zheng I-120
Liang, Chengchao I-169, II-18, II-327
Liang, Juejia II-120
Liao, LuShuang II-110
Lin, Weiqin I-259
Lin, Zhipeng I-16
Liu, Bei I-93, I-248
Liu, Canpu I-203, II-223

Liu, Guangyi I-56
Liu, Heng I-82, II-136
Liu, Hongshidi I-169
Liu, Lin II-177
Liu, Qianwen II-291
Liu, Xin I-46
Liu, Yuru II-3, II-62
Liu, Ziyi II-291
Lu, Yueming II-190
Luo, Yuyang I-169
Lv, Ke I-134
Lv, Tiejun I-16

M

Ma, Buyun II-318
Ma, Yuanhao I-29
Ma, Zheng I-82
Miao, Wang II-33
Miao, Xinyu II-318

N

Namugenyi, Ephrance Eunice II-241
Nie, Yuming II-3
Ning, Zhaolong II-276
Nsabagwa, Mary II-241

O

Oju, Joseph U. I-184
Onwodi, Gregory O. I-184
Otim, Julianne Sansa II-241

Q

Qi, Yiwei I-29
Qiao, Yaojun II-190, II-318
Qin, Guangjun II-78

R

Ren, Jiaxin I-218

S

Shao, Kai I-218
Shen, Bin II-18, II-306
Shen, Hongrui I-152
Shi, Xiaowei II-47
Su, Jinshu II-177
Su, Xin I-16, I-93, I-248
Sun, Gangcan I-120
Sun, Haoyun II-3, II-62

T

Tang, Shouze I-218
Tao, Qihui I-93
Tong, Jianfei I-82
Tugume, David II-241

V

Vincent, Olufunke R. I-184

W

Wang, Bianzheng II-306
Wang, Jiakai II-3
Wang, Kaihao I-120
Wang, Shengchu I-68
Wang, Xiaojie II-276
Wang, Xiaoqian I-56
Wang, Xin II-306
Wang, Zhengkang II-318
Wang, Zixin II-306
Wang, Ziyu II-62
Wei, Ziling II-177
Wolthusen, Stephen II-241
Wu, Xiaoyu I-93
Wu, Yu I-218, II-276, II-291

X

Xi, Rongyan I-56
Xia, Liang I-56
Xiao, Hongyujie II-136
Xiao, Yali II-18
Xiong, Bing II-33
Xiong, Xuanrui I-203, I-233, I-259, II-223, II-291
Xu, Chen II-262
Xu, Jiayi I-152
Xu, Xibin I-93, I-248
Xue, Longxiang II-47

Y

Yang, Chao II-110, II-120
Yang, Haiyan I-82
Yang, Liu II-136
Yang, Lulu II-93
Yang, Yang II-163
Yang, Yifan II-262
Yang, Zheng II-262
Yao, Xiujuan I-29

Author Index

Yao, Yiyi II-318
Yao, Yuanyuan I-134
Ye, Julei II-136
Yi, Ling II-276
Yu, Zhengxin II-33
Yuan, Peiyan II-148
Yuan, Yong II-177

Z

Zeng, Jie I-16, II-262
Zennaro, Marco II-241
Zhang, Baoyu II-3, II-62
Zhang, Junjie II-33, II-47
Zhang, Mingjun I-82
Zhang, Shiyu I-16
Zhang, Weishan II-3, II-62
Zhang, Yuan II-223
Zhang, Yushu I-203, I-233, II-223
Zhang, Yuting I-16
Zhang, Yuzhen I-218, II-291
Zhao, Hongwei II-3, II-62
Zhao, Long I-152, II-206
Zhao, Yan I-152
Zhao, Zhonghui II-276
Zheng, Juntian II-148
Zheng, Kan II-206
Zheng, Lin II-110, II-120
Zhou, Li I-218, II-276
Zhu, Hailin II-276
Zhu, Zhengyu I-108, I-120
Zhuo, Junsheng I-82

MIX
Papier aus verantwortungsvollen Quellen
Paper from responsible sources
FSC® C105338

If you have any concerns about our products,
you can contact us on
ProductSafety@springernature.com

In case Publisher is established outside the EU,
the EU authorized representative is:
**Springer Nature Customer Service Center GmbH
Europaplatz 3, 69115 Heidelberg, Germany**

Printed by Libri Plureos GmbH
in Hamburg, Germany